Japanese Subsidiaries in the New Global Economy

NEW HORIZONS IN INTERNATIONAL BUSINESS

Series Editor: Peter J. Buckley
Centre for International Business,
University of Leeds (CIBUL), UK

The New Horizons in International Business series has established itself as the world's leading forum for the presentation of new ideas in international business research. It offers pre-eminent contributions in the areas of multinational enterprise – including foreign direct investment, business strategy and corporate alliances, global competitive strategies, and entrepreneurship. In short, this series constitutes essential reading for academics, business strategists and policy makers alike.

Titles in the series include:

Globalizing America
The USA in World Integration
Edited by Thomas L. Brewer and Gavin Boyd

Information Technology in Multinational Enterprises
Edited by Edward Mozley Roche and Michael James Blaine

A Yen for Real Estate
Japanese Real Estate Investment Abroad – From Boom to Bust
Roger Simon Farrell

Corporate Governance and Globalization
Long Range Planning Issues
Edited by Stephen S. Cohen and Gavin Boyd

The European Union and Globalisation
Towards Global Democratic Governance
Brigid Gavin

Globalization and the Small Open Economy
Edited by Daniel Van Den Bulcke and Alain Verbeke

Entrepreneurship and the Internationalisation of Asian Firms
An Institutional Perspective
Henry Wai-chung Yeung

The World Trade Organization in the New Global Economy
Trade and Investment Issues in the Millennium Round
Edited by Alan M. Rugman and Gavin Boyd

Japanese Subsidiaries in the New Global Economy
Edited by Paul W. Beamish, Andrew Delios and Shige Makino

Globalizing Europe
Deepening Integration, Alliance Capitalism and Structural Statecraft
Edited by Thomas L. Brewer, Paul A. Brenton and Gavin Boyd

China and its Regions
Economic Growth and Reform in Chinese Provinces
Edited by Mary-Françoise Renard

Emerging Issues in International Business Research
Edited by Masaaki Kotabe and Preet S. Aulakh

Japanese Subsidiaries in the New Global Economy

Edited by

Paul W. Beamish

Nortel Networks Director, Asian Management Institute,
Ivey Business School,
The University of Western Ontario, Canada

Andrew Delios

Department of Business Policy,
National University of Singapore

Shige Makino

Department of Management,
The Chinese University of Hong Kong

NEW HORIZONS IN INTERNATIONAL BUSINESS

Edward Elgar
Cheltenham, UK • Northampton, MA, USA

Published by
Edward Elgar Publishing Limited
Glensanda House
Montpellier Parade
Cheltenham
Glos GL50 1UA
UK

Edward Elgar Publishing, Inc.
136 West Street
Suite 202
Northampton
Massachusetts 01060
USA

A catalogue record for this book is available from the British Library

Library of Congress Cataloguing in Publication Data

Japanese subsidiaries in the new global economy / edited by Paul W. Beamish, Andrew Delios, Shige Makino
    p. cm. -- (New horizons in international business)
  Includes bibliographical references and index.
  1. International business enterprises--Japan. 2. Corporations, Japanese--Management. 3. Subsidiary corporations--Japan. 4. Industrial management--Japan. I. Beamish, Paul W., 1953- II. Delios, Andrew, 1965- III. Makino, Shige, 1962- IV. Series.

HD2907.J3452 2001
338.8'8952--dc21

                                                        2001040115

ISBN 1 84064 735 3
Printed and bound in Great Britain by MPG Books Ltd, Bodmin, Cornwall

Contents

PART III   JOINT VENTURES

PART IV   MANAGEMENT STRATEGY

List of Figures

List of Tables

About the Editors

Paul W. Beamish is Associate Dean of Research, Professor of International Business and Nortel Networks Director of the Asian Management Institute at the Ivey Business School, The University of Western Ontario, London, Canada. He is the author or co-author of 33 books and over 75 articles or contributed chapters. His books are in the areas of International Management, Strategic Management, and especially Joint Ventures and Alliances. His articles have appeared in the three *Academy of Management* journals, *Strategic Management Journal, Journal of International Business Studies (JIBS)*, and elsewhere. He has received best research awards from the Academy of Management, the Academy of International Business, and the Administrative Sciences Association of Canada (ASAC). He served as Editor-in-Chief of *JIBS* from 1993 to 1997 and is a Fellow of the Academy of International Business. Professor Beamish has worked on Asia-specific issues for many years.

Andrew Delios is Associate Professor at the National University of Singapore. He is the author or co-author of more than 40 published journal articles, case studies, book chapters and conference proceedings. His articles have appeared in *Academy of Management Journal, Strategic Management Journal, Journal of International Business Studies, Columbia Journal of World Business* and *Asian Case Research Journal*. He is a co-author of the book *Japanese Multinationals in the Global Economy*, which analyzes the structure and performance of Japanese multinational corporations. His doctoral dissertation, which he completed at the Ivey Business School, The University of Western Ontario, examined how foreign market entry strategies influenced the performance of Japanese foreign subsidiaries. Professor Delios has worked and lived in Asia for many years. He has lived and/or worked in Australia, China, Hong Kong, Japan, India, and Finland. He has written case studies and conducted research involving China, India, Italy, Japan, Sweden and Viet Nam.

Shige Makino is Associate Professor at the Chinese University of Hong Kong, where he teaches courses on strategic management and international business. He received his Ph.D from the Ivey Business School, The

University of Western Ontario, and his BA and MBA from Keio University in Japan. His current research interests include strategy and structure of strategic alliances, foreign market entry strategy (i.e., entry mode choice, entry timing, and foundations and exits of overseas subsidiaries), cross-border technology sourcing, and Japanese foreign direct investments in emerging markets. His research has appeared in *Academy of Management Journal, Journal of International Business Studies, Management International Review, European Management Journal, Asia Pacific Journal of Management,* and *Academy of Management Executive,* among others. He is on the editorial board of *Journal of International Business Studies, Journal of International Marketing,* and *Asia Pacific Journal of Management.*

List of Contributors

Jaideep Anand is an Assistant Professor, University of Michigan

Witold J. Henisz is an Assistant Professor, The Wharton School, University of Pennsylvania

Andrew C. Inkpen is a Professor, American Graduate School of International Management

C. Patrick Woodcock is an Associate Professor, Faculty of Administration, University of Ottawa

Acknowledgements

The authors are grateful to the Social Science and Humanities Research Council of Canada (SSHRC) for funding the data collection which underpinned most of the papers in this volume; to Shelley Bellyou and Mary Roberts for their usual masterful job in pulling this entire manuscript together; and to Nortel Networks for its support of Ivey's Asian Management Institute. In addition, Chapters 5, 9, 10 and 13 were partially supported by a grant from the Research Grants Council of the Hong Kong Special Administrative Region (Project no. CUHK 4093/98H).

Chapter 4 is a later version of Woodcock, C. Patrick, Paul W. Beamish and Shige Makino. "Ownership-based Entry Mode Strategies and International Performance," *Journal of International Business Studies,* 1994, Vol. 25, No. 2, pp. 253-273.

The following chapters have been reprinted with permission:

3. Delios, Andrew and Paul W. Beamish, 'Geographic Scope, Product Diversification and the Corporate Performance of Japanese Firms', *Strategic Management Journal,* 1999, **20**, (8), 711-727. Reproduced with permission from John Wiley & Sons Limited.

5. Makino, Shige and Paul W. Beamish, 'Local Ownership Restrictions, Entry Mode Choice and FDI Performance: Japanese Overseas Subsidiaries in Asia', *Asia Pacific Journal of Management,* Special Issue on 'Government-Business Relations in Asia,' 1998, **15**, (2), 119-136. Reprinted with permission from John Wiley & Sons (Asia) Pte Ltd.

6. Anand, Jaideep and Andrew Delios, 'Location Specificity and the Transferability of Downstream Assets to Foreign Subsidiaries', *Journal of International Business Studies,* Third Quarter, 1997, **28**, (3), 579-603. Reprinted with permission.

7. Delios, Andrew and Witold J. Henisz, 'Japanese Firms' Investment Strategies in Emerging Economies', *Academy of Management Journal*, 2000, **43**, (3), 305-323. Reprinted with permission from Copyright Clearance Center.

8. Delios, Andrew and Paul W. Beamish, 'Ownership Strategy of Japanese Firms: Transactional, Institutional and Experience Influences', *Strategic Management Journal*, 1999, **20**, (10), 915-933. Reprinted with permission from John Wiley & Sons Limited.

9. Makino, Shige and Paul W. Beamish, 'Performance and Survival of Joint Ventures with Non-Conventional Ownership Structures', *Journal of International Business Studies*, Fourth Quarter, 1998, **29**, (4), 797-818. Reprinted with permission.

10. Makino, Shige and Andrew Delios, 'Local Knowledge Transfer and Performance: Implications for Alliance Formation in Asia', *Journal of International Business Studies,* Special Issue, 1996, **27**, (5), 905-927. Reprinted with permission.

11. Anand, Jaideep and Andrew Delios, 'How Japanese MNCs Have Matched Goals and Strategies in India and China', *Columbia Journal of World Business*, 1996, **31**, (3), 50-62. Reprinted with permission from Elsevier Science.

12. Beamish, Paul W. and Andrew C. Inkpen, 'Japanese Firms and the Decline of the Japanese Expatriate', *Journal of World Business*, 1998, **33**, (1), 35-50. Reprinted with permission from Elsevier Science.

13. Makino, Shige and Paul W. Beamish, 'Matching Strategy with Ownership Structure in Japanese Joint Ventures', *Academy of Management Executive*, 1999, **13**, (4), 17-28. Reprinted with permission from Copyright Clearance Center.

1. Introduction

Andrew Delios and Paul W. Beamish

Japan became a dominant economic force in the 1960s and 1970s. At that time, Japan received widespread praise for its sterling domestic economy and its formidable strengths as a competitor in export markets. The prominence that Japan's companies achieved led to a flood of books on Japanese business management, which focussed mainly on the unique aspects of the internal operations of Japanese businesses. Other management scholars devoted their efforts to explaining Japan's strengths in foreign markets, mainly as driven by its trading activities.

Since the 1970s, there have been many changes in the ways in which Japanese firms have done business. Most of the external change has been in Japan's foreign markets. Through the 1980s and 1990s, Japanese firms have transformed their strategies for foreign markets. The export-driven strategy of the 1960s and 1970s has been replaced by a great reliance on foreign direct investment (FDI), as a means to serve and produce in foreign markets.

Now, as a new decade begins, Japan has established a position as one of the leading foreign investors in the world. Its largest multinationals – Toyota Motor, Mitsubishi Corp., Nissan Motor, Mitsui and Co., and Sony – have become as well-recognized in foreign markets, as leading domestic firms are at home. But Japan's strength as a foreign investor is not just the story of these large multinational enterprises. Thousands of Japanese firms, both large and small, have contributed to Japan's 1990s emergence as one of the foremost sources of FDI outflows.

The impact of Japan's FDI activity on the world has been dramatic. More than 19,000 subsidiaries of some 5,000 Japanese firms had been established worldwide by the end of 1998. These subsidiaries had a paid-in-capital of nearly US$500 billion and employed more than 3,000,000 people, across half of the world's countries. Further, 54,000 Japanese managers worked overseas in these subsidiaries. These numbers come from information published by the leading compiler of foreign investment information in Japan, Toyo Keizai, Inc. It is numbers like these that spurred our program of research into the strategies of Japanese subsidiaries in the new global economy.

ORGANIZATION OF BOOK

Our research on the strategies of Japanese multinational enterprises began in the early 1990s. We have followed an integrated approach, trying to balance both descriptive information with analytical studies that elucidate the theory and larger patterns on the FDI activities of these firms. The primary objective of this research has been to understand the "why" of the strategy, and the subsidiary-level and corporate-level implications of the implementation of these strategies.

This research project has already led to the publication of nearly 20 journal articles, seven doctoral dissertations, one book, numerous book chapters and dozens of conference presentations and proceedings. Our purpose in compiling the best of these papers in this volume is to present our research in integrated form. Published as an individual paper, each study has its merits, within the narrower confines of its research question. However, those same confines impose limits on the broader implications of each individual paper. By grouping the papers together in this volume, we hope to present a more comprehensive picture of the actions of Japanese multinational enterprises and their implications.

Several aspects of FDI form the focus of this investigation into the international strategy of Japanese subsidiaries. Firm performance, foreign market entry strategy, management strategy in foreign subsidiaries, and country-by-country descriptions of the organizational characteristics of foreign subsidiaries are all salient aspects of FDI. Each chapter in this volume deals with one or two of these aspects. However, space limitations found in the production and publication of academic research has constrained our ability to cover all of these aspects within a single study. In fact, even a country-by-country description of subsidiaries is a commanding enough task to require a book in itself (see Beamish, Delios and Lecraw, 1997).

The aggregation of the chapters in this volume into four sections organizes these aspects of international strategy into more coherent groups. Each section in this volume deals with a specific aspect of international strategy. Part I addresses the overall nature of Japanese investment in international markets, and its broader level corporate performance implications. Part II is concerned with one specific international strategic dimension, the entry mode choice. Additionally, it presents the results of analyses into the performance ramifications of entry mode choices. Part III is devoted to the study of joint ventures – a major differentiating component of Japanese multinationals' foreign market entry strategy. Part IV is involved with investigating the management strategies that Japanese firms have used in their foreign subsidiaries.

PART I WHY INTERNATIONALIZE? MORE SUBSIDIARIES RESULTS IN SUPERIOR PERFORMANCE

In recent years, the form of Japanese foreign investment, both in absolute amounts and in terms of its location has changed considerably. This section establishes the context of Japanese investment in the late 1990s. It identifies the trends in FDI by Japanese firms through the 1990s. Furthermore, it examines the performance consequences of this investment. The second part of this section addresses performance issues in internationalization. The basic conclusion is that internationalization matters for the performance of the firm, with firms that are more internationalized exhibiting higher performance.

But before this, in Chapter 2, we detail the nature of Japanese investment worldwide. This chapter provides an overview of Japanese foreign investment as of 1999. Using a sample of 19,000+ subsidiaries and the accompanying firm-level data on the global operations of Japanese MNEs, this chapter presents in summary form data on entry date, subsidiary industry, host country, sales, equity ownership, employment of local and Japanese workers (including expatriate management), ownership patterns, mode of entry, and performance. With this context, subsequent papers (or sections) explore why Japanese firms internationalize, the relationship between entry mode choice and performance, the use of joint ventures, management strategy considerations, and country specific characteristics.

In Chapter 3, we move to an exploration of the performance consequences of internationalization. This chapter extends research on the geographic scope, product diversification and performance relationship by exploring both the antecedents and consequences of geographic scope. In so doing, it addresses a fundamental criticism of the geographic scope-performance relationship; namely, that the observed positive relationship between geographic scope and performance is spurious because it is the possession of proprietary assets that are the foundation of superior performance, not expansion into international markets per se. We tested the research model with data on the corporate performance of 399 Japanese manufacturing firms. In the Partial Least Squares analyses used to examine the study's six main hypotheses, we demonstrate that internationalization (geographic scope) was positively associated with firm profitability, even when the competing effect of proprietary assets on firm performance was considered. Further, we find that performance was not related to the extent of product diversification; although investment levels in rent-generating, proprietary assets were related to the extent of product diversification.

PART II   ENTRY MODE CHOICE AND PERFORMANCE

When expanding internationally, there are a number of important decisions that must be made. Among the most important strategic decisions are (1) the timing of the investment – when should the foreign subsidiary be established? (2) the location of the investment and (3) the mode of the investment. The preceding section outlined the basic characteristics of subsidiaries in terms of several of these important decisions. This section focuses on explaining the entry mode decision, and the relationship of entry mode to subsidiary performance. In looking at the relationship between entry mode and performance, this section attempts to establish overall trends in the performance of various modes. One of the most important conclusions drawn from this chapter is that contrary to their notorious reputation, joint ventures on average do not perform worse than wholly owned subsidiaries. The other investigations found in this section delve further into the "why" of performance by proposing moderating effects, such as government ownership restrictions and the nature of the firm's ownership advantages, on the entry mode choice and performance relationship.

Chapter 4 begins this section by establishing the overall trends in the entry mode and performance relationship. The ownership entry modes examined are the wholly owned modes of acquisition and new venture entry, and the non-wholly owned mode of joint venture entry. A theoretical relationship is developed for international entry modes that is based on the contingency characteristics of resource requirements and organizational control factors. This model suggests that different entry modes have different performance outcomes based upon their resource and organizational control demands. The theoretical model, although developed using the eclectic theoretical approach, is based largely on concepts and relationships previously delineated in contingency theory. Our hypotheses suggest that new ventures should outperform joint ventures, and joint ventures should outperform acquisitions. An empirical test using a sample of 321 Japanese firms entering the North American market provides supporting evidence.

Chapter 5, which is the second chapter in this section, moves the analysis on the entry mode and performance section forward. It does this by examining the moderating effects of a host government's local ownership restrictions on the linkage between the choice of foreign entry mode and its performance, using a sample of 917 Japanese foreign subsidiaries in Asia. The chapter focuses on two foreign entry modes, joint ventures (JVs) and wholly-owned subsidiaries (WOS), and two performance measures, financial performance and termination rate. The results suggest that the extent of local ownership restrictions is negatively and significantly associated with the financial performance of WOS, whereas it does not directly influence that of JVs. There is no clear association between the extent of local ownership restrictions and the termination rate for the JV and WOS samples.

Chapter 6 continues in the same vein as Chapter 5 but in this case it looks at internal influences on the entry mode-performance relationship rather than external influences, as in the previous chapter. In this chapter, we investigate the effect of firm-specific advantages being "local" in scope, and the influence of subsequent location-specific disadvantages, on the choice of foreign entry mode and subsidiary performance. To look into this issue, we examine Japanese FDI data from the wholesale and retail industries – two sectors that have productive activity concentrated in downstream processes and location-bound resources. Our theoretical and empirical analyses demonstrate that, in situations where required capabilities must be developed through local experience and where location-specific resources were subject to market failure, acquisition and joint venture strategies were preferred. Greenfield entries were successful in industries that permitted the offsetting of location-specific disadvantages with firm-specific advantages. From our results, we draw implications for the entry mode literature and offer a perspective on the performance of the entry mode choice.

PART III   JOINT VENTURES

A subset of the entry mode choice issue is the ownership decision. This decision concerns the percentage equity holding that a firm will take in its overseas subsidiary. A prominent feature of Japanese firms' investment patterns worldwide is the prevalence of the use of joint ventures. As Chapter 2 pointed out, joint ventures are implemented in nearly half of all Japanese foreign subsidiaries. This propensity of joint venture usage far outstrips that of other multinational enterprises from other major investing countries such as the United States or the United Kingdom. This section investigates why this is the case. The first two chapters in this section delve into the why of the case by adopting standard conceptual models, developed with reference to US-based firms, to the prediction of the ownership decision of Japanese firms. As Chapters 7 and 8 show, these models require adaptation to fully explain the ownership strategy of Japanese foreign investors. The latter two chapters in this section focus more specifically on the joint venture form.

Joint ventures can take considerable variance in form. Further, joint ventures may have a limited period of operational effectiveness because of learning on the part of the Japanese partner. Chapters 9 and 10 provide insight into why this might be the case.

The study reported in Chapter 7 jointly examines the effects of organizational capabilities and public and private expropriation hazards on the level of equity ownership chosen for foreign subsidiaries in emerging markets. Specifically, we explore the mechanisms by which 660 Japanese multinational corporations draw upon capabilities developed via industry-specific, country-specific and total international experience to mitigate these hazards for their 2,827 subsidiaries in 18 emerging markets. Results strongly support a novel specification that forges a link between the capabilities and the public and private expropriation hazards literatures.

In Chapter 8, we compare the effects of transactional, institutional and experience influences on the ownership strategies of Japanese investors. Our theoretical development suggests that the equity position of a foreign investor should increase as the specificity of the assets transferred to the foreign affiliate increases, but a lower equity position should be assumed when the foreign investor requires complementary assets to establish a foreign entry. International experience and a strong institutional environment also should lead to increases in the equity position of the foreign investor. These relationships were tested with data on more than 1,000 Japanese investments in nine countries of East and South East Asia. The results demonstrate that experience and institutional factors were the most important influences on the ownership position taken in the foreign investment, while transactional factors had a much less important and a more ambiguous role.

In Chapter 9 we explain the joint venture form in more detail. The international joint venture literature has focused on two parent JVs formed between one foreign and one local firm. Yet other types of JVs exist. This chapter identifies four distinct forms of JVs based on the JV partners' nationality and equity affiliation. These are (i) JVs that are formed between affiliated home-country based firms; (ii) JVs that are formed between unaffiliated home-country based firms; (iii) JVs that are formed between home-country based and local firms; and (iv) JVs that are formed between home-country and third-country based firms. Our analysis of 737 Japanese JVs in Asia demonstrates that the conventionally assumed form of JV represented only 30 percent of the total. Further, each of the four JV forms significantly differed in terms of incidence, performance, and survival likelihood.

Chapter 10 moves the discussion of joint ventures from the examination of the motivations to their use, to a consideration of what time means for the efficacy of this organizational form. We begin this chapter with the observation that foreign firms in host country environments frequently face location-based disadvantages. This chapter proposes three means (channels) of overcoming local knowledge disadvantages. Based on a sample of 558 Japanese JVs located in Southeast and East Asia, we find that partnering with local firms (the first channel) can be a primary strategy for accessing local knowledge and improving JV performance. JV experience in the host country (the second channel) also mitigates local knowledge disadvantages and leads to increased JV performance. The third channel, the foreign parent's host country experience, leads to increased performance in the absence of a local partner. However, when a JV is formed with a local partner, increased parent experience in the host country leads to decreased performance suggesting that the need for a local partner declines as parent experience in a host country increases.

PART IV   MANAGEMENT STRATEGY

The preceding sections have described the form and performance of Japanese investment and analyzed the motivations for the various forms of investment. While these sections have provided a good picture of the strategy involved in making these investments, it has not looked at the processes found in managing these subsidiaries. Yet, firms face formidable obstacles to successfully manage subsidiary operations and integrate the operations of these subsidiaries with those of the parent multinational. Several options exist for the firm in deciding how to manage its subsidiary. These include the degree of ownership and control, the extent of localization of management, and the use of expatriates. The three chapters in this section address each of these issues in detailing the management strategy of Japanese firms for their foreign subsidiaries.

  Chapter 11 explores the issue of integration between the subsidiary and the multinational parent. It looks at the structural mechanisms that can promote such integration, and also considers whether the multinational even had the objective of integration at the outset, when the subsidiary was founded. China and India form the empirical base for this investigation. China has been a major recipient of Japanese FDI, while investment in India has grown much more slowly. We argue that the differences extend much beyond the levels of investment – Japanese involvement in India and China is qualitatively different. Japanese FDI in China was motivated by access to location-specific production resources, and it involved a high degree of technology, management skills and organizational knowledge transfer. The Japanese subsidiaries in China were integrated with the network of international subsidiaries as a part of the MNC's global strategy. Japanese

FDI in India, however, was motivated by the desire to access local markets. It involved less transfer of technology and management skills, and Japanese subsidiaries in India operated independently as part of a multi-domestic strategy. We conclude that foreign entrants to the region should be aware and able to respond to the unique advantages of each host country and to the different strategies and capabilities of the subsidiaries of Japanese MNCs.

As the analysis in the preceding chapter revealed, Japanese expatriate employment is a critical consideration in devising management strategy. In fact, expatriates are regarded as being so critical to successful subsidiary operation that conventional wisdom holds that Japanese firms use large numbers of expatriates and are reluctant to allow local nationals a significant role in subsidiary management. Japanese firms have been criticized for their unwillingness to capitalize on the internal diversity in their international managerial ranks. It has been suggested that a rice paper ceiling in Japanese firms restricts local managers from advancement opportunities and involvement in the corporate-level decision making. The research reported in Chapter 12 directly challenges the notion that Japanese firms are unwilling to reduce their use of expatriates. This chapter shows that the number of Japanese expatriates is declining and has been for some time. One explanation for this decline is that Japanese firms have had no choice because of a limited supply of managers for expatriate positions. A second explanation is that Japanese firms are beginning to recognize the importance of empowering local management and are becoming more truly global in how they compete.

The employment of expatriates is just one form of control in foreign subsidiaries. Another form of control is the ownership structure of the foreign subsidiary. Chapter 13 addresses issues found in the use of various ownership and control structures. Research has tended to treat this issue as whether to use a joint venture or a wholly owned subsidiary. Although many international joint ventures (JVs) are formed between foreign and local firms, increasingly, non-traditional forms are utilized to a considerable extent. This chapter identifies four distinct types of JV ownership structure based on partner nationality and affiliation. In-depth interviews with senior executives of two large Japanese MNEs suggested three distinct strategies corresponding to the choice of JV ownership structure. These involve (1) the exploiting of competitive advantage specific to a parent firm; (2) exploiting the competitive advantage relating to a pre-existing relationship; and (3) complementing local partners' competitive advantage. We consider several key issues regarding JV partner selection and the development of a sustainable relationship between JV partners which are relevant to both American executives, and those from other countries.

CONCLUDING COMMENTS

In producing this volume, we had the goal of providing a more complete picture of the international strategy of Japanese firms. If we have been at all successful at achieving this goal, we hope that a more complete picture will lead to a greater appreciation of what this group of firms has been doing on the international stage. At a minimum, this recognition means cognizance of the fundamental position that Japanese subsidiaries hold in the service and manufacturing sectors of such diverse economies as China, the United States, Thailand, Hong Kong, and Germany. At a more ambitious level, this recognition would place the empirical and conceptual significance of Japanese firms on par with that of American multinational enterprises.

Some of our most fundamental insights into multinational enterprises were supported by data collected as part of the Harvard Multinational Enterprise (HMNE) project, led by Raymond Vernon of Harvard University in the late 1960s. The volume of data collected at that time resulted in the creation of the largest and most valuable database on multinational enterprise at that time, and indeed for the next twenty years. The Toyo Keizai (TK) database on which the studies in this volume are based (see Chapter 2) exceeds the HMNE in numbers of subsidiaries and parent firms, and in its longitudinal scope. Much of our understanding of multinational enterprises is driven by studies of the US-based firms that comprised the HMNE dataset. As the papers in this volume show, the Japanese case is very often different from the American one.

Yet, while we have compiled some evidence of Japanese firms' international strategies, the implementation of studies using this database is still at a young stage. The collected papers in this volume represent a start, not a conclusion, to this line of research. We hope that the papers in this book help spur scholars to extend the depth of research on Japanese multinationals. An extension of the domain of research, to firms from other nations, would likewise provide new insights into the multinational enterprise. Only by extending the depth and domain of research can we truly understand the strategies of firms in international markets.

PART I

Why Internationalize? More Subsidiaries
Results in Superior Performance

2. The nature of Japanese investment worldwide

Andrew Delios, Paul W. Beamish and Shige Makino

Foreign direct investment (FDI) flows from Japanese firms showed considerable variance in the 1990s. The decade began with near record levels of outward investment in 1990. The next three years saw successive declines in FDI levels which only rebounded to a new high in 1995. This mid-1990s peak in outward FDI was followed by another period of decline as the 1990s drew to a close (Toyo Keizai, 1999). While the 1990s exhibited considerable fluctuation in yearly FDI levels, the decade as a whole saw Japan maintain its position as one of the leading sources of FDI. In particular, Japan's leading role in Asia, and in the People's Republic of China (China), became more prominent as greater proportions of Japan's FDI outflows were directed to these countries (UNCTAD, 1997).

The result of the 1990s re-focussing of Japanese FDI from European and North American countries to Asia created a substantially different picture of the characteristics of Japanese foreign investment at the end of the 1990s. This chapter develops a snapshot of several salient characteristics of Japanese foreign subsidiaries – geographic distribution, equity ownership and entry mode, sales, capitalization, employment and subsidiary performance – to provide a backdrop for the more in-depth analyses found in later chapters in this book.

One of the most prominent characteristics of Japanese FDI is its continued growth through the 1990s. This growth occurred in the face of a protracted slowdown in Japan's domestic economy, and during a time of a severe economic downturn in many Asian countries. As an example, during the height of the Asian financial crisis (1997 to 1999), the number of foreign subsidiaries reported in Toyo Keizai's *Kaigai Shinshutsu Kigyou Souran* increased by more than 1,000, which was five percent growth over 1997.

As with any research, caution should accompany any conclusions drawn from a single source. As a check on the veracity of the numbers reported in

Kaigai Shinshutsu Kigyou Souran, we compared the foreign subsidiary information reported in this source with other sources for publicly-listed firms, namely annual reports and industry and company reports published by such bodies as the Wright Research Center. When we compared Toyo Keizai's list of foreign subsidiaries in *Kaigai Shinshutsu Kigyou Souran* for firms listed on the first and second section of the Tokyo stock exchange to these other sources, we found that all but 33 firms (about 1.5 percent) of first and second section firms that had foreign subsidiaries were listed in *Kaigai Shinshutsu Kigyou Souran*. Further, the 33 firms that were not listed had 70 foreign subsidiaries, which was less than 0.5 percent of all foreign subsidiaries of first and second section listed firms.

Based on this comparison, we can be confident that *Kaigai Shinshutsu Kigyou Souran* reports on a near population-level sample of Japanese foreign investment activity. Hence, the tabulations below reflect a fairly accurate picture of the state of Japanese foreign investment at the end of 1998.

VARIABLES

Toyo Keizai publishes two versions of *Kaigai Shinshutsu Kigyou Souran*. One version (*kaisha betsu*) lists subsidiaries by parent company ownership. Another version (*kuni betsu*) lists subsidiaries by the host country in which the subsidiary was established. The two versions report almost identical information. To facilitate grouping the data by host country, the tables in this chapter report on the information found in the latter source, the 1999 *kuni betsu* version of *Kaigai Shinshutsu Kigyou Souran*.

For each subsidiary listed in *Kaigai Shinshutsu Kigyou Souran* several key characteristics are reported. These characteristics are summarized in Table 2.1, and described in more detail in the following section. As can be seen in the table, not all items were reported with the same frequency. There was full information on the host country of the 19,030 subsidiaries listed in the 1999 edition. More than 98 percent of the listed subsidiaries identified their entry mode, equity ownership levels and foundation date. Another 96 percent had figures for the capital invested to establish the subsidiary. The number of employees was the next most commonly reported item, with 84 percent of the subsidiaries identifying the total number of employees, and 78 percent stating the number of expatriate employees. Performance information in terms of sales and profitability was also given, with 47 percent and 43 percent response rates to the sales and profitability items respectively.

Table 2.1 Summary of the data

Variable	Mean	Standard deviation	Range	No. of responses	Response rate (%)
Host country	n.a.	n.a.	n.a.	19,030	100.00
Equity ownership	n.a.	n.a.	n.a.	18,670	98.11
Entry mode	n.a.	n.a.	n.a.	18,700	98.27
Foundation date	1,988	8.55	1929-1999	18,700	98.27
Annual sales ($m)	65.68	492.70	0-25,343	8,912	46.83
Subsidiary capitalization ($m)	17.05	7,140.29	0-8,000	18,290	96.11
Total number of employees	192.62	723.17	0-45,010	15,977	83.96
Number of expatriate employees	3.69	7.43	0-188	14,762	77.57
Subsidiary performance	2.39	0.79	1 (loss) to 3 (profit)	8,240	43.30

Variable Definitions

Host country
This variable identifies the host country or region in which the subsidiary was established. In 1999, Japanese companies had established foreign subsidiaries in 123 different countries/regions outside of Japan. This represented an increase of 31 countries over the number listed in the 1994 version of the databook (Beamish, Delios and Lecraw, 1997).

Equity ownership
This variable is the percentage equity ownership level possessed by each partner in the foreign subsidiary. Partners are also identified by nationality (Japanese or a host country partner) and by affiliation (Japanese partners related at the parent company level or not).

Entry mode

Four entry modes can be identified using the information reported in *Kaigai Shinshutsu Kigyou Souran*. These are (i) wholly owned subsidiary, (ii) joint venture, (iii) acquisition and (iv) capital participation. A wholly owned subsidiary is a greenfield operation in which the Japanese parent holds a 95 percent or greater ownership position in the subsidiary. A joint venture is also a greenfield operation, however two partners each hold at least 5 percent of the subsidiary's equity. In joint ventures, there may be multiple partners, from different country origins, such as the host country, Japan or a third country (see Chapter 13). An acquisition is the purchase of an ownership position in an existing entity in the host country. It can be a complete or partial purchase. Capital participation can also be referred to as a plant expansion. It is a foreign entry made by the expansion of an existing domestic operation as funded by the foreign investor. The foreign investor possesses an ownership position in the domestic operation as a result of this funded expansion.

Foundation date

This is the year and month the subsidiary was established.

Annual sales

Sales levels are reported in yen, local currencies and US dollars. Using exchange rates provided in *Kaigai Shinshutsu Kigyou Souran*, all sales and equity levels were converted to US dollar amounts. This facilitates comparability across subsidiaries established in different host countries. Sales levels mark annual sales revenues for the subsidiary for the most recent reporting period (1998).

Capitalization

This is the US dollar amount of capital invested in the foreign subsidiary by all partners.

Total number of employees

This is the number of employees working in the subsidiary in 1998, inclusive of expatriate employees.

Number of expatriate employees

This is the number of expatriate (Japanese) employees working in the subsidiary in 1998.

Performance
This variable identifies the profitability of the foreign subsidiary in 1998. It is reported as the subsidiary general manager's assessment of the subsidiary's financial performance. It is a categorical assessment in which there are three possible responses: loss, break-even, and gain. We coded loss responses with a value of 1, break-even with 2, and gain as 3.

Industry
While not listed in Table 2.1, the subsidiary's industry of operation can be identified from the information provided in *Kaigai Shinshutsu Kigyou Souran*. In the databook, there is a verbal description of the subsidiary's industry. This written description can be converted to an industrial classification code, such as the Standard Industrial Classification (SIC) code used in the United States, or other industrial classification systems like Nikkei's or the one used by the Daiwa Institute of Research for the *Analyst's Guide*. When using the SIC system from the United States, a three-digit level of coding can be achieved in most cases, and in a minority of subsidiaries, enough information is available to classify subsidiary operations at the four-digit SIC level.

Address
Written information is also provided on the address of the subsidiary. This includes the mailing address, telephone and fax numbers, and the name of the subsidiary's general manager. Not all address information is reported for all subsidiaries, but the information is close to complete.

GEOGRAPHIC DISTRIBUTION OF SUBSIDIARIES

Turning to the first of the variables listed in Table 2.1, we use Tables 2.2, 2.3 and 2.4 to describe the geographic distribution of Japanese foreign subsidiaries. In 1999, 123 different countries/regions were host sites for Japanese foreign investments. The number of subsidiaries in the host countries ranged from 1 (in 17 host countries) to 3,733 in the United States (Table 2.2). After the United States, the next five most popular destinations for Japanese foreign investment were China (2,424 subsidiaries), Thailand (1,306), Hong Kong, SAR (1,176), Singapore (1,165) and the United Kingdom (918). The mean number of foreign subsidiaries per host country was 154.

Table 2.2 Geographic distribution of foreign subsidiaries

Country / region	Number of subsidiaries	Percentage of total formed in country / region
Algeria	1	0.01
Angola	1	0.01
Argentina	36	0.19
Australia	510	2.68
Austria	55	0.29
Bahamas	11	0.06
Bahrain	11	0.06
Bangladesh	6	0.03
Belgium	157	0.83
Bermuda	24	0.13
Bolivia	3	0.02
Brazil	314	1.65
Brunei	9	0.05
Bulgaria	3	0.02
Cambodia	2	0.01
Cameroon	3	0.02
Canada	321	1.69
Cayman Islands	41	0.22
Chile	58	0.30
China	2,424	12.74
Colombia	22	0.12
Costa Rica	10	0.05
Croatia	2	0.01
Cyprus	1	0.01
Czech Republic	31	0.16
Dem.Rep. Of Congo	1	0.01
Denmark	23	0.12
Dominican Republic	2	0.01
Dutch Antilles	14	0.07
Ecuador	10	0.05
Egypt	9	0.05
El Salvador	5	0.03
Ethiopia	2	0.01
Fiji	2	0.01
Finland	16	0.08
France	348	1.83

Table 2.2 Geographic distribution of foreign subsidiaries (continued)

Country / region	Number of subsidiaries	Percentage of total formed in country / region
Germany	632	3.32
Ghana	2	0.01
Greece	9	0.05
Guam	53	0.28
Guatemala	8	0.04
Honduras	3	0.02
Hong Kong	1,176	6.18
Hungary	43	0.23
India	152	0.80
Indonesia	665	3.49
Iran	13	0.07
Ireland	42	0.22
Israel	10	0.05
Italy	181	0.95
Ivory Coast	2	0.01
Jordan	1	0.01
Kazakhstan	1	0.01
Kenya	2	0.01
Korea	453	2.38
Kuwait	5	0.03
Laos	3	0.02
Lebanon	1	0.01
Liberia	45	0.24
Luxembourg	36	0.19
Macao	5	0.03
Madagascar	2	0.01
Malaysia	845	4.44
Maldives	1	0.01
Malta	1	0.01
Mariana Islands	3	0.02
Mauritius	4	0.02
Mexico	200	1.05
Mongolia	4	0.02
Morocco	2	0.01
Mozambique	1	0.01
Myanmar	17	0.09

Table 2.2 Geographic distribution of foreign subsidiaries (continued)

Country / region	Number of subsidiaries	Percentage of total formed in country / region
Nepal	3	0.02
Netherlands	400	2.10
New Caledonia	1	0.01
New Zealand	102	0.54
Niger	1	0.01
Nigeria	15	0.08
Norway	19	0.10
Oman	1	0.01
Pakistan	20	0.11
Palau Islands	6	0.03
Panama	126	0.66
Papua new Guinea	3	0.02
Paraguay	2	0.01
Peru	19	0.10
Philippines	409	2.15
Poland	34	0.18
Portugal	34	0.18
Puerto Rico	5	0.03
Romania	11	0.06
Russia	42	0.22
Saipan Island	21	0.11
Samoa	3	0.02
Saudi Arabia	16	0.08
Singapore	1,165	6.12
Slovak	6	0.03
Slovenia	2	0.01
Solomon Islands	3	0.02
South Africa	25	0.13
Spain	165	0.87
Sri Lanka	23	0.12
Suriname	1	0.01
Swaziland	1	0.01
Sweden	56	0.29
Switzerland	81	0.43
Taiwan	845	4.44
Tanzania	5	0.03

Table 2.2 Geographic distribution of foreign subsidiaries (continued)

Country / region	Number of subsidiaries	Percentage of total formed in country / region
Thailand	1,306	6.86
Trinidad & Tobago	3	0.02
Tunisia	1	0.01
Turkey	30	0.16
United Arab Emirates	24	0.13
Ukraine	4	0.02
United Kingdom	918	4.82
Uruguay	1	0.01
United States	3,733	19.62
Vanuatu	4	0.02
Venezuela	26	0.14
Vietnam	170	0.89
Virgin Islands	24	0.13
Zambia	2	0.01
Zimbabwe	2	0.01
Total worldwide	19,030	100

Moving to a more aggregate level of geographic analysis, Asia had the largest stock of Japanese foreign subsidiaries in 1999 (Table 2.3). More than 50 percent of Japanese foreign subsidiaries, a number approaching 10,000 in 1999, were situated in Asia. North America, with 21 percent of all Japanese foreign subsidiaries, and Europe, with 17 percent, followed Asia as prominent recipients of Japanese FDI. Both North America and Europe reached their peak in terms of the proportion of FDI received from Japan in the 1980s. Prior to 1980, foreign investment levels were highest in Asia, with the exception of subsidiaries formed in the pre-1960 period. At that time, most subsidiaries were situated in the two American continents. By the 1990s, Asia had returned to its leading position, but with inward investment levels at their highest absolute level and at their highest relative (proportional) level in the last four decades.

In the 1990s, the most rapid growth in the foreign investment positions of Japanese firms has been in China. In the first half of the 1980s, just 44 Japanese subsidiaries were formed in China. However, one decade later, nearly 1,400 subsidiaries were established in the same five-year interval. The annual rate of subsidiary formation in China had slowed in the last half of the 1990s, but it was still the most popular site for Japanese foreign subsidiary establishment in the 1996-99 period (Table 2.4).

The rate of subsidiary formation in China mirrored that in Asia as a whole, and South-East Asia in particular. Despite the severe economic downturn that struck many Asian countries in the 1997-1999 period, Japanese investment levels continued at a comparatively high level. Among the most popular destinations for foreign investment in Asia in the latter part of the 1990s were Thailand, Singapore, Indonesia, the Philippines and Malaysia.

Outside of Asia, Japanese foreign investment levels were strong in the United States. However, investment into the United States continued to show a decline from peak levels recorded in the 1986-1990 period, which also marked the height of the equity market bubble in Japan. Similar patterns could be observed in Western European countries. Prominent host sites such as Germany, the Netherlands, the United Kingdom and France saw declines in received foreign investment in the 1990s as compared to the 1980s.

Meanwhile, the emerging economies in Eastern Europe showed a different trend, albeit from a very small base. Foreign investment levels in countries such as Russia, Poland, Hungary and the Czech Republic were greater in the first half of the 1990s than in the 1980s. However, as with the case for Japanese investment in much of the rest of the world, investment levels into Eastern European countries declined in the 1996-99 period.

Outside of Europe, North America and Asia, Japanese foreign investment levels remained low. South America, which experienced its greatest prominence as a host site for Japanese FDI in the 1970s, had not yet returned to that level of prominence by the close of the 1990s. However, there had been a slight recovery of Japanese FDI beginning in the 1985-90 period which was driven by strong growth in investment in Chile. Unlike in the rest of the world, the level of investment in 1985-90 was matched by inbound Japanese FDI in the 1991-95 and 1996-99 periods.

This trend was most pronounced in Latin America (principally Mexico and Panama in Central America). As a region, Latin America showed strong growth in Japanese FDI levels from 1976 to 1995. The peak in investment levels reached in the 1990-95 period, exceeded the previous 1971-75 period peak, although it was followed by a decline in 1996-99. However, the decline in the latter part of the 1990s was less than that recorded for Japanese FDI overall. As a proportion of all Japanese investment outflows, the amount received by Latin America grew from 3.7 percent in the first half of the 1990s, to 4.7 percent in the latter half.

Oceania, like the Latin American region, was a modest destination for Japanese foreign subsidiaries. The peak investment period in Oceania was the same as the peak in worldwide Japanese FDI, namely the 1986-90 period.

Table 2.3 Number of subsidiaries: Entry date by world region

World region	Pre-1960	1961-5	1966-70	1971-5	1976-80	1981-5	1986-90	1991-5	1996-9	Total
North America	64	57	122	254	266	502	1446	741	531	3983
	41.30%	27.00%	23.30%	18.70%	22.40%	30.30%	29.10%	14.00%	15.90%	21.30%
Latin America	36	15	49	155	93	81	162	195	155	941
	23.20%	7.10%	9.40%	11.40%	7.80%	4.90%	3.30%	3.70%	4.70%	5.00%
Europe	20	34	73	256	239	381	1040	875	390	3308
	12.90%	16.10%	14.00%	18.90%	20.20%	23.00%	20.90%	16.50%	11.70%	17.70%
Africa/Middle East	2	5	13	18	23	27	30	41	44	203
	1.30%	2.40%	2.50%	1.30%	1.90%	1.60%	0.60%	0.80%	1.30%	1.10%
Asia	19	94	233	595	503	588	2069	3323	2141	9565
	12.30%	44.50%	44.60%	43.90%	42.40%	35.50%	41.60%	62.60%	64.30%	51.10%
Oceania	14	6	33	77	61	79	227	134	69	700
	9.00%	2.80%	6.30%	5.70%	5.10%	4.80%	4.60%	2.50%	2.10%	3.70%
All subsidiaries	155	211	523	1355	1185	1658	4974	5309	3330	18700

Notes:
1. 330 subsidiaries did not report a date of foundation.
2. The first number is a count, the second is a column percentage.

Table 2.4 Number of subsidiaries: Entry date by country/region

Country or region	Pre-1960	1961-5	1966-70	1971-5	1976-80	1981-5	1986-90	1991-5	1996-9	Total
North America	64	57	122	254	266	502	1446	741	531	3983
Canada	5	3	20	30	16	60	103	51	30	318
United States	59	54	102	224	250	442	1343	690	501	3665
Latin America	36	15	49	155	93	81	162	195	155	941
Mexico	4	1	6	11	12	17	44	59	43	197
Central America	0	2	9	19	14	17	26	36	19	142
Costa Rica	0	1	3	1	1	0	1	0	3	10
El Salvador	0	0	2	1	1	1	0	0	0	5
Guatemala	0	1	0	1	5	0	0	1	0	8
Honduras	0	0	0	2	0	0	0	1	0	3
Panama	0	0	4	14	7	16	25	34	16	116
Caribbean	0	2	1	13	8	5	26	36	24	115
Bahamas	0	0	0	1	1	1	6	1	1	11
Bermuda	0	0	0	4	3	2	4	5	4	22
Cayman Islands	0	0	0	3	0	1	11	15	9	39
Dominican Republic	0	0	1	0	1	0	0	0	0	2
Dutch Antilles	0	1	0	2	3	0	2	5	1	14
Puerto Rico	0	1	0	2	0	1	0	1	0	5

Country or region	Pre-1960	1961-5	1966-70	1971-5	1976-80	1981-5	1986-90	1991-5	1996-9	Total
Suriname	0	0	0	1	0	0	0	0	0	1
Virgin Islands	0	0	0	0	0	0	3	9	9	21
South America	32	10	33	112	59	42	66	64	69	487
Argentina	4	0	3	1	7	3	2	9	6	35
Bolivia	0	0	0	1	1	0	0	0	1	3
Brazil	24	5	18	96	39	31	28	29	40	310
Chile	3	0	0	1	5	2	25	15	6	57
Colombia	0	0	2	5	0	2	5	2	6	22
Ecuador	0	0	0	0	5	2	1	1	1	10
Paraguay	0	0	0	1	0	0	0	0	1	2
Peru	0	1	7	2	0	1	0	4	4	19
Trinidad & Tobago	0	1	0	0	0	0	0	1	1	3
Uruguay	0	0	0	0	0	0	0	1	0	1
Venezuela	1	3	3	5	2	1	5	2	3	25
Europe	20	34	73	256	239	381	1040	875	390	3308
Western Europe	20	34	73	256	239	380	1025	774	332	3133
Austria	0	1	1	4	2	10	18	15	3	54
Belgium	1	3	9	23	16	20	34	39	9	154
Cyprus	0	0	0	0	0	0	1	0	0	1
Denmark	0	0	0	3	1	5	8	3	3	23
Finland	0	0	0	1	2	1	4	5	3	16

Table 2.4 Number of subsidiaries: Entry date by country/region (continued)

Country or region	Pre-1960	1961-5	1966-70	1971-5	1976-80	1981-5	1986-90	1991-5	1996-9	Total
France	2	6	10	28	24	34	103	89	45	341
Germany	8	16	23	56	66	94	164	147	47	621
Greece	0	0	1	2	3	2	1	0	0	9
Ireland	0	0	0	2	3	1	14	14	7	41
Italy	1	3	3	9	16	15	62	44	20	173
Luxembourg	0	0	0	5	4	5	16	6	0	36
Malta	0	0	0	0	0	0	0	1	0	1
Netherlands	1	1	6	37	17	41	152	98	38	391
Norway	0	0	0	2	2	3	6	3	2	18
Portugal	1	0	1	3	1	3	13	6	4	32
Spain	0	0	4	10	11	12	54	54	19	164
Sweden	1	0	3	5	5	9	10	14	7	54
Switzerland	2	2	0	13	10	18	19	10	6	80
Turkey	0	0	0	0	0	1	10	10	7	28
United Kingdom	3	2	12	53	56	106	336	216	112	896
Eastern Europe	0	0	0	0	0	1	15	101	58	175
Bulgaria	0	0	0	0	0	1	0	2	0	3
Croatia	0	0	0	0	0	0	0	1	1	2

Country or region	Pre-1960	1961-5	1966-70	1971-5	1976-80	1981-5	1986-90	1991-5	1996-9	Total
Czech Republic	0	0	0	0	0	0	1	22	7	30
Hungary	0	0	0	0	0	0	6	22	15	43
Poland	0	0	0	0	0	0	2	16	15	33
Romania	0	0	0	0	0	0	0	9	2	11
Russia	0	0	0	0	0	0	6	23	12	41
Slovakia	0	0	0	0	0	0	0	2	4	6
Slovenia	0	0	0	0	0	0	0	1	1	2
Ukraine	0	0	0	0	0	0	0	3	1	4
Africa/Middle East	2	5	13	18	23	27	30	41	44	203
Middle East	2	1	4	8	12	16	11	12	15	81
Bahrain	0	0	0	0	1	6	3	0	1	11
Iran	2	0	4	4	2	0	0	1	0	13
Israel	0	0	0	0	0	0	4	3	3	10
Jordan	0	1	0	0	0	0	1	0	0	1
Kuwait	0	0	0	0	2	2	0	0	0	5
Lebanon	0	0	0	1	0	0	0	0	0	1
Oman	0	0	0	0	0	0	0	0	1	1
Saudi Arabia	0	0	0	1	5	6	2	0	2	16
United Arab Emirates	0	0	0	2	2	2	1	8	8	23

Table 2.4 Number of subsidiaries: Entry date by country/region (continued)

Country or region	Pre-1960	1961-5	1966-70	1971-5	1976-80	1981-5	1986-90	1991-5	1996-9	Total
Africa	0	4	9	10	11	11	19	29	29	122
Algeria	0	0	0	0	0	0	0	0	1	1
Angola	0	0	0	0	0	0	0	1	0	1
Cameroon	0	0	0	0	0	2	0	0	0	2
Dem. Rep. of Congo	0	0	0	1	0	0	0	0	0	1
Egypt	0	0	0	0	1	1	2	1	4	9
Ethiopia	0	0	2	0	0	0	0	0	0	2
Ghana	0	1	0	0	0	0	0	0	1	2
Ivory Coast	0	0	1	0	0	1	0	0	0	2
Kenya	0	0	0	2	0	0	0	0	0	2
Liberia	0	0	0	5	2	2	14	15	5	43
Madagascar	0	0	1	0	0	0	0	1	0	2
Mauritius	0	0	0	0	0	1	0	1	0	2
Morocco	0	0	0	0	1	0	1	0	2	4
Mozambique	0	0	0	0	1	0	1	0	0	2
Niger	0	0	0	0	1	0	0	0	0	1
Nigeria	0	1	3	1	4	4	0	1	0	14
South Africa	0	0	0	0	0	0	1	8	13	22

Country or region	Pre-1960	1961-5	1966-70	1971-5	1976-80	1981-5	1986-90	1991-5	1996-9	Total
Swaziland	0	0	0	0	1	0	0	0	0	1
Tanzania	0	1	1	1	0	0	0	1	1	5
Tunisia	0	0	0	0	0	0	0	0	1	1
Zambia	0	1	1	0	0	0	0	0	0	2
Zimbabwe	0	0	0	0	0	0	1	0	1	2
Asia	19	94	233	595	503	588	2069	3323	2141	9565
South Asia	2	4	3	7	7	20	39	50	70	202
Bangladesh	0	0	0	0	1	1	1	2	1	6
India	2	4	2	4	3	13	25	39	59	151
Kazakhstan	0	0	0	0	0	0	0	1	0	1
Nepal	0	0	1	0	1	0	0	1	0	3
Pakistan	0	0	0	1	0	1	9	3	4	18
Sri Lanka	0	0	0	2	2	5	4	4	6	23
East and South-East Asia	17	90	230	588	496	568	2030	3273	2071	9363
Brunei	0	0	0	1	2	3	1	0	1	8
Cambodia	0	0	0	0	0	0	0	2	0	2
China	0	0	0	0	0	44	205	1363	770	2382
Hong Kong	2	22	47	125	100	96	276	366	121	1155
Indonesia	1	0	13	75	45	29	95	230	171	659
Korea	0	0	12	66	31	29	135	93	79	445
Laos	0	0	0	0	0	0	1	1	0	2

Table 2.4 Number of subsidiaries: Entry date by country/region (continued)

Country or region	Pre-1960	1961-5	1966-70	1971-5	1976-80	1981-5	1986-90	1991-5	1996-9	Total
Macao	0	0	0	0	1	0	1	2	1	5
Malaysia	1	5	8	62	46	82	255	259	116	834
Maldives	0	0	0	0	0	0	0	1	0	1
Mongolia	0	0	0	0	0	0	0	2	2	4
Myanmar	0	0	0	0	0	0	0	7	10	17
Philippines	1	2	4	28	28	11	63	135	129	401
Singapore	2	7	11	95	147	127	291	285	186	1151
Taiwan	2	22	85	47	59	76	287	153	104	835
Thailand	8	32	50	89	37	71	419	317	272	1295
Vietnam	0	0	0	0	0	0	1	57	109	167
Oceania										
Australia	14	6	33	77	61	79	227	134	69	700
New Zealand	12	6	23	48	47	60	151	96	57	500
Papua New Guinea	2	0	6	9	5	11	39	21	9	102
Samoa	0	0	1	2	0	0	0	0	0	3
Vanuatu	0	0	0	0	0	1	3	0	0	4
Solomon Islands	0	0	0	1	0	1	1	0	0	3
New Caledonia	0	0	0	0	0	0	1	0	0	1

Country or region	Pre-1960	1961-5	1966-70	1971-5	1976-80	1981-5	1986-90	1991-5	1996-9	Total
Guam	0	0	3	13	3	2	19	11	1	52
Palau Islands	0	0	0	1	0	2	2	0	1	6
Saipan Island	0	0	0	1	5	2	11	1	1	21
Fiji	0	0	0	1	0	0	0	1	0	2
Mariana Islands	0	0	0	1	1	0	0	1	0	3
All subsidiaries	155	211	523	1355	1185	1658	4974	5309	3330	18700

Note: 330 subsidiaries did not report a date of foundation.

Most Japanese FDI in Oceania (about two-thirds) was situated in Australia. New Zealand was the second most popular location, but it had investment levels about one-fifth of those in Australia.

Other regions in the world, namely Africa and the Middle East, received minor amounts of FDI in all periods. Only Liberia, mainly for ship registration, the United Arab Emirates and South Africa had received FDI of any significance in the 1990s.

EQUITY OWNERSHIP

One means of looking at ownership in foreign entries is to identify if single or multiple firms have ownership positions in the foreign subsidiary. If multiple firms are involved, the equity ownership position can be defined as majority (where the foreign investing firm possesses at least 51 percent but less than 95 percent of the subsidiary's equity), as co-owned (where two firms each possess 50 percent of the subsidiary's equity), or as minority (where the foreign investing firm possesses at least 5 percent but less than 50 percent of the subsidiary's equity).

One of the most notable characteristics of Japanese foreign investment is the prevalence of shared ownership modes. Approximately 45 percent of all Japanese foreign subsidiaries involved at least two partners that possessed five or more percent of the subsidiary's equity (Table 2.5). When comparing the level of equity ownership, majority-owned and minority-owned joint ventures were used with nearly equal frequency, while co-owned joint ventures accounted for almost 6 percent of all foreign subsidiaries formed.

While much literature indicates that joint ventures are a useful form of foreign market entry during the early stages of foreign market entry (Johanson and Vahlne, 1977), Japanese firms as a whole have relied on shared ownership modes to a greater extent in the 1990s. Whereas the percentage of wholly-owned subsidiaries was 60 percent or greater throughout the 1976-90 period, the frequency with which wholly-owned subsidiaries were used declined to below fifty percent in the 1990s. Part of the reason for this may rest with the greater concentration of Japanese investment in Asia in the 1990s, where shared ownership modes were encouraged by local governments. Part of this trend may also be related to changes in Japanese firms' international strategies in the 1990s.

MODE OF ENTRY

A second means of looking at ownership in foreign entry is to identify whether the entry was made by building a new subsidiary (a greenfield entry) or by purchasing a partial or full ownership position in an existing domestic operation. As defined earlier in this chapter (see p. 16), this classification identifies four forms of foreign entry: greenfield (wholly owned subsidiary), greenfield (joint venture), acquisition and capital participation.

While much attention has been devoted to the growing use of international mergers and acquisitions as a means of undertaking foreign direct investment (UNCTAD, 1997: Chapter 1), Japanese firms have a marked preference for greenfield entries, whether wholly owned or joint venture (Table 2.6). The distribution between wholly owned and joint venture among greenfield entries has been fairly even with an overall slight preference towards wholly owned subsidiaries (47 percent WOS versus 43 percent JV). However, as the trends in Table 2.5 corroborate, the 1990s has seen a shift away from the wholly owned mode towards joint ventures. In the 1990s, slightly more than half of all foreign entries were made by the greenfield joint venture mode. This is up from an average of 35-38 percent in the preceding three decades.

Meanwhile, acquisition and capital participation have remained relatively minor components of Japanese foreign investment. The capital participation mode enjoyed its greatest prominence in the 1960s, when 7.5 percent of entries were made by this mode. Since then, however, the use of capital participation has declined. Acquisitions, in contrast, grew in frequency of use through the 1970s and 1980s reaching a peak in the 1985-90 period. In the 1990s, Japanese firms' propensity to use acquisitions declined from the 1980s, but the propensity in this period was about equal to the mean propensity.

ANNUAL SALES

Japanese foreign subsidiaries averaged US$66 million in annual sales in 1998. The distribution of subsidiary sales by world region, and the distribution of subsidiary sales within each world region, showed considerable variance (Table 2.7). The largest subsidiaries, as defined by sales, were found in Africa and the Middle East. Mean sales for subsidiaries in Africa/Middle East was US$210 million. However, with the small number of subsidiaries reporting sales (85), this average is skewed upwards by a few very large subsidiaries involved in natural resource extraction. If the

Table 2.5 *Number of subsidiaries: Entry date by ownership category*

Ownership at entry	Pre-1960	1961-5	1966-70	1971-5	1976-80	1981-5	1986-90	1991-5	1996-9	Total
Wholly owned: 95-100%	125	118	299	796	751	1048	2969	2528	1537	10171
	80.60%	56.20%	57.60%	59.10%	64.10%	63.60%	60.50%	48.80%	47.60%	55.40%
Majority owned: 51-94%	16	36	91	216	159	219	816	1186	770	3509
	10.30%	17.10%	17.50%	16.00%	13.60%	13.30%	16.60%	22.90%	23.90%	19.10%
Co-owned: 50%	1	14	27	51	47	92	262	329	221	1044
	0.60%	6.70%	5.20%	3.80%	4.00%	5.60%	5.30%	6.30%	6.80%	5.70%
Minority owned: 5-49%	13	42	102	284	215	290	861	1141	700	3648
	8.40%	20.00%	19.70%	21.10%	18.30%	17.60%	17.50%	22.00%	21.70%	19.90%
All subsidiaries	155	210	519	1347	1172	1649	4908	5184	3228	18372

Notes:
1. 965 subsidiaries reported incomplete ownership information
2. 360 subsidiaries did not report any ownership information.
3. 330 subsidiaries did not report a date of foundation.
4. The first number is a count, the second is a column percentage.

Table 2.6 Number of subsidiaries: Entry date by mode of entry

Mode of entry	Pre-1960	1961-5	1966-70	1971-5	1976-80	1981-5	1986-90	1991-5	1996-9	Total
Greenfield (WOS)	109	109	282	724	668	909	2443	2137	1287	8668
	70.30%	51.90%	54.30%	53.70%	57.00%	55.10%	49.60%	41.10%	39.70%	47.10%
Greenfield (JV)	41	82	192	512	412	574	1848	2610	1676	7947
	26.50%	39.00%	37.00%	38.00%	35.20%	34.80%	37.50%	50.20%	51.70%	43.10%
Acquisition	3	4	4	16	24	58	297	195	118	719
	1.90%	1.90%	0.80%	1.20%	2.00%	3.50%	6.00%	3.70%	3.60%	3.90%
Capital participation	2	15	41	95	68	108	336	261	160	1086
	1.30%	7.10%	7.90%	7.10%	5.80%	6.50%	6.80%	5.00%	4.90%	5.90%
All subsidiaries	155	210	519	1347	1172	1649	4924	5203	3241	18420

Notes:
1. 330 subsidiaries did not report a date of foundation.
2. The first number is a count, the second is a column percentage.

proportion of subsidiaries in various sales categories is compared across regions, the distribution in Africa/Middle East is quite consistent with other world regions, with the exception of a high proportion of subsidiaries (18 percent) in the over US$100 million category.

Like the Africa/Middle East region, North America also had a relatively high proportion of subsidiaries (16 percent) with sales exceeding US$100 million. Among regions which had received large amounts of Japanese foreign investment, mean sales in North America were the highest (US$ 128 million). Subsidiaries in Europe and Latin America had the next greatest sales, while those established in Asia had the lowest at US$33 million. The low sales of subsidiaries in Asia might represent their relative newness as compared to those established elsewhere in the world. It might also represent a systematic smaller size of subsidiaries in Asia. The accuracy of this latter point can be gauged by making comparisons across world regions using other indicators of subsidiary size, such as subsidiary employment and subsidiary capitalization.

SUBSIDIARY CAPITALIZATION

Japanese foreign subsidiaries averaged a capital investment level of US$17 million at the end of 1998. Across four world regions – Europe, Asia, Oceania and Africa/Middle East – subsidiary capitalization varied marginally. However, Japanese subsidiaries in Latin America and North America were notably larger in terms of the mean capitalization, with North American subsidiaries the largest (Table 2.8).

The mean amount of capital invested in North American subsidiaries stood at US$31 million in 1999. As might be expected given the large mean, nearly half of the subsidiaries established worldwide in the over US$100 million category were located in North America. However, Asian subsidiaries, which accounted for approximately 50 percent of all Japanese foreign subsidiaries had just 17 percent of those with a capitalization greater than US$100 million. Most of the Asian subsidiaries had smaller levels of capital investment. Fully 75 percent of all Asian subsidiaries had a capitalization of less than US$5 million.

Latin American subsidiaries, which were the second largest by the capitalization measure, exhibited trends in the distribution across capitalization categories similar to subsidiaries situated in Europe. As in the Asian case, more than 60 percent of subsidiaries were formed with a capital base of less than US$5 million. However, several very heavily capitalized subsidiaries pushed the mean capitalization value (US$23 million) closer to the mean for North America, than to the population mean. Meanwhile, in an interesting contrast to their largest size as measured by subsidiary sales, African and Middle Eastern subsidiaries had the lowest mean capitalization at US$11 million.

TOTAL NUMBER OF EMPLOYEES

Japanese foreign subsidiaries are important sources of employment in several world regions. In North America, Japanese subsidiaries employed more than 660,000 people. In Asia, the number employed was even greater standing at nearly two million people in 1999. The large number of people employed in the Asian-based subsidiaries of Japanese firms was a reflection of both the large number of subsidiaries situated in Asia, and the high employment levels found within those subsidiaries (Table 2.9). Despite the comparatively smaller size of subsidiaries placed in Asia, as measured by subsidiary sales and capitalization, those located in Asia were the largest by the total employment measure. The average Asian-based Japanese subsidiary had 228 employees in 1999. Further, nearly 400 subsidiaries had more than 1,000 employees. This represented nearly two-thirds of the worldwide subsidiaries that had a size greater than 1,000 employees. A similar proportion of worldwide subsidiaries employing between 100 and 1,000 employees was also situated in Asia.

Next to Asia, the largest subsidiaries by the employment measure were located in North America (mean of 196 employees) and Latin America (186 employees). The regions with the smallest subsidiaries, Europe and Oceania, had subsidiaries with just half the mean employment of those in Asia. The highest percentage of subsidiaries in the '10 and under' employees categories were also found in Europe and Oceania.

When comparing the size of subsidiaries by the three measures, sales, capitalization and employment, the trends across the world regions vary by each measure. For example, the largest subsidiaries by the sales measure are found in Africa/Middle East, the largest by the capitalization measure are in North America and the largest by the employment measure are in Asia. These differences illustrate the importance of using multiple measures when comparing subsidiary size. The variance across measures also points to interesting differences in the orientation of the subsidiaries established in each region. The relatively large amount of sales compared to employment and capitalization for African and Middle Eastern subsidiaries represents in part the natural resource extraction and sales (non-manufacturing) strategic orientation of these subsidiaries. The disproportionately large number of employees in Asian subsidiaries points to a manufacturing orientation for Japanese subsidiaries based in Asia, particularly in labor-intensive

Table 2.7 Number of subsidiaries: Annual sales by world region

World region	Average ($m)	Under $1m	$1-5m	$5-10m	$10-25m	$25-100m	Over $100m	Total
North America	128	178	340	233	362	487	309	1909
		9.30%	17.80%	12.20%	19.00%	25.50%	16.20%	100%
Latin America	70	95	103	45	59	51	41	394
		24.10%	26.10%	11.40%	15.00%	12.90%	10.40%	100%
Europe	81	300	245	191	268	295	150	1449
		20.70%	16.90%	13.20%	18.50%	20.40%	10.40%	100%
Africa/Middle East	210	11	25	15	6	13	15	85
		12.90%	29.40%	17.60%	7.10%	15.30%	17.60%	100%
Asia	33	902	1458	746	786	605	235	4732
		19.10%	30.80%	15.80%	16.60%	12.80%	5.00%	100%
Oceania	59	55	93	54	55	60	26	343
		16.00%	27.10%	15.70%	16.00%	17.50%	7.60%	100%
All subsidiaries	66	1541	2264	1284	1536	1511	776	8912
		17.30%	25.40%	14.40%	17.20%	17.00%	8.70%	100%

Notes:
1. 10,118 subsidiaries did not report annual sales.
2. The first number is a count, the second is a row percentage.

Table 2.8 Number of subsidiaries: Capitalization by world region

World region	Average ($)	Under $1m	$1-5m	$5-10m	$10-25m	$25-100m	Over $100m	Total
North America	31	1237	1086	398	453	455	202	3831
		32.30%	28.30%	10.40%	11.80%	11.90%	5.30%	100%
Latin America	23	415	201	100	84	67	29	896
		46.30%	22.40%	11.20%	9.40%	7.50%	3.20%	100%
Europe	14	1381	862	349	331	260	106	3289
		42.00%	26.20%	10.60%	10.10%	7.90%	3.20%	100%
Africa/Middle East	11	122	35	9	10	5	3	184
		66.30%	19.00%	4.90%	5.40%	2.70%	1.60%	100%
Asia	12	3874	3232	1049	778	408	73	9414
		41.20%	34.30%	11.10%	8.30%	4.30%	0.80%	100%
Oceania	13	278	175	79	67	60	17	676
		41.10%	25.90%	11.70%	9.90%	8.90%	2.50%	100%
All subsidiaries	17	7307	5591	1984	1723	1255	430	18290
		40.00%	30.60%	10.80%	9.40%	6.90%	2.40%	100%

Notes:
1. 740 subsidiaries did not report capitalization levels.
2. The first number is a count, the second is a row percentage.

manufacturing industries. While the regional comparisons depicted in Tables 2.7, 2.8 and 2.9 point to these interesting differences, more detailed analyses are required to disentangle explanations for the variance in broad regional and country trends in employment, capitalization and sales levels in Japanese foreign subsidiaries (Beamish, Delios and Lecraw, 1997).

NUMBER OF EXPATRIATE EMPLOYEES

Japanese expatriate employees can be found in the majority of Japanese subsidiaries located across the world. However, in perhaps a larger proportion than might be expected, 21 percent of all Japanese subsidiaries did not have an expatriate employee (Table 2.10). Proportionally, the largest number of subsidiaries without Japanese expatriate employees were located in Latin America, Africa and the Middle East and Oceania. Latin American subsidiaries are among the oldest, on average, among all Japanese subsidiaries. Given this age, it is understandable that not all subsidiaries require a Japanese expatriate. However, for subsidiaries in Africa, the Middle East and Oceania, this explanation does not apply.

Subsidiaries located in Latin America, Oceania and Africa/Middle East also had the lowest mean number of expatriate employees. Subsidiaries in these regions averaged an expatriate employment level of just more than two people per subsidiary. As a proportion of overall employment, the percentage of expatriates was slightly greater than one percent in Latin American and African/Middle Eastern subsidiaries, but two percent in subsidiaries in Oceania. The percentage in Oceania was close to the mean worldwide, which was approximately 1.9 percent. See Table 2.10.

The highest percentage of expatriate employees was found in North American subsidiaries. Nearly 2.7 percent of all employees in North American subsidiaries were Japanese expatriates. This translated into a mean expatriate employment level of 5.2 per subsidiary. This mean was nearly two expatriate employees greater than the next largest mean of 3.5 expatriates per subsidiary, found in Japanese subsidiaries in Asia. Europe was the only other region to have a mean number of expatriates greater than three.

While twenty percent of Japanese subsidiaries had no expatriate employees, nearly seven percent of subsidiaries had more than ten expatriate employees. The greatest number of subsidiaries with more than ten expatriate employees was found in Asia (459 subsidiaries). The proportion of subsidiaries with more than 10 subsidiaries was, however, greatest in North America, where more than one in ten subsidiaries had more than ten expatriate employees. Worldwide, more than 1,000 subsidiaries employed more than ten Japanese

Table 2.9 Number of subsidiaries: Total employment by world region

World region	Average	Under 5	5-10	11-25	26-50	51-100	101-1000	Over 1000	Total
North America	193	749	489	479	418	377	793	121	3426
		21.90%	14.30%	14.00%	12.20%	11.00%	23.10%	3.50%	100%
Latin America	186	213	74	98	99	101	172	31	788
		27.00%	9.40%	12.40%	12.60%	12.80%	21.80%	3.90%	100%
Europe	107	532	436	528	418	330	461	44	2749
		19.40%	15.90%	19.20%	15.20%	12.00%	16.80%	1.60%	100%
Africa/Middle East	171	46	26	23	22	12	29	9	167
		27.50%	15.60%	13.80%	13.20%	7.20%	17.40%	5.40%	100%
Asia	228	744	923	1140	1090	1236	2736	379	8248
		9.00%	11.20%	13.80%	13.20%	15.00%	33.20%	4.60%	100%
Oceania	115	182	80	87	65	72	99	14	599
		30.40%	13.40%	14.50%	10.90%	12.00%	16.50%	2.30%	100%
All subsidiaries	193	2466	2028	2355	2112	2128	4290	598	15977
		15.40%	12.70%	14.70%	13.20%	13.30%	26.90%	3.70%	100%

Notes:
1. 3053 subsidiaries did not report total employment.
2. The first number is a count, the second is a row percentage.

expatriates, and another 1,400 had between six and ten Japanese expatriates. Extrapolating mean expatriate employment values in Table 2.10 to the full sample of more than 19,000, the total number of Japanese employees working abroad exceeded 70,000 in 1999.

SUBSIDIARY PERFORMANCE

Performance of firms, whether at the corporate (parent) level or the subsidiary level, is a topic of paramount interest to managers, public policy makers and academics alike. Unlike the ready availability of corporate performance data, particularly for publicly-listed firms, subsidiary performance information is frequently lacking in consolidated reports. The profitability data listed in *Kaigai Shinshutsu Kigyou Souran* on Japanese subsidiaries provides one means of assessing the performance of these subsidiaries across world regions.

According to the managerial assessments of subsidiary performance provided in *Kaigai Shinshutsu Kigyou Souran*, 58 percent of Japanese subsidiaries had profitable operations in 1998 (Table 2.11). Among the subsidiaries that were not profitable, a slightly higher percentage achieved break-even performance as opposed to a loss (22 percent versus 19 percent). Using a value of one to represent a loss, two to mark break-even and three for a gain or profitable operations, the highest mean performance was found in subsidiaries in Europe. At a substantive level, the mean performance in Europe differed little from that in Asia. In both these regions, at least sixty percent of the subsidiaries were profitable in 1998.

In two regions, less than half of the subsidiaries were profitable. This was in the Latin American and the African/Middle Eastern regions. The lowest mean performance was for subsidiaries in Africa and the Middle East. However, mean performance in Latin America was greater than in Africa/Middle East because of the larger percentage of subsidiaries found in the gain category. With more than one-third of all subsidiaries classified as having break-even performance, Latin American subsidiaries had a mean equal to that of North American subsidiaries. Interestingly, the largest proportion of loss making subsidiaries in any region was in North America, where 22 percent of subsidiaries reported making a loss in 1998. Oceania was the only other region to have more than twenty percent of subsidiaries in the loss category.

When compared to reports in preceding years for Japanese foreign subsidiary performance, the overall mean of 2.39 represents a slight increase compared to the mean for 1993 which was 2.36 (Beamish, Delios and Lecraw, 1997: 294). Comparing the percentages in each category between

Table 2.10 Number of subsidiaries: Expatriate employment by world region

World region	Average	0	1-2	3-5	6-10	Over 10	Total
North America	5.17	650	1108	731	371	344	3204
		20.30%	34.60%	22.80%	11.60%	10.70%	100%
Latin America	2.26	236	244	137	45	25	687
		34.40%	35.50%	19.90%	6.60%	3.60%	100%
Europe	3.17	740	884	520	238	147	2529
		29.30%	35.00%	20.60%	9.40%	5.80%	100%
Africa/Middle East	2.18	57	51	31	8	4	151
		37.70%	33.80%	20.50%	5.30%	2.60%	100%
Asia	3.50	1277	3175	1978	749	459	7638
		16.70%	41.60%	25.90%	9.80%	6.00%	100%
Oceania	2.25	204	204	97	24	24	553
		36.90%	36.90%	17.50%	4.30%	4.30%	100%
All subsidiaries	3.69	3164	5666	3494	1435	1003	14762
		21.40%	38.40%	23.70%	9.70%	6.80%	100%

Notes:
1. 4268 subsidiaries did not report expatriate employment.
2. The first number is a count, the second is a row percentage.

Table 2.11 *Number of subsidiaries: Performance by world region*

Performance	North America	Latin America	Europe	Africa/ Middle East	Asia	Oceania	Total
Loss (1.0)	435	57	201	15	822	69	1599
	22.30%	17.00%	16.50%	18.80%	19.00%	21.50%	19.40%
Breakeven (2.0)	449	116	271	28	909	67	1840
	23.00%	34.50%	22.20%	35.00%	21.00%	20.90%	22.30%
Gain (3.0)	1070	163	749	37	2597	185	4801
	54.80%	48.50%	61.30%	46.30%	60.00%	57.60%	58.30%
Total	1954	336	1221	80	4328	321	8240
Average performance	2.32	2.32	2.45	2.28	2.41	2.36	2.39

Notes:
1. 10,790 subsidiaries did not report performance.
2. The first number is a count, the second is a column percentage.

1998 and 1993, there were 2.1 percent more subsidiaries in the gain category in 1998, 1.6 percent fewer in the breakeven category, and another 0.5 percent less in the loss category. This continues a trend towards higher reported Japanese foreign subsidiary performance identified in Beamish and Delios (1997b).

A second performance comparison can be made across entry modes. While it has been generally reported in the literature on foreign investment that greenfield joint ventures perform at a lower level than greenfield wholly owned subsidiaries, the performance levels across these two modes were substantively the same in 1998 (Table 2.12). Acquisitions, which have also been identified as a mode with poorer performance than greenfield joint ventures and greenfield wholly owned subsidiaries (Woodcock, Beamish and Makino, 1994), exhibited performance on par with the two greenfield modes in 1999. The highest performing mode was capital participation. Sixty-three percent of the entries made by this mode reported profitable operations in 1999.

Table 2.12 Number of subsidiaries: Performance by entry mode

Performance	Greenfield (WOS)	Greenfield (JV)	Acquisition	Capital participation	Total
Loss (1.0)	695	721	79	96	1591
	19.10%	19.80%	21.70%	17.70%	19.40%
Breakeven (2.0)	837	816	70	105	1828
	23.00%	22.40%	19.20%	19.30%	22.30%
Gain (3.0)	2109	2106	215	342	4772
	57.90%	57.80%	59.10%	63.00%	58.30%
Total	3641	3643	364	543	8191
Average performance	2.39	2.38	2.37	2.45	2.39

Notes:
1. 10,790 subsidiaries did not report performance.
2. 330 subsidiaries did not report entry mode.
3. The first number is a count, the second is a column percentage.

As with the case of performance differences by region, and the other comparisons made in this chapter, the performance comparison across entry mode begs more thorough and complete analyses to develop more substantive explanations about why these trends exist. Subsequent chapters report on studies that have explored several of these relationships in more depth. These chapters are organized by topic, and they present our findings concerning several aspects of the international strategy of Japanese firms including entry mode choice and performance, the design of joint ventures, and the management of foreign subsidiaries. The chapters also report on more in-depth analyses of the varying characteristics and strategy found in Japanese subsidiaries located in different world regions. The next chapter moves the level of analysis from the subsidiary to the corporation, as it identifies the performance implications of internationalization.

3. Geographic scope, product diversification and the corporate performance of Japanese firms

Andrew Delios and Paul W. Beamish

The study extends research on the geographic scope, product diversification and performance relationship by exploring both the antecedents and consequences of geographic scope. In so doing, it addresses a fundamental criticism of the geographic scope-performance relationship; namely, that the observed positive relationship between geographic scope and performance is spurious because it is the possession of proprietary assets that is the foundation of superior performance, not expansion into international markets per se. We tested the research model with data on the corporate performance of 399 Japanese manufacturing firms. In the Partial Least Squares analyses used to examine the study's six main hypotheses, we demonstrate that geographic scope was positively associated with firm profitability, even when the competing effect of proprietary assets on firm performance was considered. Further, we find that performance was not related to the extent of product diversification, although investment levels in rent-generating, proprietary assets were related to the extent of product diversification.

INTRODUCTION

An important question concerning the internationalization of a firm involves the relationship between geographic scope and performance. This question is particularly salient in a world in which multinational enterprises (MNEs) are accounting for larger and larger shares of worldwide production (UNCTAD, 1997). Increasingly, managers are being urged to increase the firm's geographic scope, presumably to increase its competitiveness and profitability. We explore this issue of geographic scope, defined as the international extent of a firm's operations, and corporate performance, by examining the international experiences of Japanese manufacturing firms.

Research in strategic management and international business has addressed the issue of geographic scope and performance in several ways, but with a common objective – to identify the nature of the relationship between the two. In general, the consensus in the literature is that (1) international diversification decreases the variability, or risk, of a firm's revenue stream (Rugman, 1979; Hisey and Caves, 1985; Kim, Hwang and Burgers, 1993), and (2) geographic scope is positively, although not necessarily linearly, related to performance (Geringer, Beamish and daCosta, 1989; Tallman and Li, 1996; Hitt, Hoskisson and Kim, 1997). However, a persistent criticism is that the observed relationship between geographic scope and performance is spurious. As an example of this line of critique, Dess et al. (1995) contend that geographic scope is not related to performance; rather, it is the possession of proprietary assets – which is the impetus to foreign direct investment – that is the ultimate source of superior firm performance. In this study, we address this criticism by exploring the question: Is there value intrinsic to a wide geographic scope of operations?

In addressing this question we utilize a path analytic approach that incorporates both the antecedents and consequences of geographic scope. This design is necessary because industry characteristics, diversification strategy and decisions concerning the internal development of products are inter-related with each other and corporate performance (Stimpert and Duhaime, 1997). To understand where the value arises in conducting operations internationally, it is necessary to consider the inter-relatedness of antecedent and consequent constructs, and to partial out the direct and indirect effects of these variables on corporate performance. In conducting such an analysis, this study makes several contributions. By using a causal modeling approach, this research explicitly considers the effects of the determinants of international production on both geographic scope and performance. This form of design is necessary to separately address the questions: (1) Are multinational firms more profitable? and (2) Is there value in internationalization in itself? In developing the research model, economics-based research on multinational enterprise is integrated with strategy-based research on geographic scope, product diversification and performance. As well, the study expands the context of coverage by utilizing a sample of Japanese firms, an area in which empirical research has been encouraged (Caves, 1998; Beamish, Delios and Lecraw, 1997). Finally, the study extends the model developed by Stimpert and Duhaime (1997) by including the international dimension, and by testing it with a different sample of firms.

RESEARCH MODEL AND HYPOTHESIS DEVELOPMENT

Ansoff (1965) and Andrews (1971) articulated the corporate and business-level strategic decisions faced by managers in growing firms. These decisions include the choice of the firm's vertical, product and geographic scope. The latter two choices have received much attention in the international business and strategic management literatures. For example, Stopford and Wells' (1972) pioneering study on the management of MNEs identified the extent of area diversification (i.e., geographic scope) and product diversification as two of the critical determinants of the success of the MNE's growth. Likewise, Penrose's (1956: 250) work concerned these two growth paths:

> The 'productive opportunity' which invites expansion is not exclusively an external one. It is largely determined by the internal resources of the firm: the products the firm can produce, the new areas in which it can successfully set up plants, the innovations it can successfully launch, the very ideas of its executives and the opportunities they see, depend as much on the kind of experience, managerial ability and technological know-how already existing within the firm as they do upon external opportunities open to all.

As in this quote and in the resource based literature (Penrose, 1959), the firm's optimal expansion path is governed by factors internal and external to the firm. To develop an understanding of the decisions concerning a firm's growth, and the implications of those decisions for the firm's performance, a model must consider external factors, such as the characteristics of the firm's industry, and internal factors that define the constraints and opportunities placed on the firm by its resource base. The research reported in this study attempts this form of integration. Figure 3.1 depicts this study's research model, which integrates theoretical and empirical work on the determinants of international operations with the work of Stimpert and Duhaime (1997). By bringing this model of industry, product diversification and performance into the international context, we seek to answer the question of whether there is value intrinsic to a wider geographic scope of operations.

Industry Profitability, Product Diversification and Performance

The profitability of growth by diversification is a well-explored topic in strategic management (see the reviews in Ramanujam and Varadarajan, 1989; Hoskisson and Hitt, 1990; Datta, Rajagopalan and Rasheed, 1991). Early studies on diversification and performance were guided by the IO structure-conduct-performance framework (Scherer and Ross, 1990) and explored the relationship between product diversification, market power and

firm performance.   However, little evidence was found for the hypothesis
that product diversification increased market power and firm performance
(Gort, 1962; Miller, 1973).   In fact, Montgomery (1985) found that highly
diversified firms tended to compete in less attractive markets in which they
wielded less market power and, hence, had lower performance.   The IO
framework did receive some support in Christensen and Montgomery (1981)
who presented evidence that the performance differences in Rumelt's (1974)
categories of diversified firms were attributable to market structure variables.
Along the same lines, Stimpert and Duhaime (1997) argued that firms
operating in industries characterized by low profitability and few growth
opportunities tended to expand by entering new businesses.   Hence,
diversification was a means of escaping the poor profitability of the firm's
industry (Christensen and Montgomery, 1981), and in competitive industries
with slow growth rates, product diversification may be the only prospect for
improving the profitability of the firm (Rumelt, 1974).

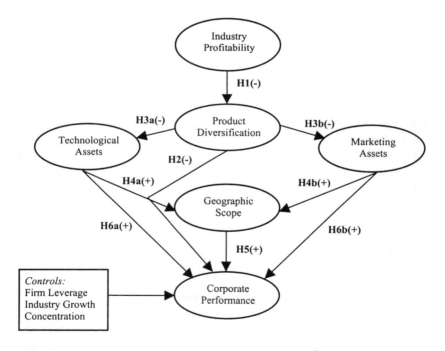

Figure 3.1 Research model

Chang (1992), in his search and selection model of firm growth, also
imputed a performance-based motive to diversification. As argued by Chang

(1992), a poorly performing firm is motivated to undertake product diversification as a means of reducing perceived performance gaps. Because the prospects for growth and profitability within related industries are limited for poorly performing firms, expansion is made into unrelated product areas (Bowman, 1982). In this sense, it can be seen why firms engage in unrelated diversification: it is the foremost means of escaping the low profitability of the firm's industry. From this, we anticipate a negative relationship between the profitability of the principal industry in which the firm operates and its extent of diversification.

Hypothesis 1. The profitability of the principal industry in which the firm operates is negatively related to the extent of diversification.

Product-Market Diversification, Proprietary Assets and Performance

In Stimpert and Duhaime (1997), diversification has an indirect, negative effect on firm performance. Similarly, we contend that a negative relationship exists; however, we further expect that the relationship involves both direct and indirect effects (see Figure 3.1). This contention is related to Rumelt's (1982) study, in which he argued that factor-based economies of scope and uncertain imitability (Lippman and Rumelt, 1982) were critical concepts in understanding diversified firms' performance. Likewise, Bettis (1981) found that superior performance in related diversified firms was associated with the development and exploitation of core skills.

The arguments of Bettis (1981) and Lippman and Rumelt (1982) run parallel to those fashioned by resource-based theorists. In the diversification literature, resource-based researchers moved the analysis of relatedness from the product-level to the resource-level. For example, Chatterjee and Wernerfelt (1991) found that unrelated diversifications that relied primarily on financial resources, had a lower performance than related diversifications that exploited a firm's intangible resources. Similar results, supporting a positive association between diversification related at the proprietary resource-level and performance, were found in Montgomery and Wernerfelt (1988); Wernerfelt and Montgomery (1988); Markides and Williamson (1994); and Anand and Singh (1997). Consistent with these findings, we expect product diversification and firm performance to be inversely related.

Hypothesis 2. The extent of product diversification is negatively related to firm performance.

The above hypothesis stipulates a direct effect between product diversification and performance. The indirect effect operates through linkages between a firm's level of diversification and its generation of proprietary assets (unique resources) by expenditures on R&D and advertising. This expectation emerges from Stimpert and Duhaime (1997) and Hoskisson and Hitt (1988) who argued that diversification can lead to lower levels of investment in new product and process technologies. Along similar lines, Bettis (1981) and Bettis and Mahajan (1985) revealed that narrowly diversified firms had higher levels of expenditures on R&D and advertising.

Hypothesis 3a. The extent of product diversification is negatively related to the R&D intensity (technological assets) of a firm.

Hypothesis 3b. The extent of product diversification is negatively related to the advertising intensity (marketing assets) of a firm.

Proprietary Assets and Geographic Scope

Theorists on multinational enterprises argue that such firms exist because the hazards associated with market-based exchange of the MNEs' proprietary assets make internalization the most efficient means of applying those assets in international markets (Hennart, 1982). That is, the governance costs of having internationally dispersed plants under common administrative control are less than the costs of having plants under separate administrative regimes, utilizing assets exchanged via inter-firm trade (Caves, 1996). Proprietary assets are those assets owned by the investing firm which are differentiable from those possessed by other firms, which can be moved between different host country markets, and which do not depreciate quickly (Caves, 1996). Possession of one or more proprietary assets provides a firm with a unique advantage, which in the case of MNEs is transferable to foreign markets. The proprietary asset can be knowledge that is unique to the firm; it might assume the form of a specific trademark or brand built up over time; or it might stem from a firm's distinctive abilities in product research and development (Caves, 1996).

Empirical work on determinants of multinational activity has examined the role of proprietary assets (see Dunning 1993: 148-154). In this research the evidence points to a positive relationship between a firm's international involvement and its possession of proprietary assets. This evidence exists for the technological assets of US-based (e.g., Pugel, 1978; Grubaugh, 1987), European-based (e.g., Swedenborg, 1979; Pearce, 1989), and Japanese MNEs (Pearce, 1989; Kogut and Chang, 1991). As well, research on downstream determinants has identified a positive relationship between a firm's marketing assets and multinational activity (Caves 1971, 1974; Lall,

1980; Kumar, 1990). Consequently, we expect the possession of proprietary technological assets and marketing assets to be reflected in more extensive international operations.

Hypothesis 4a. The R&D intensity (technological assets) of a firm is positively related to its geographic scope.

Hypothesis 4b. The advertising intensity (marketing assets) of a firm is positively related to its geographic scope.

Geographic Scope and Performance

The results of investigations into the relationship between geographic scope and performance have been more conclusive than those concerned with product diversification and performance. For the most part, studies examining geographic scope and firm performance argue that the superior performance of an MNE emerges from its ability to gain higher returns from exploiting proprietary assets, such as brand equity, patents or unique processes, across a greater number of markets. Advantages also stem from increased market power, the ability to source lower cost inputs, and the spread of risk across a number of host country settings (Kim, Hwang and Burgers, 1993). In particular, the exploitation of intangible asset advantages across international markets is promoted by imperfections found in markets for the trade of these assets. Consequently, multinational firms capitalize on market imperfections by internalizing the market for these assets and thereby achieve above normal returns when the asset is applied in international markets (Caves, 1971). Furthermore, theories of multinational enterprise do not specify limits to the optimal geographical scope of a firm (Caves, 1996), although some evidence points to decreasing returns at large levels of multinational operation (Beamish and daCosta, 1984; Tallman and Li, 1996). Even so, a consistently positive relationship has been observed between geographic scope and performance (Wolf, 1975; Rugman, 1979; Kim, Hwang and Burgers, 1989; Hitt, et al., 1997). Hence the fifth hypothesis,

Hypothesis 5. The geographic scope of a firm is positively related to corporate performance.

As the preceding paragraphs imply, influences on firm performance are not restricted to the extents of product diversification and geographic scope. We expect that the possession of proprietary assets should have a direct relationship with firm performance. This expectation is supported by research conducted in the resource-based perspective which argues that a firm's advantages in its markets stem from its unique resources, which are "all assets, capabilities, organizational processes, firm attributes, information, [and] firm knowledge" under the control of the firm and able to be utilized by the firm to design and implement strategies (Barney, 1991: 101).

Barney's (1988b; 1991) descriptions of a firm's strategic resources have a high degree of overlap with the previously identified characteristics of proprietary assets. The implication of this concordance is that proprietary assets provide a firm with unique advantages in its domestic markets and international markets, and thereby augment a firm's performance. Morck and Yeung (1991) examined the proprietary asset effect using Tobin's q as a measure of firm performance. In their study, international acquisitions were found to have a greater value for investors than domestic ones. The market's positive response to a foreign acquisition was greater when the acquiring firm's expenditures on proprietary asset generating activities (R&D and advertising) were higher. The results imply that part of the performance benefit found in expanding geographic scope comes from increased opportunities for exploiting proprietary assets. In Hypothesis 6, we propose a positive relationship between the possession of proprietary assets and firm performance.

Hypothesis 6a. The R&D intensity (technological assets) of a firm is positively related to corporate performance.

Hypothesis 6b. The advertising intensity (marketing assets) of a firm is positively related to corporate performance.

METHODOLOGY

Sample

With few exceptions, empirical studies of the corporate performance of geographic and product diversified firms have looked at the experiences of US-based multinational enterprises. Among the exceptions has been the inclusion of UK and European based MNEs (e.g., Grant, 1987; Rugman, 1979; Beamish and daCosta, 1984). Research on the corporate performance of the world's second largest group of MNEs, Japanese firms, has been inadequate by comparison, and there have been calls to extend the empirical domain of this research stream to these firms (Tallman and Li, 1996).

To extend research in this manner, we conducted our analysis on publicly listed Japanese manufacturing firms. The sample was derived from the

Analyst's Guide (Daiwa Institute of Research, 1996), which reports firm-level data gathered in a 1996 survey of 1,124 companies listed on the first section of the Tokyo Stock Exchange. Of these, 714 were manufacturing firms. We matched this list of manufacturing firms to the parent firms identified in the Directory of Japanese Firms' Overseas Operations (Toyo Keizai, 1997). This publication provided data on the foreign affiliates of private and public Japanese firms. For firms in this database, the coverage is close to the population of each firm's foreign subsidiaries (Hennart, 1991a; Yamawaki, 1991).

After this matching procedure, we were left with a sample of 399 firms. The industrial distribution of the sample closely mirrored that of the original 714 firms (Table 3.1). Firms that were involved in the chemicals industry comprised 20 percent of the sample. The next most common sectors were industrial machinery (15 percent) and electrical products (14 percent). The average firm in the sample had made 13 foreign investments, with firms in the electrical products sector the most active (18-19 foreign subsidiaries). Among the 399 parent firms, Hitachi had made the most foreign investments (111). Mean product diversification of the firms was consistent across sectors, electrical products firms having the most diversified product lines, and firms in textiles and apparels the least.

Methods

We selected the Partial Least Squares (PLS) technique for analysis. PLS is a relatively new technique that is being used with increasing frequency in strategy research (e.g., Cool et al., 1989; Birkinshaw et al., 1995). PLS is an appropriate technique when sample sizes are small, when data normality and interval-scaled data cannot be assumed, and when the goal is prediction of the dependent variables (Barclay et al., 1995). The last qualification guides the choice of PLS because an objective of this study is to identify the determinants of geographic scope and performance.

In a PLS model, relationships between constructs, and between constructs and measures, are defined beforehand by the researcher. The output from PLS provides indications of the efficacy of the measurement model, and the model's predictive power (see Hulland, 1999 for a review of PLS). Consequently, PLS tends to be superior to OLS regression because it permits simultaneous analysis of item-construct relationships along with complex causal paths (Barclay et al., 1995). PLS likewise provides the researcher with the ability to test the reliability and validity of measures within the context of their nomological network. This attribute of PLS is particularly beneficial when measures are imperfect representations of their underlying constructs, such as the R&D and advertising measures discussed below (also

Table 3.1 Characteristics of parent firms in sample

| Firm's principal industry | SIC code | Industry breakdown | | Industry Means | |
		All firms (%)	Sample (%)	Product diversification	FDI count
Food and tobacco products	20, 21	8.36	5.94	0.57	12.87
Textiles and apparel	22, 23	6.16	6.72	0.71	9.58
Chemicals	28	17.15	19.90	0.56	10.47
Rubber / stone, clay, glass	30, 32	5.87	5.17	0.57	8.30
Ferrous products	33, 34	12.32	9.04	0.70	13.97
Industrial machinery	35	14.37	14.73	0.60	12.02
Electrical products	36	12.75	14.21	0.60	18.44
Transportation equipment	37	7.92	7.75	0.54	13.23
Instruments	38	6.16	8.79	0.67	19.56
Other manufacturing industries	24–27, 29, 31, 39	8.94	7.75	0.63	10.30
Total for column		**714 firms**	**399 firms**	**0.61**	**13.12**

Notes:

1. The 'All Firms' column represents a count of the number of manufacturing firms found on the first section of the Tokyo Stock Exchange, as listed in the *Analyst's Guide* (DIR, 1996).

2. Product diversification is defined by Palepu's (1985) entropy measure, PD = $\Sigma_i[P_i \times \ln(1/P_i)]$, in which PD is the extent of product diversification, P_i is the proportion of sales made in industry i and $\ln(1/P_i)$ is the natural logarithm of the inverse of the sales (Hitt et al., 1997).

see the Appendix). As well, the estimated parameters in a PLS model allow concurrent validity and reliability concerns to be addressed (Hulland, 1999).

Variables

Dependent
As in prior studies (Beamish and daCosta, 1984; Tallman and Li, 1996; Hitt et al., 1997), we define corporate performance using accounting-based measures. From *GlobalVantage*, a companion data set to *CompuStat* that lists accounting data for non-US-based publicly listed companies, we compiled data for three performance measures: return on assets (ROA), return on equity (ROE), and return on sales (ROS). The measures had a high degree of correlation (lowest $r=0.711$, see Appendix), and we modeled a composite performance construct using the three measures as items. As with the independent variables, except geographic scope, each performance measure was computed as a five-year average (1991-95).

Industry profitability
This measure is a composite constructed from four profitability ratios listed in the *Analyst's Guide*. The four ratios are: operating income to sales, recurring profit to sales, net income to sales and industry ROE. The lowest inter-item correlation was 0.715.

Product diversification
The product diversification measure is an entropy measure based on Palepu (1985). We used the *Japan Company Handbook* as the source for determining the industries in which a firm's sales occurred and the percent of sales in each segment. Three-digit SIC codes were used to classify diversification. While a four-digit SIC classification is preferred for determining related-product diversification, limitations on industry detail at the source prevented this level of classification. We review the implications of this divergence in the discussion section.

Assets
Following Horst (1972), Grubaugh (1987), Kogut and Chang (1991), and other studies (see Caves, 1996: 5-13), a firm's possession of technological (marketing) assets was assessed using R&D (advertising) intensity. The measures were computed as the ratio of R&D (advertising) expenditures to the firm's total sales, as reported at the corporate level. The *Analyst's Guide* was the source for the advertising and one R&D term. The second R&D variable was from *GlobalVantage*.

Geographic scope

The extent of geographic operations was measured by two counts: a count of the number of foreign direct investments the firm had made by 1996 and a count of the number of countries in which FDI had occurred. These data were gathered from Toyo Keizai (1997).

Control variables

Montgomery (1985) and Christensen and Montgomery (1981) found evidence that performance differences among diversified firms were attributable in part to differences in market structures among the industries in which the firms in the sample competed. Hence, as in Grant et al., (1988) and Tallman and Li (1996), we introduced industry and firm level controls into the models. We used industry growth rates and concentration (Christensen and Montgomery, 1981; Scherer and Ross, 1990) to partial out the effect of performance variance attributable to differences in industry membership among firms (Schmalensee, 1985). Leverage (Grant et al., 1988; Tallman and Li, 1996) was the firm level control. Leverage and industry growth were derived from the *Analyst's Guide.*

RESULTS

Measurement Model: Validity and Reliability

In assessing the inner model, the principle concern is with the internal consistency and the reliability of the items in the multiple-item constructs, although it is important to evaluate the discriminant validity of all constructs. The reliability of individual items was determined by inspection of item loadings on the respective constructs. In all cases, all individual items had a high degree of reliability as each loading exceeded 0.7 (minimum = 0.844). Convergent validity, or composite reliability (see Table 3.2), was assessed using internal consistency, a measure similar to Cronbach's alpha (Fornell and Larcker, 1981). As reported in Table 3.2, all constructs had internal consistencies greater than 0.95, demonstrating strong convergent validity. Discriminant validity was gauged by comparing the correlation matrix of all constructs (Table 3.3). For each construct in Table 3.3, the diagonal elements (average variance extracted, Fornell and Larcker, 1981) were greater than the numbers in the associated row or column, which is indicative of good discriminant validity.

Table 3.2 Measurement model

Construct	Number of items	Internal consistency
Industry profitability	4	0.969
Product diversification	1	1.000
Marketing assets	1	1.000
Technological assets	2	0.984
Geographic scope	2	0.979
Corporate performance	3	0.957

Note: Internal consistency, which is analogous to Cronbach's alpha, measures the extent to which variance in each item is attributable to variance in its associated construct. The calculation is $(\Sigma\lambda_{yi})^2/((\Sigma\lambda_{yi})^2 + \Sigma Var(\varepsilon_i))$: λ_{yi} is the loading of item i on construct y, and ε_i is the measurement error in item i.

Structural Model

Given the adequacy of the measurement model, it is appropriate to proceed with interpretation of the structural model. Table 3.4 reports the outcomes of hypothesis testing and the explained variance in the model's endogenous constructs. Five of the study's nine hypotheses were supported, and the full sample model explained 14.5 percent of the variance in the performance of the firms.

The strongest support for the research model was received for the antecedents and consequences of geographic scope. R&D expenditure was positively and significantly associated with the geographic scope of the firm, supporting H4a. Geographic scope itself was significantly and positively related to performance. This relationship was observed in the presence of competing influences on performance, including the possession of marketing and technological assets, and product diversification. Among the latter, only R&D expenditure was statistically significant in its relationship with performance (supporting H6a). However, marketing expenditure (H6b) and the extent of product diversification (H2) were not significantly related to performance.

The antecedent portion of the PLS model also received some support. The path coefficient testing the first hypothesis, that industry profitability was negatively associated with product diversification, was found to be significant, as was the path testing H3b. However, two of the anticipated consequences of product diversification were not observed to be significant. The extent of product diversification was not related to the intensity of R&D expenditures, nor was it related to performance. The insignificance of the latter is surprising given the emerging consensus in the strategy literature that greater product diversification is associated with lower performance. We explored the product diversification result further using two sub-samples: one of firms with low levels of product diversification (sample mean or lower), and the other for firms with high product diversification.

We conducted this sub-sample analysis to examine if product diversification had non-linear relationships with performance. Tallman and Li (1996) observed the performance of US multinational firms to be positively related to product diversity at low levels of product diversification, and negatively related at high levels of product diversification. If the relationship was non-linear in our sample, then a full sample analysis might yield a trivial non-significant result because the positive effect of product diversification on performance at low product diversity levels would be nullified by the negative effect at high product diversity levels.

However, as reported in Table 3.4, product diversification was not related to performance either in the full sample, nor in both of the sub-samples. The insignificance of the relationship of product diversification with performance was consistent across firms with both high and low levels of product diversification. Yet, several other relationships in the model varied between the high and low product diversification sub-samples. In general, the high product diversification sample yielded results consistent with the study's hypotheses. Firms in low profit industries were more highly diversified (H1), and this diversification was associated with a lower level of expenditures on marketing assets (H3b). As well, marketing and technological assets were positively associated with geographic scope (H4a and H4b), which, in turn, was positively related to performance (H5).

Aside from the lack of significance for most of the relationship involving geographic scope or performance in the low product diversity sub-sample, the most notable difference in the two sub-samples involved the technological assets construct, specifically H3a. In the low product diversification sample, increasing product diversification was associated with lower levels of R&D expenditures, yet in the high product diversification sample, firms with a wider product portfolio had higher R&D intensities. We review the implications of this difference in the discussion section.

As for the control variables, industry growth was positively related to performance, while leverage and concentration were negatively related. While these variables were not central to the objectives or the theory underlying this study, the significance of the coefficients of the variables reaffirms the importance of controlling for industry and firm level effects when examining firm performance. Finally, it should be noted that we considered adding firm size as a second firm-level control. However, coefficient estimates were robust to the inclusion or exclusion of firm size.

Table 3.3 Discriminant validity

Construct	Correlations between constructs					
Industry profitability	0.889					
Product diversification	-0.251	1.000				
Marketing assets	0.402	-0.197	1.000			
Technological assets	0.410	-0.048	0.216	0.967		
Geographic scope	-0.010	0.122	0.093	0.258	0.959	
Corporate performance	0.431	-0.053	0.137	0.179	0.048	0.881

Note: The average variance shared by a construct and its measures (measured by the average variance extracted or $\Sigma\lambda^2_{yi}/(\Sigma\lambda^2_{yi} + \Sigma Var(\varepsilon_i))$: see variable definitions under Table 3.2). If, as in the above matrix, values in the diagonal exceed the correlations between constructs in associated rows and columns, then the measurement model has adequate discriminant validity.

Table 3.4 Summary of path estimates

Hypothesized relationships	Expected sign	Full sample	Product diversification	
			Low	High
Hypothesis				
H1 Industry profitability to product diversification	-	-0.251***	-0.225***	-0.110***
H2 Product diversification to performance	-	0.017	0.001	-0.017
H3a Product diversification to technological assets	-	-0.048	-0.099*	0.071**
H3b Product diversification to marketing assets	-	-0.197***	-0.147***	-0.152**
H4a Technological assets to geographic scope	+	0.250***	0.122	0.428***
H4b Marketing assets to geographic scope	+	0.039	0.045	0.172***
H5 Geographic scope to performance	+	0.063**	-0.035	0.162***
H6a Technological assets to performance	+	0.093*	0.045	0.112**
H6b Marketing assets to performance	+	0.026	0.045	-0.032
Controls				
Firm Leverage to performance	-	-0.302***	-0.295***	-0.339***
Industry Industry growth to performance	+	0.144***	0.149**	0.128**
Industry Industry concentration to performance	+	-0.075**	-0.109	-0.042

Hypothesized relationships	Expected sign	Full sample	Product diversification	
			Low	High
Variance explained in endogenous constructs		R^2 values for each sample		
Product diversification		0.063	0.051	0.012
Marketing assets		0.039	0.022	0.023
Technological assets		0.002	0.010	0.005
Geographic scope		0.068	0.019	0.218
Corporate performance		0.145	0.152	0.162
Number of cases		399	184	215

Note: *** $p < 0.01$; ** $p < 0.05$; * $p < 0.10$; all two-tailed tests.

Consequently, we report models exclusive of firm size because of: (1) the robustness of the estimates, (2) complicated issues of causality, and (3) the difficulty of interpreting results with firm size when it is related to other explanatory variables (Dunning, 1993: 163).

DISCUSSION

The preceding analysis of the relationships between geographic scope, product diversification and corporate performance yielded several interesting results. Principal in importance among these findings is that the geographic scope of the firm has positive repercussions for corporate performance. Increasing geographic scope is a response to the development and possession of proprietary assets at the upstream end of the value chain, as well as at the downstream end for highly diversified firms. But beyond the opportunities found in exploiting these assets in new markets, operating in foreign markets provided an added measure of value to the firm. While geographic scope was shown to be positively related to performance, the extent of product diversification was not. This result spurred additional analyses, the implications of which are discussed in the following sections.

Product Diversification

The level of product diversification was shown to be strongly influenced by the profitability of the industry of the firm's main line of business. This result suggests that the industry context of the firm is an important determinant of the level of product diversification (Stimpert and Duhaime, 1997). Several researchers in the diversification literature have argued that industry plays an important role in influencing the diversification-performance relationship and the results in this study are in agreement with prior observations that industry profitability and the level of diversification are negatively related (Rumelt, 1982; Bettis and Hall, 1982; Dess, Ireland and Hitt, 1990; Chang, 1992). When a firm is in an unprofitable industry, managers undertake product diversification to improve the prospects for higher firm performance (Bowman, 1982; Rumelt, 1974). The action of diversification itself is part of a larger set of decisions in the firm in which managers systematically undertake search and selection activities as a means of improving a firm's profitability (Chang, 1992). Diversification into unrelated product areas is part of the search process, and the firm cannot learn about its capabilities in a new product-market until it actually enters that market. The selection process involves the retention of successful new businesses, and the divestment of unsuccessful lines of business. The rate of entry into new product areas (the search process) is intensified when the firm is situated in low profitable industries. Hence, we observed that firms that competed in less attractive industries had higher levels of product diversification.

Accompanying a product diversification strategy was a general decline in expenditures used for developing unique marketing assets (for the full sample), and proprietary technological assets (for the low product diversification sub-sample). One interpretation of these results is that they concur with the thrust of the arguments in Stimpert and Duhaime (1997) and Hoskisson and Hitt (1988) – specifically that a strategy of product diversification leads to lower levels of investment in the generation of proprietary assets for use in existing lines of business. Yet, among the more highly diversified firms in the sample, a positive relationship was observed between the extent of product diversification and expenditures for the development of technological assets. This result does not concur with Stimpert and Duhaime (1997) and Hoskisson and Hitt (1988).

An alternative explanation for these results centers on the concepts of economies of scope and the fungibility of a firm's assets across lines of business. When a firm invests in a new line of business, it can attempt to take advantage of scope economies. The negative relationship between product diversification and the two asset intensity terms can be interpreted as an economies of scope effect in which firms were exploiting commonalties between lines of business at the technological or marketing ends of the value chain when investing in new lines of business. However, the extent to which scope economies were achievable was dependent on the fungibility of existing assets across product lines. From the results for the relationships between the extent of product diversification and the asset intensity constructs in the two sub-samples (i.e., consistently negative), it appeared that marketing assets were fungible across product lines regardless of the firm's extent of product diversification. But technological assets had a limited range of fungibility. Only in the low product diversification sub-sample was a negative relationship observed between the extent of product diversification and technological assets. In the high product diversification sub-sample, firms made relatively larger investments in generating technological assets as the extent of product diversification increased. This larger relative investment reflects the difficulty of applying existing technological assets (i.e. the lower fungibility) to new lines of business that were more distant from existing lines of business.

The cases of Toshiba and Nintendo help illustrate these points with respect to marketing assets. In the 1992 to 1996 period, Nintendo derived almost all of its revenues from participation in the video games segment. Its advertising expenditures on an absolute basis and as a percentage of sales were among the twenty highest in our sample. During this same period, Toshiba also had a well-recognized brand name and it was among the ten leading Japanese firms in terms of absolute levels of expenditures on advertising. However, it was also in the top quartile of the most diversified firms in the sample. With this high level of product diversification, and corresponding large size, its marketing asset intensity hovered around the sample mean. Consequently, even with Toshiba's considerable expenditures on the generation of marketing assets, compared to Nintendo, which had a narrow product line and lower sales revenues, Toshiba appeared to be a diversified firm that under-invested in the generation of marketing assets. Yet, Toshiba had developed a strong brand name which it attached to multiple product lines to achieve economies of scope in its use of marketing assets.

This line of explanation is also supported if the relationship between technological assets and product diversification is compared across the two sub-samples. As noted earlier, product diversification had a negative relationship with technological assets in the low product diversification sub-sample and a positive relationship in the high product diversification sub-sample. In the low product diversification sub-sample, 40 percent of the firms competed in essentially one line of business, the remaining 60 percent of firms had two or three principal lines of business. In this sub-sample, the observed negative relationship could extend from a diminution in R&D expenditures as a firm devoted resources towards developing new businesses. Alternatively, in an effect similar to that for marketing assets, it could have emerged as the firms in this sub-sample exploited economies of scope in moving from single-business operations to a multiple lines of business. The initial movement from a single-business entity to a multiple business firm could occur via investments in close product areas, thereby maintaining the fungibility of existing technological assets. One example is Kikkoman Corporation which derived 84 percent of its revenues from various food seasonings (sauces), and 16 percent from participation in the beverage industry. Another is Olympus Optical which obtained its revenues from participation in two similar lines of business: photographic equipment and optical instruments. Hence, an explanation for what we observed in the low product diversification sub-sample is that as firms moved into related product areas, firm size (sales) increased, but the real level of investment in the generation of technological assets did not fall. Absolute expenditures on technological assets increased, but proportionally less than sales, and the technological asset variable showed a decrease.

Meanwhile, in the high product diversification sub-sample, in which all firms had multiple lines of business, a positive relationship was observed between the extent of product diversification and expenditures on technological assets. At high levels of product diversification, developing an additional line of business would involve investments in more distant product lines. To support the development of these new product lines, the firms in this sample increased expenditures in technological assets, at a pace greater than the increase in sales revenues brought about by the expansion in product scope. Consequently, we observed a greater relative focus on developing technological assets as the product scope of the firm increased.

Interestingly, in the full sample and in the high product diversification sub-sample, increases in the level of technological assets were also matched by growth in the geographic scope of the firm. Given this result, we further explored the inter-relatedness of the investment decisions modeled in Figure 3.1 by estimating a model in which we added a path between product diversification and geographic scope. While this path was not significant in the low product diversification sub-sample, it was significant and positive in the high product diversification sub-sample. The significance of the product diversification-geographic scope relationship in the high product diversification sub-sample suggests that among Japanese firms with a wider product portfolio, the strategies of product diversification and increasing the geographic scope of the firm were being concurrently pursued. For these firms, growth into new product markets and expansion into new geographic areas were not competing or mutually exclusive activities. Rather, the two strategies were complementary, as the need for assets generated by entry into increasingly distant lines of business was met by the opportunities found to generate or acquire new assets when expanding the firm's geographic scope.

Geographic scope
In a product diversification strategy, a firm's existing assets direct its expansion as its assets are utilized in entry to new businesses. However, depending on the extent to which existing assets are applicable to the new business, the firm must also develop or acquire new assets to support its entry (Hennart and Park, 1993). Meanwhile, expanding geographic scope involves the exploitation of proprietary assets (Caves, 1996) as well as the acquisition of new assets. That is, foreign investment can be used as a means to build assets. By undertaking FDI, a firm can harness technological and marketing assets that exist in different foreign markets (Kogut and Chang, 1991). With a wider geographic scope to the firm, increased opportunities arise for sourcing dispersed knowledge-related assets, like technology, and physical assets, which can be internalized by the process of FDI and become a source of advantage for the firm. This motivation and support role for foreign investment is particularly salient in the 1990s, which has seen a growth in the geographic dispersion of knowledge-based assets (Dunning, 1998).

Expansion into new geographic markets is also driven by a motive of exploitation. The exploitation involved in geographic expansion is one of extension of the proprietary assets of the firm into new markets. The proprietary assets that form the motivation for geographic expansion might also be a source of advantage in the firm's home market, and contribute to superior corporate performance independent of the firm's investments in international markets. This reasoning, which is in accordance with the arguments of resource-based theorists, has also been the foundation for the main criticism of prior empirical studies that attempted to establish a linkage between geographic scope and performance.

One of the major limitations in prior research on the geographic scope-performance relationship is that it has not focused on the motives for international expansion when looking at this link (Dess et al., 1995). This limitation is understandable given that prior researchers were addressing the question, 'Are multinational firms more profitable?' The method of analysis that emerged in these studies was typically a correlation or regression technique. Researchers found that extensive multinational operations were associated with higher performance (Beamish and daCosta, 1984; Tallman and Li, 1996; Hitt et al., 1997) and lower levels of risk (Rugman, 1979; Kim et al., 1993). However, given that international operations encumber a firm because of the increased difficulty and costs found in operating in foreign markets, it remained at question whether the higher performance of multinational firms was attributable to a firm's possession of superior resources (i.e., proprietary assets), or to other benefits of international operations. The results of this study pointed to both effects. That is, as we observed in the full sample and in the high product diversified sub-sample, performance was positively associated with the possession of proprietary technological assets *and* with the geographic scope of the firm.

This finding suggests that there are benefits intrinsic to international operations. These benefits extend beyond the exploitation of proprietary assets, and exceed the disadvantages found in operating in foreign markets (Hymer, 1976). The advantages of geographic scope may be in part attributable to lower production costs, as firms move productive activities in response to factor price differentials, or to take advantage of other locational advantages (Dunning, 1993). Alternatively, the advantages may come from the development of new technologies as firms expand opportunities for innovation (Hitt et al., 1997), and increase opportunities for sourcing host country technological expertise (Kogut and Chang, 1991) by investing in new host countries. It is a limitation of this study that the specific benefits of geographic scope cannot be pinpointed, but it is a direction for future research.

This study has several other limitations.   The sample was limited to publicly-listed Japanese manufacturing firms.   The effect of using a sample based in Japan has been discussed to some extent, and some of the findings may be unique to the case of Japanese firms.   Generalizability is also limited by the focus on large manufacturing firms.   Future research should undertake to extend the sample to firms in the service sector, or to firms of much smaller size.   A third concern is that, even though product diversification and geographic scope have been demonstrated to have non-linear relationships with performance (e.g. Tallman and Li, 1996), the PLS analysis did not permit direct modeling of non-linearity.   Finally, the diversity in the firm's product line was assessed at the 3-digit SIC level.   This was a constraint imposed by the data source, and it resulted in an entropy measure that differed from the one developed by Palepu (1985), and employed by many researchers since.   While this study's entropy measure was not identical to Palepu (1985), it was comparable to Rumelt's (1974) original conceptualization of unrelated diversification.

CONCLUSION

This study has added much to our understanding of the relationship between product diversification, geographic scope and performance.   The path analytic approach taken in the study emphasized the integrated nature of these relationships and pointed to the different performance outcomes as the firm undertook investments in new product areas, in proprietary assets and in international markets.   Returning to the two questions raised at the outset of this study, first, we found performance to be higher in more multinational firms.   That is, geographic scope and proprietary assets, particularly in the more highly product diversified firms in Japan, had strong positive associations with the performance of Japanese firms.   Secondly, we conclude there is value in internationalization itself because geographic scope was found to be related to higher firm profitability, even when controlling for the competing effect of the possession of proprietary assets.   This finding demonstrates that expansion into new geographic markets was an effective strategy for improving the performance of Japanese firms.

ACKNOWLEDGEMENTS

This research was supported by a Social Sciences and Humanities Research Council of Canada Grant (#411-98-0393), and by the Asian Management Institute at the University of Western Ontario.   This manuscript benefited from comments received from two anonymous reviewers as well as seminar participants at the Richard Ivey School of Business, the Hong Kong University of Science and Technology, and the Fisher College of Business. We would like to thank Ayako Kira, Jo Jo Lam, Jimmy Miyoshi and Nancy Suzuki for assistance in data collection and coding.

Appendix: *Means, standard deviations and correlations*

Variable	1	2	3	4	5	6	7	8	9	10
Industry profitability										
1. Operating income / sales	1.000									
2. Recurring profit / sales	0.953	1.000								
3. Net income / sales	0.906	0.950	1.000							
4. Return on equity (industry)	0.715	0.751	0.838	1.000						
Product diversification										
5. Product diversification	-0.236	-0.277	-0.254	-0.143	1.000					
Technological assets										
6. R&D intensity (*Analyst's Guide*)	0.456	0.455	0.386	0.163	-0.060	1.000				
7. R&D intensity (*GlobalVantage*)	0.432	0.431	0.374	0.162	-0.048	0.942	1.000			
Marketing assets										
8. Advertising intensity	0.408	0.440	0.384	0.251	-0.200	0.197	0.181	1.000		
Geographic scope										
9. Total FDI count	-0.040	-0.023	-0.018	-0.025	0.138	0.243	0.258	0.055	1.000	
10. Country count	-0.005	0.026	0.012	-0.020	0.102	0.243	0.260	0.099	0.918	1.000

Variable

Corporate performance

Variable	1	2	3	4	5	6	7	8	9	10	11	12	13
11. Return on assets	0.382	0.410	0.458	0.451	-0.059	0.183	0.174	0.162	0.031	0.032	1.000		
12. Return on equity (firm)	0.272	0.290	0.329	0.400	-0.045	0.142	0.132	0.083	0.058	0.035	0.803	1.000	
13. Return on sales	0.389	0.417	0.467	0.422	-0.051	0.189	0.182	0.147	0.041	0.062	0.947	0.711	1.000
Control variables													
14. Leverage	-0.168	-0.280	-0.252	-0.197	0.175	-0.065	-0.050	-0.205	0.157	0.133	-0.294	-0.307	-0.234
15. Industry growth	0.350	0.304	0.317	0.296	-0.056	0.215	0.216	0.183	0.058	0.037	0.184	0.132	0.169
16. Industry concentration	-0.155	-0.136	-0.094	-0.013	0.072	-0.230	-0.221	-0.003	0.076	0.062	-0.090	-0.059	-0.105
Mean	4.00	3.92	1.75	3.29	0.61	0.024	0.023	0.011	13.12	7.28	0.83	1.13	0.97
Standard deviation	3.05	3.46	1.78	2.66	0.45	0.028	0.026	0.019	15.81	6.13	2.69	8.95	4.47

Note: Correlations > 0.098 significant at $p < 0.05$.

PART II

Entry Mode Choice and Performance

4. A review and update of the relationship between performance and ownership-based entry mode selection

C. Patrick Woodcock and Paul W. Beamish

This chapter reviews previous theoretical and empirical literature that relates entry mode performance to different ownership-based entry modes: the acquisition, the internal development, and the joint venture modes. It then develops a contingency-based eclectic model that assimilates the various theoretical notions. The contingency model is based on the characteristics of resource requirements and organizational control factors inherent in the selected entry modes. This model suggests that different entry modes have different performance outcomes based upon their resource and organizational control demands. The model, although developed using the eclectic theoretical approach, is based largely on concepts and relationships previously delineated and tested in prior entry mode studies. The relationships in the model are tested by comparing the predicted performance of the entry modes using two data sets. The results provide some support for the notion that internal developments outperform joint ventures, and joint ventures outperform acquisitions.

INTRODUCTION

A number of previous studies have theoretically and empirically related entry mode performance to the selection of ownership-base entry modes, the acquisition, the internal development, and the joint venture modes (Simmonds, 1990; Buckley and Casson, 1998; Shaver, 1998; Woodcock et al., 1994; Nitsch et al., 1996). Several of these studies have compared all three modes, while others have compared only the two wholly-owned modes, the acquisition and internal development modes. The results from these studies have been mixed, with some supporting the theorized relationship, while others have not supported the postulated relationship. This study re-examines this theoretical relationship, and then re-tests the theorized relationship using two new international data sets. The chapter then provides conclusions based upon all of the prior empirical and theoretical work as well as the results found in this analysis on the topic.

REVIEW OF LITERATURE

The vast majority of performance-based entry mode research has focused on the study of a single entry mode, and only recently have researchers focused on comparative entry mode performance. The prior single-mode research generally asserted that international ownership-based entry modes performed rather poorly. Caves (1989), in his review of the acquisition mode research found strong evidence that the majority of acquisitions were not financially viable for the acquirer. Furthermore, researchers have criticized the joint venture mode for its poor performance record (Janger, 1980; Killing, 1983). Finally, research on the internal development mode has been described as risky, and having a highly variable performance outcome (Burgleman, 1983, 1985; Drucker, 1974; Hill and Jones, 1989). These normative results highlight the performance enigma confronting managers and academics when they are confronted with an entry mode selection decision, particularly when these entry modes are being used more and more frequently.

A vast comparative entry mode literature exists that does not specifically include performance. This research suggests that entry mode selection is contingency-based and relates industry, environment, and firm characteristics to the selected mode, rather than relating the mode to performance directly. These studies provide us with important contingency-based characteristics for entry mode selection, some of which can be related ultimately to the performance of the selected entry mode.

Some comparative contingency research has focused on wholly-owned entry modes. For example, Caves and Mehra (1986) found that entry mode selection was influenced by a number of industry and firm-specific factors, including firm size, advertising intensity, research intensity, industry growth, and industry concentration. A subsequent study by Zejan (1990) confirmed many of Caves and Mehra's results.

Other studies have compared the joint venture and wholly-owned entry modes. Gatignon and Anderson (1987) found that locational factors, the degree of multinationality, and research and advertising intensity influence the selection decision between joint ventures or wholly-owned entry modes. Kogut and Singh (1988) found that industry, firm, and country-specific factors influence the selection decision between the three ownership-based entry modes: joint venture, acquisition, and internal development. More recently, Kim and Hwang (1992), and Agarwal and Ramaswami (1992) examined a wide variety of entry modes. They found that locational, ownership, and internalization advantages contingently influenced all of the various entry modes. In conclusion, there is considerable theoretical and empirical support for the contingency entry mode selection process. In this chapter, these contingency-based results are used to develop a performance-based theoretical model.

A profusion of non-comparative, domestic-based research has examined the acquisition mode performance relationship. In general, two approaches have been used: ex ante financial event studies, and ex post studies. The numerous ex ante studies, in general, suggest that acquisitions tend to provide value, but that all of the value accrues to the stockholders of the acquired firm (Caves, 1989; Jensen and Ruback, 1983; Ravenscraft and Scherer, 1989).

Ex post financial studies examine the longer-term returns available to the acquiring firm, and these studies have concluded that negative returns accrue to acquiring firms (Ravenscraft and Scherer, 1989; Caves, 1989). A study by Agarwal and Ramaswami (1992) exhaustively studied acquirers over several decades from a sample on the New York and American Stock Exchanges, and the study found that acquiring firms suffer a statistically significant loss of about ten percent of their stock value over a five-year period subsequent to the acquisition. From this empirical evidence it can be concluded that there is strong evidence that the acquisition mode does not benefit the stockholders of acquiring firms.

Non-comparative studies of domestic joint ventures, in general, conclude that joint venture performance is contingent upon industry and firm-specific factors. One of the most thorough studies on this topic is Harrigan's (1985), in which she found that industry-specific and strategic factors contingently influence the success of joint ventures.

Comparative entry mode research explicitly measuring performance is relatively sparse, and it can be broken into two types of research: those that consider only the two wholly-owned modes, the acquisition and internal development modes, and those that consider all three ownership-based modes. A number of researchers have examined the performance relationship between the two wholly-owned entry modes. Simmonds (1990) compared the two ownership-controlled entry modes, acquisition and internal development, in a domestic setting. He had several data sets and found that the relationship was in the correct direction (i.e., the internal development mode outperformed the acquisition mode) in all data sets, but only some were statistically significant. Woodcock also investigated these two entry modes and similarly found that the internal development mode outperformed the acquisition mode (Woodcock, 1994). More recently, Busija et al., (1997) attempted to replicate Simmonds' (1990) study which looked at domestic modes and controlled for business diversification. Busija et al., (1997) found that the relationships were in the correct direction, but none were statistically significant.

Several theoretically based studies have compared the difference between the two wholly-owned modes. McCardle and Viswanathan (1994) compared the two entry modes using a game theoretical model and found that the internal development mode outperformed the acquisition mode because the acquisition mode was always used in situations where high barriers to entry had to be overcome and this had a detrimental effect on the value of that mode. Buckley and Casson (1998) comparatively examined the two modes using a transaction cost theoretical model. They then solved the resulting model for a number of different cases, and in all cases, the internal development mode outperformed the acquisition mode.

Other studies have compared all three modes. A study by Li and Guisinger (1991) defined performance as the failure rate of the individual entry modes in the US market. The study hypothesized that internal developments would have the lowest failure rate, acquisitions the highest, and joint ventures a median rate. The empirical results found the relationship between internal developments and acquisitions to be both in the hypothesized direction and significant. However, joint venture was in the middle of the other two modes, but it was not significantly different from the other two. More recently, Woodcock, Beamish and Makino (1994) investigated Japanese entries into North America and found that the internal development mode significantly outperformed the acquisition mode and that the joint venture mode had a median performance compared to the other two modes. Nitsch, Beamish and Makino (1996) attempted to replicate this study using entries into the European market. Their results indicated that most relationships were in the correct direction, but only several of the results were significant.

We will now develop a theoretical model relating entry mode to performance, and we will use this model to empirically analyze our two new datasets. The theoretical model developed uses a contingency-based and eclectic theoretical approach to differentiate between the performances of the three different modes. The theoretical framework is then tested using six sub-samples from two data sets.

THEORY DEVELOPMENT

The theoretical model proposed uses the eclectic theory approach to develop arguments explaining entry mode performance differences, and to account for why poorer performing modes are selected by firms. Some arguments originate from previous entry mode research, although most have been conceptually and theoretically abstracted to ensure methodological parsimony.

The theoretical development of the eclectic model employs ownership and internalization advantages (see Figure 4.1). Locational advantage is not theoretically considered, but it is controlled for in the empirical testing of the model.

The ownership advantage explains a firm's resource commitment, and the internalization advantage explains a firm's organizational control difficulties. Historically, resource commitment and organizational control, or at least close proxies of these concepts, have been studied extensively by contingent entry mode researchers. Resource-based concepts or proxies that have been empirically supported in entry mode contingency studies include country experience, competitive position, and firm size (Caves and Mehra, 1986; Kim and Hwang, 1992; Kogut and Singh, 1988). Organizational control concepts or proxies that have been empirically supported include ownership control, organizational culture, and managerial transfers (Agarwal and Ramaswami, 1992; Amit, Livnat, and Zarowin, 1989; Caves and Mehra, 1986; Kim and Hwang, 1992; Kogut and Singh, 1988; Li and Guisinger, 1991; Wilson, 1980; Yip, 1982). Variables that relate to both concepts and which have been supported in contingency entry mode research include product diversification and multinational experience (Caves and Mehra, 1986). Thus, resource commitment and organizational control have been shown to support the contingency factor and entry mode relationship.

Two general theoretical arguments are made in this study through the resource commitment and organizational control theoretical approaches. The first is that firms should contingently select entry modes in a manner that best suits their situation, and the second is that contingent factors as well as the inherent characteristics of the entry mode tend to produce different performance levels. These two arguments are interdependent, otherwise firms would always select the best performing entry mode. Consequently, to produce a realistic theory both arguments must be made simultaneously.

Many researchers have suggested that different entry modes require different ownership advantages, herein called resource commitments. Among the first to outline a relationship between resource commitments and international business growth were Daniels (1970) and Vernon (1983). Anderson and Gatignon (1986) developed a model that considered the tradeoff between the costs of control and the costs of resource commitment. Hill, Hwang and Kim (1990) elaborated on this idea of resource commitment when they differentiated between licensing, joint ventures and wholly-owned entry modes. They defined resources as dedicated assets that cannot be redeployed to alternative uses without cost (p. 118). Resources in this context could be either tangible resources such as plant and capital, or intangible resources such as market or operational know-how. The argument that a firm's entry mode is contingent upon the required resources is further developed in this chapter to include the relationship between entry mode and performance.

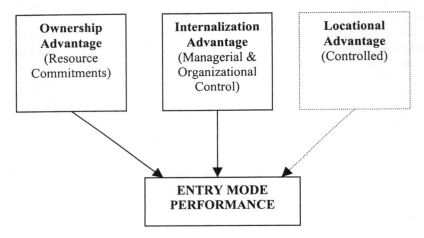

Figure 4.1 Eclectic theory model

Entry Mode Selection Based on Ownership Advantages

Ownership advantages have been used widely to differentiate between joint ventures and wholly-owned entry modes. Many studies have used the degree of ownership control as a proxy for resource commitment. The greater the degree of ownership in the entry mode, the larger the resource commitment. For example, in a joint venture, a firm's resource commitment is minimized relative to a wholly-owned entry mode because of the shared resource commitment between firms (Anderson and Gatignon, 1986). A firm not having the resources, and wishing to share the risks associated with having such resources is thus compelled to enter the market through a joint venture. Other entry mode studies have empirically corroborated the above resource-dependent relationship using proxy measures for such resource commitment. Erramilli (1991) and Erramilli and Rao (1990) used market knowledge to explain why firms use specific entry modes, and Davidson (1982) found that firms having lower market knowledge tended to reduce the strategic risk by entering these markets through licensing agreements or joint ventures rather than wholly-owned modes. Therefore, ownership advantages or resource-based contingency theory has been used extensively to differentiate between joint venture and wholly-owned entry mode selection.

The resource commitment concept can also be used to differentiate between the wholly-owned entry modes. Firms that use the acquisition entry mode are procuring a new set of resources, while firms using the internal development mode are relying on their historic and previously developed set of resources. This difference suggests that firms having suitable resources will use the internal development mode, while firms not having suitable resources will use the acquisition mode and trade financial resources for the required resources. The necessary and appropriate resources may range from tangible resources such as product characteristics to intangible resources such as market experience. Empirical evidence of a relationship between resource commitment and wholly-owned entry mode selection has been found by Caves and Mehra (1986), who observed that multinational experience was related to wholly-owned entry mode selection. Further evidence is found in Shaver's (1998) research that found the internal mode, when compared to the acquisition mode, was associated with higher performance in both the mode and the parent firm. He attributed the higher performance to an abundance of resources in the parent firm using the internal development mode compared to the firm using the acquisition mode.

The above theoretical argument and evidence provide a model for the contingent selection of internal development entries relative to the two other modes. Differentiating between the acquisition and joint venture modes requires one to distinguish between the nature and type of resources required. Two types of resource requirements are used to make this differentiation; the first is the perceived inimitability or transferability of the resources, and the second is the core nature of the resources in the parent firm.

The important difference between the acquisition and joint venture modes is that firms in a joint venture share and provide access to some of their internal resources, while in the acquisition mode no such external access is provided. A firm will use the joint venture mode to rectify a resource deficiency only if it is willing to risk providing external access to such resources, and can find a willing and suitable partner(s) having appropriate resources to share or provide reciprocal access (Hill, Hwang and Kim, 1990). The critical factor in the joint venture is finding partners that are predisposed to providing such access to resources. This predisposition must be based on inter-firm trust, and a perception that access and sharing of resources will not negatively impact the firm strategically (Daniels and Magill, 1991). A firm will tend to favor an acquisition entry mode if it cannot find a suitable partner predisposed to providing access or sharing the required resources, or if it is not itself predisposed to providing access to internal resources.

A firm's predisposition to providing another firm with access to its resources will depend upon its perception of the risk of exposing its critical resources. The risk of such resource access is perceived by management to be lower when the exposed resources are non-core, or if the resources are difficult to imitate or transfer to the partnering firm. A firm unnecessarily exposing critical resources to either imitation or transfer may provide their partnering firm with a competitive, or ownership advantage, in the future. Therefore, the perceived nature and type of resources being exposed is important to the entry mode selection process.

A variety of researchers have suggested that core resources or competencies are vital to long-term competitive advantage (Collis, 1991; Hamel and Prahalad, 1990; Prahalad and Bettis, 1986; Stalk, Evans, and Shulman, 1992). Collis (1991, p. 52) defines core competencies as "the irreversible assets along which the firm is uniquely advantaged." These are the type of resources that a firm would tend to be unwilling to share or expose unnecessarily to a potential competitor. The critical element is the perceived risk of either exposing or sharing the resources, and the resulting loss of future competitive advantage, given the benefits of the joint venture mode. If firms want to protect these vital core resources and the perceived risks of having them transferred to the second firm are high but require resources to enter the new market, then they should procure the needed resources through an acquisition.

A variety of studies have provided evidence that these core resource contingencies influence entry mode selection. In particular, the inimitability of the core resources has been examined. Singh and Kogut (1989) examined the contingent relationship between acquisition and joint venture selection and found that joint ventures were favored in research-intensive firms and industries. This relationship, they concluded, suggests that firms having research and development core competencies are less susceptible to losing them in joint ventures because of their inimitable nature. Their argument was similar to that put forward by Teece (1982) who suggested that research and development resources are tacit in nature, and therefore, more difficult to transfer and imitate. Other researchers have shown that the long-term viability of a joint venture and a firm's competitive position are threatened by sharing or exposing core resources (Hamel, 1991; Inkpen, 1992). Therefore, differentiating between core and non-core as well as the inimitability and transferability of resources by managers is critical to the selection of an entry mode.

Another stream of research has looked at the effects of risking core resources on the selection of joint venture and wholly-owned modes. Agarwal and Ramaswami (1992) empirically examined whether contractual risk influenced the choice of entry mode. They found that the higher the risk the more the ownership control desired. Kim and Hwang (1992) investigated the effects of the value of firm-specific knowledge and the tacit nature of firm knowledge on a firm's entry mode selection. They found that the value of firm-specific knowledge was not significantly related to entry mode selection, but the tacit nature of the knowledge was significantly associated with the selection of wholly-owned entry modes. These studies provide considerable evidence of a relationship between the exposure of core competencies in various entry modes and the selection of these modes.

In conclusion, resource requirements or ownership advantages influence the contingent selection of entry modes. These contingent decisions are illustrated in Table 4.1.

Table 4.1 Resource requirement contingency decision matrix

Entry mode	New resources are deemed necessary for entry mode	Concern over exposure to, or sharing of, core resources
Internal development	No	Not applicable
Joint venture	Yes	No
Acquisition	Yes	Yes

Performance Implications of Ownership Advantage Requirements

The contingency relationships delineated above not only influence the selection of the entry modes, but also their profitability. In particular, firms already having the appropriate ownership advantages incur minimal resource-based costs during market entry. However, firms not having the required ownership advantages must procure them using a joint venture or acquisition. Such a transaction will have an associated cost.

A firm using an acquisition entry mode will have several costs associated with procuring the necessary resources for market entry, particularly in the inefficient market situation, which is what an acquisition tends to represent (i.e., a single and unique market transaction). First, the firm incurs the cost of searching for an appropriate acquisition target. Second, the acquiring firm has a cost associated with the risk of paying too much for the target firm, and therefore the resources being procured. The cost of this risk is associated with the asymmetric information problem confronting the acquiring firm due to the firm's inferior knowledge of the resources being purchased. The firm to be acquired, on the other hand, has an information advantage because of its superior knowledge about its industry, its internal resources, and the market for these resources. This puts the acquiring firm at a disadvantage for evaluating the value of the resources being purchased. The seller may ask a price in excess of the value of the business and resources, or the acquirer may overbid for them.

An additional problem makes the economic transaction even more risky for the acquiring company. This problem is related to the singular nature of the transaction, which allows the sellers to cheat an acquirer, and provides the acquirer with little or no recourse to exact retribution from the sellers. Such a situation puts the seller at an advantage relative to the acquirer. Therefore, an acquisition specific risk or cost premium is associated with information asymmetry combined with the singular nature of the acquisition transaction process. Increasing initial search costs can lower risk or premium costs, but this again is an added cost that is associated with an inefficient market.

Teece (1982) makes a similar argument for a firm that selects the acquisition mode compared to the internal development mode by suggesting that a firm using the internal development has excess or slack resources which can be expended on the creation of a new internal development. Utilizing these slack resources more fully improves the overall effectiveness and efficiency of the firm. Furthermore, Teece's thesis is applicable to the whole firm while the theoretical argument in this paper is focused only on the entry mode itself. Other researchers have made similar information asymmetry arguments specific to the acquisition entry mode (Yip, 1982).

Joint ventures, on the other hand, have minimal risks associated with resource overpayment because of the symmetrical and ongoing nature of the transaction process. The risk of paying too much for these resources is limited because all partners face the same potential information asymmetry problem. Therefore, neither partner has a clear ability to induce the other partner to overpay or overcommit without incurring the same problem for itself. This leads to a situation where neither party wants to induce the other to retaliate. For instance, the other firm(s) can retaliate if one firm attempts to cheat because of the ongoing relationship or multiple transactions present in a joint venture. In such an economic transactional dilemma (called a prisoner's dilemma), all parties can hold the other parties in line with the threat of reciprocal retaliatory action in future transactions.

In addition to the above potential retaliatory game, a positive motivational economic game is also present. Given that firms in a joint venture are benefiting from either sharing resources or remuneration, all parties will be reticent to cheat for fear they will lose these benefits. Therefore, all parties attempt to actively support the joint venture and do not cheat. This positive economic game dilemma (called a stag hunt) produces a non-cheating environment based on the accruing benefits to all parties. These two economic dilemmas or games tend to discourage cheating in joint ventures.

The only situation where cheating becomes advantageous is when an asymmetric retaliatory position exists between two partnering firms. In this situation, one firm can cheat and the other cannot retaliate in an equal and reciprocal manner. It is assumed, however, that joint venture partners have appropriately selected their partners to avoid such a position. This argument highlights the one resource-based cost that joint ventures incur. This is the search and examination cost related to selecting a partner with the required resources, as well as a partner with a symmetrical retaliatory position so that cheating is minimized. It should be noted that a symmetrical retaliatory position not only includes considerations such as strategic position, but also organizational culture, and managerial values and attitudes.

On the basis of the above assessment, the total cost of procuring necessary resources in a joint venture is more than that in an internal development because of search costs, but less than that in an acquisition, as shown in Table 4.2.

Table 4.2 The costs associated with utilizing the entry modes

Entry mode	Ownership advantages *Costs of procuring additional resources*	Internalization advantages *Ownership and managerial control costs*	Total advantages *Total costs*
Internal development	Low	Low	Low
Joint venture	Medium	High	Medium
Acquisition	High	High	High

Entry Mode and Internalization Advantages

Internalization advantages or organizational control costs are also dependent upon the entry mode selected. In this study, organizational control is defined as the efficient and effective management of the relationship between the parent and entry entity, something which enables the parent to best meet its overall goals and objectives.

Organizational control has frequently been associated with different entry modes. Previous research has suggested that entry modes having different ownership levels are associated with specific control capabilities and capacities (Anderson and Gatignon, 1986; Calvet, 1984; Caves, 1982; Davidson, 1982; Gatignon and Anderson, 1988; Root, 1987). In a joint venture, the multiple ownership arrangement has costs associated with negotiating an initial control relationship between the parents, as well as costs associated with the ongoing management of the relationship (Beamish and Banks, 1987; Killing, 1983). Thus, based on management control issues, the wholly-owned modes appear to be intrinsically distinct from the joint venture mode.

The costs associated with managing organizational control mechanisms are related to the type of control mechanism used and the number of control relationships required. Schaan and Beamish (1988) delineated over two dozen non-ownership control mechanisms used in joint ventures. Such a large number of alternative mechanisms were deemed necessary and applicable because of the lack of direct ownership control. Killing (1983) similarly believed that non-ownership control mechanisms were slower and less efficient than the more direct mechanism of ownership control in subsidiaries. Non-ownership control mechanisms are often considered more costly because ultimately the various parties have greater scope to act opportunistically or cheat, given that there is no ultimate legal control mechanism such as ownership control. Furthermore, non-ownership control mechanisms require that behavioral-based values such as trust and respect be developed over a period of time before an effective control relationship results. Effort is expended in initially installing and then maintaining these control mechanisms.

The joint venture mode also has more relationships to be managed. Ensuring that control mechanisms produce maximum synergies between the various entities requires that the parents not only establish a relationship with the joint venture, but also with the other parent(s). These multiple relationships increase the probability that one of the parties will act in an opportunistic manner. All of these relationships incur organizational and management control costs.

Several researchers have found evidence of such control differences between joint ventures and wholly-owned entry modes. Agarwal and Ramaswami (1992) empirically found that joint ventures were positively associated with the contractual risks associated with different degrees of ownership. In addition, Kim and Hwang's (1992) empirical study on global entry modes discovered that wholly-owned modes were associated with more effective and efficient control mechanisms relative to the joint venture mode.

Acquisitions also incur supplementary control costs. In particular, the perceptions of resource deficiency that constrain a firm to contingently select the acquisition mode also tend to cause management control problems. The information asymmetry created by such a resource deficiency may limit the firm's ability to understand and effectively control newly acquired entities in several ways. First, organizational culture differences may exacerbate the management control problem between the two merging entities. In particular, cultural differences may limit the effectiveness of behaviorally-based control mechanisms that rely upon trust, value congruence, and respect. This may force the acquiring company to use a restricted set of control mechanisms, which in turn may decrease the implementation efficiency of the organizational control process and increase the risk of opportunistic action by the acquired company's work force. Organizational culture differences may also impede organizational integration, yet executives often erroneously predict that organizational integration will produce post-acquisitional synergies. The opportunity costs of not gaining these synergies immediately may be significant.

Organizational cultural problems of this sort have been reported by a variety of researchers (Adler and Graham, 1989; Alstom and Gillespie, 1989; Balakrishnan, 1988; Caves and Mehra, 1986; Conn and Connell, 1991; Datta, 1991; Harrison, Hitt, Hoskisson, and Ireland, 1991; Hopkins, 1987). Datta (1991) correlated acquisition performance with the degree of similarity between the management styles in the entities before acquisition. He found that similar management styles, a proxy measure for organizational cultural characteristics, led to better performance. The costs of controlling for an organizational cultural gap are incurred both prior to acquisition, when significant searching costs are required to differentiate appropriate from inappropriate organizational cultures, and subsequent to the acquisition, when a variety of management and organizational integration techniques must be used to merge the two cultures.

The second problem associated with acquisitions is that of maximizing synergies and minimizing redundancies in the new entity. Many researchers have investigated the potential for different types of synergies in acquisitions. However, the vast majority of these studies have found no significant relationship between synergies and post-acquisitional performance (Caves, 1989). Chatterjee (1992) found that synergies, in general, do not create value in acquisitions. The more significant value-creating strategy is management restructuring, a tactic that could be implemented by the previous management independently of the acquiring firm. Furthermore, for every synergy created in an acquisition there are several costly redundancies. An empirical study by Chatterjee (1990) found that, from a resource-based perspective, acquisitions have the potential to create more resource redundancies or duplications than synergies. Despite this evidence, most managers continue to suggest that acquisitions are made for synergistic reasons (Walter and Barney, 1990). This enigma of managers claiming synergies, which often are not present, to justify an acquisition is further evidence of the information asymmetries present in this mode. Based on these management control problems, it can be concluded that control costs are higher for acquisitions than for internal developments.

Table 4.2 summarizes the management control inefficiencies associated with various entry modes. Internal developments are least inefficient while both acquisitions and joint ventures incur considerable management control costs.

Hypotheses Development

These resource deficiency and management control arguments produce the hierarchy of entry modes illustrated in Table 4.2. The internal development mode is the most efficient because it incurs the lowest ownership advantage costs. The joint venture is the next most efficient because, although it incurs management control costs, it does not incur high resource deficiency costs. Acquisitions, however, incur both high direct resource deficiency costs and high management control costs and therefore, are deemed the most inefficient mode.

Based on this analysis the following hypotheses are derived:

Hypothesis 1.   Internal development entry modes will on average outperform the joint venture and acquisition modes of international market entry.

Hypothesis 2. Joint ventures will on average outperform the acquisition mode of international market entry.

Data and Methodology

The data sets used in this study originated from a survey of all Japanese manufacturing subsidiaries in North America (i.e., Canada and United States) whose parent companies were listed on the Tokyo, Osaka, or Nagoya stock exchanges in 1991 for the first data set and in 1996 for the second data set (Toyo Keizai, 1992a; Toyo Keizai, 1997). The information in the data sets was compiled using public information and a survey of the top Japanese manager in each foreign subsidiary during 1991 and 1996 (Toyo Keizai, 1992a; Toyo Keizai, 1997). The effects of locational advantage were controlled for by using only Japanese entries into the North American market. Industry-specific effects were partially controlled for by using only entries that involved manufacturing firms with established manufacturing operations in North America.

The data sets under-represent small firm entries and over-represent larger firms due to the public nature of the database source. This may reduce the generalizability of the study, but it helps control for organizational size influences, particularly influences of an entrepreneurial nature. Although no organizational variables were used in the model, the three modes appear to include cases having comparable operational scope and scale. An analysis of variance indicates that sales volume, total employment, and capitalization values were not significantly different between the three modes in each data set. This analysis also tends to confirm that radically different industries (i.e., capital intensive versus non-capital intensive industries) were not present in the three mode sub-samples. The 1992 sample consisted of subsidiaries having average sales of $51 million, average investment of $30 million and an average of 197 employees; while the 1997 sample consisted of subsidiaries having average sales of $181 million, average investment of $34 million and an average of 387 employees. The difference in the average size of subsidiaries is reflected also in the increased average age of the subsidiaries in the second sample set, having been 8.3 years old in the 1992 data set and moving to 10.5 years old in the 1997 data set.

The operational definition of the modes are as follows: an internal development was defined as an entry that involved only one parent, which built and operationally equipped the plant; an acquisition was defined as an entry that involved only one parent, and its plant and equipment were purchased from the previous owner; and a joint venture was defined as an entry that involved more than one parent, and its plant was built and operationally equipped by these parents.[1] These definitions ensure that the entry modes are mutually exclusive.

The data sets contained information on the initial entry mode type, the initial entry mode objective, and the present ownership structure of the entity. From this information only those modes that appeared to fit the defined operational types were used in the study. In the 1992 data set, a total of 321 database entries or market entries were used in this study; 166 of these were internal developments, 79 were joint ventures and 76 were acquisitions.[2] In the 1997 data set, a total of 955 market entries were used; 525 of these were internal developments, 371 were joint ventures and 159 were acquisitions.

The measurement of performance was taken from a survey question that asked the top Japanese manager in the subsidiary to evaluate their overall financial performance in terms of financial profitability for the entry mode. The scale for the performance indicator had only three choices: profitable (1), break-even (0), or a loss (-1).[3] This financial performance measurement, although limited, represents the only information Japanese firms were willing to provide given their very private nature. The use of different accounting approaches and individual assessments of performance is likely to be minimized because respondents are from the same country and from the same level in the organization. Furthermore, the analysis eliminated startup period variations caused by when unusual one-time accounting charges and operational delays and adjustments that might create anomalous performance variations.

Chi-squared, Spearman's Rank Correlation and Kruskal-Wallis tests were used to assess the relationship between performance and entry mode. Pearson's Chi-squared is the most commonly used test for the relationship between categorical variables. The measure is based on the differences between actual and expected frequencies in a multi-way table (Freund and Walpole, 1980). The Kruskal-Wallis and Spearman's Rank Correlation tests are used to further test the relationship using tests that are specific to interval-based and categorical variables. The Kruskal-Wallis test is a non-parametric alternative to the one-way analysis of variance test. It is based on the generalized rank-sum test that investigates the null hypothesis and it tests whether the samples come from the same population (Freund and Walpole, 1980). Spearman's Rank Correlation is a measure of variance accounted for in the relationship and is computed from the ranks of the variables present (Freund and Walpole, 1980). These three statistical tests were employed to ensure the results were duplicable, and were not the result of an inherent mathematical bias within one statistical technique.

Analytical Approach

When investigating the relationship between performance and entry mode, one must consider the effects of entry age. The internationalization literature has consistently shown that entry into a new international market requires a learning period over which entering firms establish themselves (Cardozo, Reynolds, Miller, and Phillips, 1989; Forsgren, 1989; Johanson and Vahlne, 1977; Johanson and Wiedersheim-Paul, 1975; Juul and Walters, 1987; Newbould, Buckley, and Thurwell, 1978). During this startup period, performance is depressed because the new entrant is trying to establish market penetration and achieve economies of scale and scope. At this time, financial performance may be poor for a variety of reasons. First, new entrants require time to adjust to new markets, new organizational processes and systems, or new competitive factors in the entered market. A lag effect would probably be most pronounced in internal development and joint venture entry modes because of their newness and initial vulnerability. Time would be required for these two modes to establish their ownership advantages. Second, the average performance of an entry may be low at first because some firms have selected the wrong entry mode or market, and thus require time to readjust or abandon their entry strategy. This study attempts to control for these effects by defining and excluding the initial adjustment period. Therefore, the data sets were examined to see if an initial adjustment period was present.

A visual check of the data indicated that all of the entry modes had an initial startup period having low unstable performance, which subsequently increased and stabilized at a higher level. Furthermore, regression analysis confirmed this relationship in both data sets, as illustrated in Table 4.3 and 4.4. The regression results showed a positive slope for all entry modes, indicating that performance was initially low, and as age increased performance increased. Furthermore, the low R^2 values suggested that the relationships may be nonlinear, possibly leveling off over time. Therefore, the influence of age had to be either controlled or eliminated. Controlling for age statistically is unworkable because it reduces the cell size to a point where statistical problems occur.

Table 4.3 The 1992 regression of entity age after entry to performance

Entry mode	Regression model	R^2
Internal development	Performance = 1.9 + 0.1 * Age	0.05
Joint venture	Performance = 1.6 + 0.1 * Age	0.15
Acquisition	Performance = 1.6 + 0.1 * Age	0.05

Table 4.4 The 1997 regression of entity age after entry to performance

Entry mode	Regression model	R^2
Internal development	Performance = 2.2 + 0.8 * Age	0.01
Joint venture	Performance = 2.1 + 0.8 * Age	0.01
Acquisition	Performance = 2.4 - 0.1 * Age	0.00

The technique used to eliminate the effects of entry age was based upon the notion that, for each entry mode, performance would initially improve and then, after several years, it would stabilize and oscillate around this new level. Thus, a technique was needed to isolate the stable period from the growth or initial startup period. We used a non-linear regression technique, piece-wise linear regression with a breakpoint.

Piece-wise linear regression with a breakpoint maximizes the correlation (R^2) by fitting two linear relationships appropriate to the data; one prior to an x axis variable breakpoint and one subsequent to the breakpoint. Thus, the technique not only searches for the best slopes and intercepts for the data, but it also searches for the best point on the x-axis for an appropriate breakpoint to occur by dividing the data into two sub-data sets. Using age as the x variable we can attempt to describe the point at which the relationship between performance and entry age stabilizes. Furthermore, we can see whether the second regression line, which describes the data beyond the solved-for breakpoint, is horizontal and thus a relatively stable performance level.

Table 4.5 and 4.6 illustrate the results from the breakpoint regression analysis for the two data sets. These analyses used all of the statistical evidence in the data to develop the breakpoint lines, and thus the significance of these relationships cannot be assessed. However, several interesting attributes provided strong evidence of an appropriate region from which to select a stable sample for subsequent analysis. First, the break points all occurred at approximately two years. Furthermore, as one would suspect, the internal development entry required a slightly longer period to stabilize than the joint venture or acquisition modes in all analyses. Second, the linear relationships subsequent to the breakpoints were flat, suggesting that a stable relationship between entry mode, age, and performance was established after the second year in all analyses. Therefore, the sub-samples used in the subsequent analysis stages were limited to entities over two years old.

Table 4.5   The 1992 break point regression of entity age after entry to performance

Entry mode	Regression model #1	Break point	Regression model #2	R^2
Internal development	Perf.= 1.4 + 0.0 * Age	2.1 years	Perf.= 3.0 + 0.0 * Age	0.80
Joint venture	Perf.= 1.0 - 0.0 * Age	2.0 years	Perf.= 2.5 + 0.0 * Age	0.84
Acquisition	Perf.= 1.0 - 0.0 * Age	1.9 years	Perf.= 2.5 - 0.0 * Age	0.80

RESULTS

Results for both data sets are illustrated in Table 4.7 and 4.8. In the 1992 results, all tests were statistically significant; and in the correct direction supporting the hypotheses. The results for the 1997 data were in the correct direction, but were not statistically significant.

Table 4.6 The 1997 break point regression of entity age after entry to performance

Entry mode	Regression model #1	Break point	Regression model #2	R^2
Internal development	Perf.= 1.5 + 0.1 * Age	2.2 years	Perf.= 3.0 + 0.0 * Age	0.81
Joint venture	Perf.= 1.3 - 0.0 * Age	2.3 years	Perf.= 3.0 + 0.0 * Age	0.86
Acquisition	Perf.= 1.1 - 0.0 * Age	2.3 years	Perf.= 3.0 - 0.0 * Age	0.86

Table 4.7 The 1992 performance difference in entry modes for entries over 2 years of age (given as performance frequency per entry mode in percent)

Entry mode	Performance gain	Performance break-even	Performance loss	Mean
Internal development	44%	29%	27%	2.17
Joint venture	39%	20%	39%	2.02
Acquisition	25%	32%	43%	1.82

Notes:
1. Chi-square: $p=0.04$
2. Kruskal-Wallis Test: $p=0.03$
3. Spearman's Rank Correlation: $p=0.01$
4. Mean is based on 3 being gain, 2 being break-even and 1 being loss.

DISCUSSION AND CONCLUSIONS

The results provide some evidence that different entry modes have different performance levels. The 1992 results support the hypotheses suggesting that the internal development mode outperforms the joint venture mode and the joint venture mode outperforms the acquisition mode, but the 1997 results do not statistically support the hypothesized relationships, although they are in the correct direction. These equivocal results can be explained by either a theoretical misspecification of the model, or alternatively, a methodological or statistical flaw.

A misspecification of the theoretical relationships within the model is entirely possible due to the parsimony of the relationships developed. Certainly a more complex theoretical model could be developed to account for other potential influences on the various entry mode's performance.

Other research has certainly found evidence of different performance levels are inherent in the different entry modes because of either organizational, country, or industry level effects. For example, several recent studies have found that different types of joint venture incurred different levels of performance based on organizational and country effects (Makino and Beamish, 1998; Makino and Delios, 1996). Other studies have found that the performance of acquisitions are influenced by organizational considerations (Chatterjee, 1992; Datta, 1991). And Buckley and Casson's (1998) examination of the theoretical complexities of relating performance to internationalization modes of the firm clarifies for researchers the problems of trying to develop a theoretical model that encompasses all of the theoretical nuances present. Thus, it would be helpful to develop a more complex model that more fully explained the performance of the different modes.

Table 4.8 The 1997 performance difference in entry modes for entries over 2 years of age (given as performance frequency per entry mode in percent)

Entry mode	Performance gain	Performance break-even	Performance loss	Mean
Internal development	50%	28%	22%	2.28
Joint venture	54%	19%	27%	2.27
Acquisition	53%	19%	28%	2.25

Notes:
1. Chi-square: $p=0.15$
2. Kruskal-Wallis Test: $p=0.96$
3. Spearman's Rank Correlation $p=0.96$
4. Mean is based on 3 being gain, 2 being break-even and 1 being loss.

A more important question for this particular study is to assess whether this particular theoretical model had any particular systematic bias, and thus, caused one mode to preferentially outperform another mode when the results were statistically significant. The researchers examined the data carefully and could not find any systematic bias that might have occurred. In fact, the methodology used the breadth of the data to provide improved validity to insure that the analysis would not be biased, but would be more generalizable.

An alternative, and possibly concurrent, explanation for why the 1997 results are not significant may be a result of statistical or methodological problems. After reviewing the data, the researchers found evidence that the

1997 data set is statistically more constrained than the 1992 data set. This could provide an explanation for why one data set provides significant results and the other does not. The variance in performance for the 1992 data set was suitable for a statistical analysis with almost one third of the modes being in each of the respective performance categories: loss, breakeven, and profit. However, performance variance in the 1997 data set was constrained with the majority of sample points indicating profitable. This constraint means that the 1997 data will intrinsically have difficulty developing a result that is statistically significant because there is not enough variance for the results to show a significant difference.

Busija et al., (1997) also were confronted with a non-significant result when they compared wholly-owned mode performances. One of their conclusions was that during certain economic periods both modes may perform very well, and therefore, no statistical differences are discernable during those economic periods. Our data set in 1997 presents a potentially similar situation in that the excellent economy in North America during this period tended to make all entry modes perform relatively well, and thus, statistical analysis had difficulty differentiating them.

How do the results in this study compare with results in other studies? Studies that compared all three ownership-based entry modes have consistently found mixed results with some data sets showing a significant difference between the three modes in the predicted direction, while other data sets have provided insignificant results (Li and Guisinger, 1991; Woodcock et al., 1994; Nitsch, 1996). Studies that have compared only the two wholly-owned entry modes have also provided us with mixed results. Most studies have found some statistically significant evidence that the internal development mode outperforms the acquisition mode (Woodcock, 1994; Simmonds, 1990; Li, 1995). A number of the analyses have found no statistically significant results, however none of the studies have found any evidence that the acquisition mode outperforms the internal development mode (Busija et al., 1997). Therefore, on balance the statistical evidence indicates that the relationships hypothesized in this paper are supported almost 50% of the time they have been tested, and contrary relationships have never been statistically supported.

Nevertheless, this paper exposes the potential limitations inherent in this and previous studies on this topic. More specifically, these studies are limited because they do not fully control for other potential influential effects. For example, firm-specific contingency variables such as strategic intent, size, and organizational characteristics are not controlled for in the analytical model. These variables may provide further insight into the above relationships. In addition, industry-specific factors, such as barriers to entry and exit, may improve the ability of the models to explain the variance in the performance data. Some firm, industry, and country-specific variables were partially controlled for in this study, but clearly, a preferred methodological approach would include controls for more of these variables.

In conclusion, the study provides some support for the theoretical model developed in this study. However, this study also points out the limitations of the theoretical model and statistical data used. Clearly, future research must focus on improving the measurement of these variables as well as developing a more complex model that considers both within and between mode influences. Finally, this study points out the importance of researching comparative entry mode performance. Managers are continuously having to make entry mode selection decisions and ultimately performance is an important driving factor in this decision process. To date, these comparative studies represent rather coarse analyses of the issue. However, they have established a base theoretical model and some preliminary evidence upon which subsequent work can be based. Further analysis should concentrate on developing more generalized models that include other contingent influences and incorporate the complexities of within-mode differences.

NOTES

1. The joint venture mode in this study was limited to the internal development case. Therefore, joint ventures that were established through acquisitions were not included.
2. The sample performance variance for the 1992 data set was as follows: 38 percent reported profitable, 26 percent reported break-even, and 36 percent reported a loss. For the 1997 data set the performance variance was as follows: 52 percent reported profitable, 23 percent reported break-even, and 25 percent reported a loss.
3. It should be noted that an analysis using the total 1992 data set including entities having an age of less than 2 years also provides evidence supporting the hypotheses. The Chi-squared was non-significant at $p=0.11$, Spearman's Rank Correlation was significant at $p=0.05$, and the Kruskal-Wallis test was significant at $p=0.02$. The directions of the results also supported the hypotheses.

5. Local ownership restrictions, entry mode choice and FDI performance: Japanese overseas subsidiaries in Asia

Shige Makino and Paul W. Beamish

This study examines the moderating effects of a host government's local ownership restrictions on the linkage between the choice of foreign entry mode and its performance, using a sample of 917 Japanese foreign subsidiaries in Asia. The study focuses on two foreign entry modes, joint ventures (JVs) and wholly-owned subsidiaries (WOS), and two performance measures, financial performance and termination rate. The results suggest that the extent of local ownership restrictions is negatively and significantly associated with the financial performance of WOS, whereas it does not directly influence that of JVs. There is no clear association between the extent of local ownership restrictions and the termination rate for the JV and WOS samples.

INTRODUCTION

The importance of government restrictions on the choice of foreign entry mode has frequently been discussed in the international business literature (Fagre and Wells, 1982; Lecraw, 1984; Beamish, 1985; Kobrin, 1988; Contractor, 1990). The literature has generally suggested that foreign firms tend to choose joint ventures over wholly-owned subsidiaries when investing in restrictive countries. For example, Beamish (1985) reported that 57% of North American multinational enterprises (MNEs) chose JVs when entering less developed countries (LDCs) due to government suasion. Kobrin (1988) suggested that about 76% of US multinational corporations (MNCs) chose JVs when investing in restrictive countries in which local ownership restrictions were imposed on all foreign inward investments, whereas only

30% chose JVs when investing in countries in which no such restrictions were imposed.

However, what is not well understood is the impact of host governments' restrictions on the performance of foreign subsidiaries. Few studies have been conducted in this area. The lack of performance implications of host government restrictions implies a missing source of practical information for both managers of MNEs and host country policy makers. For foreign managers, how host country restrictions affect their subsidiary performance is a critical issue for their choice of investment site. For policy makers in a host country, the question of what types of inward investment restrictions should be implemented is directly associated with the issue of how to attract inward investment. Therefore, the primary purpose of this study is to examine the relationship between the extent of local ownership restrictions, the choice of entry mode (greenfield JVs vs. greenfield WOS) and its performance. The first part of the chapter reviews previous studies on the relationships between: (1) local ownership restrictions and the choice of foreign entry mode; (2) local ownership restrictions and foreign subsidiary performance; and (3) the choice of foreign entry mode and its performance. The second part of the chapter involves the empirical investigation, using a sample of Japanese MNCs in Asia.

LITERATURE REVIEW

Local Ownership Restrictions and Choice of Foreign Entry Mode

Previous studies have suggested that the choice of entry mode would be influenced by the host government's local ownership restrictions (Fagre and Wells, 1982; Lecraw, 1984; Contractor, 1990; Padmanabhan and Cho, 1996). These studies generally suggested that when investing in highly restrictive countries, foreign firms were more likely to have a shared-ownership form such as equity JVs, rather than a sole-ownership form such as wholly-owned subsidiaries.

Fagre and Wells (1982) viewed the extent of foreign ownership as an outcome of negotiation between foreign MNCs and host governments – the bargaining power of the two parties. Drawing from a sample of US MNCs in Latin America, they found that the bargaining power between foreign firms and host country would be influenced by the resources brought by the foreign firms and by the number of competitors offering similar resources. Lecraw (1984) replicated and extended Fagre and Wells' study using a sample of 153 subsidiaries of MNCs based in the USA, Europe, Japan, and other less developed countries located in Southeast Asia, and confirmed their findings.

Contractor (1990) examined the impact of a liberalization of local ownership restriction on the ownership position of US foreign subsidiaries across the world. Contractor found a clear reduction in the number of 50-50 and minority JVs from US affiliates as the liberalization of host government regulations proceeded in the 1980s. Similarly, Franko (1989) found that US MNCs tended to adopt more minority or 50-50 JVs in less developed countries than in developed countries in the mid-1970s, due in part to the increased host country restrictions during the period. Padmanabhan and Cho (1996) also found Japanese MNCs tended to prefer full ownership to shared ownership when they invested in less restrictive host countries.

The relationship between local ownership restrictions and equity ownership position is not always as straightforward as suggested by these earlier studies because the choice of ownership position may also be influenced by foreign firms' preference. Lecraw (1984), for example, pointed out that the relationship between the extent of equity ownership and the degree of control would not always be linear. Lecraw found that the relationship between the two was actually a J-curve shape. Many researchers in fact have suggested equity ownership would be one, but not the sole, control mechanism (Geringer and Hebert, 1989; Schaan, 1988; Yan and Gray, 1994; Madhok, 1995).

Gomes-Casseres (1990) examined the impact of both local ownership restrictions and firm preference on the choice of foreign entry mode, using 1,877 foreign subsidiaries of US MNEs across the world. He found that the US firms tended to form more JVs than WOS when investing in highly restrictive countries, but this relationship was moderated when some industry- and firm-specific factors (i.e., type of industry, parent firms' familiarity with local country, size of subsidiary, and the GDP growth of host country) were controlled. Based on the results of the analysis, he concluded that the choice of ownership position for a foreign subsidiary would depend on both firm preference and local ownership restrictions.

Blodgett (1991) examined the hypothesis that the relative ownership position between foreign and local JV partners was associated with the relative importance of contributions specific to each partner. Consistent with Gomes-Casseres' claim, she found that the level of equity position of the JV partner was significantly influenced by the extent of partner contributions, but this relationship did not hold when host government suasion existed.

In sum, previous literature has suggested that the level of equity position would be influenced by local ownership restrictions, by foreign firms' preference, and by the relative contributions from each partner. While the ownership position is directly influenced by local ownership restrictions, foreign firms may still have an incentive to share the remaining equity share – the equity ownership after the share requested by local ownership restrictions was left out – with local partners if they preferred to do so. This is because foreign firms may obtain more benefits from sharing ownership with local partners than the costs of losing their bargaining power over local partners (see Contractor and Lorange (1988) for a comprehensive discussion on both costs and benefits of cooperative venture formation).

Local Ownership Restrictions and FDI Performance

While a handful of studies have discussed the impact of the local ownership restrictions on the ownership structure of foreign affiliates, its effect on subsidiary performance has not been well investigated. Few previous studies have looked at this issue. Theory suggests there are three potential arguments regarding local ownership restrictions and subsidiary performance.

The first argument postulates that local ownership restriction has a negative impact on subsidiary performance. The argument implies that a "forced JV" does not represent an ideal ownership structure, and hence, may not achieve the ideal performance that the foreign firms originally intended. In a study of JVs in developing countries, Beamish (1984) found that JVs operating in countries where shared local ownership policy was imposed upon foreign investing firms performed less successfully than those where no such regulations existed. Thus, the first perspective suggests that a host government's local ownership policy leads to lower performance and a higher probability of termination.

The second argument suggests that a host government facilitates a foreign firm's resource access opportunities. This view implies that a host government assists a foreign firm's access to location-specific resources by providing a wide range of subsidies and fiscal incentives (see the review Guisinger et al., 1985, pp. 2-4), and protects the JV from threats of competitors both within and outside the host country in exchange for local ownership or control of the JV (Oman, 1988). In many cases, such incentives and supports from host governments, coupled with market size and local skill attractions, are critical factors which influence foreign firms' choice of location (Guisinger et al., 1985; Franko, 1989). This view implies that local ownership is a means of circumventing host country conditions and that JVs in the countries with local ownership restrictions tend to obtain more support from the local government than those operating in the countries with no local ownership restrictions.

The third argument suggests that local ownership restriction itself does not affect JV performance. This view postulates that the foreign market entry decision is essentially a foreign firm's choice (Shenkar and Tallman 1993). The assumption underlying this view is that since most foreign firms have many alternative overseas investment opportunities, a decision to invest in any given country must be based on a careful evaluation of the costs and benefits of a particular investment project. For example, foreign firms which have a hurdle-rate ROI may not invest unless expected ROI exceeds their hurdle-rate. This example illustrates that foreign firms do *not* have to invest in countries employing local ownership restrictions, which implies that the host government does not have any direct effect on the performance of foreign subsidiaries.

In summary, local ownership restrictions can either hinder, facilitate, or do nothing for subsidiary operations in a host country, and hence, be a negative, positive, or a neutral influence on subsidiary performance. Each of the three explanations may be as likely as the others. Nonetheless, previous studies have provided no insights regarding which perspective can predict more effectively than the others the relationship between local restrictions and subsidiary performance, and when.

Foreign Entry Mode and Performance

The choice of entry mode has been one of the core areas of study in the international business literature. However, while many previous studies have identified a variety of contingency factors that influenced entry mode choice decision (for a comprehensive review, see Anderson and Gatignon, 1986; Hill, Hwang and Kim, 1990; Padmanabhan and Cho, 1996), the relationship between entry mode and performance has not been well investigated. Among the few studies, Woodcock, Beamish and Makino (1994) examined the relationship between performance and three entry modes, new venture (WOS), JV, and acquisition, of Japanese MNCs in North America. Controlling for subsidiary age, they found that new ventures and JVs attained significantly higher financial performance than acquisition, but no significant difference was found between performance of new ventures and that of JVs. Nitsch, Beamish and Makino (1996) examined this relationship, using a sample of Japanese foreign subsidiaries in Western Europe. They also found that new ventures and JVs outperformed acquisitions, but the difference in performance between new ventures and JVs was not statistically significant. Li and Guisinger (1991) examined the performance of new ventures (WOS), JVs, and acquisitions using failure rate as a performance measure. They found that acquisitions had a significantly higher failure rate than WOS. However, the failure rate of JVs was not significantly different from either of the others.

These studies generally suggested that: (1) foreign subsidiaries entering through acquisitions were less likely to be successful, compared with WOS and JVs; and (2) there was no clear difference between performance of WOS and that of JVs. However, these previous studies have some limitations. First, they focused only on foreign subsidiaries in developed countries such as those in North America and Western Europe, and ignored those in other non-Western regions such as Asia. Second, they did not identify and control for contingency factors that might affect the relationship between foreign entry mode and performance: they simply compared performance differences between the three entry modes. Thus, the identified association between entry mode and subsidiary performance is conditional, particularly in its application to those subsidiaries under regulatory environments.

In sum, previous literature has not provided a systematic explanation of the relationship between local ownership restrictions, foreign entry mode choice, and performance. Many of the prior studies have focused on the impact of local ownership restrictions on foreign entry mode choice. Fewer studies have investigated performance implications of both local ownership restrictions and foreign entry mode – particularly for those subsidiaries in non-Western host countries such as Asia. The principal purpose of this study is to examine this overarching relationship using a sample of Japanese foreign subsidiaries in East and Southeast Asia. In the analysis, we focus on two entry modes, JVs and WOS, and two performance measures, financial performance and termination rate. The subsequent sections discuss the background and measures of local ownership restrictions, followed by a detailed description of the data and the analytical methods used in the analysis. The results and implications of the analysis are discussed in the final section of the study.

METHODOLOGY

Sample Selection

The sample was collected from a survey of Japanese subsidiaries at the end of 1991 that appeared in the *Kaigai Shinshutsu Kigyou Souran* (Toyo Keizai 1992a). Toyo Keizai lists about 13,500 subsidiaries of 3,332 Japanese parents with 5 percent or more equity ownership. From the original survey, the sample selected for this study included: (1) manufacturing subsidiaries formed by at least one Japanese parent firm that owns 5 percent or more of the equity in Taiwan, Hong Kong, Thailand, Singapore, Malaysia, the Philippines, Indonesia, and South Korea; and (2) those subsidiaries terminated during 1985 - 1991. In this study, joint ventures that were formed as a result of either acquisition or capital participation were excluded in order to eliminate the possible confounding effects of acquisition and capital participation. Terminated samples are defined as those cases that had disappeared from the list of *Kaigai Shinshutsu Kigyou Souran* during 1985 - 1991.[1]

Based on the above criteria, 1,732 cases were available. Of the 1,732 cases, 116 were ventures which had been terminated during the 1985 to 1991 period, and 801 cases included financial performance information for the subsidiaries. The balance (815 cases) represented ventures that were active in 1991, but did not have performance information.

Variables

Local ownership restrictions

Host governments' local ownership restrictions are measured in terms of the extent to which foreign ownership is either prohibited or restricted. Judgement of whether a given host country adopts open or restrictive local ownership restrictions is quite complex. First, local ownership restrictions differ among countries. Some countries, such as Thailand and Indonesia, use a general ownership criterion which is applied to all foreign investments. Another group of countries, such as Taiwan, use either industry- or project-based restrictions. Yet other countries, such as South Korea, Malaysia and Philippines, use a combination of both.

Second, host governments often use differential local ownership policies toward foreign firms. In many cases, host governments impose various ownership restrictions on foreign firms based on type of business, size of investment, level of technology, level of outward exports, content of raw materials, age of the subsidiaries, and so forth. Therefore, it is likely that subsidiaries owned by the same foreign firm have different ownership restrictions even though they operate in the same host country (Poynter 1982).

Third, some host governments impose no restrictive local ownership restrictions on foreign firms, but impose a strict pre-investment screening process. Those countries may accept only *desirable* inward investments, allowing foreign investors to possess full ownership.

In this study, we measured the degree of openness of local ownership restrictions for each country by using two different measures. The first measure (OWN_USC) was from the data from the Benchmark Surveys conducted by the US Department of Commerce in 1982. The data include the fraction of the number of respondents that felt a country was restrictive, using responses of over 17,213 US affiliates in 1982 (Contractor 1990). The data are the most recent years available from the survey (Contractor, 1990;

Shane, 1994). The same survey data have been used as a proxy for local ownership restriction in previous studies (e.g., Contractor, 1990; Gomes-Casseres, 1990; Shane, 1994; Padmanabhan and Cho, 1996).

Some weaknesses of using this measure should be noted. First, the survey data involve the subjective assessments on local ownership restrictions from American managers' point of view.   Japanese managers might assess it differently. Second, the survey data do not include the assessment of local ownership restrictions in the People's Republic of China (PRC). By using the survey data, these data must be classified as missing. Finally, and most importantly, the survey data only represent a particular political environment as of 1982. As previous studies suggested, many countries (particularly less developed countries) have changed, usually liberalized, their local ownership restrictions over time (Contractor, 1990; and European Round Table of Industrialists, 1994). The survey data cannot capture such changes in local ownership policies.[2]

The second measure (OWN_IMD) was from the data reported in the *World Competitiveness Report 1995*. The data were based on the questionnaire survey, conducted by the IMD International & World Economic Forum, with the respondents of 3,292 C.E.O. and economic leaders in 49 countries. In the original data, the degree of local ownership restrictions was measured by the average value of respondents' rating (0 - 10), with 0 indicating the highest and 10 indicating the lowest degree of local ownership restrictions.   The scale of the second measure was reversed so that the higher (lower) value represents the higher (lower) degree of ownership restrictions.

Two of the distinctive characteristics of using these data are as follows: first, the data were obtained from a large sample survey; and second, the data are coded as a continuous measure which makes it easier to compare local ownership policies on a country-by-country basis. Table 5.1 provides the summary of the survey data and brief overview of local ownership restrictions by country.

Other regulatory variables
Besides the above two measures of local ownership restriction, we used six variables which measure other regulatory factors in host countries. These variables include the extent of unequal treatment towards foreigners (TREAT), the extent of difficulty in forming cross-border ventures without local government imposed restraint (CROSS), the lack of available investment protection schemes for foreigners (SUPPORT), the extent of national protectionism against foreign products and services (PROTECT), the extent of state control of enterprises (CONTROL), and the extent of state interference over the development of business in a host country (INTERFERE).   These variables were all from the data provided in the

World Competitiveness Report 1995 (IMD International & World Economic Forum, 1995). The scale for all of the above measures was reversed so that a smaller (larger) value in the scale reflects less (more) regulatory environment for Japanese subsidiaries in the host countries.

Entry mode

This study focuses on two foreign entry modes: JVs and WOS (new ventures). A sample of JVs used in the analysis includes subsidiaries formed between at least one Japanese- and one local-firm that own 5% or more of the equity ownership respectively; and a sample of WOS includes those subsidiaries formed by one Japanese parent firm that owns more than 95% of its equity. Although there is no consensus on a cut-off point that should be used to distinguish a JV from a WOS (Horaguchi 1992), the international business literature has used 95% as a cut-off point to differentiate a JV and a WOS. For example, major studies that have used the 95% cut-off point include Anderson and Gatignon (1986), Franko (1971), Gomes-Casseres (1989), Hennart (1991a), Padmanabhan and Cho (1996), and Stopford and Wells (1972). Therefore, this study follows the above convention and uses a 95% cut-off point.

Performance

Performance is operationalized using two measures: (1) financial performance and (2) survival (termination) rate. Financial performance is measured according to that reported in the Toyo Keizai survey: a three-item scale with 1 indicating a financial loss, 2 indicating break-even, and 3 indicating a financial gain. The scale of financial performance was used as a continuous measure.

There are several reasons why subjective measurements are appropriate. First, many foreign subsidiaries do not disclose their performance data. Second, even when financial performance data are available, it is difficult to compare them when the foreign subsidiaries operate in different industries and countries that have different accounting systems and customs (e.g., Brown, Soybel and Stickney 1994). Finally, the subjective assessment of financial performance may be a better proxy for performance than the objective measure of financial profit, particularly when the parent firm adopts transfer pricing policies towards its foreign subsidiaries.

While survival (or termination) rate has been frequently used in previous studies, no consistently used measure exists. In most studies, JV survival has been measured by the ratio of the number of subsidiaries terminated during a certain period of time relative to that of surviving subsidiaries at a certain point of time (Curhan, Davidson and Suri, 1977; Davidson and McFetridge, 1984; Gomes-Casseres, 1987; Kogut, 1988b, 1989). Our definition of

Table 5.1 Summary of local ownership restrictions by country

Country	The extent of local ownership restriction [1]		Summary of local ownership restrictions (as of 1992)[2]
	Benchmark survey data	IMD data	
Hong Kong	0.01	0.67	No distinction between local and foreign firms.
Taiwan	0.08	3.78	There is no restriction on the percentage of foreign ownership for most manufacturing companies. Foreign ownership is prohibited or restricted in some government controlling industries (e.g., armaments/munitions, tobacco and wine, public utilities). Foreign Investment Approved (F.I.A.) status is required to invest in certain industries. However, the F.I.A. is not a legal requirement, and foreign firms are technically able to invest in domestic companies.
South Korea	0.28	5.16	Foreign ownership must be less than 50%. Foreign ownership is prohibited or restricted in state monopoly industries (tobacco and ginseng) and other business areas including public utilities and services as well as other government-related activities, high energy consumption businesses, certain developing industries, and others.
Singapore	0.00 (negligible)	1.79	No distinction between local and foreign firms.
Malaysia	0.18	5.10	The level of foreign ownership will be determined by the Malaysian Industrial Development Authority (MIDA). Foreign ownership of up to 100% will be allowed depending upon factors such as level of exports, level of technology, content of raw materials, types of industry, share holders' value, employment structure.

Table 5.1 Summary of local ownership restrictions by country (continued)

Country	The extent of local ownership restriction [1]		Summary of local ownership restrictions (as of 1992)[2]
	Benchmark Survey data	IMD data	
Indonesia	0.19	3.78	Typically, local ownership is 20% or more, but in many cases, it may be 5% either when projects require large capital, when they contribute significantly to export, or when they are located in remote areas. Local partners are generally supported to attain majority ownership over a 15 to 20 year period.
Thailand	0.10	4.79	Local ownership must be 51% or more. A few majority-owned foreign investments in certain industries are allowed if the activities cannot be competently carried on by an entity whose majority is Thai.
Philippines	0.14	4.02	Foreign ownership of certain service industries such as retail trade, rural banks, and mass media is prohibited or restricted; foreign ownership of manufacturing sectors is basically open but needs to get the approval of the Board of Investments when it exceeds 40%. Foreign ownership of up to 100% will be allowed depending upon level of exports.

Notes:
1. Source: The number in the left column represents the "RATIO 1" in *The Benchmark Surveys* of the US Dept. of Commerce (1982), and that in the right column represents the item #. 2.43 in the *World Competitiveness Report 1995* (IMD International & World Economic Forum 1995). The original scale of the latter measure was reversed so that a smaller (larger) value in the scale would reflect less (more) strict local ownership restrictions.
2. Sources: Price Waterhouse (1990), *Corporate taxes, individual taxes, foreign exchange investment regulations: An Asia Pacific region summary*; and the *Economist* (1988), *Business Traveller's Guides: South-east Asia.*

termination rate follows this tradition. In our study, termination rate was measured as a fraction of the number of subsidiaries which had dissolved or had been acquired during the period of 1986 - 1991 relative to those which existed at the end of 1991. The samples were collected from *Kaigai Shinshutsu Kigyou Souran* (Toyo Keizai, 1986, 1987, 1988, 1989, 1990, 1991, and 1992a). The Toyo Keizai database listed the foreign investments that appeared in the database but then disappeared subsequently. The foreign subsidiaries which disappeared in the database between 1986 and 1991 are considered part of the terminated sample. Due to the limited size of the sample, the termination rate used in the analysis may not reflect the actual occurrence of termination. To examine the validity of the sample, we compared the termination rate obtained from our sample with that reported in the recent published comprehensive survey on the termination of Japanese foreign investments by country (Toyo Keizai, 1995). The Wilcoxon Signed-Ranks Test was used to examine whether the termination rate in our sample was associated with that reported by the recent survey. The result was statistically significant ($Z=2.24$; $p=.025$). The analysis also indicated that the termination rate in our sample somewhat underestimated the actual termination rate due to the fact that our sample defined the terminated subsidiaries as those terminated during a five-year period of time (i.e., 1986 - 1991), while the survey included those subsidiaries terminated since 1970.

It should be noted that, while some recent studies suggested the significant association between termination and poor financial performance of alliances (Pearce, 1997; Olk and Young, 1997), the termination rate used in this study may not necessarily measure "failure" of investment. In fact, termination of investment sometimes involves successful completion of cross-border projects. The results of the analysis, therefore, should be interpreted with caution.

Analysis

The statistical analyses in the present study examined: (1) whether financial performance and termination rate differed between entry modes (i.e., JVs and WOS); (2) whether financial performance and termination rate differed across host countries for each entry mode; and (3) whether the degree of local ownership restrictions was significantly associated with the financial performance and termination rate of JVs and WOS. The differences in financial performance and termination rate between entry modes across host countries were examined by t-tests and ANOVA (for financial performance) and Chi-square analyses (for termination rate). Spearman correlation analysis was used to examine the relationship between performance measures and the degree of ownership restrictions for each entry mode.

One may argue that the financial performance measure utilized in the present study should be characterized as an ordinal- rather than a continuous-measure, which may not be suited to parametric statistical analysis. In this study, therefore, we used non-parametric analyses (e.g., Kruskal-Wallis one-way ANOVA) to confirm all the results obtained from the parametric analyses.

RESULTS

Table 5.2 provides the summary of financial performance by entry mode for each country. The average financial performance of the Japanese subsidiaries, both JVs and WOS, was more than 2.0, indicating that these subsidiaries generally performed well (i.e., more than "breakeven"). The financial performance of WOS in Indonesia was not available due to the lack of cases.

The right column provides the t-test results which examined the difference in financial performance between JVs and WOS. In the total sample, the financial performance of JVs (2.56) was significantly higher than that of WOS (2.45) (t=1.97; p<.05). At a country level, this result was most obvious in Malaysia (t=2.36; p<.05). In contrast, the financial performance of JVs was significantly lower than that of WOS in Hong Kong (t=1.68; p<.10).[3] There were no significant differences in financial performance between JVs and WOS in the other individual countries.

Table 5.3 provides the results of ANOVA that examined the difference in financial performance by country for each entry mode. The results suggested that financial performance significantly differed across countries for the WOS sample (F=3.05; P<.01), yet was not significant for the JV sample (F=3.06; P>.10). A multiple comparison of financial performance by country was examined using Scheffe's posthoc analyses. The results of the analyses showed that WOS in Hong Kong had a significantly superior financial performance to WOS in Malaysia. No significant difference in financial performance was found for pairs of countries in the JV sample.[4]

The summary of termination rate by entry mode is provided in Table 5.4. The termination rate was 7.0% for the JVs, 6.0% for WOS, and 6.7% for the total sample. There was no significant difference in termination rate between JVs and WOS (Chi-square= .41). However, significant results were found at an individual country level. The termination rate for JVs was significantly higher than that for WOS in Singapore and Malaysia, and significantly lower in Korea.

The termination rate of each entry mode was also compared between countries. The summary of the results is provided in Table 5.5. The results suggested that the termination rate for JVs, WOS, and the total sample all significantly differed between countries (Chi-square=29.14, 75.06, and

Table 5.2 Financial performance of entry mode by country

Nation	Entry Mode		Total (A+B)	Financial performance by entry mode: The results of T-test (t-value)
	(A) JV	(B) WOS		
1. Taiwan	2.57 (n=133)	2.48 (n=47)	2.55 (n=180)	.68
2. Hong Kong	2.45 (n=20)	2.77 (n=27)	2.63 (n=47)	1.68* [1]
3. Thailand	2.50 (n=128)	2.50 (n=16)	2.50 (n=144)	.00
4. Singapore	2.57 (n=31)	2.56 (n=61)	2.56 (n=92)	.14
5. Malaysia	2.53 (n=43)	2.12 (n=54)	2.30 (n=97)	2.36**
6. Philippines	2.72 (n=17)	2.70 (n=10)	2.71 (n=27)	.02
7. Indonesia	2.68 (n=80)	n.a. (n=0)	2.68 (n=80)	n.a.
8. Korea	2.54 (n=118)	2.25 (n=16)	2.51 (n=134)	1.30
Total	2.56 (n=570)	2.45 (n=231)	2.53 (n=801)	1.97**

Notes:
** $p<0.05$; * $p<0.10$
1. Non-parametric analysis (Kruskal-Wallis one-way ANOVA) did not detect a significant difference.

58.88, respectively). The difference in termination rate was then compared by each pair of countries for each entry mode. The results suggested that the termination rate for JVs and WOS both significantly differed across countries. Specifically, the termination rates for both JVs and WOS were constantly higher in Philippines and Korea, and lower in Hong Kong and Thailand.

Table 5.6 provides the result of correlation analysis between financial performance, termination rate, local ownership restrictions (OWN_USC and OWN_IMD) and six other regulatory variables (TREAT, CROSS, SUPPORT, PROTECT, CONTROL, and INTERFERE).

Table 5.3 Financial performance by country: Results of ANOVA

Financial performance by country	F	Pairs of countries which revealed significant differences[1]
JV cases only	.67	n.a.
WOS cases only	3.05***	Hong Kong (2.77) > Malaysia (2.12)
Total cases	2.25***	Indonesia (2.68) > Malaysia (2.30)

Notes:
*** $p<0.01$
1. Results based on Scheffe's posthoc comparison at $p=.05$ level.

The degree of local ownership restrictions was negatively (and significantly) associated with the financial performance of the WOS sample for both the Benchmark Survey and IMD measures (-.197; $p<.01$ for OWN_USC, and -.230; $p<.01$ for OWN_IMD), yet no significant association was found for the JV sample. All other regulatory variables except SUPPORT were all negatively and significantly associated with financial performance for the WOS sample. These variables (except SUPPORT) were also all positively associated with that for the JV sample, yet this association was not statistically significant.

Both measures of local ownership restrictions and other regulatory variables were all positively associated with the termination rates for both the JV and WOS samples (except the JV sample with SUPPORT), suggesting that the extent of regulations in a host country had a negative impact on survival likelihood of both JVs and WOS. However, this relationship was statistically significant only for the WOS sample with one measure of the degree of local ownership restrictions (OWN_USC) and with the extent of state interference (INTERFERE). Other regulatory variables were not significantly associated with termination rate for both the JV and WOS samples.

DISCUSSION

The results of the analyses are threefold: First, the significance and the direction of the association between performance (financial performance and termination rate) and entry mode differed across host countries; second, the degree of local ownership restrictions itself did not have a direct impact on subsidiary performance; and finally, the financial performance of WOS was significantly lower than that of JVs when they operated in restrictive host countries.

Entry mode choice and performance

Table 5.4 Termination rate of entry mode by country (%)

Nation	Entry Mode		Total (A+B)	Termination rate by entry mode: Results of Chi-square analysis (Chi-square)
	(A) JV	(B) WOS		
1. Taiwan	4.9	5.9	5.2	.13
2. Hong Kong	2.8	1.7	2.1	.12
3. Thailand	1.1	1.8	1.3	.15
4. Singapore	11.8	4.4	6.9	3.77**
5. Malaysia	9.3	0.0	4.9	11.53***
6. Philippines	13.3	22.7	16.4	.95
7. Indonesia	10.1	n.a.	10.1	n.a.
8. Korea	10.4	33.3	13.8	14.72***
Total	7.0	6.0	6.7	.41

Notes: *** $p<0.01$; ** $p<0.05$

The study suggests several implications. First, the relationships between entry mode and both financial performance and survival likelihood may not be as straightforward as has been suggested by the prior literature. While previous literature has tended to examine the linear relationship between entry mode and performance in relatively developed economic regions such as North America and Western Europe (Woodcock et al., 1994; Nitsch et al., 1996), our results showed that there was no consistent association between entry mode and financial performance across host countries in Asia. The present study, for example, found that WOS attained significantly higher financial performance than JVs in Hong Kong, yet significantly lower financial performance in Malaysia. There were no significant differences in financial performance between JVs and WOS in other countries. Termination rates also varied across the host countries. The study found that JVs had a significantly higher termination rate than WOS in Singapore and Malaysia, yet a significantly lower termination rate in Korea. The cross-national differences in termination rate for each entry mode and for the total sample also differed significantly across the host countries. Thus, future studies of the performance and survival of entry modes should take account of differences in country specific factors such as local ownership restrictions.

Second, the study showed that WOS in restrictive countries tended to attain less successful financial performance than WOS in open countries. This finding may add new insights to the literature on foreign entry strategy. In general, previous studies have suggested that firms would prefer to form a WOS over a JV particularly when they possess stronger ownership advantages over indigenous competitors. This is because, by establishing a WOS, the firms can (1) appropriate the benefits brought by exploiting their advantages in a host country; and (2) avoid exposure of its proprietary resources to JV partners. However, our finding suggests that a simple exploitation of ownership advantages by establishing a WOS may not always be the best strategy for foreign investments to be financially successful in restrictive countries. One possible explanation for this result may be that it is more difficult for WOS in restrictive countries to build legitimacy and recognition in the host countries (particularly from the local government) than in the open countries. Such legitimacy and recognition may be more critical in restrictive countries with regard to attaining superior financial performance than in open countries.

Third, local ownership restrictions *per se* are not necessarily an obstacle for the success of FDI. Our findings suggest that there was not a clear relationship between the extent of local ownership restrictions and subsidiary performance (financial performance and termination rate) for the total sample. This implies that the likelihood for success of foreign subsidiaries in restrictive countries is equal to that for those in open countries. MNC managers should recognize that the key for FDI success is not the extent to which a foreign firm controls a subsidiary, but rather whether it can choose the right partner with which to form a cooperative relationship in a regulated local environment.

Finally, it should be noted that there were some host countries in which the average financial performance and the survival likelihood of foreign subsidiaries were *both* lower than others. While local ownership restrictions may facilitate the country's industrial development and technology transfer, if the performance of foreign investments is less successful compared with that in other countries, foreign firms may become quite reluctant to increase the number and amount of investments in the long run. The government officers in such countries should identify the major causes for unsuccessful performance of the inward investments and take appropriate measures.

While the present study provides important evidence and implications regarding the linkage between entry mode, the extent of local ownership restrictions, and subsidiary performance, it does have several limitations. First, financial performance was measured using managers' subjective assessment of financial performance. It may not directly measure the actual financial performance, but may measure the attitudes of managers. Also, the

Table 5.5 Termination rate by country: Results of Chi-square analysis

Termination rate by country	Chi-square	Pairs of countries which revealed significant differences[1]
JV cases only	29.14***	Taiwan &(Thailand, Singapore, Philippines, Indonesia, and Korea) Hong Kong & Philippines Thailand & (Singapore, Malaysia, Philippines, Indonesia, and Korea)
WOS cases only	75.06***	Taiwan & (Malaysia, Philippines, and Korea) Hong Kong & (Philippines and Korea) Thailand & (Philippines and Korea) Singapore & (Malaysia, Philippines, and Korea) Malaysia & (Philippines and Korea)
Total cases	58.88***	Taiwan & (Hong Kong, Thailand, Malaysia, and Philippines) Hong Kong & (Singapore, Philippines, Indonesia, and Korea) Thailand & (Singapore, Malaysia, Philippines, Indonesia, and Korea) Singapore & (Philippines and Korea) Malaysia & (Philippines, Indonesia, and Korea) Philippines & Indonesia

Notes:
*** $p < 0.01$
1. Results based on the Chi-square analysis at $p = .10$ level.

termination rate used in this study was calculated for each group of subsidiaries for the same entry mode. While this measure examined subsidiary survival at the *group* level, not at the *firm* level, the questions of how and why some subsidiaries with the same entry mode survive longer than others remain unresolved. Also, the degree of a host government's local ownership restriction could be criticized in terms of reliability of the measure. The actual effect of local ownership restrictions is a complex phenomenon because the content of local ownership restrictions differs significantly between countries. We used two single-scale measures to operationally define the concept. Although these measures were based on large sample surveys conducted by established research institutes, the

Table 5.6 Correlation between local ownership restrictions and performance of entry mode: Results of Spearman correlation analysis[1]

		Spearman correlation coefficients							
		OWN_USC	**OWN_IMD**	**TREAT**	**CROSS**	**SUPPORT**	**PROTECT**	**CONTROL**	**INTERFERE**
		The degree of local ownership restriction (Benchmark Survey data)	The degree of local ownership restriction (IMD data)	The extent of unequal treatment towards foreigners	The extent of difficulty in forming cross-border ventures	The lack of available investment protection schemes for foreigners	The extent of national protectionism against foreign products and services	The extent of state control of enterprises	The extent of state interference over the development of business in a host country
Financial performance									
a. Total sample	801	-.034	-.08**	-.04	-.05	.05	-.03	.01	.01
b. JV sample	570	.02	-.03	.02	.01	.04	.03	.04	.02
c. WOS sample	231	-.20***	-.23***	-.23***	-.24***	.05	-.20***	-.17***	-.17***
Termination rate (by country)	n								
a. Total sample	8	.58	.31	.46	.41	-.13	.57	.58	.68*
b. JV sample	8	.37	.16	.31	.26	-.51	.33	.39	.38
c. WOS sample	7	.70*	.38	.60	.57	.19	.59	.58	.73*

Notes:
1. The sample of WOS in Indonesia was removed from the analysis due to the lack of data.
2. * $p<0.10$; ** $p<0.05$; *** $p<0.01$

reliability of the measures and their applicability to a Japanese context are unknown.

Also, we did not allow for country specific factors. Among possible country specific factors, the present study focused on local ownership restrictions and six other regulatory variables. Clearly, future research should investigate other country factors such as market size, market growth, infrastructure, and socio-cultural environments which would affect such differences.

Another limitation may involve the nature of the analysis. The analyses conducted in this study were cross-sectional in nature. The study did not always capture the longitudinal changes in the choice and performance of entry mode.

Finally, the generalizability of the results of the study is limited. This study focused exclusively on Japanese MNEs investing in manufacturing sectors in eight Asian countries. A further study should be conducted to verify the results obtained in this study using different research settings such as nationality of investing firms (i.e., non-Japanese parent firms), business scope (i.e., service industries) and geographic regions (i.e., non-Asian host countries).

NOTES

1. The same method was used by Horaguchi (1992).
2. The average age of the JVs in our sample was 10.3 years as of 1991 (standard deviation = 8.1 years). In other words, the JVs in our sample were, on average, formed early in the 1980s, thus their political environment might be closely characterized by that of 1982.
3. This result was not supported by non-parametric analysis (Kruskal-Wallis one-way ANOVA).
4. These results were also confirmed by non-parametric analyses (Kruskal-Wallis one-way ANOVA).
5.

ACKNOWLEDGEMENTS

The authors wish to thank N Rao Kowtha and two anonymous reviewers for comments on earlier drafts. We also thank the participants of the Asia Pacific Journal of Management Conference for their comments and suggestions.

6.   Location specificity and the transferability of downstream assets to foreign subsidiaries

Jaideep Anand and Andrew Delios

We investigate the effect of firm-specific advantages being 'local' in scope, and the influence of subsequent location-specific disadvantages, on the choice of foreign entry mode and subsidiary performance. To look into this issue, we examine Japanese FDI data from the wholesale and retail industries – two sectors that have productive activity concentrated in downstream processes and location-bound resources. Our theoretical and empirical analyses demonstrate that in situations where required capabilities must be developed through local experience and where location-specific resources were subject to market failure, acquisition and joint venture strategies were preferred. Greenfield entries were successful in industries that permitted the offsetting of location-specific disadvantages with firm-specific advantages. From our results, we draw implications for the entry mode literature and offer a perspective on the performance of the entry mode choice.

INTRODUCTION

Theories of foreign direct investment (FDI) focus on the importance of firm-specific or intangible asset advantages as factors that determine which firms invest abroad and levels of international activity (e.g., Caves, 1971; Buckley and Casson, 1976). Much of this research points to the important role that technological factors play as determinants of FDI and foreign entry mode (see Caves (1996: Chapter 1)). Technology tends to be fungible across borders and is not intrinsically location-specific; that is, it is a global skill. Once a firm has developed and applied technological knowledge, the marginal cost of applying that technology in other locations is close to zero. The intangible, fungible and public goods nature of firm-specific knowledge like technology provides the firm with its advantage when investing abroad. However, other resources within the firm are less fungible across borders and the limited transferability of these capabilities encumbers a firm in its foreign operations.

Hymer (1976) explicitly recognized the location-specific disadvantages faced by a foreign firm, and attributed much of the disadvantage to a lack of knowledge of host country political, economic and social conditions. But location-specific disadvantages may also arise from the inapplicability of the firm's existing resource and capabilities base to the market requirements in the host country. In contrast to globally specific skills, such as technology, other skills in the firm may have a restricted geographical scope because of intrinsic differences in host country markets (Buckley and Casson, 1996). Such locally specific skills are not fungible across borders and represent an impediment to foreign market entry. To effect successful entry, the foreign firm must overcome its disadvantage in locally specific skills. An interesting question is how a firm structures its foreign entry in response to this form of location-specific disadvantage. In this paper, we investigate the entry mode determinants of firms in two industries – wholesale and retail trade – that are particularly susceptible to the need to configure activities to local market demands. Our research centers around the questions: How do location-specific disadvantages vary by industry, and, how are locally specific skills acquired in foreign market entry?

We consider acquisitions, joint ventures and greenfield establishments as alternative entry modes. In examining the choice between these modes, as influenced by the need to develop locally specific skills, we hope to make several contributions to the literature. First, the paper investigates the role that acquisitions play in gaining the resources and developing the capabilities necessary to ameliorate location-specific disadvantages. It also presents several arguments as to when and why acquisitions would be a preferred mode of gaining location-specific capabilities. Second, the paper illustrates and develops a conceptual framework that is useful for identifying the relative magnitude of location-specific disadvantages, and the relationship of location-specific disadvantages to entry mode and performance outcomes. Third, the paper concentrates on two sectors – wholesale and retail trade – that have received little attention in the international and entry mode literature, and are part of the rapidly internationalizing service sector (Boddewyn, Halbrich and Perry, 1986; Dunning, 1993).

To address the issue of location-specific disadvantages and foreign market entry, we structure the paper as follows. The next section reviews literature on location-specific disadvantages and entry mode. In the third section, we discuss hypotheses concerning relationships between entry mode determinants and their variance across wholesale and retail entries. The fourth section describes the data, variables and empirical tests. We conclude with a discussion of the results.

LOCATION-SPECIFIC DISADVANTAGES AND FOREIGN ENTRY MODE

When a firm undertakes FDI, the firm's managers expect firm-specific advantages to outweigh the disadvantages of being foreign (Hymer, 1976). However, as we argue in this paper, the proportion of a firm's production that must occur at the time of consumption affects the magnitude of these disadvantages and the optimal entry mode strategy. Typically, earlier entry mode studies considered the variance in the proportion of production that must occur at the time of production (and in the host country) to be equal across firms. Hence, prior researchers argued that location-specific disadvantages varied inversely with the firm's amount of international experience (Hymer, 1976; Beamish, 1988; Barkema, Bell, Pennings, 1996). Where the host country was idiosyncratic from the foreign firm's perspective, new knowledge and skills had to be learned, and the level of international experience thereby affected the entry mode decision.

Process views of international expansion such as the Scandinavian School (e.g. Johanson and Vahlne, 1977) and the Product Cycle approach (Vernon, 1979) relate the level of international experience to foreign market entry behavior.[1] A firm's initial foreign involvement encompasses markets that are culturally and geographically proximate. The internationalization process is also one of increasing commitment to foreign markets. Firms move sequentially from no international involvement to exporting, to an overseas sales subsidiary and, ultimately, to overseas production. International expansion and growth is a learning process on the firm's part. Increasing levels of involvement in foreign markets relate to a firm's accumulation of experiential knowledge and the accumulation of local knowledge generally requires the participation of a local firm. Typically, joint ventures (JVs) with local firms represent the bridge between no equity involvement and equity involvement in a host country. The firm may also undertake the acquisition of a domestic incumbent to gain the knowledge of a local firm.

Thus, two entry modes – JVs with local firms and acquisitions – facilitate the procurement of host country knowledge, resources and capabilities. Conceptually, JVs and acquisitions are organizational choices that bring together the resources of two firms: those of the local firm and those of the foreign firm. Since Stopford and Wells' (1972) pioneering study on MNEs, researchers have argued that JVs with local firms are an effective means of overcoming location-specific disadvantages because the JV provides the foreign firm with a ready stock of the local firm's location-specific resources. As such, local partner JVs can be used as a means to access or acquire local knowledge and resources (Beamish and Inkpen, 1995), and thereby overcome location-specific disadvantages. Several empirical studies demonstrate the important role that local partners play in providing local knowledge. Beamish (1988) identified local firms as supplying critical local knowledge resources that positively affected the performance of international JVs. In Gomes-Casseres' (1989; 1990) transaction cost analyses of US-owned foreign subsidiaries, market failure for location-specific resources led to the formation of JVs with local firms. Similarly, Hennart (1988; 1991a) argued that the provision of complementary location-specific resources by local firms was an important factor influencing the formation of JVs.

Like the formation of a local partner JV, acquisitions can serve as a means of overcoming location-specific disadvantages. An acquisition of a domestic incumbent represents the purchase of a stock of location-specific resources and capabilities that are bundled with the other resources that comprise the local firm. While an acquisition provides a firm with several benefits, such as an immediate stock of capabilities, it also comes with a high cost that may outweigh the sum of the expected benefits (Barney, 1988a). Information asymmetry between the target and the foreign acquirer regarding the value of the target's resources makes the pricing of acquisitions problematic, and the level of integration required to achieve expected gains is often difficult to achieve (Jemison and Sitkin, 1986; Nayyar, 1993). These difficulties have led to the view that acquisitions may be a less-efficient entry mode compared to greenfields and JVs (Woodcock, Beamish and Makino, 1994). However, in cases where local partners are unavailable, and where a firm must obtain new resources, such as local competence, to overcome formidable location-specific disadvantages, acquisitions may represent the only viable means of foreign market entry.

The potency of acquisitions in obtaining new resources arises out of obstacles firms face in internally developing or purchasing new resources. Internal development is constrained by a firm's history of past investments and its limited range of available routines which form a repertoire of fixed responses (Nelson and Winter, 1982). A firm is restrained in its ability to use outside knowledge by its level of previous experience within a technological domain or in a particular product market (Cohen and Levinthal, 1990). Further, the tacit and embedded nature of resources hampers duplication of the processes of competing firms (Dierickx and Cool, 1989). The tacitness and organizational embeddedness of resources also makes market valuation and transfer difficult. Resources tend to lose value when removed from their organizational context (sold discretely apart from the firm), and these resources are subject to market failure. While a firm searching for discrete resources, such as a firm encountering location-specific disadvantages, prefers to buy a discrete resource rather than acquire the whole firm, it is difficult to ascertain the value of discrete resources (Hennart, 1982). Even if the acquiring firm can value discrete resources accurately, the quality of transfer is subject to the discretion of the selling firm's managers [Chi 1994]. In such situations, acquisitions can be an efficient means of acquiring new resources that are indivisible from the firm (Mitchell, 1994).

Whether a firm requires new resources on foreign entry depends on the magnitude of the firm's existing firm-specific advantages and location-specific disadvantages. In discerning the extent of location-specific disadvantages, it is useful to determine the transferability of the firm's existing resources. Transferability may be restricted by the physical boundedness of firm-specific advantages or by the applicability of firm-specific advantages in the host country environment. For example, service sector firms have lower levels of international activity than manufacturing firms because the activities of service firms tend to be more location-bound (Carman and Langeard, 1980). The extent to which conditions in the host country market are similar to those in the home country can also limit the transferability of firm-specific advantages to the host country. Where products have to be adapted to a greater extent to suit the demands and tastes of local consumers, lower levels of foreign activity are observed (Boddewyn et al., 1986). Fundamentally, the importance of the location-specificity of resources to the foreign entrant depends on the proportion of the firm's productive activity that must occur in the host country.

Hirsch's (1988) description of how the productive activities of a firm need to be divided between the home and host country helps to identify the proportion of production that must occur in the host country. Hirsch (1988) makes the point that a product is produced partly in isolation (independent of the presence of the consumer) and, in part, simultaneously with consumption. A firm's activities can be defined by the extent to which the direct interaction between consumer and producer (the simultaneity of production and consumption) accounts for the total cost of delivery. The fraction of the total economic value associated with the service component (i.e., production at the time of consumption) is the simultaneity or S-factor.[2] The greater the S-factor, the greater the amount of production that occurs at the site of consumption.

The S-factor is a propitious concept for identifying how susceptibilities to location-specific disadvantages vary across industries. In sectors in which the S-factor is high, a large proportion of the firm's productive activities must be located at the site of the consumer. When FDI occurs in a high S-factor industry, less of the firm's production can occur in the home country, and the firm must learn how to conduct many of its activities in the host country. With increases in the S-factor, productive processes become more locally specific and location-specific disadvantages multiply concomitantly. In the next section, we operationalize differences in the S-factor by comparing Japanese investments in the wholesale and retail sectors.

HYPOTHESIS DEVELOPMENT

Japanese Wholesale and Retail Firms

In general, service businesses incur a greater simultaneity of production and consumption (a higher S-factor) than firms in the manufacturing sector; however, the S-factor is not equal across all service industries. Even wholesale and retail firms, which are engaged in similar activities – the exchange of products across a trading interface – exhibit differences in the S-factor. Retail firms provide extensive services at the point of product exchange.[3] For example, automotive dealers provide information to the consumer about makes and models of vehicles and permit the consumer to sample the product via a test-drive. In a clothing store, customers sample merchandise and solicit the assistance of sales clerks. Many computer retailers typically provide both before- and after-sales service. These activities add value to the product at the point of exchange and economic value is created in the producer-consumer interaction. Referring back to the S-factor, the producer-consumer interaction component of the retail firm's product is high and the S-factor is large.

Several cases demonstrate the challenges to international entry presented by the high S-factor in retail operations. One of the more successful firms in the US, Wal-Mart, encountered numerous pitfalls in the mid-1990s in attempting to establish a market presence in Hong Kong and China; Lane-Crawford, a Hong Kong-based retailer, failed in its attempts to set up in Singapore; and Kmart was unsuccessful in its entry to Singapore. These failed market entries were attributed to an inability to deliver value at the downstream end of the value chain (*Economist,* 1996). Even in geographically and culturally proximate countries, entrants in the retail sector face considerable challenges when crossing borders. Few Canadian retail firms have had success in entering the US (Evans, Lane and O'Grady, 1992), although a Canadian retail entrant's likelihood of success was greatest when entry was by acquisition (Lane and Hildebrand, 1990).

While international entrants into the retail sector have met numerous difficulties, entrants into the wholesale sector have encountered fewer exigencies. For example, Japanese General Trading Companies, *sogo shosha,* have had considerable success in establishing wholesale operations.

In the early 1990s, Mitsubishi, Mitsui and Sumitomo ranked consistently among the world's 40 largest MNEs (UNCTAD, 1996).[4] The wholesale subsidiaries of sogo shosha perform three basic activities: transaction intermediation, information-gathering and financial intermediation (Kojima and Ozawa, 1984). The first activity involves a producer-consumer interaction and consists of the procurement of materials for manufacturing firms and export assistance. To perform this activity, knowledge of global and local market conditions for resources and for finished goods is required as are market-making skills (information gathering). In contrast, information-gathering and financial intermediation are performed in isolation and are independent of the various host markets in which the firms operate. Consequently, the S-factor for wholesale firms is lower than that for retail firms, and the magnitude of location-specific disadvantages is smaller.

Hypotheses

We expect differences in the magnitude of the S-factor across industries to be reflected in the entry mode decision. As the process view of internationalization states, the most effective way to acquire location-specific resources is in partnership with local firms. A foreign entrant often does not have the time to internally develop downstream capabilities (Dierickx and Cool, 1989) because the resources from which location-specific capabilities are derived depend on the skills and routines of the firm's employees (Nelson and Winter, 1982: Chapter 5) and represent organizationally embedded know-how shared by the firm's employees (Caves, 1996). Moreover, the required downstream resources and capabilities tend to be subject to high transaction costs and market failure because of their tacitness and social complexity (Chi, 1994). Consequently, where the S-factor and location-specific disadvantages are high, as in retail subsidiaries, we expect entry to occur more frequently as acquisitions and JVs.

Hypothesis 1. The greater the proportion of production that must occur at the time of consumption, the greater the frequency of entry by acquisition and local partner JV.

Hypothesis 2 examines the relationship between resources and entry mode. In the wholesale and retail sectors, the firm's resources are embodied in its human assets, and the transfer of capabilities from the parent to a subsidiary requires the transfer of employees (Dunning, 1989). We expect employment patterns to be representative of embedded resources and capabilities and the increased need to source local resources when the S-factor of the subsidiary's industry is high. That is, the human resource requirements of higher S-factor industries (retail) are indicative of the demand for local content and resources.

Hypothesis 2. The greater the proportion of production that must occur at the time of consumption, the greater the proportion of local employment in the foreign subsidiary.

Hypotheses 3a and 3b examine the relationship between industry, entry mode and performance. Performance has been a central construct in many entry mode studies but there is a lack of consensus across these studies. Woodcock et al., (1994) demonstrated that among Japanese entries into the US, greenfields were the highest performing mode; however, in a study using the same performance measure, Nitsch, Beamish and Makino, (1996) found JV entries into Western Europe to be the best performing mode. Other evidence reported by Chowdhury (1992) points to the superior performance of JVs over greenfields along several performance measures, and Koh and Venkatraman (1991) found that the announcement of JV formation increased the market value of parent firms. Similarly, researchers are not in unison regarding the performance of acquisitions. Existing literature has demonstrated that domestic acquisitions tend to perform poorly (Porter, 1987); and there is evidence that international acquisitions outperform domestic ones (Swenson, 1993; Markides and Ittner, 1994).

We offer the conjecture that the lack of agreement in these studies can be explained by examining entry motives. We suggest that when the foreign firm can exploit existing resources on foreign entry, greenfields perform better. When the foreign firm must acquire new competencies on foreign entry, acquisitions and JVs perform better.

Hypothesis 3a. In the foreign subsidiary's industry, the lesser the proportion of production that must occur at the time of consumption, the better the performance of greenfield entries relative to local partner JV and acquisition entries.

Hypothesis 3b. In the foreign subsidiary's industry, the greater the proportion of production that must occur at the time of consumption, the better the performance of acquisition and local partner JV entries relative to greenfield entries.

These three hypotheses establish relationships between the proportion of production that must occur at the time of consumption and the entry mode strategy and performance of the foreign subsidiary. The greater the proportion of production that must occur at the site of consumption, the greater the need to involve local participation, in the form of an acquisition or a local partner JV, on foreign entry. The local staffing requirements for the foreign subsidiary reflect local participation demands, as we expect to find a greater proportion of local employees in subsidiaries that incur a greater requirement for local production. Finally, the relative performance of the three entry modes – greenfield, acquisition and local partner JV – is contingent on the need to source local resources and the ability to exploit existing capabilities.

METHODS

Empirical Setting

To test the preceding three hypotheses, we investigated Japanese investments in the wholesale and retail sector. In general, Japanese firms have a preference for the establishment of a new operation (greenfield or JV) over the acquisition of an existing operation (Kogut and Chang, 1991); however, "if Japanese investors require complementary inputs that can be more cheaply acquired in a going concern than in disembodied form on the market," acquisitions will be chosen (Hennart and Park, 1993: 1056). Sogo shosha play an important role in Japanese firms' international expansion. In many instances, sogo shosha act as a minority partner to the Japanese manufacturing or service firms in the same *keiretsu* undertaking FDI (Kojima and Ozawa, 1984), and provide financial assistance and general information about the host country. In our sample, at least 52% of retail subsidiaries had a parent that was a sogo shosha (e.g., Nissho Iwai) or had a parent that was affiliated with a sogo shosha (e.g., Mistukoshi is part of the Mitsui group (Toyo Keizai, 1996)). As a consequence, levels of international experience and resources across the parent firms of the wholesale and retail subsidiaries are roughly comparable, and we expect parent firm effects on entry mode strategies to vary little between entrants in the two sectors.

However, the profile of firm-specific advantages of the wholesale and retail subsidiaries are different. Sogo shosha are well recognized as leading international competitors in wholesale trade.[5] The firm-specific advantages of the wholesale subsidiaries, compared to retail subsidiaries, are likely to be stronger. Furthermore, Japanese retail firms have firm-specific advantages that tend to be specific to Japan. This specificity, along with Japan's lingual and cultural uniqueness, makes these advantages difficult to transfer overseas (Johansson, 1990), and the location-specific disadvantage is likely to be a substantial barrier for Japanese retail firms. Finally, Japanese retail firms tend to utilize international sourcing networks or *kaihatsu yunyu* systems.

These systems provide a common source of products for the different establishments of a retail firm (Davies and Fergusson, 1995). This suggests that when a new subsidiary is established, upstream activities are conducted through existing connections, and any new capabilities that need to be developed are at the downstream end of the value chain.

Data Description

The source for the wholesale and retail entries of Japanese firms is *Kaigai Shinshutsu Kigyou Souran – kuni betsu* (Japanese Overseas Investments – By Country) (Toyo Keizai, 1994). Yamawaki (1991) reported that this annual survey covers close to the population of Japanese overseas affiliates, although Anderson and Noguchi (1995) identified a few companies that had incomplete listings of overseas affiliates.   Nonetheless, the major trading companies in Japan (e.g., Mitsui, Marubeni, Sumitomo) reported extensively in the 1994 survey. Our sample of 1,609 subsidiaries comprised all retail and wholesale subsidiaries that reported performance information and were located in North America, Western Europe and East and South East Asia. The largest number of entries were in North America (38%); 32% of entries were in East and South East Asia, and Western Europe received the remaining 30%. As indicated in Table 6.1, JVs occurred most frequently in Asia, and the highest frequency of acquisitions was in Europe. Table 6.2 provides descriptive statistics and correlations for all variables used in this study.

Table 6.1 Entry mode by world region

Region	Greenfield	Local partner JVs	Acquisitions	Total entries
East and South East Asia	340	151	26	517
Western Europe	389	37	53	479
North America	536	30	47	613
Total	1,265	218	126	1,609

Analytical Procedures

We examined the first hypothesis with two operationalizations of the amount of production that must occur at the site of consumption. The first operationalization of this concept is the industry in which the subsidiary was established. *Chi*-square analysis of entry mode patterns across the two sectors is the first test of Hypothesis 1. The second test of Hypothesis 1 involves multinomial logit analysis in which we model the entry mode choice as a function of the intensity of activity that must occur in downstream functions (the second operationalization). In both tests, the dependent variable is the entry mode: greenfield, JV or acquisition.[6] Multinomial logit analysis is an appropriate modeling procedure for qualitative dependent variables with more than two levels. The equations estimated in the multinomial logit model provide a set of probabilities for the three possible entry modes given the observed characteristics of the entrant (Greene, 1997).

We used a series of *t*-tests to explore Hypothesis 2. A second multivariate analysis examined the determinants of subsidiary performance (Hypotheses 3a and 3b). The performance measure for this series of analyses was the subsidiary general manager's assessment (loss, breakeven or gain) of the subsidiary's financial performance in 1993. In our sample, 19.8% of subsidiaries reported a loss, 25.4% breakeven and 54.8% were profitable. Because the performance variable has ordinal properties, we used ordered logit analysis as the estimation procedure.[7] Similar to multinomial analysis, ordered logit analysis estimates models in which the dependent variable has more than two discrete outcomes; however, ordered logit analysis retains the ordinal properties of the dependent variable.

Variables

Industry-level variables
The industry-level variables measure inter-industry variance in the amount of production that must occur at the site of consumption (and the accompanying location-specific disadvantage).[8] To measure this variance, we introduce three continuous industry-level measures that gauge the relative intensity of downstream, upstream and managerial processes in each sector.[9] We calculated the downstream measure as the ratio of employees in downstream occupations (e.g., sales workers, sales agents, salespersons, cashiers, demonstrators, promoters and telemarketers) to all employees. In line with Hypothesis 1, we expect a positive relationship between the magnitude of the downstream measure (location-specific disadvantages) and the propensity to enter by acquisition or JV.

Employment in upstream occupations (e.g., wholesale and retail buyers, purchasing agents, budget analysts, cost estimators, technicians, computer programmers and technical writers) measured the use of staff engaged in upstream activities such as information gathering, and other technical and skilled activities. We expect a negative relationship between the upstream

Table 6.2 Pearson correlation coefficients and descriptive statistics (N=1218)

Variables

	1	2	3	4	5	6	7	8	9	10
1. Subsidiary age (years)	1									
2. Subsidiary sales (log 1993 $ mil. sales)	.16*	1								
3. Expatriate employment (% total employment)	-.04	.02	1							
4. Cultural distance	-.08*	-.02	.02	1						
5. Region dummy: North America =1	.19*	.06*	.13*	-.17*	1					
6. Region dummy: Europe =1	-.08*	-.01	-.05	-.25*	-.51*	1				
7. Downstream (% of employment)	-.09*	.00	-.09*	.01	-.04	-.05	1			
8. Upstream (as % of employment)	.05	.00	.03	-.01	.06*	.05	-.08*	1		
9. Manager (% of employment)	.08*	.01	.07*	.01	.03	.06*	-.28*	.86*	1	
10. Industry dummy:	-.10*	.00	-.13*	-.02	.01	-.08*	.54*	-.48*	-.72*	1

Variables

Retail = 1

Variable	1	2	3	4	5	6	7	8	9	10	11	12	13
11. Mode dummy: Local partner JV = 1	-.09*	-.05	-.20*	.06	-.20*	-.09*	.11*	-.08*	-.10*	.08*	1		
12. Mode dummy: acquisition = 1	-.08*	.00	-.14*	-.05	.00	.09*	.06*	-.05	-.02	.07*	-.12*	1	
13. Performance	.12*	.03	-.05	.07*	-.09*	-.09*	-.04	.06*	.12*	-.10*	.07*	-.04	1
Mean (Greenfield: 79% of sample)	12.55	105.01	.2589	2.773	.4275	.2951	.2227	.0849	.0755	.0678	0	0	2.339
Mean (Local Partner JVs: 13% of sample)	10.21	19.88	.0990	2.944	.1341	.1829	.2503	.0779	.0726	.1402	1	0	2.482
Mean (Acquisitions: 8% of sample)	9.70	87.22	.1109	2.590	.3789	.4316	.2441	.0789	.0743	.1474	0	1	2.221
Mean (Overall)	12.02	91.86	.2258	2.781	.3842	.4866	.2281	.0835	.0750	.0837	.2126	.0780	2.349
Standard deviation	8.39	56.72	.2482	1.152	.4866	.4542	.0809	.0278	.0104	.2771	.4093	.2683	0.791
Variable	1	2	3	4	5	6	7	8	9	10	11	12	13

Notes: * $p < 0.05$.

measure (firm-specific advantages) and the propensity to enter by acquisition or JV.

The percent of employees in management occupations (e.g., administrative, general and top managers) is the measure of the managerial function. The relationship between the intensity of management employment and entry mode is less clear because the management function is dispersed throughout the value chain. However, Franko (1971) and Stopford and Wells (1972) observed in subsidiaries of US MNEs that local managers were better able to handle the local labor force and relationships with buyers, suppliers and governments. This finding suggests a greater location-specificity to subsidiary management and a higher ratio of managers in the entered industry should tend to favor entry by acquisition or JVs.

Table 6.3 summarizes mean values for the three employment measures by industry. Each retail industry employed proportionally more downstream employees and fewer upstream employees than the two wholesale industries. To inspect the validity of the upstream and downstream measures, which we constructed from US data, we compared the downstream and upstream employment ratios to industry-level upstream and downstream expenditures for Japanese firms. The same trends were evident in the two measures. Downstream employment and expenditures were greater in retail industries, while upstream employment and expenditures were greater in wholesale industries. We conclude the employment measures are valid.

Country-level controls
Three variables control for country-level variations. The first is cultural distance (Kogut and Singh, 1988). Subsidiaries established in culturally distant countries encounter larger knowledge barriers regarding local political, cultural and societal norms. Involving a local partner via a JV or an acquisition reduces this initial barrier (Gatignon and Anderson, 1988; Kogut and Singh, 1988). We expect the frequency of greenfields to be negatively related to cultural distance. The second and third country-level controls are region dummies that mark entries made into North America and Western Europe. The region dummies control for variance attributable to differences in markets for corporate control in Asia, North America and Western Europe. Arguably, acquisitions may have been more difficult to effect in Asian countries because many firms were privately held and equity markets were less active.

Subsidiary-level controls
Kogut and Singh (1988) argued that more internationally experienced firms were more likely to enter via acquisition. We anticipate subsidiary age (a proxy for entry date) to be negatively related to the frequency of entry by

acquisition.   Subsidiaries also vary in size.   Larger subsidiaries require greater resource commitments from parent firms and entail more risk.   Caves and Mehra (1986) and Hennart (1991a) found that larger subsidiaries involved more entries by acquisition than by greenfield, while Kogut and Singh (1988) observed that larger subsidiaries tended toward JVs.   We expect a positive association between subsidiary size and the frequency of entry by acquisition and JV.

Table 6.3 Trends in employment by industry

SIC code – industry	Downstream employment	Upstream employment	Managerial employment	Downstream expenses	Upstream expenses
Wholesale	**.2140**	**.0756**	**.0736**	**.1284**	**.0243**
5000 Durable goods	.2157	.0999	.0809	--	--
5100 Non-durable goods	.2123	.0512	.0662	--	--
Retail	**.5040**	**.0386**	**.0537**	**.1689**	**.0008**
5200 Building materials	.4227	.0309	.0737	.2064	.0011
5300 General merchandise	.5935	.0353	.0385	.1352	.0004
5400 Food stores	.5449	.0137	.0311	--	--
5500 Automotive dealers	.3344	.0081	.0513	--	--
5600 Apparel stores	.7671	.0248	.0555	--	--
5700 Furniture stores	.4183	.0531	.0803	--	--
5800 Eating / drinking places	.4599	.0048	.0400	.0680	.0023
5900 Miscellaneous retail	.4912	.1384	.0595	.2487	.0011

Notes: The numbers in the first three columns represent the proportion of all employees found in that occupational category. Downstream expenses were computed as the ratio of direct selling and advertising expenses to sales. Upstream expenses are the ratio of R&D expenses to sales. Source for downstream and upstream expenses: Daiwa Institute of Research Limited [1996].

Hypothesis Testing

Hypothesis 1

The first hypothesis concerns the propensity to enter by acquisition, JV and greenfield as dependent on the amount of production that must occur in the host country at the time of consumption.   Figure 6.1 depicts the frequency with which these entry modes were used in wholesale and retail entries. Eighty percent of entries in the wholesale sector were by greenfield, while only 63% of entries in the retail sector were by this mode.   Entrants in the retail sector utilized acquisitions and JVs with significantly greater frequency.   The evidence supports Hypothesis 1: entry mode varied significantly across the two industries, with entrants that incurred a greater need to locate production in the host country (retail) using proportionally more acquisitions and JVs.

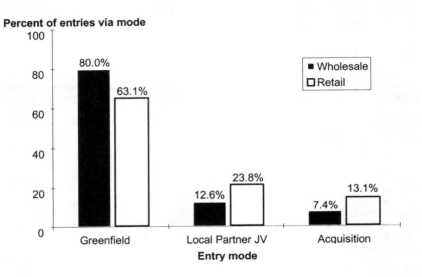

Notes: A chi-square test of independence for the distributions was significant (Pearson χ^2 = 20.384; df = 2; p < .001).   There were 1,479 wholesale entries and 130 retail entries. In the sample for the multivariate study (all cases with missing values removed: 1,218 remaining), the percentages for wholesale entries were identical to within 1%; for retail entries, percentages were identical to within 1-2%. The Pearson χ^2 statistic was significant at p<.001.

Figure 6.1   Selection of entry mode by industry category

We employed multinomial logit analysis as a second test of Hypothesis 1. Initially, we ran three restricted models that included all controls but only one of the downstream, upstream and manager variables.   In the first restricted model, the downstream variable was positively signed and significant for both the acquisition-greenfield comparison and the local partner JV-greenfield comparison.   In the second model, the upstream measure was negatively signed for both comparisons, but only significant for the acquisition-greenfield comparison.   In the third model, the manager measure was also negatively signed for both comparisons, but only significant in the local partner JV-greenfield comparison.

We next ran a full model that included the downstream, upstream and manager variables.   However, in the full model the sign on the coefficient for the manager variable reversed, and the absolute value of the coefficient for the downstream variable was much greater than the coefficient in the corresponding restricted model. This instability in the coefficients is attributable to multicollinearity (Table 6.2 indicates $r = 0.86$ between downstream and manager), and we removed the manager term from the full model. The reestimated multinomial logit model was significant, and, in the acquisition-greenfield comparison, the industry variables were significant and signed as expected (see Table 6.4). The positive coefficient on the downstream variable shows that the greater the proportion of downstream employees, the greater the propensity to acquire. The negative sign on the upstream coefficient indicates that greenfields were favored in sectors where upstream employees were more intensively used.

In regard to the effect of the other variables, older subsidiaries were more likely to be greenfields as compared to acquisitions. Larger subsidiaries tended to be formed more frequently as acquisitions than greenfields, and least frequently as JVs. At the country-level, acquisitions were effected with the greatest frequency in Europe; but the insignificance of the North America dummy indicates that acquisitions were not used with greater frequency in North America than in Asia. Cultural distance had no discernible influence on the build or buy choice.

The comparison between local partner JVs and greenfields reveals several notable differences in the determinants of entry mode. The decision to joint venture or not appears to have hinged to a greater extent on country-level determinants. The two industry-level variables were signed as predicted but only the downstream variable was significant. More intensive use of downstream employees increased the propensity to form JVs, but the levels of upstream employment did not affect the JV-greenfield choice. Meanwhile, the country-level variables were significant. The negative sign on cultural distance indicates that JVs tended to be formed in more culturally proximate countries, a result not consistent with Kogut and Singh (1988). The two region dummies show that subsidiaries formed in Asia more often took the form of a JV than subsidiaries in North America and Western Europe. Kojima (1978) and Beamish and Delios (1997b) have previously noted the high propensity of Japanese manufacturers to form JVs in Asia. The results of the greenfield-JV comparison demonstrate that Japanese investors in the wholesale and retail sectors in Asia engaged a similar entry mode strategy.

Hypothesis 2

The second hypothesis related expatriate employment levels to the subsidiary's industry. Table 6.5 displays employment patterns by sector. On average, wholesale and retail subsidiaries employed the same number of

Table 6.4 Estimation of entry mode and performance

Variables	Entry mode		Performance
	Multinomial logit analysis		Ordered logit analysis
	Comparison mode is Greenfield		Dependent variable has 3 levels:
Estimation procedure	Acquisition	Local Partner JV	1=Loss; 2=Breakeven; 3=Profit
Firm-Level Controls			
1. Subsidiary age (years)	-0.0556***	-0.0155	0.0111**
	(11.71)	(1.54)	(2.39)
2. Subsidiary sales	0.1527***	-0.1370***	0.1216***
(log 1993 $ mil. sales)	(8.09)	(4.37)	(6.06)
Country-Level Controls			
3. Cultural distance	-0.0642	-0.2083***	-0.0177
	(0.40)	(5.21)	(-0.54)
4. Region dummy: North America = 1	0.1608	-1.0421***	-0.6107***
	(0.99)	(63.41)	(-5.99)
5. Region dummy: Europe = 1	0.3555**	-0.7582***	-0.6041***
	(4.71)	(34.09)	(-6.35)
Industry-Level Variables			
6. Downstream (% of employment)	2.1783**	2.3590***	--
	(3.72)	(6.70)	
7. Upstream (% of employment)	-6.8163*	-3.9679	--
	(3.33)	(1.62)	
8. Industry dummy: Retail = 1	--	--	-0.3896**
			(-2.40)

Table 6.4 second performance column (1=Loss; 2=Breakeven; 3=Profit):

Variables	Performance (Ordered logit analysis)
1. Subsidiary age (years)	0.0112**
	(2.42)
2. Subsidiary sales	0.1170***
	(5.89)
3. Cultural distance	-0.0801
	(-0.24)
4. Region dummy: North America = 1	-0.5770***
	(-5.71)
5. Region dummy: Europe = 1	-0.5650***
	(-6.03)
6. Downstream (% of employment)	--
7. Upstream (% of employment)	--
8. Industry dummy: Retail = 1	-0.4490***
	(-3.30)

Estimation procedure	Entry mode		Performance	
	Multinomial logit analysis		Ordered logit analysis	
	Comparison mode is Greenfield		Dependent variable has 3 levels: 1=Loss; 2=Breakeven; 3=Profit	
Variables	Acquisition	Local Partner JV		
9. Mode dummy: Local Partner JV = 1	--	--	0.1658	0.2970**
			(1.55)	(2.57)
10. Mode dummy: Acquisition = 1	--	--	-0.1490	-0.2977**
			(-1.13)	(-2.24)
11. Interaction: Retail*Local Partner JV = 1	--	--	--	-0.8632***
				(-2.76)
12. Interaction: Retail*Acquisition = 1	--	--	--	1.0161**
				(2.19)
13. Intercept	-3.8339***	-0.7101	-0.6701**	-0.6866**
	(14.67)	(0.88)	(-2.09)	(-2.12)
Model Indices				
Log-Likelihood	-717.68		-1154.45	-1145.03
Model χ^2	82.78		126.24	143.06
Significance of Model	$p<0.01$		$p<0.01$	$p<0.01$
Number of Cases	1,218		1,218	1,218

Notes: Wald statistics in parentheses for multinomial, t-statistics in parentheses for ordered logistic. V.I.F.s in all equations were less than five, and multicollinearity did not threaten the estimations. *** $p<0.01$ level; ** $p<0.05$ level; * $p<0.10$ level, all two-tailed tests.

expatriates (4.13 and 3.97 respectively); however, the mean number of employees in retail subsidiaries was much larger. When we compared the proportion of expatriate employees across sectors, expatriate employment in wholesale subsidiaries was significantly greater. One in four employees in wholesale subsidiaries was an expatriate; for retail subsidiaries, this ratio was one in ten.

Table 6.5 Expatriate employment in wholesale and retail subsidiaries

Employment measure	Wholesale (N=1,413)	Retail (N=119)	*t*-value	Significance
Number of employees	41.45	173.42	8.823	.001
Number of expatriates	4.13	3.97	0.172	.896
Percent expatriate employment	23.24%	11.36%	5.150	.001

Notes: *t*-test statistics are for the comparison of row values of wholesale and retail firms. Percent expatriate employment figures are the mean value of subsidiary expatriate employment percentages in each sector.

Hypotheses 3a and 3b

The crux of Hypotheses 3a and 3b is that the performance of subsidiaries is jointly dependent on the S-factor of the industry of operation and the entry mode. In the ordered logit analyses used to test Hypotheses 3a and 3b, mode and industry were measured by dummy variables. For entry mode, one dummy indicated entry by JV, and the other indicated entry by acquisition. Two interaction terms (retail-JV and retail-acquisition) accounted for the predicted higher performance of acquisitions and JVs in the retail sector.

The first ordered logit analysis, which modeled only main effects, was significant, and in general the variables were signed as predicted (Table 6.4). The retail dummy was negatively signed and significant demonstrating that on average retail subsidiaries had a lower performance than wholesale subsidiaries. The two mode dummies were not significant indicating that, independent of accounting for the industry in which the entry was made, the entry mode had an ambiguous relationship with subsidiary performance.

The second ordered logit analysis introduced the two mode-industry interaction terms. The explanatory power of this model was significantly greater than that of the main effects model (incremental $\chi^2_{(2)}$=16.82; p<.01). In the full model, the coefficient on the retail dummy remained negative and significant, and the other two main effects became significant. The negative sign on the acquisition dummy similarly indicates that acquisitions performed more poorly than greenfield entries. JVs, not greenfields, were the mode associated with the highest level of subsidiary performance. These results provide partial support for Hypothesis 3a.

Concerning Hypothesis 3b, the retail-acquisition interaction term was positively signed and significant indicating that acquisitions made in the retail sector performed better than acquisitions in the wholesale sector, and better than greenfield entries in the retail sector. Meanwhile, the retail-JV interaction term was negatively signed. Hence, retail JVs performed worse than retail entries made via acquisition and greenfield, and worse than JVs in the wholesale sector. While the retail-acquisition result is consistent with Hypothesis 3b, the retail-JV result is not. This outcome is discussed further in the concluding section.

As for the other variables, both subsidiary age and sales were positively related to firm performance.[10] Newer subsidiaries performed more poorly suggesting a liability of newness (Stinchcombe, 1965), while more successful subsidiaries may have attracted re-investment, hence the positive relationship between sales and performance. The performance of subsidiaries in Asia was, on average, higher than that in subsidiaries in North America and Europe. In itself, this result is not surprising given the strong economic growth that the countries of Asia achieved in the 1980s and early 1990s. Cultural distance was negatively signed but not significant.

DISCUSSION

The empirical portion of this study revealed several general trends in the patterns and determinants of entry mode and performance in Japanese wholesale and retail subsidiaries. To summarize, subsidiaries in the wholesale sector had a greater incidence of greenfield entry and employed more expatriates. Retail subsidiaries were established more frequently by acquisitions and JVs with local partners and, on average, employed proportionally more local employees than wholesale subsidiaries. Acquisitions in the retail sector tended to perform better than greenfield entries, while the opposite outcome was observed in the wholesale sector.

Before discussing the results further, several cautions must be interjected into their interpretation. The downstream, upstream and management variables, while demonstrably valid measures, are imperfect measures of the concentration of activities outside of the US context. The overlap in the parent firms of the wholesale and retail subsidiaries controlled for, but in an imperfect fashion, variance in entry mode that could be attributed to parent firm differences. Finally, our sample was limited to foreign entries by Japanese firms. Whether or not the results of this study are generalizable to the experiences of wholesale and retail subsidiaries formed by firms based in other nations remains at question. Nevertheless, the results contribute much to our understanding of the nature of wholesale and retail industries, and the role of the location-specificity of assets as a determinant of entry mode and performance.

The relationship of location-specific disadvantages to the strategy of foreign entrants has generally been examined under the rubric of the 'experience effect' (Barkema et al., 1996). In this research stream, location-specific disadvantages stem from inexperience in international markets, and the incremental accumulation of international and specific host country experience reduces such disadvantages. In this paper, we suggested that location-specific disadvantages may also be rooted in the need for the foreign firm to develop a new skill base on foreign market entry. This need comes not from a lack of familiarity with host country conditions, or from product-line diversification; rather, the need for locally specific skills comes from the lack of transferability of home country skills to the host market. Hence, the location-specific disadvantage is a function of the nature of the firm's productive processes: the greater the proportion of production that must occur in the host country, the greater the extent of location-specific disadvantages.

The S-factor concept, which defines the amount of economic value created at the point of exchange, aids in identifying which industries are susceptible to location-specific disadvantages. Consistent with Hirsch [1988], we argued that high S-factor industries tend to be location-bound, because the product is not exportable. The only way to serve foreign markets in high S-factor industries is by direct investment. However, direct investment is impeded by the very factors that make FDI the only route to international involvement. If a firm must service a foreign market by producing in that market, and its existing firm-specific resources are either physically bound or not suitable to host country conditions (i.e., nontransferable), the foreign entrant faces substantial location-specific disadvantages. To overcome these disadvantages, the entrant needs to acquire locally specific resources and develop competence in the host country. Where market failure does not exist, the foreign entrant can acquire needed resources and capabilities in factor markets. Where market failure does exist, which is the more common case, the foreign entrant must access or acquire needed resources either in a JV or by an acquisition – a mode that we introduced as a means of overcoming location-specific disadvantages.

We observed that retail subsidiaries, which have a high S-factor, tended to be established more frequently by acquisitions and JVs. While this basic evidence supported the above arguments, a more in-depth examination of entry mode choice was undertaken by analyzing three employment intensities (downstream, upstream and managerial) as determinants of entry mode. In comparing the choice between acquisition and greenfield, we found transferable firm-specific advantages to be associated with entry by greenfield. These greenfield entries also tended to employ more expatriates suggesting that firm-specific capabilities were indeed transferred to the subsidiary. When the S-factor of the industry increased, as measured by an increase in the intensity of use of downstream employees, entries tended towards acquisition. From this observation, we inferred that in industries with high location-specific disadvantages, foreign entrants find the acquire option effective for building local capabilities. The evidence with respect to JVs as a vehicle for procurement of local resources was weaker but consistent with the hypotheses.

The performance results alluded to an efficiency gain in acquisitions made in highly location-specific industries.[11] When the skills of the firm were locally specific, there was a need to acquire the resources of local firms on foreign entry. Under the condition of market failure for locally specific resources, the relative efficiency of the acquisition mode increased. As a result, when entry was made in retail industries by acquisition, the performance of these subsidiaries was higher than that of greenfields in the same sector. Where the resources of the firm were less locally specific, greenfield entries had a higher performance.

The performance results for the JV mode were opposite to the direction hypothesized; that is, JVs in the retail sector performed at a lower level than JVs formed in the wholesale sector. Further, the evidence regarding the determinants of entry mode choice was weaker for the JV case than for acquisitions. These results are more understandable when we consider the local firm's perspective. A local firm will partner with a foreign firm when the foreign firm possesses unique resources that are subject to market failure (Hennart, 1988). However, in the case of Japanese entrants in the retail sector, the firm-specific advantages of the Japanese firm are weak. When a retail JV is formed with a local firm, the local firm provides the majority of resources to the JV. The asymmetry in resource contributions increases the complexity of the JV's management (Killing, 1983) and decreases the performance of this mode (Inkpen and Beamish, 1997). Moreover, the foreign firm's lack of proprietary resources may lead to partnerships being formed with weaker domestic firms, and result in poor performance. Hence, in cases where the foreign firm does not have extensive intangible resources to contribute to the subsidiary, acquisitions can be an effective entry mode.

CONCLUSION

This study analyzed data on the entry mode and performance of Japanese subsidiaries established in the wholesale and retail sectors to determine how differences in the amount of production that must occur at the site of consumption (the S-factor) are related to location-specific disadvantages and the foreign market entry strategies of Japanese investors. The main finding of this study is that entry in industries in which the foreign parent's resources and capabilities were not transferable to the host country increased location-specific disadvantages and impeded the frequency and efficacy of entry by greenfield. Therefore, when there was this strong requirement for local resources, Japanese investors preferred acquisitions and local partner JVs.

The results also show that the entry strategy of foreign firms can have important implications for the performance of the foreign subsidiary. Specifically, we found that the comparative performance of the three entry modes – greenfield, local partner JV and acquisition – was contingent on the industry of entry and the associated demands for local content. Future research should work to expand the performance and subsidiary survival implications of foreign entry strategies under differing demands for local content, particularly with the increased international prominence of service sector firms. As well, future work should continue to try to differentiate and disentangle the motives for acquisitions and local partner JVs.

NOTES

1. See Barkema, Bell and Pennings (1996) for a recent review and application of the internationalization approach.
2. More formally, the S-factor is defined as $S = (P_s + R_s)/U$, where $U = P_i + P_s + R_i + R_s$. The total value of the transaction is U, P is an activity performed by a producer and R is an activity performed by a consumer. Subscripts i and s represent, respectively, activities performed in isolation and simultaneously with consumption [Hirsch 1993].
3. The importance of the services that retailers provide is indicated in discussions of retail price maintenance (see Telser (1960) and Scherer and Ross (1990: 548-558)).
4. Not all of the sogo shosha's activities are wholesale trade. Frequently these firms take equity in the foreign subsidiaries of small manufacturers [Enderwick 1988].
5. Li and Guisinger (1992) found Japanese firms in the wholesale sector to be much more competitive internationally than similar firms based in Europe or North America. Meanwhile, retailing was argued by Enderwick (1990) to be among the least internationally competitive of Japanese service industries because of legal and cultural differences arising from Japan's distinctiveness, and because of the limited penetration of foreign retail establishments in Japan (and concurrent limited opportunity for the dissemination of new ideas and foreign practices).
6. We operationalize the entry mode as the mode of operation reported in Toyo Keizai (1994). For entries made by acquisition, the operating mode is directly equivalent to the entry mode. In the case of greenfield and JV entries, it is possible for the operating mode to differ from the entry mode because of changes in ownership positions of the parent firm(s).

However, we observed little change in the equity position of the parent firm(s) when the ownership structure of 417 subsidiaries was compared at two points in time: 1986 and 1994. In this eight-year period, only 4.3% of subsidiaries (across both industries) underwent a shift in ownership from local partner JV to greenfield.

7. See Chu and Anderson (1992) and Bell (1996) for discussions and demonstrations of the comparative merits of multinomial and ordered logit analysis.

8. Other industry level variables, such as concentration ratios, can affect the entry mode choice. However, in the case of wholesale and retail firms, competition is more atomistic than oligopolistic and the relevance of entry barriers, retaliatory behavior and the like is less likely to affect the entry mode choice (Scherer and Ross, 1990: 58-62). See Bell (1996) for a comprehensive review of entry mode determinants.

9. Employment data have been found to function well as a proxy for the availability of specific classes of labor and resources (Belderbos and Sleuwaegen, 1996), and to represent the level of processes like distribution activity (Yamawaki, 1991). In this study, the employment measures were constructed from information compiled in a 50,000 firm survey of the employment practices of US firms conducted in the 1989-1991 period by the Bureau of Labor Statistics, US Department of Labor (1992). The survey reported on employment patterns across all three-digit US service and manufacturing industries. To derive measures of employment intensity for two-digit wholesale and retail industries, employment patterns in three-digit industries were aggregated at the two-digit industry level. Within each industry, the number of employees in an occupational category (e.g., downstream) was divided by the total number of employees in all occupational categories. The resulting measure is a ratio or percentage of the total number of employees in an occupational category to total employment.

10. We ran restricted models using subsidiary age cutoffs from one to ten years. The coefficients on the country- and subsidiary-level controls were not sensitive to the cutoffs with one exception, subsidiary age. In models restricted to subsidiaries of three years or older, the coefficient on subsidiary age was non-significant. As in Woodcock, Beamish and Makino (1994), we find that subsidiary performance stabilizes after two years of operation.

11. The performance results must be interpreted with caution because of the uni-dimensionality of the performance measure, and because of the lack of data on the prior performance and capabilities of the acquired firm and on the parent firm(s) with which a JV was formed.

PART III

Joint Ventures

7. Japanese firms' investment strategies in emerging economies

Andrew Delios and Witold J. Henisz

This study jointly examines the effects of organizational capabilities and public and private expropriation hazards on the level of equity ownership chosen for foreign subsidiaries in emerging markets. Specifically, we explore the mechanisms by which 660 Japanese multinational corporations drew upon capabilities developed via industry-specific, country-specific and total international experience to mitigate these hazards for their 2,827 subsidiaries in 18 emerging markets. Results strongly support a novel specification that forges a link between the capabilities and the public and private expropriation hazards literatures.

INTRODUCTION

Foreign market entry strategy involves choices about which markets to enter and how to enter them. An important decision for the foreign investing firm is the choice of ownership level in the host country subsidiary (Li, 1995; Stopford and Wells, 1972). Studies that have addressed this choice have commonly utilized a transaction cost approach (Anderson and Gatignon, 1986; Buckley and Casson, 1976; Hennart, 1982), modeling firms as devising ownership strategies that minimize the cost of exploiting proprietary assets while protecting the rent-generation potential of those assets. As recognized in this research, one set of risks involved in deploying assets in a foreign country stems from the private expropriation hazards encountered when conducting transactions with other firms in the foreign, or host, countries (Williamson, 1996). A second set of risks arises from public expropriation hazards that are a function of the ability of a host country's institutional environment to credibly commit to a given policy or regulatory regime (North, 1990). Empirical research has found both hazards to have an impact on ownership levels. However, this research has implicitly assumed that a firm's ability to deal with these hazards is stable over time, and invariant to new capabilities developed in its investment activity.

Such an assumption is inconsistent with the substantial body of research on the effects of international experience on market entry strategy (Barkema, Bell and Pennings, 1996; Davidson, 1980b; Davidson and McFetridge, 1985; Erramilli, 1991; Hennart and Park, 1994; Johanson and Vahlne, 1977; Mody, 1993). This research demonstrates that knowledge and capabilities developed by operating in diverse environments influence ownership strategies (Barkema and Vermeulen, 1998; Chang, 1995). Drawing upon this line of research, we contend that the capabilities developed in a firm's sequence of foreign investment activities (its experience) affect its ability to mitigate public and private expropriation hazards. We demonstrate that one mechanism by which experience affects ownership strategies is by augmentation of a firm's hazard mitigating capabilities. Following prior research, we consider three types of experience: experience in a given country setting, experience in a given product setting (industry), and other international experience (Hitt, Hoskisson and Kim, 1997).

We tested our hypotheses using a sample of 2,827 foreign investments made by 660 Japanese firms in 18 emerging economies in Africa, Asia, Europe and Latin America. Japanese firms provide a suitable empirical context because they have been leading investors in emerging economies, particularly those in Asia (Belderbos and Sleuwaegen, 1996). Also, Japanese firms have been described as taking a capability development approach to foreign investment (Chang, 1995). Furthermore, the emerging economies context emphasizes public expropriation hazards because of the high variance in the institutional environments in these economies. The issue of private expropriation hazards is also highlighted in emerging economies because Japanese firms are more likely to provide the intangible assets. However, for the case of Organization for Economic Cooperation and Development (OECD) countries, Japanese foreign investment often involves an asset-sourcing motive (Carr, Markusen and Maskus, 1998; Kogut and Chang, 1991). Finally, the Japanese setting allows for a test of intrafirm capability transfer through the collection of experience data at the parent company level as well as a test of inter firm capability transfer through the collection of data on the presence of a home country partner. This latter analysis accounts for *keiretsu* (horizontal business alliances) and *sogo shosha* (general trading company) partners whose presence may also affect entry strategies (Belderbos and Sleuwaegen, 1996; Yoshino, 1976).

RESEARCH MODEL AND HYPOTHESIS DEVELOPMENT

In their seminal analysis of the ownership strategies of US multinationals, Stopford and Wells (1972) modeled the ownership decision as contingent on a parent firm's need to secure and maintain control of a foreign subsidiary, and on a need to gain new host country or industry-specific capabilities. Since Stopford and Wells, the literature on the ownership strategy of foreign investors has proceeded along two seldom converging paths. Transaction cost theorists (Anderson and Gatignon, 1986; Hennart, 1982; Oxley, 1997) have advanced knowledge of control, and Beamish and Banks (1987), Hennart (1988, 1991a), Mody (1993) and Kogut and Zander (1993, 1996) have developed and furthered research on the need for new capabilities.

These research streams have occasionally overlapped when studies explicitly identify the need for local expertise and complementary capabilities as a mechanism to reduce expropriation hazards (Chi, 1994; Hennart, 1988; Teece, 1986a). However, research has yet to demonstrate the specific mechanisms by which a firm's prior investment history affects the tradeoff between the potential gains of partnering, in the form of the acquisition of organizationally complex and tacit knowledge and capabilities, and its potential costs, in the form of expropriation of existing knowledge and capabilities. Comprehensive reviews of multinationals call for a pluralistic and integrated approach to the ownership decision (Dunning, 1993: 205-206) that balances these factors. Complicating this challenge is the time-variant profile of knowledge and capabilities, which changes as a firm makes investments and divestments across businesses (Chang, 1992), and thereby alters the calculus of decisions concerning its ownership strategy when investing (Madhok, 1997).

Our model underlying this process is laid out in Figure 7.1. Three bodies of scholarly literature – on private expropriation hazards, public expropriation hazards and organizational capabilities – underpin the relationships in this figure. We join these literatures by developing hypotheses about the mechanisms by which types of experience, and/or the presence of experienced partners, affect the choice of equity ownership levels.

Public Expropriation Hazards

Because the state possesses a legal monopoly on coercion and is present in the background of every economic transaction (North, 1981, 1990), it poses a threat to the revenue stream of all private firms. This threat may take the form of regulatory or tax policy shifts or, at the extreme, outright expropriation of private sector assets. Multinational firms face heightened exposure to these public expropriation hazards due to two main factors.

First, compared to host country competitors, they possess relatively superior knowledge of foreign factor markets, but inferior knowledge of host country factor markets. This disparity in information leads the multinational to use lower percentages of domestic content in their host country operations than host country competitors. The political costs to the host country government of expropriation (broadly defined to include administrative seizure of a portion of a subsidiary's revenue stream) – in the form of higher unemployment, lower tax revenue, lower political contributions or lower votes – are therefore lower than the costs of expropriating host country firms. A complementary argument can be found on the benefit side of the political decision calculus. Domestic constituents may support the expropriation of foreign-owned assets due to reasons of national pride or perceptions regarding national sovereignty. Such motivations may be especially powerful in periods of political or economic uncertainty.

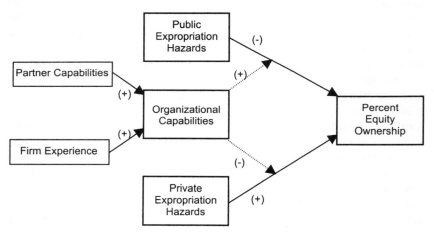

Figure 7.1 Research model

Assistance from a home country government and support from multilateral institutions may offset these disadvantages for some foreign investing firms. However, on average, host country firms or joint ventures between host country firms and foreign partners tend to be treated more favorably by the government for the reasons described above. Providing an example of this tendency, Bradley (1977) found that expropriation of joint ventures exclusively between foreign firms was eight times as likely as expropriation of joint ventures that involved local partners.

Second, in addition to the lower political costs to a government of expropriation from multinationals, the overseas subsidiaries of multinationals are disadvantaged in their ability to adapt in a manner that reduces the costs of a given expropriation. The same information disparity described above causes multinationals to be at a disadvantage in the disposal of assets compared to their host country competitors. Should a host country government alter regulatory or tax policy in a manner that makes continued operations undesirable, a multinational corporation faces a higher opportunity cost in transforming the assets to their next best use. Furthermore, subsidiaries are more likely to be required to seek permission from headquarters for adaptive moves than are joint ventures. In a static or one-shot game, these additional cost wedges provide the government with flexibility to renege on any promises of national treatment and to discriminate against foreign subsidiaries. Of course, in a repeated context, such policies will deter future investment and yield lower long-range political benefits to the host country government. However, as long as politicians have relatively short time horizons, owing to reelection constraints or the constraint of providing political benefits to non-democratic support groups such as the military or other politically powerful classes, they will face a time consistency problem in their dealings with multinationals that may result in discriminatory behavior.

Multinationals do not, however, enter into host countries without foresight. Their market entry strategies are specifically tailored to ensure that their expected profits remain higher than the next best alternative use for their capital. While other strategic options are available to them, including making the host country subsidiary dependent on the home country parent for intermediate products, technology, management skills or downstream markets (Fagre and Wells, 1982; Lecraw, 1984), we emphasize one strategic option: the percentage of equity ownership chosen for the host country operation.

By increasing the percentage of equity held by host country partners, multinationals can partially alleviate both the knowledge disparity (Hennart, 1988) and organizational rigidity (Gatignon and Anderson, 1988) described above, increasing their share of local content and shifting the political decision calculus of the governments away from expropriation. Furthermore, the reduction in the information disparity also reduces the cost of asset disposal in the event of an expropriation. Assuming that the percentage of equity ownership is positively correlated with host country partner involvement and control over day-to-day operations and, thus, the degree of knowledge transfer, decreasing the equity share of the multinational enhances this information flow and provides an important safeguard against public expropriation hazards. This relationship, which has been the subject of extensive empirical testing with generally supportive results (Agarwal and Ramaswami, 1992; Brouthers, 1995; Burton and Inoue, 1987; Gatignon and

Anderson, 1988; Henisz, 2000a; Kobrin, 1978; Kogut and Singh, 1988; Oxley, 1999; Scholhammer and Nigh, 1984; Shane, 1992), is captured in our first hypothesis.

Hypothesis 1. The greater the level of public expropriation hazards in a country, the lower the ownership position assumed by a foreign investing firm.

Private Expropriation Hazards

Partnering with a host country firm also poses hazards for multinationals. The joint venture partner may, given the necessarily incomplete nature of the joint venture agreement, behave in an opportunistic manner so as to divert the revenue stream of the joint venture away from the multinational. The feasibility of such behavior increases with certain characteristics of the activity pursued by the host country subsidiary (Williamson, 1996).

One category of private expropriation hazards is technological leakage (Pisano, 1990, 1991; Teece, 1986b, 1992). Oxley (1997) summarized several problems in contracting for technology, the majority of which vary by transaction rather than by country, including the "fundamental paradox" of information (Arrow, 1971), the tacitness of some information (Kogut, 1988b; Mowery and Rosenberg, 1989, Teece, 1986b), the absorptive capacity of the contracting partner (Cohen and Levinthal, 1990) and the exclusion of some – especially new – technologies, even in a strong intellectual property regime, from the coverage of the patent law. Such transaction-specific variance in the ability of the multinational to contract for technology gives rise to the private expropriation hazard of technological leakage. As this hazard increases, the costs of writing, monitoring and enforcing contracts increase.

A second category of private expropriation hazards developed in the extant literature is the hazard of free riding on brand name and reputation (Anderson, 1985; Anderson and Coughlan 1987; Anderson and Schmittlein, 1984; Klein and Leffler, 1981). Gatignon and Anderson argued that multinational firms with strong brand equity will assume higher equity positions in joint ventures to "prevent the local operation from diluting or confusing the international positioning of the brand" (1988: 310). Once again, the presence of an asset with a value that is difficult to protect or describe contractually increases governance costs.

In both cases, a multinational is exposed to the hazard that returns on its sunk costs (either R&D or advertising) will be devalued or expropriated by the joint venture partner. Each of these characteristics of a given transaction increases the potential returns to the host country joint venture partner of an opportunistic expropriation. Because of the condition of "bounded rationality," joint venture contracts are necessarily incomplete and these hazards cannot be reliably safeguarded through contract. Therefore, as the private expropriation hazards of technological leakage and free-riding on brand name reputation increase, the potential for maladaption that arises from contractual incompleteness in a joint venture rises.

Once again, multinationals are expected to act with foresight so as to minimize the expropriation hazards. Although a host of strategic options are available, including the careful design of joint venture contracts, we again emphasize the percentage of equity ownership chosen for the host country operation. Where private expropriation hazards are high, multinationals are expected to increase their equity shares so as to minimize the control over day-to-day operations held by their potentially opportunistic joint venture partners. This prediction, captured in our second hypothesis, has also been the subject of extensive empirical tests (Davidson and McFetridge, 1985; Gatignon and Anderson, 1988; Gomes-Casseres, 1989, 1990; Henisz, 2000a; Hennart, 1991a; Kogut and Singh, 1988; Murtha, 1991; Oxley, 1997), the vast majority of which have been supportive (see Delios and Beamish, 1999 for a recent exception).

Hypothesis 2. The greater the level of private expropriation hazards in a foreign investing firm's assets, the higher the ownership position it assumes.

Experience and the Capability to Mitigate Hazards

In addition to the study of public and private expropriation hazards, researchers have examined how capabilities developed by prior investment activity influence the strategies used for subsequent investments. In this research stream, a firm's international expansion strategy is considered to consist of a series of integrated choices through which the firm capitalizes on the best market opportunities and takes advantage of experiential learning (Kogut, 1983). Experiential learning helps to develop new capabilities, and these capabilities affect the way a firm evaluates its ownership position when making its next investments (Chang, 1995). Furthermore, capabilities developed through particular forms of investment, such as operating alliances, enhance the future value of similar ownership strategies to the firm (Anand and Khanna, 2000).

The relationship between capabilities and a firm's ownership position stems from the demands placed on the firm when it enters new product or geographic markets. The capabilities required to compete successfully in the new market can differ significantly from the ones required for success in existing markets and it becomes incumbent on the firm to develop new capabilities suited to the market into which it has expanded. This need stems from the specificity of a firm's routines (Nelson and Winter, 1982) and the bounded rationality of its managers (Simon, 1997), both of which impede deployment of a firm's capabilities outside of its current market contexts.

Because of the difficulty of deploying existing capabilities in new product and geographic markets, firms may seek required capabilities via partnerships with other firms that have experience and capabilities in the market in which the firms are making their investments. That is, foreign firms inexperienced in a given host country often partner with local firms (Inkpen and Beamish, 1997). By a similar line of reasoning, when firms invest in new product-markets, they may seek other firms with experience in that area as partners to augment existing capabilities (Hennart, 1988). This form of partnering tends to be equity-based because of the difficulties encountered in valuing and pricing the discrete tacit assets that underlie the proprietary capabilities sought in such partnerships (Chi, 1994; Hennart, 1988). Researchers have argued that inexperience in markets indicates such capability shortfalls on the part of foreign investing firms, and therefore reflects an increased propensity to share ownership with host country firms on entry.

We tested for this direct effect of experience on equity ownership levels but note that the partnerships encouraged by capability shortfalls themselves generate exposure to private expropriation hazards, which in turn complicates these relationships. Extant theory, although identifying both of these effects, has not addressed them jointly. By explicitly considering mechanisms by which experience affects equity ownership levels in foreign subsidiaries and by analyzing the magnitude of this effect under different levels of public and private expropriation hazards, we can make specific predictions about the relative magnitudes of the benefits and costs of such partnerships.

First, we posit that capability shortfalls – which initially hinder growth into new markets – can be overcome as a firm acquires new capabilities by operating in new geographic markets and/or industries (Chang, 1992; Silverman, 1998). At a broad level, the accumulation of international experience reduces the degree of foreignness faced by a firm on entry into a host country (Hymer, 1976) because it can more quickly absorb the intricacies of the economic, political, legal and cultural environment of the host country (Beamish, 1988). One specific example of this is the ability to detect and safeguard against opportunistic behavior on the part of host country governments. A specific government or a government with a specific institutional configuration may exhibit patterns in its behavior that a firm with prior experience in the same or similar countries can use to mitigate public expropriation hazards. With the development of such knowledge, a multinational can become more integrated in local factor markets as it becomes familiar with local buyers and suppliers, and it can develop capabilities more suited to dealing with local political actors.

Hypothesis 3a. The negative effect of public expropriation hazards on the level of equity ownership of a subsidiary in a given country is smaller in magnitude for foreign investing firms with greater host country, industry or international experience.

Just as the capability to mitigate public expropriation hazards can vary with the extent of multinationals' experience, these firms might differ in their ability to mitigate private expropriation hazards. For instance, assume that in each country there exists a set of joint venture partners that range from more to less opportunistic in their behavior. Furthermore, assume that channels of expropriation can vary from country to country. A multinational then faces a choice of whom to partner with and on what terms. The multinational will attempt to choose the partner that provides the largest net potential benefit when the gains of complementary capabilities are set against the potential losses from opportunistic behavior.

This partnering choice, and the ability to mitigate concomitant private expropriation hazards, varies positively with a firm's experience and capabilities in the market and industry in which it invests. These capabilities can be used to draft more complete contracts that safeguard proprietary assets (Mayer, 1999). Country experience, for example, provides important information about the reputations of various potential transaction partners. Industry and total overseas experience yield similar benefits. In each case, experience lets a firm reduce the expected variance in the opportunistic behavior of a potential joint venture partner. Prior studies corroborate this argument that firms can base routines useful for managing transactions with other firms on experience gained through prior entries (Tallman and Shenkar, 1994; Westney, 1988). Hence, we have Hypothesis 3b.

Hypothesis 3b. The positive effect of private expropriation hazards on the level of equity ownership of a subsidiary in a given country is smaller in magnitude for foreign investing firms with greater host country, industry or international experience.

Partner Capabilities

The discussion of Hypotheses 3a and 3b points out that a firm can augment existing capabilities – specifically, those that aid in hazard mitigation – through its experience in product and geographic markets. Yet a firm making a foreign investment can also benefit from the experience of other firms not directly involved in the foreign entry as equity partners (Chang 1995; Levitt and March, 1988; Shaver, Mitchell and Yeung, 1997). One particular context in which firms can benefit from the experience of other firms is through their membership in business groups. Business groups are a ubiquitous aspect of industrial organization in a variety of countries; for example, there are Korea's *chaebols*, India's family-centered industrial groups and Japan's keiretsus.

A growing literature on the economic foundation for business groups emphasizes their ability to substitute for markets that for reasons of low levels of economic development, government regulation or market size are absent in a host country (Fisman and Khanna, 1998; Khanna and Palepu, 1999). Business groups have also been hypothesized to arise because of the foreign trade and investment asymmetries that enhance the returns from the capability of "combining foreign and domestic resources – inputs, processes, and market access – to repeatedly enter new industries" (Guillen, 2000:364). In our analysis, the absent market is for hazard mitigating capabilities. The asymmetries of interest to Guillen (2000) were present in our research context, Japanese multinational activity in emerging markets. We expected that, in the absence of (or as a complement to) relevant national or industry experience, Japanese multinationals could utilize existing business group relationships – sogo shosha partnership or keiretsu membership – to obtain hazard mitigating capabilities.

Sogo shoshas have taken a leading role in the international expansion of Japanese firms (Kojima and Ozawa, 1984; Yoshida, 1986), participating as equity partners in a large percentage of Japanese firms' foreign investments (Yoshino, 1976; Toyo Keizai, 1997). When a sogo shosha is an equity partner in a foreign investment, it provides extensive knowledge and capabilities of foreign markets, built up by its wide network of foreign subsidiaries and its extensive foreign trading operations. Just as a firm's experience can reduce private and public expropriation hazards, equity participation by a sogo shosha can reduce uncertainty regarding potential proclivities toward, and avenues for, opportunistic behavior.

Membership in a keiretsu can also benefit a multinational (Belderbos and Sleuwaegen, 1996). Horizontal keiretsus are business alliances in which member firms are integrated with one another by such mechanisms as cross-appointments of directors and executives, cross-shareholdings, and joint projects. The close relationships between member firms foster good information flows (Gerlach, 1987). Imai (1987) characterized a keiretsu as a network of knowledge in which firms gain information from one another through ongoing trading relationships, collaborative projects and personnel exchanges (Gerlach, 1987). Information about foreign markets, along with resources related to finance, technology or other fields, are pooled (Helou,

1991).   A firm undertaking a foreign investment could readily obtain knowledge about the investment environment from other firms in the same keiretsu.   Consequently, we expected the experience of sogo shosha and keiretsu partners to be applied to mitigate public and private expropriation hazards.

Hypothesis 4a. The negative effect of public expropriation hazards on the level of equity ownership of a subsidiary in a given country is smaller for foreign investing firms with sogo shosha partners or keiretsu membership.

Hypothesis 4b. The positive effect of private expropriation hazards on the level of equity ownership of a subsidiary in a given country is smaller for foreign investing firms with sogo shosha partners or keiretsu membership.

METHODS

Sample

The sample of Japanese foreign subsidiaries in 18 emerging economies (see Table 7.3) was drawn from the 1997, Japanese-language edition of *Kaigai Shinshutsu Kigyou Souran – kuni betsu* (Japanese Overseas Investments – by country).   Toyo Keizai compiled these data as part of an annual survey of the overseas operations of major listed and non-listed Japanese firms. The survey data were supplemented by Toyo Keizai with information from annual reports, newspaper accounts and other media. Our initial sample totaled 18,223 subsidiaries. Because parent firm data were required for our analysis, we matched the Japanese parent firms for each subsidiary to the firms listed in the *Analyst's Guide* (Daiwa Institute of Research, 1996) and in *Kaisha Zaimu Karute* (Corporate Financial Listing; Toyo Keizai, 1998).   Both of these sources are compendiums of accounting and financial data for Japanese public firms.

Once the lists were matched, we removed nongreenfield (acquired) manufacturing operations from the sample.   Even though nongreenfield entries, particularly partial acquisitions, can be similar to joint ventures in their information asymmetry and capability transfer motivations for formation (Anand and Delios, 1997; Pisano, 1989; Hennart and Park, 1993), they accounted for just 0.6 percent of all Japanese entries in our emerging economies sample. Therefore, we removed acquisitions to facilitate our analysis and discussion. After restriction to greenfield operations, the sample consisted of 3,076 manufacturing subsidiaries of 660 large public firms. Mean sales were 458 billion yen, and mean employment stood at 4,447. In this group, 16 percent of revenues were derived from exports. On average, each parent had made foreign investments in eight countries (see Table 7.1). After "listwise" deletion of cases with missing values, our final sample numbered 2,827 subsidiaries.

Table 7.1 Descriptive statistics for Japanese parent firms

Characteristic	Number of firms	Mean	Standard deviation
Sales in billions of yen	627	457.76	1,592.01
Number of employees	625	4,447.27	8,025.85
Percentage of total sales abroad	525	16.51	17.76
Number of foreign subsidiaries as the main parent	660	13.98	29.03
Number of foreign subsidiaries as a parent	660	17.13	47.11
Number of countries invested in as the main parent	660	8.00	8.26
Number of countries invested in as a parent	660	8.26	8.58
Return on assets	609	0.81	2.72
Return on equity	611	0.43	15.30

Analysis

We tested the hypotheses using Tobit and ordered Probit analyses (Greene, 1997; Maddala, 1983). The former technique is preferred to ordinary least squares (OLS) regression when the dependent variable is "censored" at some value on the left and/or right side because OLS can lead to biased coefficient estimates. In the case of equity ownership, the dependent variable, which we defined as the sum of the equity holdings of Japanese parents that were members of the same horizontal keiretsu, has a lower limit of 0 and an upper limit of 100, hence the double-censored Tobit procedure (using Eviews 3.1) that we employed was appropriate. Ordered Probit analysis is suited for qualitative dependent variables that have more than two ordinal categories. We used ordered Probit analysis when the dependent variable was defined by ownership category. Following Curhan, Davidson and Suri (1977), we defined the three types of ownership structures by the equity holdings of the affiliated Japanese parents (in parentheses): minority joint venture (< 50 percent), co-owned or majority joint venture (>= 50 percent but < 95 percent) and wholly owned subsidiary (>= 95 percent). As the results of these analyses were qualitatively similar, we report and discuss only the Tobit results. The study's measures are discussed below (see Table 7.2).

Measures

Public expropriation hazards
We used two measures. The first, *political hazards*, taken from Henisz (2000b), is a measure of the extent to which a change in the preferences of any one branch of government (executive, lower and upper legislative chambers, judiciary and sub-federal institutions) may lead to a change in government policy. From existing political science databases, it identifies the number of independent branches of government with veto power over policy change. The preferences of each of these branches and the status quo policy are then assumed to be independently and identically drawn from a uniform, unidimensional "policy space." This assumption allows for the derivation of a quantitative measure of institutional hazards using a simple spatial model of political interaction.

This initial measure is then modified to take into account the extent of alignment across branches of government using annual data on the party composition of the executive and legislative branches for each country. Such alignment increases the feasibility of policy change. The measure is further modified to capture the extent of preference heterogeneity within each legislative branch that increases (decreases) the decision costs of overturning policy for legislatures aligned (opposed) to the executive. Possible scores for this measure range from 0 (minimal risk) to 1 (extremely risky).[1]

The second measure, *equity restrictions*, is a measure of perceived legal barriers to equity ownership by foreign firms. The variable used is the average response of a panel of 2,515 executives surveyed for the World Economic Forum's *World Competitiveness Report* to the statement 'Foreign investors are free to acquire control in a domestic company.' Table 7.3 provides average 1985-94 political hazard scores and a logarithmic transformation of the legal restrictions on equity ownership score for the 18 emerging economies.

Private expropriation hazards
Lacking microanalytic data on the private expropriation hazard of technological leakage found in Oxley (1997), we used the conventional measure – R&D expenditures as a percentage of sales (*R&D intensity*) – as an imperfect proxy. For similar reasons, we adopt the advertising-to-sales (*advertising intensity*) ratio as an imperfect proxy of the extent of private expropriation hazards of free-riding on brand name and reputation

Table 7.2 Correlations and descriptive statistics[a]

Variable	1	2	3	4	5	6	7	8	9	10	11	12	13	14	15	16	17
1. Equity ownership																	
2. Political hazards	-0.18																
3. Equity restrictions	-0.14	-0.05															
4. R&D intensity	0.15	0.03	-0.06														
5. Advertising intensity	0.06	0.03	-0.06	0.16													
6. National experience[b]	-0.08	0.08	-0.00	-0.14	-0.08												
7. Industry experience[b]	0.06	0.24	-0.08	0.04	0.09	0.32											
8. Other experience[b]	-0.03	0.31	-0.11	0.02	-0.09	0.65	0.41										
9. Unrelated entry dummy	-0.10	-0.10	0.05	-0.08	-0.10	-0.11	-0.62	-0.12									
10. Keiretsu without sogo shosha	-0.10	0.01	-0.04	0.28	-0.11	-0.02	0.02	0.02	0.01								
11. Sogo shosha as primary	-0.24	0.05	0.02	-0.31	-0.20	0.58	0.12	0.51	-0.01	-0.20							
12. Sogo shosha as secondary	-0.19	0.13	0.03	0.02	0.03	-0.08	-0.00	-0.08	0.00	0.13	-0.11						
13. Export intensity	0.24	-0.03	-0.04	0.13	-0.02	-0.03	0.12	0.11	-0.09	-0.07	-0.13	-0.08					

Variable	1	2	3	4	5	6	7	8	9	10	11	12	13	14	15	16	17
14. Relative subsidiary size	0.09	-0.01	0.09	-0.06	-0.02	-0.08	0.01	-0.12	-0.09	-0.06	-0.03	-0.02	0.22				
15. Parent size[b,c]	-0.19	0.10	-0.05	0.00	-0.12	0.62	0.23	0.69	0.07	0.71	-0.02	-0.07	0.01	-0.16			
16. Per capita GDP[b]	-0.03	0.12	0.05	-0.01	-0.01	0.11	0.11	0.22	-0.02	0.06	0.06	-0.02	0.02	0.06	0.11		
17. Population	-0.01	0.09	0.24	0.02	-0.02	-0.09	-0.06	-0.11	0.02	-0.05	-0.02	0.01	-0.04	-0.01	-0.10	-0.53	
Mean	61.00	0.66	1.61	0.03	0.01	1.33	1.73	4.25	0.28	0.25	0.11	0.13	0.18	0.11	12.90	8.26	8.69
Median	52.80	0.73	1.64	0.02	0.00	0.00	1.59	4.44	0.00	0.00	0.00	0.00	0.13	0.03	12.60	8.44	8.43
Standard deviation	29.50	0.30	0.25	0.03	0.02	1.69	1.74	2.29	0.45	0.43	0.31	0.34	0.18	0.34	1.760	0.76	1.62
Maximum	100	1.00	1.93	0.17	0.23	7.11	5.87	9.31	1.00	1.00	1.00	1.00	0.98	10.0	16.70	9.39	11.56
Minimum	0.13	0.16	0.48	0.00	0.00	0.00	0.00	0.00	0.00	0.00	0.00	0.00	0.00	0.00	9.07	6.85	4.20

a. $N=2,827$. Correlations greater than 0.03 or less than -0.03 significant at $p < 0.05$.
b. Logarithm
c. Annual sales, in billions of yen.

Table 7.3   Public expropriation hazard scores[a]

Country	Political hazard	Legal restrictions on equity ownership
Argentina	0.57	0.48
Brazil	0.16	1.44
People's Republic of China	1.00	1.39
India	0.55	1.34
Indonesia	1.00	1.79
South Korea	0.68	1.93
Malaysia	0.30	1.79
Mexico	0.76	1.30
Philippines	0.75	1.83
Poland	0.31	1.45
Singapore	0.32	1.11
South Africa	0.68	0.96
Taiwan	0.29	1.64
Thailand	0.73	1.82
Turkey	0.60	0.75
Vietnam	1.00	n.a.

[a] These are 1985-1999 averages.

(see Gatignon and Anderson, 1988; Gomes-Casseres, 1989; Hennart, 1991a; Hennart and Park, 1993; Kim and Hwang, 1992; Kogut and Singh, 1988). Both measures were five-year (1992-96) averages of data from *Kaisha Zaimu Karute*. Both measures are also proxies for firm-level capabilities (research and marketing). Although we acknowledge the limits of these proxies, we stress that, at least in the emerging market context, these capabilities are more in need of protection from opportunistic behavior than in need of complementary capabilities.

Capabilities
We measured experience at the firm level by examining a firm's foreign investment activity in a given host country, in a given industry and in countries other than the focal host country. The variables *national (host country) experience, industry experience* and *other (international) experience,* were based on the extent of a firm's investment activity at the date of a subsidiary's founding. Each variable was the logarithm of the number of subsidiary years of relevant (host country, industry and other) experience. A subsidiary year was one year of operations by one subsidiary.

In calculating these measures, we included the experience of current subsidiaries and of subsidiaries that a Japanese parent had owned and exited by 1997. We identified exits by searching several earlier versions (1986, 1989, 1992 and 1994) of *Kaigai Shinshutsu Kigyou Souran.*

Three dummy variables captured the effect of sogo shosha or keiretsu participation. The first *sogo shosha as primary partner* was coded 1 when a sogo shosha was the largest Japanese equity holder. The second, *sogo shosha as secondary partner*, was coded 1 when a sogo shosha had an ownership position lower than that of another Japanese firm. We identified nine sogo shoshas (Itochu, Kanematsu, Sumitomo Corporation, Tomen, Nichimen, Nissho Iwai, Marubeni, Mitsui and Co., and Mitsubishi Corporation), as listed in the *Analyst's Guide* under industry code 40101 (general trading companies). To separate the effects of keiretsu membership from sogo shosha ties, we created a dummy variable for overseas operations in which a keiretsu partner from one of the big six horizontal keiretsu (Mitsubishi, Mitsui, Sumitomo, DKB, Fuyo and Sanwa, see Dodwell (1996/1997)) took an equity stake, but no sogo shosha was active (*keiretsu without sogo shosha*).

Control Variables

We determined whether the subsidiary was in a core business of the focal Japanese parent by first developing a profile of the parent firm's businesses by searching through Toyo Keizai's *Japan Company Handbook* and *Principal International Businesses: The World Marketing Directory, 1996* (Dun and Bradstreet, 1995). If the subsidiary's industry did not match one of the parent firm's businesses it was coded as an *unrelated entry* (1).

Following established practice, we controlled for *export intensity* (Chang, 1995; Terpstra and Yu, 1988), *relative subsidiary size* (subsidiary's number of employees/parent firm's number of employees) and *parent size* (the size of the Japanese parent measured as annual sales in billions of yen) (Agarwal and Ramaswami, 1992; Delios and Beamish, 1999; Gatignon and Anderson, 1988; Kogut and Singh, 1988, Oxley, 1997), purchasing power adjusted *per capita level of GDP* (Delios and Beamish, 1999; Gomes-Casseres, 1989; 1990; Green and Cunningham, 1975; Kobrin, 1976) and the *population* of the host country (Green and Cunningham, 1975; Kobrin, 1976). Logarithmic transformations of data were used for all the control variables but unrelated entry, relative subsidiary size, and export intensity.

RESULTS

Models 1-4 of Table 7.4 display the results of the Tobit analyses for our emerging country sample with (1) no experience interactions, (2) public sector expropriation hazard and parent firm experience interactions, (3) public and private sector expropriation hazard and parent firm experience interactions and (4) public and private sector expropriation hazard and parent firm experience and partner firm presence interactions. The coefficient estimates on the nonexperience variables were correctly signed and significant with p-values of 0.01 or lower with the exception of firm size and relative size (insignificant), advertising intensity (correctly signed with p values of .24, .22, .14 and .07) and R&D intensity (correctly signed with p values of .02, .02, .34 and .19). The experience variables, and the sogo shosha and keiretsu variables were highly significant in the base specification (column 1). However, consistent with our hypotheses, much of the impact of these variables on the predicted level of ownership occurs through indirect channels – by mitigating the impact of public and private expropriation hazards. Finally, the industry and regional dummies were jointly significant ($F = 11.23$, log-likelihood ratio $= 238.94$). The adjusted multiple squared correlation coefficient (R^2) ranges from .24 to .25. Using an F-test, one can reject the hypothesis that the set of coefficients on the newly included variables in columns 2, 3, or 4 are equal to zero; p-values are .03, .24, and .004. As well, a test for the inclusion into model 4 of the interactions introduced in model 3 allows rejection of the null hypotheses that the omitted variables are redundant ($p = .09$).

Focusing on the results in model 4, we review the tests of our hypotheses in turn. First, the negative and significant coefficient estimates for both measures of public expropriation hazards ($p < .001$) support the hypothesis that as these hazards increase, firms increasingly rely upon host country partners to increase domestic content, maintain compliance with existing legal statutes, ease the disposal of assets and provide information and access to the domestic political system. Second, although the coefficient estimates on R&D and advertising intensity were consistently positive providing partial support for the traditional transaction cost hypothesis that as private expropriation hazards increase, Japanese multinationals favor higher levels of equity control, neither estimate was statistically significant in model 4.

Next, in contrast to the model 1 results, industry and national experience have no direct impact on equity ownership levels in the results for model 4, which included the full set of experience interactions. The positive and significant coefficient estimates on the interaction of the parent firm's industry experience ($p = .03$) with the host country's level of political

Table 7.4 Results of TOBIT analysis on equity ownership[a]

Variable	Model 1	Model 2	Model 3	Model 4
Public expropriation hazards				
Political hazards	-20.72** (2.33)	-31.39** (7.16)	-31.52** (7.16)	-26.23** (7.62)
Equity restrictions	-17.06** (2.74)	-32.61** (9.01)	-31.73** (9.02)	-42.45** (9.67)
Private expropriation hazards				
R&D intensity	66.07* (28.73)	69.76* (28.73)	103.31 (107.33)	138.47 (107.78)
Advertising intensity	57.53 (49.23)	59.67 (49.17)	201.23 (136.16)	253.36 (138.11)
Parent firm experience				
Other experience[b]	2.24** (0.55)	-7.27** (2.65)	-7.30** (2.66)	-9.42** (2.91)
Industry experience[b]	-1.11* (0.56)	-4.76 (3.56)	-3.30 (3.60)	-2.43 (3.66)
National experience[b]	-2.23** (0.63)	7.16 (4.29)	6.18 (4.32)	5.46 (4.52)
Presence of partner capabilities				
Keiretsu without sogo shosha	-5.60** (1.53)	-5.86** (1.54)	-5.85** (1.54)	-12.63 (10.09)
Sogo shosha as primary	-18.15*** (2.92)	-18.28*** (2.91)	-17.07*** (3.03)	-4.58 (17.72)
Sogo shosha as secondary	-12.36** (1.78)	-12.35** (1.78)	-12.62** (1.78)	-34.60* (14.34)
Experience/capabilities and public expropriation hazards				
Other experience X Political hazards		0.75 (1.22)	2.39 (1.75)	-0.91 (1.33)
Industry experience X Political hazards		2.44 (1.67)	-0.32 (1.75)	3.71* (1.71)

Table 7.4 Results of TOBIT analysis on equity ownership[a] (continued)

Variable	Model 1	Model 2	Model 3	Model 4
National experience X Political hazards		0.13 (2.13)	-1.30 (2.22)	-2.01 (2.22)
Keiretsu without sogo shosha X Political hazards				11.03* (4.77)
Sogo shosha as primary X Political hazards				26.48** (7.83)
Sogo shosha as secondary X Political hazards				4.30 (6.48)
Other experience X Equity restrictions		5.59** (1.52)	6.01** (2.16)	7.59** (1.68)
Industry experience X Equity restrictions		1.14 (1.94)	1.05 (2.07)	-0.20 (1.97)
National experience X Equity restrictions		-5.90** (2.35)	-1.65 (2.72)	-4.40 (2.46)
Keiretsu without sogo shosha X Equity restrictions				-0.60 (5.85)
Sogo shosha as primary X Equity restrictions				-20.82* (9.90)
Sogo shosha as secondary X Equity restrictions				13.55 (7.76)
Experience/capabilities and private expropriation hazards				
Other experience X R&D intensity			-2.24 (15.61)	-0.32 (16.16)
Industry experience X R&D intensity			-44.57* (22.87)	-51.46* (22.86)
National experience X R&D intensity			45.10 (24.09)	48.23* (24.35)
Keiretsu without sogo shosha X R&D intensity				-50.41 (57.37)
Sogo shosha as primary X R&D intensity				n/a n/a
Sogo shosha as secondary X R&D intensity				-118.87 (88.11)
Other experience X Advertising intensity			7.03 (27.72)	8.74 (20.09)
Industry experience X Advertising intensity			-68.73 (38.23)	-72.76 (38.17)
National experience X Advertising intensity			-22.80 (38.51)	-1.81 (40.49)

Variable	Model 1		Model 2		Model 3		Model 4	
Keiretsu without sogo shosha X Advertising intensity							159.36	(131.60)
Sogo shosha as primary X Advertising intensity							n/a	n/a
Sogo shosha as secondary X Advertising intensity							-154.53	(137.07)
Control variables								
Relative subsidiary size	1.30	(1.81)	1.24	(1.82)	1.38	(1.82)	1.51	(1.81)
Parent size[b,c]	-0.85	(0.82)	-0.82	(0.82)	-0.71	(0.82)	-0.62	(0.82)
Export intensity	17.19**	(3.87)	17.38**	(3.87)	17.23**	(3.87)	16.64**	(3.85)
Unrelated entry	-8.01**	(1.54)	-7.85**	(1.55)	-7.98**	(1.55)	-7.92**	(1.54)
Per capita GDP[b]	5.27**	(1.14)	5.10**	(1.17)	5.13**	(1.17)	5.15**	(1.17)
Population[b]	3.70**	(0.57)	3.48**	(0.58)	3.49**	(0.58)	3.49**	(0.58)
Constant	36.79	(21.10)	79.53**	(26.60)	74.50**	(26.66)	88.45**	(27.25)
Adjusted R^2	0.24		0.24		0.24		0.25	
Log likelihood	-11,337.89		-11,329.00		-11,324.51		-11,309.26	
Number of observations	2,827		2,827		2,827		2,827	

a. Values in parentheses are standard errors. Coefficient estimates for industry and regional dummies not reported.
b. Logarithm.
c. Annual sales, in billions of yen.
* $p < .05$
** $p < .01$

hazards, as well as the interaction between other international experience and the level of equity restrictions ($p < .001$) support the prediction (Hypothesis 3a) that parent firm experience can reduce the sensitivity of a multinational corporation to public expropriation hazards. Only parent firm industry experience appears to aid in the development of mitigating private expropriation hazards ($p = .02$). This result partially supports Hypothesis 3b, which argued that the total years of experience in an industry may improve partner screening abilities and provide more knowledge regarding the most likely avenues of expropriation.

Mirroring the results for parent firm experience, the coefficient estimates on keiretsu or direct sogo shosha participation that were significant in model 1, are insignificant in column 4, once we take into account the indirect effect of hazard mitigation. However, secondary sogo shosha participation (empirically always observed in addition to the presence of a keiretsu partner) still has a significant impact on the choice of equity ownership. The positive and significant coefficient estimates on the interaction of the dummy variables for keiretsu presence ($p = .02$) and the sogo shosha as primary partner ($p < .001$) with political hazards provides partial support for Hypothesis 4a, stating that partner firm experience can reduce the sensitivity of a firm to public expropriation hazards. The multiple relationships between sogo shoshas and host country governments seem to restrain opportunistic behavior by the latter. Such constellations of transactions were found to mitigate private expropriation hazards by de Figueiredo and Teece (1996). No support was found for Hypothesis 4b.

Figures 7.2 and 7.3 illustrate the variable effects of public expropriation hazards by plotting the predicted level of equity ownership for varying levels of pairs of independent variables of interest (with all other variables held constant at their means). These two figures provide evidence of the quantitative significance of the results. In Figures 7.2 and 7.3, we observe that under all categories of experience, and with or without keiretsu or sogo shosha participation, increasing public expropriation hazards reduces the predicted level of equity ownership. Furthermore, the difference obtained in the predicted level of the dependent variable from a one standard deviation increase above its mean level ranges from 15.1 to 38.7 per cent of one standard deviation of the dependent variable (29.2 percentage points), depending on the level of experience or presence of keiretsu and/or sogo shosha partners. These results lend further support to Hypothesis 1.

Figure 7.2 also depicts the strong support found for Hypotheses 3a; more experienced firms are less sensitive to increases in public expropriation hazards. Firms with levels of national, industry and other experience one standard deviation below the mean are twice as sensitive as firms with experience levels one-standard-deviation above the mean to a one-standard-deviation increase in public expropriation hazards. Similarly, as indicated by the coefficient estimates for the experience and private expropriation hazards terms found in Table 7.4, inexperienced firms are much more sensitive than experienced firms to changes in private expropriation hazards (the nonsignificance of the main effect of private expropriation hazards prohibits a plot of these interactions). These results are consistent with the hypotheses that firms with more experience possess advantages in affecting the political decision calculus of host country governments (Hypothesis 3a), in screening potential counterparties, and in writing, monitoring and enforcing contracts with private sector counterparties (Hypothesis 3b). Experienced firms are thus less likely to rely upon the relatively crude safeguard of adjusting their level of equity control in their foreign subsidiaries to safeguard against public and private expropriation hazards.

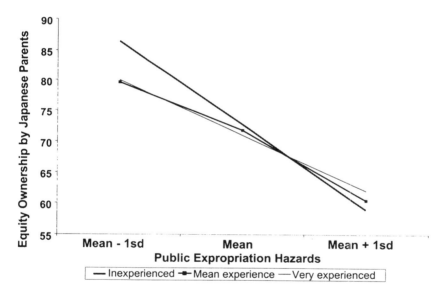

[a]All independent variables held constant at their mean levels with the exception of the dummies for diversification (0) and for no keiretsu or sogo shosha participation. Values on the vertical axis are percentages.

Figure 7.2 Own experience, public expropriation hazards and ownership[a]

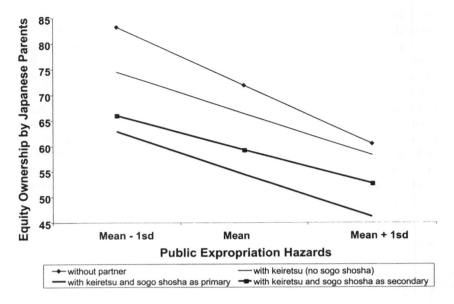

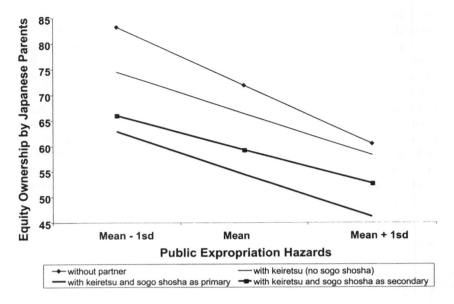

^aAll independent variables held constant at their mean levels with the exception of the dummy
for diversification (0). Values on the vertical axis are percentages.

Figure 7.3 Partner presence, public expropriation hazards and ownership^a

Finally, Figure 7.3 provides qualified support for Hypothesis 4a, in that
firms without keiretsu or sogo shosha partners are marginally more
susceptible to increases in public expropriation hazards. Reliance on partners
with the requisite industry, host country and international experience appears
to be a substitute for own firm experience in the mitigation of these hazards.

Turning to the control variables, the negative and significant coefficient
estimate ($p < .001$) on the unrelated entry dummy indicates that firms with no
experience in a specific line of business are more likely to yield equity
control to their host country partners so as to gain the knowledge and
capabilities necessary to compete in the new industry. We interpret the
negative sign and significance ($p < .001$) of the other international experience
term in conjunction with a positive and significant coefficient estimate on
export intensity ($p < .001$) as evidence of an important omitted but,
unfortunately, unavailable variable from our analysis. Multinationals that
produce abroad for export to their home country markets (thus exhibiting low
export intensity and high total experience) tend to be less willing or see
fewer benefits to sharing it. In contrast, firms that produce abroad for
overseas consumption may be more willing to share equity ownership and

may see larger benefits from doing so, because the local partners' knowledge of the host country distribution system and local tastes and preferences are of higher value to the parent firm.

Finally, national per capita GDP ($p < .001$) and population ($p < .001$) were positively associated with equity ownership levels. These results suggest that Japanese multinationals entering wealthier markets – which tend to be more similar to Japan than poorer markets – rely less heavily upon the information provided by host country partners at the times of entry. Larger markets may be too important to the firms for them to risk entry failure due to disputes with a local partner. Hence, Japanese firms invest the resources necessary to acquire the information internally rather than rely upon potentially opportunistic host country partners.

To insure that our results were not spurious owing to a sample selection bias, we undertook several tests for the effect of unobserved firm-level heterogeneity on the entry mode choice (Shaver, 1998). Space constraints preclude discussion and presentation of these tests, but we concluded that the results in Table 7.4 possessed strong explanatory power, independent of the factors that led firms to choose to enter these emerging economies.

DISCUSSION

This study offers an integrated approach for examining the ownership decisions of foreign investors. We demonstrate that a firm's capabilities, in terms of its experience in an industry and a country of expansion as well as elsewhere, influence the level of equity ownership the firm chooses in a foreign subsidiary by increasing its stock of hazard mitigating capabilities and thus reducing its sensitivity to public and private expropriation hazards. These hazard-mitigating capabilities were shown to both develop with a parent firm's own experience and to be transferred to the firm through the participation of keiretsu or sogo shosha partners.

Experience and the Capability to Mitigate Hazards

A primary contribution of this study is its application of the organizational capabilities approach to multinational entry strategy in combination with more traditional perspectives from the private and public expropriation hazards literatures. Received theory on multinationals emphasizes the important impetus to, and support of, foreign direct investment that is provided by advantages rooted in proprietary assets. According to the dominant transaction cost and internalization paradigms, a firm moves into an international market by direct investment when it can displace the transaction costs of operating via arm's length in that market by the establishment of a foreign subsidiary. Yet, in placing proprietary assets in the host country, the firm exposes those assets to public and private expropriation hazards. The observed effects of these hazards on ownership strategies were broadly consistent with extant theory, yet our findings point to an important dynamic in the foreign investment behavior of firms.

This dynamic emerged from our tracing of firms' investment history, as mirrored in the time sequence of the establishment of foreign subsidiaries. We tracked how entry mode strategies varied with the extent of experience in international markets. By studying a cross section of firms with variation in the level of host country, industry and other experience, we examined hypotheses that bridge the capabilities and hazards literatures. Our tests of these hypotheses demonstrate that Japanese firms' strategic responses to private and public expropriation hazards were contingent on their levels of experience in foreign markets and particular industry segments. The results also show that public and private expropriation hazards had the strongest effect for firms that were relatively inexperienced.

Our combination of these literatures helps point to ways in which inconclusive empirical results concerning the relationship between experience and ownership can be resolved. The so-called experience-effects literature is rich in the number of empirical studies that have been conducted, and in the industrial and geographic contexts that have been studied. These studies show a variety of contradictory effects including a negative relationship between a firm's experience and local equity ownership levels (Davidson, 1980b; Gatignon and Anderson, 1988; Johanson and Vahlne, 1977), a positive relationship (Davidson and McFetridge, 1985; Stopford and Wells, 1972) and curvilinear effects of experience on ownership (Erramilli, 1991).

Our results suggest that the inconsistent results may have stemmed from a misspecification of the relationship. As suggested in our arguments and as demonstrated in our empirical results (see, in particular, Figure 7.2), the net effect of experience depends crucially on the profile of an overseas investment. For investments in countries with high public expropriation hazards, experience generates information on local factor and political markets, that may aid in the implementation of safeguards other than the formation of alliances with local partners. Hence, we see higher levels of equity ownership for experienced firms relative to less experienced firms. Similarly, for investments with high private expropriation hazards, industry experience provides firms with better information on partner type and the likely avenues of expropriation by opportunistic partners. This experience aids in the implementation of safeguards other than taking higher levels of ownership.

Although our theory and evidence suggest that experience and hazards interact to influence the choice of ownership levels, it also provides corroborating evidence concerning the importance of differentiating among different forms of experience and capabilities (Miller and Shamsie, 1996). By specifically identifying firms' levels of experience in international markets, host countries and the industries in which the firms were investing, the analyses captured both geographic and product scope aspects of firm growth (Barkema and Vermeulen, 1998). Like earlier researchers, we found that the extent of geographic and product line expansion (Chang, 1995; Barkema et al., 1996; Johanson and Vahlne, 1977; Pennings, Barkema and Douma, 1994) influenced an investing firm's ownership strategy. In sum, these effects point to the importance of understanding the extent of product and multinational diversity in a firm's operations when examining foreign ownership choices (Hitt, Hoskisson and Kim, 1997).

Partner Capabilities

In addition to a foreign investing firm's operations, conditions in its home country likewise influenced ownership strategies. In our theoretical and empirical analyses, we considered the domestic context by evaluating the role of keiretsu affiliation and sogo shosha partnership. Our study identified sogo shosha affiliation as a means by which public expropriation hazards could be mitigated. A sogo shosha's equity participation in a foreign venture provided the subsidiary with a parent that had relatively extensive knowledge of, and political connections in, the host country. Sogo shoshas fulfilled various roles such as finding appropriate local partners where needed and negotiating with host country governments (Ozawa, 1979; Yoshino, 1976). Membership in a horizontal keiretsu presented firms with an alternative hazard mitigation mechanism. Member firms could draw upon the massed investment experience of other member firms, and exploit alliances forged in the domestic context, in the international setting (Reddy, Osborn and Pratap, 1998).

Limitations and Future Directions

Our analysis pointed to an important temporal component in the foreign entry strategy of Japanese firms. A limitation of the analysis, however, is that we used cross-sectional rather than panel data. Given the encouraging results obtained herein, a useful extension would be for researchers to examine the evolution of foreign investment using a cross-sectional time series framework. This would allow for explicit modeling of the impact of experience on market entry strategy by looking at one firm over time rather than similar firms with varying experience levels.

Ideally, we would like to extend the depth as well as the coverage of our data. Murtha (1991) and Oxley (1997) demonstrated that microanalytic measures of private expropriation hazards outperformed commonly used accounting-based proxies such as advertising and R&D intensity. Our accounting-based proxies for various capabilities did not let us identify specific internal routines or processes that can affect entry strategy.

Additionally, our analysis suffers from at least two errors of omission. Our sample is biased towards profitable overseas opportunities because we did not have data on the countries that were not chosen for entry. Furthermore, we explicitly limited our analysis to the choice of the level of equity control made by Japanese parent firms. We set aside consideration of alternative hazard mitigation strategies including licensing, exporting (which serves the dual purpose of generating hard currency and creating dependence on tacit knowledge of the parent company regarding international distribution channels), hiring additional domestic workers, sourcing additional intermediate products, hiring political risk management services, writing more detailed contracts, utilizing international arbitration in the event of disputes or employing more generic, rapidly depreciating or mobile assets.

A further line of analysis is suggested by the consistent role that sogo shoshas and keiretsu occupied in these foreign investment decisions. The robust effect of these variables highlights the importance of considering the domestic context of the firm when conducting international business research (Barkema et al., 1996). One of the more interesting, and limiting, aspects of international business research has been its isolation from a firm's domestic activities. Likewise, discussions of growth in the domestic context have been isolated from discussions of growth, often concurrent, in foreign markets. Although researchers have treated domestic and foreign strategy and growth as separate phenomena, in the minds of managers and in the actions of firms, there is certainly considerable interrelatedness between the two.

CONCLUSIONS

Despite these limitations, we believe our results demonstrate that a multinational's hazard mitigating capabilities – developed over time with experience in a given industry, host country or other international market, or alternatively, transferred from keiretsu and/or sogo shosha partners – affect its chosen levels of equity control over its subsidiaries in emerging markets. Our research extends previous studies by explicitly examining two mechanisms by which experience affects entry strategy. In countries with high public expropriation hazards, experience substitutes for local knowledge of host country factor and political markets provided by local partners, thereby increasing equity ownership levels. In contrast, for investments with high private expropriation hazards, experience facilitates the writing, monitoring and enforcement of contracts and aids in partner selection, thereby reducing the tendency to take a higher equity stake in a foreign subsidiary to guard against opportunistic behavior.

By demonstrating the differential impact of experience on investment in countries with various levels of public expropriation hazards and on investments with various levels of private expropriation hazards, we have modeled one dimension of a firm's capabilities as an analytically tractable component of its foreign entry strategy. Given the level of public and private expropriation hazards inherent in emerging market investment opportunities, these findings should be salient to multinationals considering entry into these countries as well as to host country policymakers seeking to encourage and influence the level of equity ownership in such entries.

NOTES

1. The political constraint index data set is available from *http://www-management.wharton.upenn.edu/henisz/*.

ACKNOWLEDGEMENTS

Thanks to Chung Ming Lau, Bruce Kogut, Myles Shaver, Bennet Zelner and the participants in the 1999 Strategy Research Forum in Gloucester, Massachusetts for their comments on drafts. This research was supported in part by a Social Sciences and Humanities Research Council of Canada Grant (# 411-98-0393), by a Direct Allocation Grant (DAG 98/99.BM51) and by the Asian Management Institute at the University of Western Ontario. We would like to thank Connie Lun, Jo Jo Lam, Jimmy Miyoshi and Nancy Suzuki for assistance in data collection and coding.

8. Ownership strategy of Japanese firms: Transactional, institutional and experience influences

Andrew Delios and Paul W. Beamish

We compare the effects of transactional, institutional and experience influences on the ownership strategies of Japanese investors. Our theoretical development suggests that the equity position of a foreign investor should increase as the specificity of the assets transferred to the foreign affiliate increases, but a lower equity position should be assumed when the foreign investor requires complementary assets to establish a foreign entry. International experience and a strong institutional environment also should lead to increases in the equity position of the foreign investor. These relationships were tested with data on more than 1,000 Japanese investments in nine countries of East and South East Asia. The results demonstrate that experience and institutional factors were the most important influences on the ownership position taken in the foreign investment, while transactional factors had a much less important and a more ambiguous role.

INTRODUCTION

A firm entering a foreign market must make a decision concerning the degree of ownership if investing. The ownership strategy, commonly subsumed under the broader topic of entry mode strategy, is critical for foreign entrants as it affects both the foreign affiliate's likelihood of success (Stopford and Wells, 1972) and its probability of survival (Li, 1995). Since early studies by internalization theorists (Buckley and Casson, 1976; Hennart, 1982), most conceptual and empirical work in this area has sought to identify the firm-specific, transaction-related motives for full or shared-ownership. However, there have been fewer empirical studies concerning how non-transactional factors have affected the ownership strategy.

The past focus on transaction-related motives is understandable. In making a direct investment in a foreign market, a firm is transferring firm-specific advantages to that market (Hymer, 1976). The assets that form the basis of the advantage are often proprietary and the degree of ownership assumed in the foreign operation confers a proportional degree of control over the uses to which the firm-specific assets can be put (Grossman and Hart, 1986). But the protection of firm-specific assets is just one consideration in structuring a foreign market entry. The need to acquire new assets on foreign entry (a second transactional influence), the international experience levels of the foreign firm and the institutional environment of the host country are important influences on ownership strategies in themselves. The principal objective of this paper is to empirically investigate the relative importance of these three factors – transactional, experience and institutional – on the ownership strategies of Japanese investors in East and South East Asia.

In this analysis, ownership strategy is defined as the choice concerning the degree of ownership (percent equity holding) taken when a foreign investment is made. The implications of the transactional, experience and institutional influences can be effectively determined by examining their relationship with the ownership levels in foreign investments. The TOBIT analyses that are conducted in this study shed light on the foreign ownership strategies of Japanese firms in Asia, an area that has received scant attention in the empirical literature despite the leading position of Japanese firms as foreign investors and Asian countries as recipients of foreign direct investment (UNCTAD, 1996). As well, this study contributes to the growing debate surrounding transaction cost theory (Kogut and Zander, 1993; Ghoshal and Moran, 1996; Madhok, 1997) by testing the predictions of this theory in a non-North American context, in a model with improved measures of asset specificity, and against competing explanations (institutional and experience influences).

This paper proceeds as follows. In the next section, we review developments in entry mode research, with particular emphasis on asset-related concerns, to identify key groups of variables that influence the ownership strategy of foreign investors. The third section develops hypotheses that relate ownership strategies to transactional and experience characteristics as well as to host country institutional factors. The fourth section introduces the data, methods and variables used for hypothesis testing. The final two sections discuss implications of the empirical results, summarize the main conclusions and suggest avenues for future research.

PREVIOUS RESEARCH

The entry mode choice has long been considered a critical decision for a firm expanding into international markets (Stopford and Wells, 1972; Wind and Perlmutter, 1977) and several studies have demonstrated that the entry mode choice has critical implications for the foreign investment's performance (Root, 1987; Woodcock, Beamish and Makino, 1994) and its survival (Li, 1995). A variety of mode choices exist for a firm. The choices range from no international involvement, to exporting/licensing, to direct investment via joint venture (minority, co- or majority) or by wholly-owned subsidiary. One of the principal issues faced by early researchers was understanding why differing degrees of ownership were utilized by multinational enterprises (e.g., see Vernon and Wells, 1976).

Early entry mode studies by internalization theorists concentrated on the choice between licensing and direct investment (Buckley and Casson, 1976; Rugman, 1982), although scholars soon began to concentrate on the level of ownership question, specifically the choice between wholly-owned subsidiaries and the joint venture mode (Hennart, 1982). The level of ownership in these and other studies in the internalization stream explained higher ownership levels as being a response to the need to protect firm-specific knowledge (essentially technological and R&D expertise) from unwanted dissemination. Hence, internalization theory stated that full ownership and control would be observed when a firm transferred unique, firm-specific knowledge to the host country when making its foreign investment.

The ideas of internalization theorists ran parallel to the precepts of transaction cost (TC) theory (Williamson, 1975; 1985). TC theory is concerned with explaining what is the most efficient governance structure – markets, hierarchies or a hybrid – under which to govern a specific set of transactions. TC theory enriched internalization theory by providing several key concepts with which the entry mode choice could be more rigorously modeled. Scholars writing on the theory of multinational enterprise (Teece, 1986a), on theories of joint ventures (Beamish and Banks, 1987; Hennart, 1988; Kogut, 1988a) and on entry mode strategies (Anderson and Gatignon, 1986) melded the ideas of TC theory with the previous work of internalization theorists.

In conceptual and empirical entry mode studies, TC theory has been particularly useful in understanding the determination of ownership levels (e.g., Anderson and Gatignon, 1986; Gatignon and Anderson, 1988; Gomes-Casseres, 1989). In bringing the ideas of TC theory to the entry mode question, Anderson and Gatignon (1986) provided an extensive review of the ownership literature. In this literature, the amount of equity ownership was equated with the amount of control that a firm could exert over its subsidiary's operations.   Control was considered important because it provided the foreign parent with the ability to influence systems, methods and decisions (Anderson and Gatignon, 1986) and with a means to resolve disputes that could arise in the joint management of an enterprise (Davidson, 1982). However, with greater control came increased resource commitments and increased risk.   Hence, the ownership decision involved a tradeoff between control and resource commitments made under different levels of risk and uncertainty (Anderson and Gatignon, 1986).   Based on the conceptual developments made in these writings, various researchers empirically examined the ownership strategies of US firms investing in developed and developing economies (e.g., Gatignon and Anderson, 1988; Gomes-Casseres, 1989) and the ownership strategies of Japanese firms investing in the US (e.g., Hennart, 1991a). Consistently, in these studies, support was found for the TC-based hypotheses.

While the need to safeguard assets transferred to the foreign investment was recognized as an important determinant of foreign ownership levels in the aforementioned conceptual and empirical studies, a second asset-related influence concerns the need to acquire complementary assets on foreign entry.   When a firm expands into international markets, it is often faced with the need to acquire new assets (Stopford and Wells, 1972).   However, these assets may be subject to market inefficiencies which make the cost of market-based exchange prohibitive.   Hence, a common strategy of a foreign firm on foreign entry is to form a joint venture with a local partner to secure locally based assets (Hennart, 1988).   Several empirical studies (Beamish and Banks, 1987; Gomes-Casseres, 1989; 1990; Hennart, 1991a) explored this influence on entry mode strategies and found that the foreign parent's level of ownership declined with increased need to source complementary host country assets.

One critical locally based asset is knowledge of the host country environment.   Deficiencies in knowledge of the local environment constitute a significant competitive disadvantage for the foreign firm (Hymer, 1976), and the accumulation of host country experience alleviates the foreign firm's local-knowledge disadvantages (Johanson and Wiedersheim-Paul, 1975; Johanson and Vahlne, 1977). The internationalization approach argues that a firm's level of commitment to investments in a foreign market increases with greater knowledge of that market.   A firm's internationalization process is one of experience and knowledge accretion – as experience and knowledge are gained in a host country the firm can make better strategic decisions and it develops the capability to operate independently in the host country. However, because of the difficulty of acquiring local knowledge, firms with little host country experience often must acquire local knowledge by partnering with local firms (Barkema, Bell and Pennings, 1996).

Local knowledge encompasses a broad array of host country characteristics – political and legal rules and the social norms for business transactions. These variables constitute the host country's institutional environment, which defines the conditions under which business occurs (North, 1990). Aspects of the institutional environment can have a direct effect on a foreign firm's entry mode strategy. For example, legal restrictions on the foreign ownership of domestic enterprises establish definitive limits on foreign equity holdings and induce shared ownership structures (Contractor, 1990; Gomes-Casseres, 1990). Other aspects of the institutional environment have an indirect effect on entry mode strategy. These aspects relate to hazards that can accompany transactions because of weaknesses in the institutional environment (North and Weingast, 1989). Weaknesses in the institutional environment refer to conditions which undermine property rights and increase risks in exchange. Where property rights are weaker and environmental risks are greater, firms are less likely to make investments because assets face greater transactional hazards and returns are less predictable and certain (Williamson, 1996). In this manner, the nature of the institutional environment influences the comparative efficiency of governance structures. That is, the security of property rights in the broader institutional environment is as important a concern for foreign entrants as the protection of proprietary assets in an exchange between two firms (Oxley, 1995). Hence, consistent with the need to minimize transaction costs when constructing institutional arrangements for exchange, the firm's entry mode strategy varies with the need to safeguard assets and minimize risks across differing institutional environments.

This section reviewed the extant literature to identify broad classes of influences on the relative efficiency of asset transfer across alternative governance structures. The review points to the considerable explanatory power of the standard TC model in explaining the ownership strategies of US investors or of foreign investors in the US. However, experience and institutional variables can be critical determinants of entry mode strategies as well, and the comparative efficacy of these three viewpoints on the determinants of ownership strategies has not been tested within the same empirical setting. In the remainder of this study, we develop and test a conceptual model that compares the explanatory power of the three viewpoints in a non-US, multi-country research setting. The next section develops this study's hypotheses.

HYPOTHESIS DEVELOPMENT

In this section, we develop four main hypotheses about the effects of transactional, experience and institutional variables on ownership strategy. We consider transactional variables to comprise both assets transferred by the foreign firm to the host country (contributed assets), and assets required by the foreign firm upon investment in the host country (complementary assets). To be consistent with previous empirical studies of transaction cost theory, and to provide an evenhanded test, the conceptual model discussed in the contributed assets and complementary assets sections develops hypotheses in line with the standard predictions of TC theory. However, in the empirical models we offer improved measures of the asset specificity construct.

Contributed Assets

The main contribution of TC theory to the analysis of ownership levels has been the concept of asset specificity. A basic tenet of TC theory is that as asset specificity increases, the greater will be the hazards associated with market-based exchange and the greater the incentives to internalize the transaction (Williamson, 1975; 1985). Anderson and Gatignon (1986), who modeled their TC framework on that of internalization theorists, considered the optimal degree of control (level of ownership) to be positively related to the degree of asset specificity. Davidson and McFetridge (1985), in comparing the licensing versus direct investment option, provided some of the earliest evidence that asset specificity leads to higher ownership levels. Gatignon and Anderson (1988), in an empirical study of many of the propositions outlined in Anderson and Gatignon (1986), found the TC framework to be robust in explaining the ownership decisions of US MNEs; that is, industries with high asset specificity were positively related to larger numbers of entries by high ownership modes. Other studies found similar relationships. For example, Anderson and Coughlan (1987) used the logic of TC to examine the propensity of foreign entrants to integrate forward into distribution. Increasing asset specificity was associated with greater integration (internalization). While Osborn and Baughn (1990) found less compelling evidence for the asset specificity-internalization relationship, Kim and Hwang (1992) and Erramilli and Rao (1993) observed a positive relationship between asset specificity and the level of ownership. The first hypothesis examines the relationship between asset specificity and the level of ownership.

Hypothesis 1. The greater the degree of asset specificity in the foreign investing firm's assets, the higher the ownership position assumed in the foreign investment.

Complementary Assets

The preceding hypothesis concerns the relationship between the foreign firm's assets and the level of ownership. A separate but related aspect of the ownership decision concerns the foreign firm's need to acquire new assets on foreign entry (Stopford and Wells, 1972). Hennart (1988) and other scholars argue that joint ventures are organizational modes that combine the complementary assets of two partners when exchange for these assets in factor markets is subject to high transaction costs. Put another way, joint ventures are an efficient organizational structure for acquiring assets for which there are factor market imperfections (i.e., high market transaction costs). Consequently, firms are motivated to structure foreign entries as joint ventures, and to take lower equity positions, when faced with the need to acquire complementary assets that can not be obtained efficiently in factor markets. The second hypothesis examines this aspect of a firm's ownership strategy.

Hypothesis 2. The greater the degree of market imperfections for complementary assets, the lower the ownership position assumed in the foreign investment.

Institutional Environment

Host country political and economic risk is the aspect of the institutional environment that has received the most attention in conceptual and empirical studies of entry mode choice. As put forward in Anderson and Gatignon (1986: 15), in more externally uncertain and volatile environments, firms are better off utilizing low control and ownership modes (e.g., joint ventures instead of wholly-owned subsidiaries) because of the increased flexibility provided to the firm by the low control mode. Similarly, Hennart (1988) and Hill, Hwang and Kim (1990) argued that firms can reduce the level of host country risk and incur lower transaction costs by utilizing lower ownership modes in host countries with greater political risk and uncertainty. Empirical studies by Vernon (1983), Shan (1991) and Kim and Hwang (1992) also identified a negative relationship between political and economic risk and the level of ownership in the foreign investment. Hypothesis 3a outlines a relationship consistent with the above studies.

Hypothesis 3a. The greater the degree of risk in the host country, the lower the ownership position assumed in the foreign investment.

The effect of host country restrictions on foreign and local ownership has received considerable attention in entry mode studies. Government policies can effectively influence foreign ownership levels, and legal and political constraints in the host country may bring about local ownership, even where TC theory does not predict the existence of joint ventures (Contractor, 1990; Gomes-Casseres, 1989, 1990). We expect legal limits on foreign equity participation in domestic enterprises to be reflected in lower ownership levels in the foreign investment.[1]

Hypothesis 3b. The greater the legal restrictions on foreign equity participation, the lower the ownership position assumed in the foreign investment.

A third aspect of the institutional environment concerns property rights protection. Property rights protection has received much attention as an influence on levels of foreign direct investment, but less attention has been given to its relationship with ownership levels. Effective property rights protection ensures that the owner of an asset has discretion over the uses to which the asset is put and is able to appropriate returns from the asset. Where the value of assets protected by patents and trademarks cannot be fully realized by the owner, then the incentives to make investments involving these technological or marketing-based assets are reduced (Teece, 1986b). Under an institutional setting in which the protection of property rights is weaker, the cost of contracting and the cost of using a hybrid such as a joint venture increases because of the increased risk of leakage or unwanted dissemination of proprietary technological and marketing assets to rivals, suppliers and buyers (Williamson, 1996). Given differences in host country environments with respect to the degree of protection for patented technology or trademarks, ownership strategies of foreign investors should vary accordingly. Under a weak property rights regime, higher ownership modes are more efficient because of the reduction in costs of unwanted dissemination. Where property rights protection is greater, lower ownership modes are more efficient as the risk of asset expropriation is less and costly governance structures do not need to be constructed to protect assets. Hypothesis 3c reflects these stated relationships.

Hypothesis 3c. The lower the level of intellectual property protection, the higher the ownership position assumed in the foreign investment.

International Experience

When firms make international investments, specific knowledge of the host country is gained as is more general knowledge of conducting international operations (Barkema, Bell and Pennings, 1996). As argued by the internationalization theorists, firms with more experience in a host country have developed organizational capabilities suited to that country, and are able to make greater commitments to foreign investments (Johanson and Vahlne, 1977). This argument is supported by Chang (1995) who suggested that more internationally experienced firms face fewer local knowledge disadvantages. Further, Makino and Delios (1996) found that the comparative utility of structuring a foreign investment as a local partner joint venture, as opposed to a wholly-owned subsidiary, decreased with greater levels of international experience because of the foreign firm's development of local knowledge. Finally, empirical research points to a positive relationship between the level of ownership and the level of host country experience (Davidson, 1980b; Li, 1995). Hence, we construct the following hypothesis.

Hypothesis 4. The greater the level of international experience, the higher the ownership position assumed in the foreign investment.

METHODOLOGY

Sample

The majority of TC-based entry mode studies have involved an empirical setting in which the US was either the host or the home country for the foreign direct investment. To expand the empirical context, we conducted our analysis on investments made by Japanese firms in nine countries of East and South Asia (Asia). The sample included all Japanese manufacturing subsidiaries located in China, Hong Kong, Indonesia, Malaysia, Philippines, South Korea, Singapore, Taiwan and Thailand as listed in *Kaigai Shinshutsu Kigyou Souran – kuni betsu* (Toyo Keizai, 1994). This annual publication provides information on the foreign affiliates of private and public Japanese companies. The coverage of this dataset is reputed to be close to the population of Japanese foreign affiliates (Hennart, 1991a; Yamawaki, 1991).

From the 1994 edition of this data source, we identified 2,594 greenfield manufacturing investments in Asia in which the Japanese parent held at least five percent of the equity. We next identified the Japanese parent firm for each investment and parent company information was collected from the

Analyst's Guide (Daiwa Institute of Research, 1996). The *Analyst's Guide* reports firm-level data gathered in a 1996 survey of 1,124 companies listed on the first section of the Tokyo Stock Exchange. Aggregates of industry-level information, also reported in the *Analyst's Guide*, are based on a survey of 1,515 firms.

After merging the information from Toyo Keizai (1994) with the parent company information from the *Analyst's Guide,* the sample size became 1,424. Table 8.1 compares the number of entries by country between the full and reduced samples. In Table 8.1, China and Thailand are depicted as the two most popular host sites for Japanese manufacturing investment in Asia. The distribution of entries by country does not exhibit much variation between the two samples, although Thailand received proportionally more investment in the reduced sample than in the full sample, and China proportionally less. The proportion of wholly-owned subsidiaries is approximately equal in the two samples, and the mean equity holding of the Japanese parent is almost identical. While the demographics of the two samples are similar, the findings of this study's empirical section are likely to be more applicable to the foreign investment experience of public Japanese firms listed on the first section of the Tokyo Stock exchange.

Table 8.1 Distribution of entry by country

Country	Full sample		Reduced sample	
	Number	**Percent**	**Number**	**Percent**
China	478	18.4	228	16.0
Thailand	453	17.5	273	19.2
Taiwan	415	16.0	199	14.0
Malaysia	320	12.3	196	13.8
Korea	256	9.9	127	8.9
Indonesia	224	8.6	151	10.6
Singapore	223	8.6	122	8.6
Hong Kong	139	5.4	73	5.1
Philippines	86	3.3	55	3.9
Total	2,594	100.0	1,424	100.0
Number which were wholly-owned	598	23.0	305	21.4
Mean % equity of Japanese parent (all investments)	61.76		61.27	

Methods

We used the TOBIT regression procedure to test the hypothesized effects of the independent variables on the ownership position of the Japanese parent. TOBIT analysis is more suitable than OLS regression because the dependent variable takes a maximum value of 100% ownership. When the dependent variable is truncated at some value, OLS regression can lead to biased estimates of the coefficients (Greene, 1997). Using TOBIT analysis, we estimated several models that tested the individual and combined contributions of the four groups of independent variables.[2] Table 8.2 defines each of the variables, and we describe these variables in more detail below. Descriptive statistics and inter-item correlations are provided in the Appendix.

Variables

Dependent

The dependent variable in all analyses is the percentage ownership of the Japanese parent(s) in the foreign investment. When more than two Japanese firms possessed equity in the foreign investment, we identified whether the firms shared a keiretsu affiliation. If the firms were part of the same keiretsu, the dependent variable was the sum of the equity holdings of the keiretsu affiliated firms; otherwise the dependent variable was the percentage ownership of the main Japanese parent.

Contributed asset variables

The specificity or proprietary nature of the Japanese parent's assets was measured by two variables which were in turn operationalized in four ways. Following standard operationalization (e.g., Gatignon and Anderson 1988; Gomes-Casseres, 1989), two industry-level variables – advertising intensity and R&D intensity – measure the degree of proprietary content in the firm's technological and marketing assets. Both intensity variables were calculated as the ratio of the respective yen expenditure to total sales in the two-year period prior to 1994 (1992 and 1993). Values were also determined for these variables from firm-level data. As well, a normalized intensity term was created for the two variables. As an example, the advertising normalized intensity term was calculated in the following manner:

normalized advertising intensity =

$$\frac{(\text{firm-level advertising intensity} - \text{industry-level advertising intensity})}{\text{industry-level advertising intensity}}.$$

Table 8.2 Variable descriptions and expected signs

Variable	Definition	Hypothesis	Expected relation to level of ownership
Contributed assets			
1. Advertising intensity	Advertising expenses / sales	H1	(+)
2. R&D intensity	R&D expenses / sales	H1	(+)
Complementary assets			
3. Resource industry	Entry into resource-based industry (resource-based=1; otherwise = 0)	H2	(-)
4. Relatedness	Investment made in parent's main line of business (not related =1; related = 0)	H2	(-)
5. Relative size	Affiliate employment / parent employment	H2	(-)
Institutional environment			
6. Host country risk	Extent of political and economic risk	H3a	(-)
7. Host country restrictiveness	Extent of restrictions on foreign ownership	H3b	(-)
8. Intellectual property protection	Extent of intellectual property protection	H3c	(+)
International experience			
9. Export intensity	Export revenue / sales	H4	(+)

Variable	Definition	Hypothesis	Expected relation to level of ownership
10. Number of foreign investments	Total number of Japanese parent's foreign investments	H4	(+)
11. Years of host country experience	Number of years of operational experience in the host country	H4	(+)
12. Sogo shosha as partner	General Trading Company is a partner (GTC main parent = 1; otherwise = 0)		
Dependent			
13. Equity ownership	Percentage ownership by affiliated Japanese firms		

Further, a dummy variable was created for the advertising and R&D variables. For each dummy variable, a value of one was assigned when a firm-level intensity was greater than the corresponding industry-level intensity. The normalized intensity terms and the dummy variables were used to identify those firms that had marketing and technological assets with a greater proprietary content than the industry mean.

The two variables, at both the industry and the firm-level, were collected from the *Analyst's Guide*. We obtained the principal industry or main line of business of the parent firm from the same source; hence, coding of the firm's industry was based on Daiwa's five-digit industrial classification. This level of classification is similar to the three-digit SIC level, and it divides all manufacturing industries into 112 coherent industrial groups. The number of companies in a five-digit group ranged from 68 in automobile parts to 1 in motorcycles (mean=8.62).

Complementary asset variables

As identified in Hypothesis 2, the foreign firm may be motivated to reduce its ownership position in the foreign investment to secure complementary assets via shared equity arrangements in its foreign investment. Complementary assets that foreign firms require can take a variety of forms and include such things as knowledge of markets, tacit technology, distribution systems, and other intermediate inputs (Hennart, 1988). We define three commonly utilized measures of requirements for complementary assets.

The first variable measuring requirements for complementary assets is the foreign firm's need for raw material inputs supplied in non-competitive local markets. A local firm is more likely than a foreign firm to have preferred access to these resources, and a JV with such a local firm is necessary to secure access to these raw material inputs. This form of JV, analogous to the link JV identified in Hennart (1988: 362), is expected to occur with greater frequency when entry is in resource-based industries such as food and beverages, textiles, wood, petroleum, rubber, primary metals and pulp and paper (Gomes-Casseres, 1989). We used a dummy variable coded as 1 to identify investments made in resource-based industries.

A second resource requirement concerns the new knowledge and resources required to compete when the entry is a diversification from the parent firm's main line of business. Foreign firms that expand into a product market not related to the parent's main line of business incur a greater need for new knowledge and assets as well as a greater risk of unsuccessful entry (Li, 1995). To mitigate the need for new knowledge and assets, an entry into an unrelated industry is expected to utilize the JV option to a greater extent than a non-diversifying entry (Gomes-Casseres, 1989; Hennart, 1991a). To establish whether the entry was in an unrelated industry, we compared the main line of business of the Japanese parent with the affiliate's industry as described in Toyo Keizai (1994). Unrelated entries were coded as 1 in this dummy variable.

The third variable measuring the need for complementary assets is the size of the investment as compared to the parent firm. If the investment is large relative to the parent firm, the parent is less likely to possess all the assets required on entry. Consequently, the larger the relative size of the investment, the greater the need to acquire complementary assets (Hennart, 1991a). Initially, we computed two relative size measures: one was the ratio of total employment in the investment to that in the parent, and the other was a similar ratio computed from sales values. The two variables were moderately correlated ($r=0.501$; $p<.01$) and exhibited identical effects in the models. However, we used the employment-based relative size variable in all reported models because there were fewer missing values for this variable.

Institutional environment variables

We used three variables to assess the relationship between the institutional environment and the ownership strategy of Japanese investors. The first variable measured the level of host country political and economic risk in 1993. The risk variable was derived from the host country risk index published in *Euromoney* in 1993. Cosset and Roy (1991) demonstrated that *Euromoney*'s risk index is replicable using objective host country economic and political factors. The second variable accounted for the effects of local ownership restrictions and was constructed from the *World Competitiveness Report, 1994* (IMD and World Economic Forum, 1994). This yearbook provided information on the openness of 47 countries (including the nine host countries in this study) to foreign equity participation in domestic enterprises in 1993. The *World Competitiveness Report* was also the source for the third variable which measured the degree of intellectual property protection in the host country environment.[3]

International experience variables

Three variables measured the extent of international experience of the Japanese parent. The first two measures accounted for general international experience and the third identified the degree of host country experience. The first variable, the export ratio, indicates the extent of a firm's international trade activity and its international experience (Terpstra and Yu, 1988; Chang, 1995). It was computed as the ratio of foreign sales (exports) to total sales for the years 1992 and 1993. The second international experience variable is based on the extent of the firm's international investment activity. As the incremental value of more international experience is greater when a firm has fewer international investments, this variable is the log of the count of the number of foreign direct investments in which the firm is involved either as a majority or minority equity partner.

The third experience variable measures host country experience. This variable is based on the firm's international investment activity and was computed as the log of the total number of firm-years of experience in the host country. A firm-year represents one-year of operating experience in the host country for one foreign investment. To determine the total number of firm-years of experience for a firm, the number of years of operating experience for each of the firm's investments in the host country were summed.

RESULTS

In the models reported in Tables 8.3 and 8.4 positive signs on a coefficient point to a positive relationship between that variable and the equity holding of the Japanese parent. Discussion of the models reported in Table 8.3 identifies the effects of the four groups of independent variables. But as the effects of the latter three groups of variables (Complementary Assets, Institutional Environment and International Experience) were consistent across all specifications, discussion of the models reported in Table 8.4 focuses on the role of Contributed Assets group of variables.

Table 8.3

The five models reported in Table 8.3 are nested models, and the chi-square tests show that each subsequent model is an improvement on the preceding model. We begin the analysis with transactional variables because this group of variables has received the most support in the empirical literature. All models in Table 8.3 estimate Japanese ownership levels using industry-level variables as measures of the proprietary content in the Japanese parent's assets. Each model was significant, and, as indicated by the 0.32 adjusted R^2 value for the corresponding OLS regression, the full model was a substantive predictor of the Japanese firm's ownership level. Advertising Intensity and R&D Intensity, the measures of the specificity of the Japanese firm's assets, had positive and significant effects on ownership levels. As suggested by TC theory, a greater degree of proprietary content in marketing and technological assets both lead to higher ownership levels in the foreign operation.[4] However, the two variables accounted for just four percent of the variance in ownership positions.

The addition of the variables indicating the need for the Japanese firm to secure new assets on entry improved the explanatory power of the model (incremental $\chi^2_{(3)}$=52.34, p<.01). Resource Industry and Relative Size were significant, while Relatedness was not significant in any of the models. Consistent with the case of US firms investing abroad (Gomes-Casseres, 1989) and Japanese firms investing in the US (Hennart, 1991a), the negative sign on the coefficient for Resource Industry reveals that Japanese firms in Asia took lower ownership levels and joint ventured with local firms to secure access to raw-material inputs. Counter to the complementary assets argument, subsidiaries large in size relative to the Japanese parent had a higher ownership level by the Japanese parent overall. As in Hennart (1991a), large investment size did not induce the Japanese parent to reduce ownership either to secure assets or to secure additional sources of capital; rather, investments in which the foreign firm had a large stake were accompanied by higher ownership levels. Finally, the insignificance of Relatedness indicates that whether the entry was in the Japanese parent's main line of business did not affect ownership levels.[5]

As in the case of the Complementary Asset variables, the addition of the Institutional Environment variables improved the explanatory power of the models significantly (incremental $\chi^2_{(3)}$=175.40, p<.01) and two of the three variables were significant. The negative sign on the Host Country Restrictiveness coefficient indicates that in countries in which there were more stringent controls on foreign equity participation, the ownership levels of Japanese firms were indeed lower. A similar effect was observed concerning the degree of intellectual property protection. Higher ownership levels by the Japanese parent occurred in countries which had better protection of intellectual property. Host country risk did not have a significant effect in Table 8.3, although its insignificance is related to its correlation with host country restrictiveness.[6]

The International Experience variables contributed positively to the explanatory ability of the models (incremental $\chi^2_{(3)}$=121.80, p<.01). The positive sign on the export intensity term indicates that firms with extensive international business activity and more international experience had a higher ownership position in foreign subsidiaries. More host country experience was also associated with higher ownership levels as indicated by the positive sign on the Years of Host Country Experience variable. Counter to expectations, however, the Number of Foreign Investments had a negative relationship with Japanese firm ownership levels.

The negative sign on the Number of Foreign Investments variable becomes more understandable when the role of the *sogo shosha* (General Trading Companies) is considered. Nine sogo shosha were involved in almost 20 percent of Japanese investments worldwide, and sogo shosha possess

Table 8.3 Japanese firm ownership levels: Industry-level data (N=1,043)

Independent variables	TOBIT analysis: Percent equity ownership as dependent Industry-level				
Contributed assets					
1. Advertising intensity (industry-level)	274.97***	257.94***	214.90***	284.85***	177.79***
	(3.16)	(3.00)	(2.70)	(3.76)	(2.36)
2. R&D intensity (industry-level)	224.75***	178.26***	192.82***	108.12***	102.78**
	(4.72)	(3.80)	(4.43)	(2.57)	(2.24)
Complementary assets					
3. Resource industry	–	-15.67***	-13.14***	-6.84***	-4.32*
		(-5.92)	(-5.36)	(-2.86)	(-1.83)
4. Relatedness	–	-2.93	-2.77	-1.69	-0.72
		(-1.31)	(-1.34)	(-0.82)	(-0.36)
5. Relative size	–	3.89***	7.54***	5.76***	4.88***
		(2.98)	(3.45)	(2.75)	(2.41)
Institutional environment					
6. Host country risk	–	–	-0.84	7.48	6.71
			(-0.07)	(0.64)	(0.58)
7. Host country restrictiveness	–	–	-53.22***	-50.62***	-46.00***
			(-6.18)	(-6.15)	(-5.74)
8. Intellectual property protection	–	–	60.96***	58.58***	58.99***
			(6.98)	(7.03)	(7.27)

Independent variables	TOBIT analysis: Percent equity ownership as dependent				
			Industry-level		
International experience					
9. Export intensity	–	–	–	–	67.91***
					(9.92)
10. Number of foreign investments	–	–	–	-2.64***	-0.42
				(-3.18)	(-0.49)
11. Years of host country experience	–	–	–	0.76***	0.67**
				(2.34)	(2.12)
12. Sogo shosha as partner	–	–	–	–	-18.04***
					(-7.17)
13. Constant	56.48***	61.45***	56.23***	53.35***	47.22***
	(27.81)	(18.33)	(5.75)	(6.07)	(6.51)
Model Indices					
Significance of model	<.01	<.01	<.01	<.01	<.01
Adjusted R²	0.04	0.08	0.21	0.28	0.32
Model chi-square	41.26	93.60	269.00	390.80	441.18
Incremental chi-square	–	52.34	175.40	121.80	50.38
Significance of additional variables	–	<.01	<.01	<.01	<.01

Notes:
1. *t*-statistics in parentheses.
2. *** *p*<0.01; ** *p*<0.05, * *p*<0.10, all two-tailed tests.
3. Adjusted R² derived from corresponding OLS analysis.

considerable international experience.[7]   To account for any effects
attributable to sogo shosha, we introduced a dummy variable, coded as 1
when a sogo shosha was an equity partner in a foreign investment. This
model is reported in the right-most column of Table 8.3. The sogo shosha
variable takes a negative sign in this model, and the Number of Foreign
Subsidiaries coefficient is no longer significant. This indicates that when a
sogo shosha was an equity partner in a foreign investment, the level of
ownership taken by Japanese firms was lower. The role of the sogo shosha
will be reviewed to a greater extent in the discussion section.

Table 8.4

The models in Table 8.4 are similar to the fifth model in Table 8.3 (the one
with the greatest explanatory power) but with one important difference: the
proprietary content of the Japanese firm's assets are measured at the firm
level. Most striking in the first model in Table 8.4 is the insignificance of the
two firm-level intensity variables – Advertising and R&D. Even though the
Contributed Assets group of variables were not significant in this model, the
other three groups of variables maintained signs and significance levels
consistent with the results in Table 8.3.

  We explored the role of Contributed Assets further using dummy variable
and normalized firm-level intensity operationalizations. In the second model
in Table 8.4, dummy variables were entered for Advertising and R&D
Intensity. The Advertising dummy was insignificant while the R&D dummy
was significant and negatively signed indicating that when a firm expended a
lower than industry average of its sales on R&D, its ownership level in the
investment was higher. Likewise, Hennart (1991a) found non-significant
relationships between firm-level measures of the specificity of R&D and
advertising assets and the ownership position of Japanese firms.

  The fourth and fifth models in Table 8.4 were run using firm-level
normalized intensities for advertising and R&D expenditures. In both
models, the normalized advertising and R&D intensities were significant and
negatively signed. Contrary to Hypothesis 1, the negative signs on the asset
specificity variables indicate that firms with a higher level of proprietary
content in marketing and technological assets (as compared to industry
counterparts) tended to have a lower level of ownership in their foreign
investments.   Even when we included industry-level controls (the fifth
model) the two normalized intensity variables remained negatively signed
and significant. The implications of these results are discussed in the next
section.

DISCUSSION

This study reported new empirical evidence on determinants of ownership strategies. The results were obtained from data on 1,043 foreign investments in Asia by Japanese firms. The evidence consistently supported a key tenet of the internationalization approach: increased international experience was accompanied by an increased ownership position in foreign investments. As well, the institutional environment played a substantive role in influencing ownership strategies. The evidence was less supportive of predictions derived directly from transaction cost theory.

In the international entry mode literature, several studies provide convincing evidence supporting TC theory.[8] Consistently, these studies reported a positive relationship between measures of the specificity of assets and the level of ownership (Gatignon and Anderson, 1988; Gomes-Casseres, 1989, 1990, among others). This study diverged from previous TC-based entry mode studies in two ways. First, the empirical setting did not involve the US as a home country or as a host country for the foreign direct investment. Second, we developed an improved measure of asset specificity. One of the reasons for the divergence of this study's empirical findings may be related to differences in the operationalization of asset specificity.

Most large-sample, archival studies of entry mode determinants have utilized industry-level measures. In this study, the first set of models (Table 8.3) employed similar industry-level measures of the specificity of marketing assets (advertising intensities) and technological assets (R&D intensity). The results of these models tended to be consistent with the predictions of TC theory and consistent with the results of prior studies. However, when we employed firm-level measures of the specificity of assets – as absolute measures or as measures relative to industry averages – either no relationship was observed between asset specificity and ownership, or the relationship observed was opposite to the direction hypothesized (see also Hennart, 1991a).

One implication of this discrepancy between the results obtained for industry-level and firm-level measures concerns the interpretation of previous empirical research on entry mode. Studies that have reported positive relationships between the intensity of industry-level advertising and R&D expenditures and the level of ownership as an asset specificity-degree of ownership relationship (e.g., Gatignon and Anderson, 1988; Gomes-Casseres, 1989) may just have identified the sector-specific trends in entry mode behavior previously uncovered in early research on US multinationals (Franko, 1971; Stopford and Wells, 1972; Lecraw, 1984). In light of the new evidence presented in this study, the results of these previous TC-based entry mode studies should be interpreted cautiously.

Table 8.4 Japanese firm ownership levels: Firm-level data (N=708)

Independent variables	TOBIT analysis: Percent equity ownership as dependent				
	Firm-level untransformed	Firm-level dummies	Firm-level normalized	Firm-level dummies	Firm-level normalized
Contributed assets					
1a. Advertising intensity (firm-level)	41.25 (0.52)	-4.15 (-1.58)	-3.81*** (-2.61)	-4.17 (-1.60)	-3.64*** (-2.50)
2a. R&D intensity (firm-level)	23.18 (0.56)	-4.85* (-1.88)	-1.87*** (-2.51)	-4.01 (-1.53)	-1.63** (-2.14)
1b. Advertising intensity (industry-level)	—	—	—	116.78 (1.22)	101.71 (1.06)
2b. R&D intensity (industry-level)	—	—	—	62.04 (1.29)	48.84 (1.01)
Complementary assets					
3. Resource industry	-8.45*** (-2.79)	-8.11*** (-2.69)	-8.43*** (-2.82)	-7.81*** (-2.60)	-8.15*** (-2.72)
4. Relatedness	-2.30 (-0.92)	-3.31 (-1.33)	-2.57 (-1.04)	-2.85 (-1.14)	-2.25 (-0.91)
5. Relative size	1.65 (1.59)	1.08 (0.58)	0.85 (0.47)	1.17 (0.62)	0.94 (0.51)
Institutional environment					
6. Host country risk	24.28 (1.59)	27.30* (1.80)	27.72* (1.85)	23.45 (1.54)	24.33 (1.61)
7. Host country restrictiveness	-48.19*** (-4.63)	-49.70*** (-4.79)	-47.80*** (-4.65)	-49.52*** (-4.79)	-47.74*** (-4.66)
8. Intellectual property protection	66.01*** (6.24)	65.92*** (6.26)	66.46*** (6.36)	64.77*** (6.17)	65.44*** (6.26)

TOBIT analysis: Percent equity ownership as dependent

Independent variables	Firm-level untransformed	Firm-level dummies	Firm-level dummies	Firm-level normalized	Firm-level normalized
International experience					
9. Export intensity (firm-level)	59.64***	55.46***	55.36***	59.08***	58.93***
	(7.87)	(7.27)	(7.21)	(8.00)	(7.87)
10. Number of foreign investments	0.75	0.61	0.61	0.23	0.25
	(0.68)	(0.50)	(0.50)	(0.21)	(0.22)
11. Years of host country experience	0.96***	0.88**	0.90**	0.80**	0.83**
	(2.34)	(2.17)	(2.22)	(1.98)	(2.05)
12. Sogo shosha as partner	-18.62***	-19.96***	-18.65***	-19.78***	-18.69***
	(-5.66)	(-6.24)	(-5.73)	(-6.24)	(-5.78)
13. Constant	50.57***	54.24***	51.74***	49.09***	47.47***
	(5.01)	(4.63)	(4.85)	(5.21)	(-5.36)
Model indices					
Significance of model	<.01	<.01	<.01	<.01	<.01
Adjusted R^2	0.31	0.31	0.32	0.32	0.33
Model chi-square	289.00	294.72	298.90	302.26	305.10
Incremental chi-square	–	–	4.18	–	2.84
Significance of additional variables	–	–	Not significant	–	Not significant

Notes:
1. *t*-statistics in parentheses.
2. *** $p<0.01$, ** $p<0.05$, * $p<0.10$, all two-tailed tests
3. Adjusted R^2 derived from corresponding OLS analysis.

A second implication of this result concerns the predictability of the ownership patterns in Japanese subsidiaries in Asia using TC theory. When asset specificity was operationalized by firm-level measures, the observed patterns in ownership levels in the Asian subsidiaries of Japanese firms were not consistent with the predictions of TC theory. When measured at an absolute level, the specificity of the Japanese parent's assets did not have any relationship to ownership levels. When compared to industry norms concerning the degree of specificity, if anything, an inverse relationship was observed with the ownership level in the foreign investment. Further, even when industry-level measures were used, the explanatory power of these measures was low (adjusted R^2 = 0.04, compared to 0.33 for the fully-specified model).

While the evidence in Tables 8.3 and 8.4 suggests that the ownership strategies of Japanese firms in Asia were not strongly influenced by transaction cost minimization objectives, we explored a number of alternative explanations for the insignificance of the Contributed Assets set of variables.[9] The first exploration emerges from a limitation of the operationalization of the R&D and advertising intensity items. The technological and advertising intensity of the investments was gauged using expenditure data from the parent firm. While this measure provides a good indication of expenditure patterns at the aggregate or corporate level within the home country, it imperfectly represents the technological sophistication or marketing capabilities for activities carried out in the subsidiary in the host country. That is, the foreign subsidiaries established in East and South East Asia by Japanese investors may not have involved the same degree of technological or advertising intensity as the parent firm. This is likely to have been the case particularly in early investments in East and South East Asia when Japanese firms' investments in these countries were oriented more towards securing lower cost inputs, such as labor, as compared to later investments which would have involved a greater degree of technology and management skills transfer (see Beamish, Delios and Lecraw, 1997).

We tested for this effect by partitioning our sample by the age of the subsidiary, with the expectation that more recent entrants would have made more technologically intensive investments. We utilized a variety of age cutoffs beginning with a subsidiary age of 14 years (i.e., subsidiaries established before 1980 or after 1980) and continuing to a cutoff for a subsidiary age of 4 years. Using these cutoffs, the results of the models depicted in Table 8.4 remained essentially unchanged. However, models limited to the Contributed Assets variables defined at the firm-level (not normalized) did show that the intensity of R&D was significantly related ($p<0.05$) to ownership levels for investments made after 1984, but not for investments made prior to 1984.

We next explored the advertising results by partitioning the sample by the industry in which the investment was made. We followed two forms of industry classification. The first was a partition into convenience and non-convenience goods industries (Porter, 1976) and the second was a partition into consumer and producer industries (following Kohn, 1988 and Hennart, 1991a). In the first partition, firms competing in convenience goods tend to be associated with high advertising expenditures because of the need for product differentiation and the need to develop a strong brand image (Porter, 1976). We expect that firms in convenience goods industries would be more likely to transfer specific marketing assets to the foreign subsidiary. Likewise, in the second partition, firms in consumer goods industries may be more sensitive to the transfer of advertising assets, and more likely to protect those assets by securing higher ownership levels. The empirical results of these two partitions were not materially different from those depicted in Table 8.4, although in a convenience goods model in which only the Contributed Assets variables defined at the firm-level (not normalized) were entered, the advertising variable was significant. In the case of the industry-level variables, they were consistently signed and in the correct direction for the consumer goods sample but not for the producer goods sample.

The first two forms of partition were made along temporal and sectoral lines. The third partition was made along a geographical dimension. The host country context for this study comprised nine countries. It is possible that the mix of firm strategies by country could have contributed to the insignificance of the advertising and R&D items. We tested for this by examining the models in Table 8.4 on a country-by-country basis, and by dividing the sample into two groups: newly-industrializing economies, or NIEs (Hong Kong, Korea, Singapore and Taiwan), and a second group composed of the remaining five countries (i.e., non-NIEs). The country-by-country results did not reveal any substantive changes in the full models, nor did the NIE versus non-NIE comparison, with one exception. However, in models restricted to the Contributed Assets group of variables, entries made in NIEs had higher Japanese ownership levels as advertising intensity increased, whereas in non-NIEs, we found a positive relationship between R&D intensity and ownership levels, but not between advertising and ownership.

Finally, the home country context of the study may have contributed to the lack of support for the transaction cost set of variables in another way. That is, part of the reason for the weak influence of asset specificity on the level of ownership may be related to the link between ownership levels and control in Japanese firms. As is well-reported in the academic and practitioner literature (Abegglen and Stalk, 1985; Gerlach, 1987), Japanese firms are often linked by cross-equity holdings; they have strong inner-group corporate networks and are further connected by close buyer-supplier relationships. These inter-organizational linkages, when replicated in foreign investments, provide the foreign firm with a secondary means of operational control, independent of the level of ownership, because the linkages establish markets for the firm's outputs and sources for the firm's inputs. Sogo shosha in particular are "able to exercise a great deal of managerial control without holding majority ownership, since they provide such critical services as supplies of inputs and working capital and access to markets" (Kojima and Ozawa, 1984: 42-43). Hence, consistent with the findings of Kojima (1978) and Kojima and Ozawa (1984), we observed lower equity holdings by sogo shosha because of their ability to exercise control independent of ownership. Furthermore, because ownership levels may not directly equate to the amount of control exercised by Japanese firms in foreign investments, the observed effect of transactional variables is weak.

Like the influence of Contributed Assets, the need to secure new assets was a comparatively minor influence on the Japanese firm's ownership strategy. When a direct investment entry was made in a resource dependent industry, the ownership position of the Japanese firm was lower. However, the insignificance of the Related variable and the positive sign on the Relative Size variable may be artifacts of the composition of the sample. The Japanese parents comprised public firms listed on the first section of the Tokyo Stock Exchange. These firms were large and well diversified, and often were connected to other Japanese firms via cross-equity arrangements. The need for complementary assets when making a diversifying entry outside of the parent's main line of business may not have been a substantive consideration for the Japanese parent. This is reflected in the insignificance of the Related variable. Similarly, larger subsidiaries did not lead to reduced ownership levels as a means to secure additional assets, financial or otherwise. The positive sign on the Relative Size variable indicates the need to hold greater ownership, and to reduce risks concomitant with shared ownership, when more of the firm's assets are located in the host country.

The institutional environment exerted a strong influence on the level of ownership. Legal restrictions on foreign ownership effectively reduced the equity holdings of Japanese firms. The higher ownership levels associated with weaker intellectual property rights regimes suggest that the need to safeguard proprietary assets from suppliers, buyers and competitors was more stringent when less effective regulations existed to protect patents and trademarks. While weaker intellectual property rights appeared to increase the threat of asset appropriation, and thereby induced higher ownership levels, increasing host country political and economic risk did not consistently lead to reduced ownership levels. As in Gatignon and Anderson (1988), host country risk was a less important institutional consideration than legal sanctions on foreign ownership perhaps because of the reduced threat of expropriation (Minor, 1994).

The results of this study also suggest a strong experience effect on ownership strategy. Firms more experienced in international markets and in the host country market took a higher ownership position when making a foreign investment. The role of the local partner diminished when experience levels were higher, suggesting that experience was positively associated with learning and the development of knowledge about the host country environment. This observed effect corroborates findings of previous studies that experiential knowledge is important, and that it affects the entry mode strategy (Johanson and Vahlne, 1977) even in later stages of the internationalization process (Barkema, Bell and Pennings, 1996).

CONCLUSION

This study analyzed data on manufacturing investments of Japanese firms made in nine countries in East and South East Asia to determine how transactional, experience and institutional factors influenced the ownership strategy of these firms. The principal finding in this study is that experience and institutional factors were the most important determinants of the ownership strategy. The results show that the institutional environment affected ownership levels both at a regulatory level and at a risk level. Foreign investors responded to the increased risk of unwanted dissemination of proprietary assets in countries in which intellectual property rights were less secure by taking a higher ownership position. Japanese firms also secured higher ownership levels when they had more experience in international markets and more experience in the host country market.

Transactional factors were a less important influence than experience and institutional factors. While firms that operated in technologically and marketing intensive industries tended to take higher ownership positions when making foreign investments, this effect was relatively weaker than institutional and experience related effects. Further, within industry variance, and across firm differences, in the proprietary content of firms' technological and marketing assets had an ambiguous relationship with the degree of ownership taken in the foreign investment. Finally, the insignificance and ambiguous effect of technological and marketing assets persisted in more fine-grained analyses involving samples divided along temporal, sectoral and geographical lines, although these analyses also pointed to potential differences in firm strategies depending on the time, industry and region in which the investment was made.

One of the main tenets of the internalization approach and transaction cost theory concerns the positive relationship between the proprietary content of a firm's assets and the level of ownership. While the results were consistent with past research when we used industry-level indicators, no evidence was found in support of this relationship using absolute and relative firm-level indicators of asset specificity. A remaining empirical question is to identify if the null effect of transactional variables is unique to Japanese firms, perhaps because of the attenuated relationship between ownership and control that can exist in these firms, or if transactional variables, when operationalized as in this study, also have a weak effect for the foreign investments of firms based in other nations. Hence, future research should continue to examine the relative importance of transactional, institutional and experience factors on the ownership and entry mode strategies of firms across a variety of host and home country settings.

NOTES

1. The binding power of legal restrictions on foreign investors' ownership positions is subject to the bargaining power of the host country government and the foreign firm. Hence, the amount of local ownership actually induced by formal government policies varies by country and by firm (Stopford and Wells, 1972). Accordingly, we present the legal restrictions relationship with ownership levels as an hypothesis, rather than as a control.
2. To test the sensitivity of the results to the selection of the modeling procedure, we also ran OLS regressions and LOGIT regressions (the choice between wholly-owned subsidiaries and joint ventures). The results were strongly consistent across OLS, LOGIT and TOBIT specifications. We report the TOBIT results because it is the most appropriate modeling procedure.
3. The *World Competitiveness Report* contains information on 381 criteria used to assess a nation's international competitiveness. Individual criteria were developed from statistical indicators of international organizations and national institutions and from responses by 2,850 executives worldwide to questionnaires concerning their perceptions of the international business community.
4. The five most R&D intensive manufacturing industries were: pharmaceuticals, communications equipment, computerized office equipment, optical and copy machines and heavy-duty electrical equipment. The five most advertising-intensive industries were cosmetics and toiletries, liquor, sporting and entertainment goods, instant foods and beverages.
5. All entries that had a sogo shosha as a main parent were coded as not related because the sogo shosha's main line of business is wholesale trading. We removed all sogo shosha entries to test if the insignificance of the relatedness variable was due to the inclusion of sogo shosha in the sample. The variable was not significant in the sub-sample.
6. The insignificance of the host country risk variable may be attributed, in part, to its correlation with the host country restrictiveness variable ($r=-0.609$). When host country restrictiveness is removed from the equation, host country risk becomes significant.
7. These nine firms, and the worldwide number of foreign investments in which they had an equity stake, were: Itochu (331), Kanematsu (122), Sumitomo (326), Tomen (289), Nichimen (103), Nissho Iwai (242), Marubeni (395), Mitsui & Co. (633), and Mitsubishi Corporation (442).

8. Extensive empirical support of transaction cost theory exists in studies reported in the economics, marketing and strategic management literature (for a review see Masten, 1994).
9. We thank an anonymous reviewer for many insightful suggestions for tests of alternative explanations concerning the results for the Contributed Assets set of variables.

ACKNOWLEDGEMENTS

This research was supported by a Social Sciences and Humanities Research Council of Canada Grant (#411-98-0393), and by the Asian Management Institute at the Richard Ivey School of Business. The manuscript benefited from comments received from Tony Frost, Brian Golden, Rod White, an anonymous reviewer and seminar participants in the 1997 Nordic IB workshop in Helsinki, Finland. An earlier version of this paper was presented at the 1997 Academy of Management meetings in Boston.

Appendix: *Pearson correlation coefficients and descriptive statistics*

Variable	1	2	3	4	5	6	7	8	9	10	11	12	13
1. Advertising intensity		0.199	0.029	-0.131	-0.052	0.075	-0.064	0.028	-0.105	-0.008	-0.098	-0.148	0.039
2. R&D intensity	0.232		-0.071	-0.025	-0.081	0.063	0.028	-0.052	0.094	0.172	0.076	-0.070	0.052
3. Resource industry	-0.039	-0.109		0.101	-0.052	0.024	-0.055	-0.045	-0.240	0.076	0.013	0.188	-0.211
4. Relatedness	-0.179	-0.134	0.147		0.067	-0.002	-0.005	-0.042	0.084	0.161	0.174	0.076	-0.016
5. Relative size	-0.017	0.048	-0.038	0.038		0.060	-0.061	0.016	0.238	-0.067	-0.054	-0.052	0.103
6. Host country risk	0.008	-0.003	0.079	0.035	0.037		0.327	-0.618	0.043	0.146	0.041	0.262	-0.183
7. Host country restrictiveness	-0.044	0.045	0.027	-0.023	-0.044	0.339		-0.467	-0.041	-0.067	0.019	0.156	-0.278
8. Intellectual property protection	0.023	0.011	-0.090	-0.049	0.014	-0.609	-0.443		0.041	-0.063	-0.085	-0.193	0.347
9. Export intensity	-0.037	0.176	-0.241	-0.028	0.075	0.059	-0.032	0.026		0.216	0.072	-0.163	0.350
10. Number of foreign investments	-0.172	-0.185	0.136	0.302	-0.092	0.193	-0.045	-0.092	0.131		0.352	0.165	0.063
11. Years of host country experience	-0.136	-0.077	0.114	0.254	-0.074	0.109	0.011	-0.118	0.071	0.512		0.031	0.069
12. Sogo shosha as partner	-0.258	-0.204	0.246	0.232	-0.071	0.264	0.109	-0.179	-0.111	0.459	0.230		-0.314
13. Equity ownership	0.150	0.176	-0.206	-0.101	0.095	-0.223	-0.286	0.339	0.323	-0.105	-0.039	-0.365	
Mean	0.009	0.021	0.213	0.499	0.147	21.528	4.284	4.551	0.185	75.228	8.570	0.265	59.483
Standard deviation	0.013	0.024	0.410	0.500	0.769	10.482	1.344	1.531	0.155	138.166	24.321	0.441	28.414

Notes:

1. Correlations in lower half of matrix are for advertising and R&D intensities measured at the industry-level (N=1,043). Correlations > 0.049 significant at p<0.05.

2. Correlations in upper half of matrix are for advertising and R&D intensities measured at the firm-level (N=708). Correlations > 0.071 significant at p<0.05.

9. Performance and survival of joint ventures with non-conventional ownership structures

Shige Makino and Paul W. Beamish

The international joint venture (JV) literature has focused on two parent JVs formed between one foreign and one local firm. Yet other types of JVs exist. This chapter identifies four distinct forms of JVs based on the JV partners' nationality and equity affiliation. These are (i) JVs that are formed between affiliated home-country based firms; (ii) JVs that are formed between unaffiliated home-country based firms; (iii) JVs that are formed between home-country based and local firms; and (iv) JVs that are formed between home-country and third-country based firms. Our analysis of 737 Japanese JVs in Asia demonstrates that the conventionally assumed form of JV represented only 30 percent of the total. Further, each of the four JV forms significantly differed in terms of incidence, performance, and survival likelihood.

INTRODUCTION

Joint venture (JV) ownership structure has traditionally been defined by the percentage of equity held by the foreign parent. Where the foreign parent has a greater than 50 percent equity stake, the JV is called a majority-owned JV. If ownership is equal to 50 percent, the JV is considered co-owned, and if the equity holding is less than 50 percent, the JV is identified as a minority-owned. This conventional measurement assumes that: (i) the relative size of equity ownership represents the degree of control by the parent in the JV, and (ii) the JV was formed between two firms, typically a foreign and a local firm. The latter assumption is related to the first, because when there are more than two firms, one firm may have dominant managerial control (a majority equity position) even with less than 50 percent of ownership, but the collusive actions of the other two (or more) firms can affect this application of ownership towards control.

Ownership as a primary mechanism of control has been a dominant perspective in the economics literature, in which ownership is defined as "residual rights of control," or the rights to make any decision concerning an asset's use that is not explicitly assigned by law or contract to another party (Milgrom and Roberts, 1992, p. 602). Grossman and Hart (1986) explicitly posit that the extent of ownership equates to control. They suggest that decisions regarding the choice of ownership position depend on the relative importance of the investment of one firm to that of the other firm in gaining an *ex post* return for the investment. Anderson and Gatignon (1986) share a similar view. Drawing on transaction cost theory, they suggest that ownership equals control. The choice of desired ownership level reflects an interplay between the firm's desire to secure control and its attitudes towards investment risks. Finally, foreign direct investment (FDI) literature suggests that foreign firms (typically US-based firms) have tended to secure a dominant equity position to exercise control over the local partner (or the local government) (Fagre and Wells, 1982; Lecraw, 1984; Contractor, 1990).

However, other studies have criticized the ownership-control relationship for a variety of reasons. First, control can be exercised through non-ownership mechanisms such as formal contracts, management teams, and other more informal control methods (Schaan, 1983; Beamish and Banks, 1987; Yan and Gray, 1994; Mjoen and Tallman, 1997). Second, the ownership position may also represent the relative importance of partner contributions to the JV (Blodgett, 1991; Kogut, 1988b; Shan and Hamilton, 1991; Makino and Delios, 1996). Third, when shared ownership is imposed in certain host countries, the local partner(s) may not possess substantial control over the JV operation. Finally, a minority-equity holder often exercises dominant control of specific activities within a JV (Schaan, 1983; Hebert, 1994; Mjoen and Tallman, 1997).

From a different perspective, recent studies (Erramilli, 1996; Pan, 1997) have suggested that firms with different national backgrounds have different preferences in ownership positions perhaps because parent firms have differing propensities to view equity ownership as a primary control mechanism (Parkhe, 1991, 1993; Shane, 1993; Erramilli, 1996; Pan, 1996). For example, Pan (1997) suggested that North American multinational enterprises (MNEs) were more likely than Japanese MNEs to form a wholly owned subsidiary (WOS) over a JV. Yet, Japanese MNEs had a higher propensity to secure dominant ownership positions within JVs than North American MNEs (Beamish and Delios, 1997b). Pan (1996) also found significant differences in patterns in ownership among Japanese, US, and European MNEs in China.

While the conceptualization of ownership has changed in recent years, early studies, such as those using the Harvard Multinational Enterprise Project (HMNE) database (Curhan, Davidson and Suri, 1977; Vernon, 1995), classified JVs by the majority-, co-, and minority-distinction (Curhan, Davidson and Suri, 1977). Researchers using the HMNE database have developed a tradition of defining and studying JVs which are of the two-partner form (i.e., one local and one foreign partner JV) (see Table 9.1). Rarely does a study (notable exceptions include Tsurumi, 1976; Yoshino, 1976; Kojima and Ozawa, 1984; Hennart, 1988; Shan, 1991) explicitly identify and consider JVs that were formed by multiple partners, or JVs that were formed between a foreign firm and a partner *not* based in the host country.

The present study makes several contributions. First, it provides evidence that non-conventional (versus local-foreign partner JVs) forms of JVs are frequently occurring, and are important organizational forms. This research examines the performance and survival likelihood of JVs that have been rarely considered in previous studies. Second, it does so by introducing a new typology which looks at JVs formed (i) by multiple (three or more) firms; (ii) with non-local firms (home- and third-country based firms); and (iii) by affiliated firms (e.g., JVs formed between the parent firm and its domestic or foreign subsidiaries). Third, it demonstrates that international JVs formed with a third-country based partner(s) often represent a worst case scenario, with both a high termination rate and a low performance level. Fourth, it provides a comparison of the performance and survival likelihoods using the new ownership typology with the existing (minority, even, majority) ownership typology.

DEFINING JV OWNERSHIP STRUCTURE

In this study, JV ownership structure is defined by (i) partner nationality and (ii) partner affiliation. Partner nationality involves the country-of-origin of the parent firm.[1] Specifically, this study defines partner nationality in terms of whether the JV's equity is owned by *home-* (Japanese), *host-*, or *third country*-based firms.[2] Partner affiliation is defined in terms of whether the JV's equity is related between JV partners. Partners are affiliated if : (i) they are parent firms (or subsidiaries) of the other JV partners; (ii) they have cross-holdings of each others' equity; or (iii) they belong to the same *keiretsu*.[3]

Table 9.1 Selected IJV studies: 1970–1997

Researcher	Type and form of IJV study
Tomlinson (1970)	Two partner JVs, examined control issues.
Franko (1971)	Two partner JVs, examined control issues.
Friedman & Beguin (1971)	Studied Foreign-Local partner JVs. Possible to have more than two partners.
Curhan, Davidson & Suri (1977)[1]	Principally two partner JVs defined as majority, minority or co-owned JVs.
Asheghian (1982)	Two partner JVs formed with a local partner.
Fagre & Wells (1982)	Principally two partner JVs. Ownership structure was defined in terms of actual, firm-corrected, and country-corrected ownership.
Killing (1983)	Developed framework for management of two partner JVs.
Lecraw (1984)	Two partner JVs formed with a local partner.
Reynolds (1984)	Two partner JVs formed with a local partner.
Beamish (1985)	Two partner JVs formed with a local partner.
Harrigan (1985 & 1986)	Developed framework for management of two partner JVs.
Franko (1987)	Two partner JVs defined as majority, minority or co-owned JVs.
Habib (1987)	No indication of number of partners or nationality of partners provided.
Lorange & Probst (1987)	Development of two partner JV research framework.
Shenkar & Zeira (1987)	Discussed human resource management issues in both two- and multiple-partner JVs.
Buckley & Casson (1988)	Developed a theoretical framework of two partner JVs.
Hennart (1988)	Theoretical development of transaction cost theory of JVs allows for multiple and non-local partners.
Kogut & Singh (1988)	No indication of number of partners or nationality of partners provided.
Franko (1989)	Two partner JVs defined as majority, minority or co-owned JVs.
Kogut (1989)	Multiple partner JVs (including domestic JVs) formed by at least one American firm.
Gomes-Casseres (1989)	Principally two partner JVs formed with a local partner.
Contractor (1990)	Two partner JVs defined as 50:50 and minority JVs.
Blodgett (1991, 1992)	Two partner JVs defined as majority, 51:49, 50:50, 49:51, and minority.

Researcher	Type and form of IJV study
Geringer (1991)	Multiple partner JVs, identifies partner selection determinants.
Geringer & Hebert (1991)	Two partner JVs formed with a local partner.
Hennart (1991a)	Multiple partner JVs in the USA formed by at least one Japanese firm.
Shan (1991)	Two partner JVs formed by firms with different countries of origin.
Inkpen (1992)	Two partner JVs formed with a local partner.
Shenkar & Zeira (1992)	Multiple partner JVs treated as two partner JVs, management oriented study.
Parkhe (1993)	Two partner JVs formed with at least one US partner.
Lyles & Baird (1994)	Multiple partner JVs formed with a local partner.
Yan & Gray (1994)	Two partner JVs formed with a local partner.
Cullen, Johnson & Sakano (1995)	Multiple partner JVs treated as two partner JVs with a foreign and local partner.
Lee & Beamish (1995)	Two partner JVs formed with a local partner.
Madhok (1995)	Developed a theoretical framework of principally two partner JVs.
Buckley & Casson (1996)	Developed a theoretical framework of two partner JVs.
Lyles & Salk (1996)	Multiple partner JVs and two partner JVs defined as dominant and 50:50 JVs.
Makino & Delios (1996)	Multiple partner JVs formed with local and /or non-local firms.
Pan (1996)	Two partner JVs defined as majority, minority or co-owned JVs.
Pan & Tse (1996)	Two partner JVs formed by firms with multiple countries of origin.
Barkema & Vermeulen (1997)	JVs formed by at least one Dutch firm. No indication of number of partners.
Brouthers & Bamossy (1997)	Multiple partner JVs formed between western and central/eastern European enterprises.
Inkpen & Beamish (1997)	Developed a theoretical framework of two partner JVs.
Luo (1997)	Two partner JVs formed with a local partner.
Mjoen & Tallman (1997)	JVs formed by at least one Norwegian firm. No indication of number of partners.

Note: Other studies that have utilised the Harvard Multinational Database for the study of JVs have used a classification scheme similar to that in Curhan, Davidson and Suri (1977).

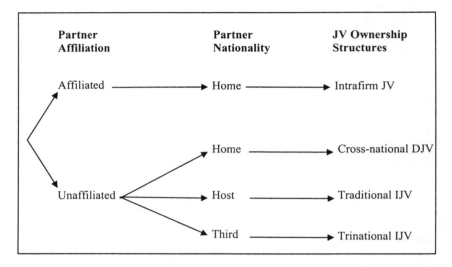

Figure 9.1 Joint venture ownership structure options from the home-country based firm perspective

This JV ownership classification scheme is depicted in Figure 9.1. The four JV ownership structures that arise out of this classification scheme are: (i) Intrafirm JV; (ii) Cross-national domestic JV (DJV); (iii) Traditional International JV (IJV); and (iv) Trinational International JV (IJV).[4] Intrafirm JVs represent those JVs formed between affiliated home-country based firms;[5] Cross-national DJVs are JVs formed between unaffiliated home-country based firms; Traditional IJVs are JVs formed between home-country based and host-country based (local) firms; and Trinational IJVs are JVs formed between home-country and third-country based firms.

JV OWNERSHIP STRUCTURE, PERFORMANCE AND SURVIVAL

In examining the performance and survival implications of JV ownership, this study focuses on two factors that characterize the choice of JV ownership structures, namely, local access (i.e., access to local market) through JV partner(s), and cultural distance at country- and corporate-levels among partners.

Local Access, Performance, and Survival

The international business literature states that foreign firms face location-based disadvantages compared to local competitors (Hymer, 1976). Formation of a Traditional IJV has often been considered an effective means of acquiring local knowledge and, hence, of overcoming location-based disadvantages, particularly when (i) the firm had no previous operational experience in the host country; and (ii) the self-development and cross-border transfer of local knowledge is difficult.

Sharing ownership with local firms can be an effective strategy, as several studies have found that JVs performed better when ownership was shared with local partners (Beamish, 1985; Beamish and Banks, 1987; Bleeke and Ernst, 1993; Blodgett, 1992; Makino and Delios, 1996). While local access may be critical for successful performance, at least at the initial stage of foreign operations, the role of local partners as a window to unfamiliar markets may eventually become redundant as the foreign partner accumulates local experience (Makino and Delios, 1996). Underlying this idea is the fact that local knowledge is a "public good" to domestic firms. Due to this characteristic, foreign firms tend to rely on local firms to gain better local access on entry to the host country. But this dependence decreases as local experience is accumulated, and the foreign firms' bargaining power over local partners may increase. As a consequence the JV can become unstable, and it may be terminated or acquired by the foreign partner (Inkpen and Beamish, 1997). Thus, all other things being equal, JVs formed as a means to gain local access are generally more unstable than those JVs formed by foreign firms that do not depend on local partners for local access.

Cultural Distance, Performance, and Survival

Cultural distance can be defined at the country and corporate levels. The concept of cultural distance at the country level has been extensively discussed in the ownership strategy literature (Kogut and Singh, 1988; Erramilli, 1991, 1996; Erramilli and Rao, 1993; Shane, 1993; Agarwal, 1994; Barkema, Bell and Pennings, 1996). Cultural distance at the corporate level has often been investigated in terms of differences in core businesses, management practices, decision making process, need, and learning capabilities between alliance partners (Killing, 1983; Makhija and Ganesh, 1997; Pearce, 1997). Further, there is some evidence that both forms of cultural distance impact alliance performance. Parkhe (1991), for example, has suggested that the diversity in the national contexts as well as in the corporate culture of alliance partners may hamper effective inter-partner collaborations and negatively affect the longevity of alliances. Barkema et al., (1996) found that the termination of JVs (and acquisitions) was more susceptible to cultural distance than WOS (and start-ups) because the former had to accommodate both national and corporate cultures, or "double-layered acculturation." Based on the case study of North American firms involved in international JVs, Killing (1983) suggested that cultural distance was a major problem in many financially unsuccessful and failed shared-management JVs.

Although a recent study found no empirical support to the positive association between cultural distance and termination (Park and Ungson, 1997), most studies have suggested that JVs with culturally distant partners incur a higher level of management complexity than those JVs formed between partners with similar cultural backgrounds. Assuming that management complexity within a JV is a major hindrance to both the stability and performance of the JV, we suggest that JVs formed between partners that share a similar national or corporate culture tend to have a higher likelihood of survival and attain superior financial performance than those that do not.

JV Ownership Structure, Local Access, Cultural Distance and Performance

In the JV ownership structures defined earlier, local access opportunities and cultural distance vary. Figure 9.2 exhibits the variance in these attributes by JV ownership structures. As in the Figure, a Traditional IJV provides the best opportunity for gaining local access through its local partner, yet is subject to the highest cultural distance between partners (high cultural distance at both the country and corporate levels). An Intrafirm JV, on the other hand, provides no local access, yet has the lowest cultural distance at both the country and corporate levels. A Cross-national DJV provides no local access, and is subject to a moderate level of cultural distance (low cultural distance at country level and high at corporate level). A Trinational IJV provides no local access and is subject to high cultural distance (high cultural distance at both country and corporate levels). If we can assume that cultural distances at both the country and the corporate levels are equal sources of management complexity, then the level of management complexity is highest in both Traditional IJVs and Trinational IJVs, moderate in Cross-national DJVs, and lowest in Intrafirm JVs.

The expected financial performance and survival likelihood of the different JV ownership structures are based on a comparison of local access opportunities and the cultural distance embedded in each form of JV. As seen in Figure 9.2, Intrafirm JVs and Traditional IJVs are expected to achieve the highest performance, followed by Cross-national DJVs and Trinational IJVs. Intrafirm JVs are expected to achieve the highest survival likelihood, followed by Cross-national DJVs, and Traditional IJVs and Trinational IJVs attain the lowest survival likelihood. Overall, this suggests:

Hypothesis 1. Intrafirm JVs and Traditional IJVs achieve higher financial performance than other JV types.

Hypothesis 2. Cross-national DJVs achieve moderate financial performance compared to other JV types.

Hypothesis 3. Trinational IJVs achieve lower financial performance than other JV types.

Hypothesis 4. Intrafirm JVs have a higher survival likelihood than other JV types.

Hypothesis 5. Cross-national DJVs have a moderate survival likelihood compared to other JV types.

Hypothesis 6. Traditional IJVs and Trinational IJVs have a lower survival likelihood than other JV types.

	Intrafirm JV	Cross-National Domestic JV	Traditional International JV	Trinational International JV
Local access through partners	No	No	Yes	No
National cultural distance	Low	Low	High	High
Corporate cultural distance	Low	High	High	High
Expected level of performance	High	Medium	High	Low
Expected level of survival likelihood	High	Medium	Low	Low

Figure 9.2 Local access, cultural distance, and joint venture ownership structure options

RESEARCH METHODOLOGY

Classification of JV Ownership Structure

To classify multiple-partner JVs into one of the four types of JVs previously defined, criteria need to be established that can differentiate the relative impact of each partner's attributes (i.e., nationality and affiliation) on the overall configuration of the JV.[6] To solve this problem, we use two continuous measures of these attributes: (i) Nationality Ratio and (ii) Affiliation Ratio. Nationality Ratio is the percentage of the JV's equity possessed by partners with the same nationality. Affiliation Ratio is the percentage of the JV's equity possessed by the largest single partner or group of affiliated home country based partners in the JV.

To measure the importance of ownership in defining Nationality and Affiliation ratios, we followed traditional accounting rules. In conventional accounting principles, firms are considered to be affiliated when one firm owns between 20 percent and 50 percent of the other. When one firm owns more than 50 percent of another, the former is considered as a parent firm of the latter, and the latter as a subsidiary of the former (e.g., accounting standards of Canada, US, etc.). When equity ownership is under 20 percent, the investment is termed a "portfolio investment." Following the principles used in accounting, we adopted a cut-off point of 20 percent or more to indicate when a partner had some influence on JV management.

Sample

This classification scheme was applied to a sample of Japanese JVs collected from a 1991 survey of Japanese subsidiaries reported in *Kaigai Shinshutsu Kigyou Souran 1992* (Toyo Keizai, 1992a). This database listed 13,500 foreign subsidiaries of 3,332 Japanese parents. From the original survey, our sample comprised the 737 subsidiaries that met the following criteria.

1. Manufacturing JVs formed by at least one Japanese parent firm.
2. JVs located in East and Southeast Asia (China, Taiwan, Hong Kong, Thailand, Singapore, Malaysia, Philippines, Indonesia, and South Korea).
3. JVs that were established on a greenfield basis.
4. JVs with financial performance information.

Using the first three criteria, a sample of 1,685 cases was obtained. The reduction in the sample size from 1,685 to 737 JVs by the inclusion of the performance item raises the spectre of non-respondent bias. To examine for the bias, several statistical tests were performed, using t-tests of size measures (the US dollar value of JV equity capital and the number of total employees of the JVs) and Chi-square tests of demographic proportion. No significant differences were detected. Hence, we conclude that the JVs with performance information came from the same population as those that did not report performance.

Variables

JV ownership structure
In the sample, 92 subsidiaries were classified as Intrafirm JVs, 81 as Cross-national DJVs, 546 as Traditional IJVs, and 18 as Trinational IJVs.

Performance
In the Toyo Keizai survey, performance was measured on a three-point scale, coded "loss," "break-even," and "gain." The same performance measure has been frequently used in previous studies (Woodcock, Beamish and Makino, 1994; Makino and Delios, 1996; Beamish, Delios and Lecraw, 1997). We used the performance measure as a categorical variable.

Survival
The terminated JV cases used in the analysis involve those JVs that had dissolved or been acquired during the 1986-1991 period. The termination rate for each JV ownership structure was calculated as the ratio of the number of the terminated cases to the number of newly formed JVs for the 1986-1991 period.[7] To construct the list of terminated JVs, we consulted consecutive editions of *Kaigai Shinshutsu Kigyou Souran* (Toyo Keizai, 1986, 1987, 1988, 1989, 1990, 1991, and 1992a). When a JV was delisted in the 1986 and 1991 database, it was considered terminated.

Data Analysis

JV ownership structure and performance
With a categorical dependent variable, we used Log-linear models (independence and row-effect models) to test the relationship between ownership and performance. In the independence model, both the JV ownership structure and performance variables were treated as nominal variables. This model tests the null hypothesis that there is no association between JV ownership structure and performance. In the row-effect model, JV ownership structure is treated as a nominal variable, and performance as an ordinal variable. The row-effect model examines how performance varies among JV ownership structures.

JV ownership structure and survival

The relationship between JV ownership structure and survival likelihood was examined by Chi-square tests. In the statistical analysis, all the cases were classified into either a surviving- or a terminated-JV category. Each count of surviving and terminated JVs was compared across the four JV ownership structures.

RESULTS

Incidence

Table 9.2 illustrates the results of the classification. In our sample, 92 (12.5%) were classified as Intrafirm JVs; 81 (11.0%) Cross-national DJVs; 546 (74.1%) Traditional IJVs; and 18 (2.4%) Trinational IJVs. The first column from the left lists the number of JV partners. In this sample, the number of two-partner JVs represented less than 50% of the total cases. More than the half of the cases were JVs with three or more partners, and those JVs with four or more represented 20% of the total. This suggests that a two-partner JV is not the typical form of JV ownership structure which the JV literature has assumed.

A striking result in Table 9.2 is that JVs formed between a foreign and a local firm (i.e., two-partner Traditional IJVs), the type thought to typify most international JVs, represented only 31.5 percent of all JVs in the sample. The remaining nearly 70 percent of JVs were classified as non-conventional forms of JVs. Contrary to popular belief, this evidence shows that most (Japanese) JVs were formed by more than two partners, or by partners that were affiliated with each other, and that JV partners might be based in a third country.

JV Ownership Structure and Performance

Table 9.3 provides the results of the first Log-linear analysis which examined the relationship between financial performance and JV ownership structure. Marginal frequencies show that 65.5 percent of the JVs were profitable, while 17.1 percent had a loss in 1991. Traditional IJVs had the best performance. Nearly 70 percent of Traditional IJVs were classified as profitable, or "gain." Among the other three JV types, Intrafirm JVs had the second best performance, followed by Cross-national DJVs. Trinational IJVs were the worst performers.

Table 9.2 Comparison of JV formation incidence by JV ownership structure

	JV ownership structures				
Number of JV partners	Intrafirm JV	Cross-national DJV	Traditional IJV	Trinational IJV	Row total
2	64 (8.7%)	29 (3.9%)	232 (31.5%)	9 (1.2%)	334 (45.3%)
3	20 (2.7%)	29 (3.9%)	199 (27.0%)	7 (0.9%)	255 (34.6%)
4	5 (0.7%)	13 (1.8%)	79 (10.7%)	1 (0.1%)	98 (13.3%)
5	2 (0.3%)	6 (0.8%)	23 (3.1%)	1 (0.1%)	32 (4.3%)
6	1 (0.1%)	3 (0.4%)	9 (1.2%)		13 (1.8%)
7 or more		1 (0.1%)	4 (0.5%)		5 (0.6%)
Total	92 (12.5%)	81 (11.0%)	546 (74.1%)	18 (2.4%)	737 (100.0%)

Note: The figures in brackets represent the total-count percentage.

The independence model was compared with the row-effect model to examine whether financial performance significantly varied among JV ownership structures. The goodness-of-fit of the independence model was poor, with $\chi^2 = 31.17$ based on d.f. = 6. The difference in the Pearson's Chi-squares between the independence model and the row-effect model resulted in a change in χ^2 of 28.55 (d.f. = 3), indicating that the inclusion of the row-effect parameters significantly improved the fit of the model. These results suggest that there was a significant difference in performance among the four JV ownership structures.[8]

Given the significant association between JV ownership structure and performance, we then examined how performance varied among the four JV ownership structures. To examine this, the row-effect parameters for each JV type were estimated. The bottom row in Table 9.3 provides the estimated row effect parameters for each JV ownership structure. The more positive (negative) the parameter is, the greater the likelihood for JV structures to be at the more successful or "gain" (unsuccessful or "loss") end of the performance scale. The parameter was largest for Traditional IJVs (.433); then Intrafirm JVs (.242) and Cross-national DJVs (.036) follow, and the lowest and only negative parameter was for Trinational IJVs (-.711). The result implies that Traditional IJVs are the most successful JV ownership structure of the four JV ownership structures, and Intrafirm JVs are the second most successful JV ownership structure. With the parameter close to zero, Cross-national DJVs are not as successful as the preceding two JV ownership structures. Trinational IJVs are the least successful JV ownership structure. These results support the hypotheses.

Table 9.3 JV ownership structure and performance: Result of log-linear analysis

Performance category	Intrafirm JV (n=92)	Cross-national DJV (n=81)	Traditional IJV (n=546)	Trinational IJV (n=18)	Total (n=737)
Loss	16 (17.4)	22 (27.2)	78 (14.3)	10 (55.5)	126 (17.1)
Break-even	20 (21.7)	13 (16.0)	92 (16.8)	3 (16.7)	128 (17.4)
Gain	56 (60.9)	46 (56.8)	379 (68.9)	5 (27.8)	483 (65.5)
Estimated row-effect parameters	.242	.036	.433	-.711	

Notes:
1. The figures in brackets represent the column-count percentage.
2. Goodness-of-fit test for the Independence model: Pearson χ^2: 30.17 (d.f.=6; p=.000)
3. Goodness-of-fit-test for the Row-effect model: Pearson χ^2: 1.62 (d.f. = 3; p= .654)
4. Improvement in Pearson χ^2: $\Delta\chi^2$ = 28.55 (Δd.f.= 3)

JV Ownership Structure and Survival

The summary of the frequency for terminated and surviving cases for each of the four JV ownership structures is provided in Table 9.4. The termination rate for the four JV ownership structures was 12.7 percent for Intrafirm JVs, 10.9 percent for Cross-national DJVs, 31.3 percent for Traditional IJVs, and 35.7 percent for Trinational IJVs. As expected, JVs that were formed between Japanese partners (Intrafirm JVs and Cross-national DJVs) tended to survive longer than those formed by non-Japanese partners (Traditional IJVs and the Trinational IJVs).

Pearson's Chi-square tests rejected the null hypothesis that performance and JV ownership structure are independent ($\chi^2 = 16.72$), indicating that they are significantly associated with each other. Using Chi-square tests, we then examined whether survival likelihood differed for each pair of the four JV ownership structures. The results of the analyses suggested that the termination rates of both Intrafirm JVs (12.7%) and Cross-national DJVs (10.9%) were significantly lower than those of Traditional IJVs (31.3%) and Trinational IJVs (35.7%). There was no significant difference in termination rates between Intrafirm JVs and Cross-national DJVs, nor between Traditional IJVs and Trinational IJVs. These results are generally consistent with the hypotheses.

Table 9.4   JV ownership structure and survival: Results of Chi-square analyses

Survival category	Intrafirm JV	Cross-national DJV	Traditional IJV	Trinational IJV	Total
Terminated JVs (JVs terminated between 1986 and 1991)	7	6	105	5	123
New JVs (JVs newly formed between 1986 and 1991)	48	49	230	9	336
Total (termination rate, %)	55 (12.7)	55 (10.9)	335 (31.3)	14 (35.7)	459 (26.7)

Notes: Chi-square tests:
1. Total category: Pearson χ^2: 16.72 (d.f.=6; p=.00081)
2. Each pair of JV ownership structures:
   (1) Intrafirm JV vs. Cross-national DJV: Pearson χ^2: .08 (d.f.=1; p=.767)
   (2) Intrafirm JV vs. Traditional IJV: Pearson χ^2: 7.99 (d.f.=1; p=.004)
   (3) Intrafirm JV vs. Trinational IJV: Pearson χ^2: 4.10 (d.f.=1; p=.042)
   (4) Cross-national DJV vs. Traditional IJV: Pearson χ^2: 9.68 (d.f.=1; p=.001)
   (5) Cross-national DJV vs. Trinational IJV: Pearson χ^2: 5.12 (d.f.=1; p=.023)
   (6) Traditional IJV vs. Trinational IJV: Pearson χ^2: 0.11 (d.f.=1; p=.730)

For comparison purposes, we also examined both the performance and termination rate of JVs using the conventional ownership classification. In this analysis, we used only two-partner Traditional IJVs – JVs formed between one Japanese parent with 5 percent or more of equity, and one local firm with 20 percent or more equity. Tables 5 and 6 provide the summary of the results. There was no conspicuous difference in performance among the three JV groups ($\chi^2 = 3.87$; p = .423), though co-owned JVs had a higher percentage of JVs that were classified as profitable than the other JVs. The Chi-square analyses suggested that the termination rate for majority-owned JVs (15.2%) was significantly lower than those of minority-owned (38.5%) and co-owned JVs (37.1%) . No significant difference in termination rate was detected between minority-owned and co-owned JVs.

Table 9.5 Conventional JV ownership structure and performance: Result of log-linear analysis

Performance category	Minority-owned JV (n=113)	Co-owned JV (n=54)	Majority-owned JV (n=65)	Total (n=232)
Loss	17 (15.0)	5 (9.3)	14 (21.5)	36 (15.5)
Break-even	21 (18.6)	9 (16.7)	12 (18.5)	42 (18.1)
Gain	75 (66.4)	40 (74.0)	39 (60.0)	154 (66.4)
Estimated Row-effect parameters	-.015	.252	-.237	

Notes:
1. The figures in brackets represent the column-count percentage.
2. Goodness-of-fit test for the Independence model: Pearson χ^2: 3.87 (d.f.=4; p=.423)
3. Goodness-of-fit-test for the Row-effect model: Pearson χ^2: 0.18 (d.f. = 2; p= .912)
4. Improvement in Pearson χ^2: $\Delta\chi^2 = 2.69$ (Δd.f.= 2)

DISCUSSION

This study identified four distinct JV forms based on the JV partners' nationality and equity affiliation, and examined their incidence, financial performance and termination rate. With regard to JV incidence, the results of the analysis showed that the number of JVs taking the form of the conventionally assumed JVs represented less than one third of our sample. Seventy percent of the sample involved JVs formed by multiple partners or JVs formed by non-local firms. This evidence suggests that the JV ownership structure varied in terms of the number of partners, the nationality of the partners, and the organizational affiliation of the partners.

Table 9.6 Conventional JV ownership structure and survival: Results of Chi-square analyses

Survival category	Minority-owned JV	Co-owned JV	Majority-owned JV	Total
Terminated JVs (JVs terminated between 1986 and 1991)	25	13	5	43
New JVs (JVs newly formed between 1986 and 1991)	40	22	28	90
Total (termination rate, %)	65 (38.5)	35 (37.1)	33 (15.2)	133 (32.3)

Note: Chi-square tests :
1. Total category: Pearson χ^2: 5.93 (d.f.=2; p=.051)
2. Each pair of JV ownership structures:
   (1) Minority-owned JV vs. co-owned JV: Pearson χ^2: .01 (d.f.=1; p=.896)
   (2) Minority-owned JV vs. majority-owned JV: Pearson χ^2: 5.59 (d.f.=1; p=.017)
   (3) Co-owned JV vs. majority-owned JV: Pearson χ^2: 4.22 (d.f.=1; p=.039)

This result raises a note of caution with respect to the use of the conventional definition of IJV ownership structure. If researchers focus only on JVs that are captured by the conventionally assumed type (i.e., two-partner JVs formed between local and foreign firms), a significant number of JVs will be excluded from their samples. Empirical research that focuses on conventional JVs will not reflect the reality of most foreign direct investment decisions.

Before discussing the results of the statistical analyses, several limitations must be addressed. First, we did not control for potential contingency factors which might moderate the impact of JV ownership structure on performance and survival. Second, we did not directly measure the actual levels of both local access opportunity and management complexity for each JV ownership structure. As was discussed earlier, some non-ownership based factors may better represent these constructs than ownership structure. Third, the scope of the analysis was limited to Japanese JVs in East and Southeast Asia in manufacturing sectors. The generalizability of the results of our study therefore remains unknown. Finally, several measures used in the analysis may need further refinement. For example, the performance and survival measures used in the study may capture only part of the multidimensional aspects of JV performance. Future studies should examine whether the same results can be obtained by using different performance measures, such as a satisfaction measure. However, even with an imperfect performance measurement, significant differences in both the performance and survival likelihood were found among the four JV ownership structures.

Our analysis revealed that (i) Traditional IJVs provided the greatest opportunity to achieve superior performance, yet, apart from Trinational IJVs, had the greatest likelihood of termination; (ii) Intrafirm JVs provided the second highest opportunity to attain superior performance, and had a lower likelihood of termination than either Traditional or Trinational IJVs; (iii) Cross-national DJVs provided a lower opportunity, compared to Traditional IJVs and Intrafirm JVs, for attaining superior performance, yet had the lowest likelihood of termination; and (iv) Trinational IJVs provided the fewest opportunities for attaining superior performance and had the highest likelihood of termination.

These results suggest that local access and management complexity stemming from inter-partner cultural distance may have a significant impact on both the performance and survival of the JV. Our evidence suggests that a local access opportunity through local JV partners was the critical factor that improved performance of the JV; and cultural distance at both country and corporate levels was strongly related to the survival likelihood of the JV.

Figure 9.3 graphically illustrates the relationship between JV ownership structure, performance (percentage of the frequency counts classified in the "gain" category) and termination rates. As is shown in Figure 9.3, the choice of JV ownership structure may be made based on the trade-off between longer-term and shorter-term orientations for JV success. In general, an Intrafirm JV and a Cross-national DJV represent longer-term solutions (i.e., lower termination rate with moderate-to-high performance) for attaining JV success, and a Traditional IJV as a varying solution (i.e., high termination rate yet with the highest performance). A Trinational IJV is usually the least desirable of the ownership-structure types, as it incurs the highest termination rate and achieves the lowest performance.

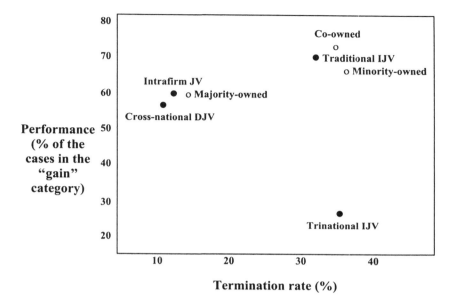

Figure 9.3 JV ownership structure, performance, and termination rate

The long-term focus strategy puts a relative emphasis on the long-term survival of the JV by reducing the level of managerial complexity; and the shorter-term focus strategy involves gaining quick access to local markets through local partners, and attaining higher performance in a relatively short term. It should be noted, however, that in our analysis there was not one JV ownership structure that attained both the highest performance and had the lowest termination rate. The question of which strategy is more successful, therefore, still remains unclear from the analysis, particularly when both performance measures are considered simultaneously.

Figure 9.3 also depicts both the performance and termination rate of the three conventional JV types, minority-, co-, and majority-owned JVs. Figure 9.3 suggests several implications with regard to the use of the conventional ownership classification in examining performance and survival of JVs. First, Majority-owned JVs had similar performance and survival consequences as Intrafirm JVs and Cross-national DJVs. Second, Co- and Minority-owned JVs had similar performance and survival consequences to Traditional IJVs. Finally, none of the three conventional JV types had the performance and survival consequences similar to Trinational IJVs. In other words, the conventional ownership measure cannot fully capture the performance and survival implications of JVs formed with a third-country based firm.   These results generally suggest that nationality of JV ownership does matter in predicting both the performance and survival likelihood of JVs.

CONCLUSION

In sum, this study provides new evidence concerning JV ownership structures. Specifically, the study demonstrates that JVs are not homogenous organizational forms. As our sample shows, the conventionally assumed form of JV – a JV formed between one foreign and one local firm – is not the most common form of shared ownership mode of foreign subsidiaries. Actual IJVs have complex ownership structures in terms of the number of JV partners, their equity affiliation and their nationality. The four identified JV ownership structures differed in their incidence and performance and survival likelihood.

NOTES

1. We define the nationality of the firm in terms of the country of origin, not the location, of the firm.   We used this definition because (i) home-country effects of foreign firms tend to persist for long periods of time due to the fact that the founding conditions and the basis for competitive advantages of the parent firms strongly reflect the home-country conditions (Stinchcombe, 1965; Porter, 1990); and (ii) recent studies have defined the nationality of a foreign parent in terms of the national origin of the firm, not in terms of its location of operation (Kogut and Singh, 1988; Erramilli, 1996).
2. Difficulties in defining the nationality of a partner occur when a parent firm is wholly or partly a subsidiary of another parent firm, or a third firm with a different nationality. To simplify and clarify partner nationality, the following criteria were established for defining partner nationality.   First, when the JV partner is an independent firm, partner nationality is defined as the national origin of the parent firm.   Second, when the JV partner is a subsidiary, partner nationality is defined as the national origin of the parent firm. Finally, when the JV partner is itself a JV, partner nationality is defined as the national origin of the firm that possesses the largest share of its equity.
3. The keiretsu membership was defined based on *Kigyou Keiretsu Souran* (Toyo Keizai, 1992b) in which the *keiretsu* membership was defined in terms of the origin of the owner of the firm, the affiliated main-banks, and the conventional buyer-supplier links. We assume that firms in the same *keiretsu* group are affiliated because, as Burton and Saelens (1982) have identified, international JVs formed by Japanese firms often function as a part of a larger industrial group relationship, and many JVs are formed between firms within the same *keiretsu* group.   In this study, we focused on both horizontal and vertical keiretsu groups. Horizontal keiretsu groups include Mitsubishi, Sumitomo, Mitsui, and Fuyo.   Vertical keiretsu groups include the buyer-supplier alliances in major industrial company groups such as Toyota, Nissan, Matsushita, Hitachi, and so forth.   It is assumed that firms within the same keiretsu group are better informed, share similar organizational cultures, and exchange both tangible and intangible resources, regardless of the size of cross-ownership.
4. Note that the definition of JV ownership structure is based on *a home-country based firm perspective* (or a Japanese parent firm perspective).   Therefore, when JV partners are classified as affiliated, their nationality is considered home-country.   For this reason,

Intrafirm JVs are considered to be formed by parent firms which are both home-country (Japan) based.

5. An Intrafirm JV can be viewed as either a wholly owned subsidiary or a JV. For example, if a JV is defined in terms of whether equity is shared, an Intrafirm JV can be defined as a JV. However, if a JV is defined in terms of whether equity is shared by *independent firms* that have an origin different from that of the owner, Intrafirm JVs are defined as wholly owned subsidiaries. In this study, we use the first definition.

6. Although the 20 percent criterion is suggested by the traditional accounting rules, some studies have used different criteria. For example, some studies have used 5 percent as a cut-off point to differentiate between JVs and wholly owned subsidiaries (e.g., Franko, 1971; Stopford and Wells, 1972; Anderson and Gatignon, 1986; Beamish, 1988; Gomes-Casseres, 1989; Hennart, 1991a; and Chowdhury, 1992).

7. While survival (or termination) rate has been frequently used in previous studies, no consistently used measure exists. First, the scope of measurement differs among studies. For example, in some studies, JV survival has been measured in terms of "instability" – changes in the division of ownership between partners (Blodgett, 1992; Franko, 1971). In most studies, JV survival has been measured by the ratio of the number of terminated JVs relative to that of surviving JVs (Curhan, Davidson and Suri, 1977; Davidson and McFetridge, 1984; Gomes-Casseres, 1987; Kogut 1988b, 1989). We adopted the latter operational definition of JV termination.

8. To confirm these results, we conducted the same analysis using the dataset as of 1988. The 1988 dataset included 321 cases with performance information. The result suggested that the number of JVs classified into the "gain" category was highest in Traditional IJVs, followed by Intrafirm JVs and Cross-national DJVs, and lowest in Trinational IJVs. This order is consistent with that provided in Table 9.3.

ACKNOWLEDGEMENTS

The authors wish to thank Andrew Delios for his comments on an earlier version of this paper. The comments of anonymous referees are gratefully appreciated. The financial supports of the Social Sciences and Humanities Research Council of Canada and the Chinese University of Hong Kong are gratefully acknowledged.

10. Local knowledge transfer and performance: Implications for alliance formation in Asia

Shige Makino and Andrew Delios

Foreign firms in host country environments frequently face location-based disadvantages. This study proposes three means (channels) of overcoming local knowledge disadvantages. Based on a sample of 558 Japanese joint ventures (JVs) located in Southeast and East Asia, we find that partnering with local firms (the first channel) can be a primary strategy for accessing local knowledge and improving JV performance. JV experience in the host country (the second channel) also mitigates local knowledge disadvantages and leads to increased JV performance. The third channel, the foreign parent's host country experience, leads to increased performance in the absence of a local partner. However, when a JV is formed with a local partner, increased parent experience in the host country leads to decreased performance suggesting that the need for a local partner declines as parent experience in a host country increases.

INTRODUCTION

Foreign direct investment (FDI) has often been conceptualized as a firm's response to advantages. Firms that possess advantages invest abroad (Caves, 1971; Hymer, 1976); countries that have an advantageous resource endowment and a favorable geographical position are sites of inbound FDI (Dunning, 1977); and where there is market failure in the trade of a firm's proprietary knowledge, advantages are conferred to the firm that internalizes the transfer of this knowledge (Buckley and Casson, 1976; Rugman, 1981; Hennart, 1982). The Eclectic Paradigm (Dunning, 1993) melds these views, and argues that location and internalization advantages, as well as ownership advantages shape multinational enterprises' (MNE) actions and the patterns of FDI. As noted by Kogut and Zander (1993), since Hymer's (1976) thesis was received, the central issue in FDI has been this notion of advantages, or, more precisely, ownership advantages. The quintessence of the investing firm's advantage is the knowledge it transfers to the host country. Conceptualized as such, knowledge is an intangible asset (one type of ownership advantage in Eclectic Theory), and comprises the organization of work, non-codifiable knowledge, marketing and finance know-how, and product innovations; that is, the resource structure of the firm (Dunning, 1988a, 1993).

However simplistically presented, inside this framework of advantages – whether the advantages are tangible or intangible, or firm or location specific – resides a deficiency. Principally, this lacuna results from the singular focus on advantages. The notion of advantages is credited to Hymer (1976), but within his work resides a second notion, that of the location-based disadvantages faced by foreign firms in the host country environment. He writes:

National firms have the general advantage of better information about their country: its economy, its language, its law, and its politics. To a foreigner the cost of acquiring this information may be considerable. But note that it is a fixed cost; once incurred by establishing a foreign operation, it need not be incurred again. (p. 34)

In sum, a firm which invests abroad has an ownership advantage which is transferred across borders but as a consequence of investing abroad, the firm has the disadvantage of being foreign (Hymer, 1976). This disadvantage stems from a lack of local knowledge of social, political and economic conditions in the host country (Beamish, 1984). Thus a stock of local knowledge is required to mitigate such disadvantages. It is our thesis that overcoming such disadvantages, in essence becoming less foreign, will improve international joint venture (JV) performance. In sum:

(Advantages of foreign parent) - (Disadvantages of competing in a foreign environment) $\prod$ JV performance

In examining this thesis, first we review internationalization theory and elaborate on the concept of location-based disadvantages. Next we develop and test three sets of hypotheses which posit the existence of three means (channels) of local knowledge acquisition. We follow this with a discussion of the implications and the limitations of our approach.

THEORETICAL BACKGROUND AND HYPOTHESIS DEVELOPMENT

Location-Based Disadvantages

The related notions of location-based disadvantages and local knowledge acquisition are fundaments of internationalization theory. This theory of incremental international expansion views FDI motives as being related to the accumulation of international experience and the concomitant reduction in location-based disadvantages (e.g., Johanson and Vahlne, 1977; Davidson, 1980a; Johanson and Mattson, 1987). The core idea in this research stream is that foreign firms increase their resource commitments to investments abroad as they accumulate local experience. Many previous empirical studies support this claim. The level of a foreign firm's pool of local knowledge and operational experience has been found to have had a positive influence on the level of resource commitment in FDI (Johanson and Vahlne, 1977; Davidson, 1980a; Erramilli and Rao, 1990; Erramilli, 1991; Li, 1994).

In internationalization theory, local knowledge is usually defined in terms of *general* knowledge. Local knowledge comprises information and know-how about the local economy, politics, culture and business customs of a region; information on local demands and tastes; as well as information on how to access the local labor force, distribution channels, infrastructure, raw materials and other factors required for the conduct of business in a region. Since such general knowledge usually takes the form of location-based intangible assets, its acquisition results from local operating experience. However, the literature generally ignores the fact that some forms of local knowledge or resources are difficult to internalize by themselves through the mere accumulation of experience in a host country. This difficulty arises because some forms of local knowledge or resources are *specific* to particular local firms as well. Examples of such knowledge are a local firm's skills and capabilities to negotiate with the local government; its access to and skills in negotiating with the local elite; its ability to manage the local labor force and unions; and its competence with respect to local market access, product quality, branding, market reputation, and so forth. These forms of local knowledge and skills are *both* location- and firm-specific in nature (Rugman and Verbeke, 1992) and, due to the latter characteristic of this knowledge (i.e., firm-specificity), it may not be readily acquired through the accumulation of experience nor the hiring of local managers alone.

Recently, some researchers have focused on the role of JVs as a means of local knowledge acquisition (e.g., Beamish, 1984, 1988). These researchers have implicitly assumed that some forms of required local knowledge can be accumulated neither through market transactions nor through experience.

Knowledge of this sort is more readily transferable through JVs or other non-equity forms of alliances with local firms than through experience. For example, Beamish (1984, 1988) found that the need for a local firm was a significant factor influencing JV performance. This need became more critical when MNEs operated in less developed countries rather than in developed countries (Beamish, 1985). Gomes-Casseres' (1989, 1990) study of US-owned foreign subsidiaries revealed that access to information about the local environment was the most important criterion for US firms forming JVs with local firms. Inkpen (1992) examined US-Japanese auto-parts JVs in North America and concluded that many were formed because of complementary needs between American and Japanese firms. North American firms desired technical and manufacturing knowledge and Japanese firms required local knowledge. Finally, Makino (1995) in interviews with executives of Japanese firms, each with several alliances in Southeast Asia, found that the primary motive for alliance formation with local firms was to access local knowledge.

While many previous studies have examined firm experience and JV formation as a means of local knowledge acquisition, the relationship between these constructs remains unclear. Generally, when local knowledge acquisition has been examined, it has been done tangentially under the heading of the experience effect. The accumulation of operational experience in a host country, considered to be the means of local knowledge acquisition, has been postulated to free the firm from the need for a local partner, allowing for higher control modes. However, the amount of experience has an inconclusive effect on control with support being found for positive (Johanson and Vahlne, 1977; Davidson, 1980a; Gatignon and Anderson, 1988), neutral (Sharma and Johanson, 1987; Kogut and Singh, 1988) and negative (Stopford and Wells, 1972; Daniels, Ogram, and Radebaugh, 1976, Davidson and McFetridge, 1985) effects of experience on the amount of desired control. Erramilli (1991) provides a good review of these studies in an empirical study which identifies a non-linear (U-shaped) relationship between experience and control. However, rather than examining the relationship between experience and control, we differentiate between JV and parent experience and use JV performance, not the extent of equity ownership, as our dependent variable.

Local Knowledge Acquisition Channels

The theoretical explanation for the relationship between knowledge acquisition and JV performance centers on the question of which channel(s) (means) – within or between firms – provides for the most efficient acquisition of knowledge (Kogut and Zander, 1992, 1993). Notwithstanding the debate about their complex conceptualization of the firm (Kogut and Zander, 1995; Love, 1995; McFetridge, 1995), it is compelling to view MNEs as social communities that create and internally disseminate knowledge. While Kogut and Zander (1993) empirically tested the transference of technological knowledge, we argue that the same underlying characteristic (intangibility) defines local knowledge. As a consequence, the internal development of local knowledge occurs via the incremental accumulation of experience (Kogut and Zander, 1993). As identified in Chang (1995), firms can learn from experience or they can learn from other firms. We expand this definition to include learning from other bodies with strong connections to the same firm (i.e., the parents of a JV). Thus, the acquisition of local knowledge can occur by three distinct local knowledge acquisition channels. A JV can acquire local knowledge: (1) by forming a JV with a local firm; (2) by transference from the foreign parent's stock of past host country experience; or (3) by the accumulation of operational experience in the host country.

Foreign parent's host country experience to the joint venture

The first channel is a within-firm transfer of local knowledge from the foreign parent to the JV. In this knowledge acquisition channel, both the provider (the foreign parent)[1] and the receiver (the JV) of local knowledge are effectively the same firm. Internalization theory suggests that a firm has an incentive to internalize markets for its intangible assets (Caves, 1971; Magee, 1977; Rugman, 1981; Hennart, 1982). Such intangible assets, once internalized, have the characteristics of a public good. The asset, in this case local knowledge, can be internally transferred at zero marginal cost to the firm. Underutilized assets, such as knowledge about the conditions in a particular host country, can be applied to new businesses, such as an entry to a foreign market, exploiting the public goods nature of this knowledge (Chang, 1995). An available stock of local knowledge, accumulated in the parent's experience in the host country, is hypothesized to increase JV performance.

Hypothesis 1. The length of the foreign parent's past host country experience is positively associated with the performance of its joint ventures.

JV's host country experience to the joint venture

The second channel is also a within-firm acquisition of knowledge where local knowledge is accumulated by a JV in a learning-by-doing process. The resource-based perspective postulates that a firm's competitive advantage depends on how quickly and how efficiently a firm can develop or acquire inimitable knowledge and skills which convey advantage to the firm (e.g. Wernerfelt, 1984; Dierickx and Cool, 1989). A JV's local knowledge can be a source of advantage, when it is uniquely developed or accumulated through its learning-by-doing process of operating in the host country.

Hypothesis 2. The length of a joint venture's host country experience is positively associated with its performance.

Local partner to the joint venture
The third channel is a between-firms channel in which local knowledge is transferred from a local JV partner to the JV. Local firms are generally more familiar with local market conditions such as government policies, the local economy and the culture of the region. As such, they are immediate sources of local knowledge which can complement the investing firm's ownership advantages. Some types of local knowledge may be imperfectly transferable in the market interface between firms. When local knowledge is specific to local firms; it can be accessed more efficiently when it is shared by formation of a JV between foreign and local firms (Makino, 1995) and its acquisition will lead to higher JV performance.

Hypothesis 3a. In general, a joint venture formed with one or more local firms attains superior performance compared to other forms of joint ventures.

However, the efficacy of the local partner channel may be conditional on levels of other indicators of local knowledge acquisition (parent and JV experience). For example, when a foreign firm has previous operational experience in a local country, a JV with a local partner may not be required to obtain local knowledge. Similarly, a foreign firm which has established a JV with a local partner may view its JV partner as redundant as it accumulates local knowledge (Hamel, 1991). Hence, under conditions in which the JV exhibits evidence of substantive local knowledge acquisition (high levels of JV or parent experience), the transaction costs stemming from partner opportunism (e.g., Hennart, 1988) and the operational difficulties inherent in JVs (Killing, 1983) begin to outweigh the local knowledge benefits of the local partner. In effect, the foreign parent's or JV's host country experience makes the local partner's local knowledge contribution redundant. Hypotheses 3b and 3c incorporate this conditionality.

Hypothesis 3b. As the foreign parent's host country experience increases, the relative performance benefit of having a local joint venture partner decreases.

Hypothesis 3c. As the joint venture's host country experience increases, the relative performance benefit of having a local joint venture partner decreases.

RESEARCH DESIGN

Scope of Study

The sample comprises Japanese manufacturing JVs established in eight countries of Southeast and East Asia.[2] The use of subsidiary level data is somewhat unique as most studies have utilized country or industry level analyses (Chang, 1995). The sample is restricted to manufacturing JVs in Southeast and East Asia to control for the potential confounding effects of inter-industry and inter-country differences on the performance of each firm. Performance distributions across country and industry are provided in Table .10.1. A chi-square analysis revealed no significant performance differences across industries. Although the Pearson χ^2 statistic was significant in the country grouping, it should be noted that the dispersion around the sample's distribution was small. On average 32 percent of all JVs reported low performance. No individual country exceeded 45 percent in counting low performers, and the minimum low performer count was 15 percent. Despite the significance of the chi-square statistic, the range is small with little between country variation in performance.

The second restriction concerns the mode of entry. The sample comprises JVs established between a foreign firm and local partners, third country partners, or home country partners. The entry mode is restricted to JVs to isolate the contribution that local partners make in the knowledge acquisition process. If the modality of investment was permitted to differ, variation in the dependent variable may arise because of entry mode differences. Several studies (e.g. Li and Guisinger, 1991; Woodcock, Beamish and Makino, 1994; Nitsch, Beamish and Makino, 1996), have demonstrated that performance differs systematically by entry mode.[3]

Sample

The data used in this study are a subset of the Toyo Keizai (1992a) dataset. This information has been published annually since 1970. Although it has not been used extensively by researchers, perhaps because it is published in Japanese, the Toyo Keizai survey is enjoying increasing acceptance among academic researchers.[4] The information in the survey is compiled from publicly available information and a survey of the top Japanese manager of

Table 10.1 Performance distributions by country and industry

Country	Low performance	High performance	Industry	Low performance	High performance
Taiwan	36 (29%)	86 (71%)	Foods	6 (29%)	15 (71%)
Hong Kong	4 (15%)	22 (85%)	Textiles	10 (26%)	29 (74%)
Thailand	44 (40%)	66 (60%)	Apparel	2 (67%)	1 (33%)
Singapore	12 (21%)	45 (79%)	Lumber and wood products	0 (0%)	1 (100%)
Malaysia	34 (45%)	42 (55%)	Furniture	1 (14%)	6 (86%)
Philippines	13 (45%)	16 (55%)	Paper	1 (25%)	3 (75%)
Indonesia	12 (22%)	42 (78%)	Printing and publishing	1 (100%)	0 (0%)
Korea	26 (31%)	58 (69%)	Chemicals	32 (36%)	58 (64%)
All Countries	**181 (32%)**	**377 (68%)**	Petroleum	3 (100%)	0 (0%)

Industry	Low performance	High performance
Rubber and plastics	16 (47%)	18 (53%)
Stone, clay, and glass	3 (19%)	13 (81%)
Primary metals	7 (32%)	15 (68%)
Fabricated metals	15 (50%)	15 (50%)
Industrial machinery	19 (36%)	34 (64%)
Electronics	38 (30%)	89 (70%)
Transportation equipment	18 (24%)	58 (76%)
Instruments	4 (25%)	12 (75%)
Miscellaneous manufacturing	5 (33%)	10 (67%)
All industries	**181 (32%)**	**377 (68%)**

Note: The first number in a cell is a count, the second is the row percentage.

each foreign subsidiary during 1991 (Toyo Keizai, 1992a).[5] Supplementary parent company information was collected from *Kaisha Shikiho* (Japanese Company Handbook) (Toyo Keizai, 1991).

Variables

Dependent variable
The dependent variable is a dichotomous variable constructed from the JV's top Japanese manager's categorical assessment of its financial performance.[6] While categorical performance measures have limitations, there are several arguments in support of this type of measure. First, many JVs do not report financial performance. Second, where available, financial measures of performance are not directly comparable across industries and countries with different accounting systems and customs (Brown, Soybel and Stickney, 1994). Because the survey respondent is the top Japanese manager in each JV, we expect that each manager reports JV performance from a similar reference point. Finally, managers' perceptions of performance have been demonstrated to be correlated with objective financial measures (e.g., Geringer and Hebert, 1991).

Independent variables
The independent variables used in this study are: LOCAL – a dummy variable indicating the existence of a *local* JV partner; the foreign parent's past local country experience measured in years (PARENT) and the JV's operational experience (i.e., JV experience) in the local country measured in years (JV-EXP). As LOCAL, PARENT and JV-EXP might have different slopes when they interact in concert with each other, four interaction variables are defined to test for this complementary aspect of knowledge acquisition channels. LOCAL_PAR is the interaction between LOCAL and PARENT. PAR_JV and LOCAL_JV similarly represent the two other two-way interactions. LOCAL_JV_PA is the three way interaction between these terms.

Control variables
A country-level variable (RESTRICT) derived from the Benchmark Surveys conducted by the US Department of Commerce in 1982 controls for national variations in legal restrictions about foreign equity ownership (Gomes-Casseres, 1990). The other control variables are firm level and were derived from Toyo Keizai and the Japanese Company Handbook. EXPORT is the ratio of the foreign parent's export sales to total sales. R_&_D refers to the foreign parent's R&D expenditure as a percentage of total sales in 1991. SALES is the foreign parent's total sales in 1991. R&D expenditure and

foreign parent size have frequently been used as proxies for a parent firm's ownership advantages (see Dunning (1993) and Caves (1996)). EQUITY is the JV's 1991 equity capital reported in millions of US dollars and is used to control for variations in JV size. The final two variables concern employment practices. J_RATIO is the ratio of Japanese expatriate managers to total employees for each JV (referred to as the intensity of Japanese employment). The variable JRA_PAR is the interaction between parent firm experience and intensity of Japanese employment.[7] Descriptive statistics and inter-item correlations are found in Table 10.2.[8]

DATA ANALYSIS

Performance and Local Knowledge Acquisition Channels

We first test for the presence of local knowledge acquisition channels by examining the primary relationships between the presence or level of each channel and JV performance. Table 10.3 reports the results of the three *t*-tests of means.[9] The first relationship examined is that between the presence of a local partner and JV performance. The performance of local partner JVs is significantly greater than that of JVs formed with home country or third country partners. Similarly, the performance of JVs with greater than the mean number of years of experience (12 years) is much greater than that of JVs with less than the mean. However, parent experience exhibits a result counter to what was predicted in Hypothesis 1. The performance of JVs formed when the parent had less than the mean number of years of experience in the host country (seven years) is significantly greater than the performance of JVs formed when the parent had more experience. But as the other two channels vary across levels of parent experience, it is premature to conclude that parent experience has an overall negative influence on JV performance. The larger negative effect of parent experience on performance in local partner JVs suggests a more complex relationship. These relationships are examined in a multivariate model.

The Model

The dependent variable in this analysis is a dichotomous variable constructed from the three point performance measure. With a binary dependent variable, a logistic regression model is utilized to estimate the effects of the independent variables.[10] The model examines the effect of local knowledge acquisition channels and the indicated interactions on the likelihood of high performance as opposed to low performance. It models the probability of

Table 10.2 Descriptive statistics and correlations

Variables	Model term	Means	s.d.	1	2	3	4	5	6	7	8	9	10	11	12
1. Local partner dummy variable	LOCAL	0.72	0.44	1											
2. Parent's host country experience (years)	PARENT	6.58	7.58	-.08*	1										
3. JV's host country experience (years)	JV-EXP	12.3	7.87	.09*	-.48*	1									
4. Local partner-parent interaction	LOCAL_PAR	4.6	6.99	.41*	.73*	-.33*	1								
5. Parent-JV interaction	PAR_JV	51.25	60.89	-.02	.64*	.02	.51*	1							
6. Local partner-JV interaction	LOCAL_JV	9.42	8.9	.64*	-.35*	.73*	-.06*	-.01	1						
7. Local ownership restriction	RESTRICT	0.13	0.09	.22*	.11*	-.06	.15*	.12*	.11*	1					

Variables	Model term	Means	s.d.	1	2	3	4	5	6	7	8	9	10	11	12
8. Parent firm R&D rate (percentage)	R_&_D	3.15	2.85	.10	.09*	.15	.09*	.13*	.18	.07	1				
9. Parent firm sales ($)	SALES	588.2	2072.45	-.01	.18	.01*	.13	.20*	.01*	.03	.23*	1			
10. Subsidiary capitalization ($)	EQUITY	10.61	105.89	.01	.11	-.03	.12	.12	.03	.07	.02	.17	1		
11. Japanese / total employment	J_RATIO	0.03	0.08	-.08*	.03	-.20	.02	-.10*	-.18*	.10*	-.04	-.05	-.04	1	
12. Employment-parent interaction	JRA_PAR	0.21	0.66	-.03	.39*	-.24*	.29*	.12*	-.17*	-.04	.04	.01	-.01	.44*	1
13. Export intensity of parent (percentage)	EXPORT	17.01	17.89	-.29*	.10	.06*	.00	.12*	-.17*	.02	.09	.25*	-.02	-.02	-.01

Note: * indicates correlation significant at 0.05 level.

Table 10.3 Local knowledge acquisition channels and performance

Local partner	Mean performance	High performance (%)
Local partner	2.51*	67
No local partner	2.35	57
JV's host country experience	Mean performance	High performance (%)
JV experience > 12 years	2.78*	83
JV experience ≤ 12 years	2.26	52
Parent's host country experience	Mean performance	High performance (%)
Parent experience > 7 years	2.36*	61
Parent experience ≤ 7 years	2.58	68
Local partner JVs only		
Parent experience > 7 years	2.34*	58
Parent experience ≤ 7 years	2.62	74

Notes:
1. * difference between performance in two categories significant at 0.05 level (*t*-test).
2. Mean performance equals average performance of all joint ventures in category.
3. High performance equals the percent of high performers in category.
4. The performance trend in Parent Experience is insensitive to the seven-year breakpoint.

high performance to that of low performance as a function of the main effects and the interaction terms. The basic equation used to estimate the three binomial logistic regression analyses is:

$$\text{Probability of high performance} = 1/(1 + \exp^{(-y)}):$$

where

$$Y = \beta_0 + \beta_1 X_1 + \beta_2 X_2 + \beta_3 X_3 + \ldots + \beta_n X_n + \varepsilon . \qquad (10.1)$$

$X_1, X_2, \ldots X_n$ are the independent and control variables and $\beta_1, \beta_2, \ldots \beta_n$ are the corresponding coefficients. β_0 is the intercept or constant and ε is a disturbance term. The parameters are estimated using the logistic regression procedure of the SPSS 6.1.3 statistical package. The predictive ability of the model can be assessed by comparison of the estimated model's classification rate to the random classification rate. Large χ^2 values and small p values indicate statistical significance. A positive sign for a regression coefficient indicates that the variable increases the likelihood of higher performance, while a negative sign indicates an increase in the likelihood of lower performance. Once the logistic regression equation is estimated, expected probabilities of high performance can be computed (Hosmer and Lemeshow 1987).

Model Estimation and Fit

Model 1 – full model

Initial runs indicated that the interaction term LOCAL_JV_PA was not significant. Therefore this term was dropped and the full model was re-estimated. In the re-estimated model, two outliers were identified. These two cases had noticeably larger influence statistics (Cook's D) and leverage when compared to other observations. The two outliers were dropped and the model was estimated a third time.[11] Table 10.4 reports that this re-estimated model is statistically significant (likelihood ratio $\chi^2_{(13)}$=90.258, p<0.0001), which suggests that the variables as a group discriminate well between high and low performing firms. Furthermore, the model correctly classifies 74 percent of the JVs which represents an improvement (18 percent fewer errors) relative to the classification based on chance alone. The model seems to have reasonable explanatory power and predictive abilities. A comparison of the full model with the main effects model reveals that the interaction terms help explain a substantial amount of variation in high and low performing firms (incremental $\chi^2_{(3)}$=19.167, p=0.0002). This stresses the important role that these interaction terms have on firm performance.

Model 2 – no local partner

The interaction terms LOCAL_JV and LOCAL_PAR were removed from this model as was the term LOCAL (which is used to define the two sub-samples). Table 10.3 reports that this re-estimated model is statistically significant ($\chi^2_{(10)}$=45.112, p<0.0001). The model correctly classifies performance in 77 percent of the JVs.

Model 3 – local partner

As in Model 2, LOCAL, LOCAL_JV and LOCAL_PAR were removed. Model 3 is significant ($\chi^2_{(10)}$=62.656, p<0.0001) and correctly classifies 76 percent of the cases.

HYPOTHESIS TESTING

Hypotheses 1, 2 and 3a state that a positive relationship is expected between the utilization of each knowledge acquisition channel and performance. A positively signed coefficient on the local partner, parent experience or JV

Table 10.4 Asia sample logistic regression results

Variables	Model term	Model 1 All JVs	Model 2 No local partner	Model 3 Local partner
1. Local partner dummy variable	LOCAL	1.5866*** (7.5064)		-.1315*** (15.1312)
2. Parent's host country experience	PARENT	-.0225 (0.4479)	.0052 (0.0127)	.0266 (1.7333)
3. JV's host country experience	JV-EXP	.0971*** (8.0229)	.1171*** (8.2254)	
4. Local partner-parent interaction	LOCAL_PAR	-.0997*** (8.7628)		
5. Parent-JV interaction	PAR_JV	.0088*** (9.9406)	.0063 (1.1681)	.0093*** (7.9888)
6. Local partner-JV interaction	LOCAL_JV	-.0708* (3.7232)		
7. Local ownership restriction	RESTRICT	-2.1134* (2.9004)	-7.2320*** (9.6890)	.0126 (0.0001)
8. Foreign parent firm R&D rate	R_&_D	.0562 (1.5894)	.2095** (5.0145)	.0017 (0.0011)
9. Foreign parent firm sales	SALES	-.0004** (5.3998)	-.0002 (0.5644)	-.0006** (6.2569)
10. Subsidiary capitalization (US$ mil.)	EQUITY	.0204* (2.9428)	.0258 (1.0525)	.0179 (2.0348)

		Model 1	Model 2	Model 3
11. Japanese / total employment	J_RATIO	-4.8217**	-.9384	-6.4772**
		(4.3333)	(0.0616)	(5.376)
12. Employment-parent interaction	JRA_PAR	.4622**	.2382	.5909*
		(4.1742)	(0.4929)	(4.5366)
13. Export intensity of parent	EXPORT	.0098	-.0006	.0242**
		(2.0545)	(0.0025)	(5.6074)
14. Constant		-.7044	-.8089	.7057*
		(1.7077)	(1.4837)	(2.8743)

Model Indices	Model 1	Model 2	Model 3
Pearson's χ^2	90.258	45.112	62.656
Significance	P < 0.0000	p < 0.0000	p < 0.0000
Random Model Classification Rate	56%	55%	57%
Overall Classification Rate	74%	77%	76%
Number of Cases	556	156	400

Notes:
1. *t*-statistics in parentheses
   * significant at the .10 level, two-tailed test
   ** significant at the .05 level, two-tailed test
   *** significant at the .01 level, two-tailed test
2. A random model's classification rate is defined as: $\alpha2 + (1 - \alpha)^2$, where α is the proportion of higher performing JVs in the sample. A model classifies well when the overall classification rate is higher than that obtained by chance.
3. Two cases were eliminated in initial runs because of high influence statistics.

experience terms would indicate support for the respective hypothesis, while a negatively signed coefficient would not be supportive. The interaction terms examine Hypotheses 3b and 3c. Where the coefficient is negatively signed on the local partner-parent experience or local partner-JV experience interaction terms, support is found for the respective hypothesis.

In Model 1, support is found for Hypotheses 2 and 3a. The positive sign on the local partner coefficient indicates that a local JV partner has a positive impact on performance; similarly, as the years of JV operational experience increase, so does performance. The interaction terms (LOCAL_PAR and LOCAL_JV) are significant and signed in the hypothesized direction indicating support for Hypotheses 3b and 3c. As in Table 10.3, the parent experience variable is negatively signed; however, it is not significant. For the control variables local ownership restrictions had a negative influence on firm performance. The size of the JV (its equity base) and the size of the parent (its sales) had positive effects on performance. The relative intensity of Japanese expatriate employment was negatively associated with JV performance, although this effect was moderated somewhat as parent firm experience increased (a positive sign on the employment-parent interaction term). All other control variables were not significant.

The interactions in this model temper the effect of parent and JV experience and merit further discussion. To gain additional insights into these interactions, expected probabilities must be computed for the terms affected by the interaction. Estimated probabilities are computed in several steps. First, an equation constant is calculated for all terms not involved in the interaction. Second, log-odds are determined for different levels of the interaction term. Third, log-odds are converted to expected probabilities. For the interaction between the presence of a local JV partner and JV experience:

$$\textit{equation constant} = b_0 + b_2(\textit{PARENT}) + b_4(\textit{LOCAL\_PAR}) + b_7(\textit{RESTRICT}) + \\ b_8(R\_\&\_D) + b_9(\textit{SALES}) + b_{10}(\textit{EQUITY}) + b_{11}(J\_\textit{RATIO}) \\ + b_{12}(\textit{JRA\_PAR}) + b_{13}(\textit{EXPORT}). \qquad (10.2)$$

All variables in this equation are continuous, therefore, in computing the equation constant, the value entered for each variable is its mean. B values are supplied in the regression output. The sum of these variables is the equation constant. The value of the log(odds: high / low performance) for the local partner-JV experience interaction is determined by inserting the LOCAL, JV-EXP, PAR_JV and LOCAL_JV terms into the regression equation at different levels of these variables. Thus,

$$Y \{log \ (odds: \ high/low \ performance)\} =$$
$$equation \ constant + b_1(LOCAL) +$$
$$b_2(JV\text{-}EXP) + b_4(PAR\_JV) + b_6(LOCAL\_JV) \qquad (10.3)$$

where LOCAL equals zero (no local partner) the regression equation is reduced to the equation constant and the JV-EXP and PAR_JV terms. Where LOCAL equals one, the regression equation includes the four variables and the equation constant. Values of Y are calculated for JV experience at two year intervals for the full range of the variable. These log-odds are converted to odds (Ω) by exponentiating the log-odds term. The odds ratio is converted to a probability using the formula, probability equals $\Omega(\Omega+1)$.

Figure 10.1 depicts the foreign parent experience-local partner interaction in graphical format. In general, JVs established with a local partner have a higher expected probability of high performance than those established with a non-local partner. This effect is most pronounced when the parent experience in a region is very low. However, as parent experience in a region increases, the utility of having a local partner decreases. If parent experience exceeds ten years, there may be disadvantages in partnering with a local firm. Thus, the negative relationship between parent experience and performance identified in Table 10.3 is contingent upon the levels of JV experience and the presence of a local partner. When there is no local partner and JV experience is constant, greater parent experience leads to higher performance. However, when there is a local partner, greater parent experience does not have a positive effect on performance.

JV experience has a similar relationship with local partners and JV performance (see Figure 10.2). New JVs benefit most from the presence of a local partner. Where a local partner is present in a new JV, the expected probability of high performance is much greater (47 percent versus 30 percent). However, as JV experience increases, the utility of partnering with local firms decreases. Where JV experience exceeds ten years, JVs formed with local partners are not expected to perform as well as those formed without. The interaction between parent experience and JV experience is less dramatic and conceptually less clear (i.e., parent experience cannot be low where JV experience is high). However, the tendency in this interaction supports Hypothesis 1. JVs that have a parent with more experience in the host country are expected to perform better than those with a parent with little experience.

In Japanese JVs in Southeast and East Asia, the effect of local knowledge channels on performance is complicated. The presence of a local JV partner benefits performance especially in the early stages of a new JV when parent experience in the host country is low. However, over time as the Japanese parent's experience increases in the host country and as the JV matures, the positive impact of having a local partner on JV performance declines to the point where the presence of a local partner may be detrimental to the performance of the JV. In cases where parent experience in a region is high (more than 10 years) and a new JV is being established, it may not be beneficial to the parent to establish a JV with a local partner. These observations support the conditionality aspect of Hypothesis 3: the impact of a local partner on JV performance is dependent upon the level of parent and JV experience.[12]

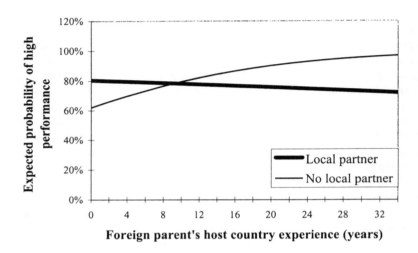

Figure 10.1 Interaction between foreign parent experience and a local partner

To further examine the effect of having a local partner, the full model (Model 1) was divided into two separate models. Model 2 examines JVs which did not have a local partner. JV experience is positively and significantly associated with performance in this model. The coefficient on parent experience, though not statistically significant, is positively signed unlike in the full sample and in Model 3. Interestingly, the host country restriction term is negatively associated with performance while the parent's R&D rate is positively associated with performance. In the absence of a local partner, technical or ownership advantages and the degree of host country restrictions become important factors impacting performance.

Model 3 examines JVs that had a local partner. Consistent with the term in Model 1, parent experience is significantly negatively associated with performance in this local partner model. The propensity of the foreign parent to export is positively related to performance while the intensity of Japanese employment to total employment is negatively related to performance. The intensity of Japanese employment interacts with parent experience such that as parent firm experience increases, the negative impact of Japanese employment decreases.

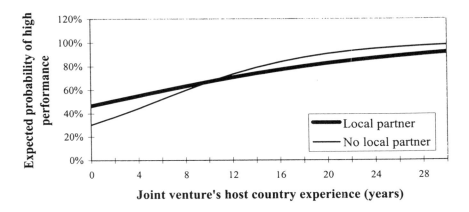

Figure 10.2 Interaction between JV experience and a local partner

DISCUSSION AND CONCLUSION

This study examined the relationship between knowledge acquisition channels and performance. Each knowledge acquisition channel was found to influence performance. However, the influence of each channel is complementary. The strong relationship between the presence of a local JV partner and higher performance suggests that a JV formed with a local firm can be a primary strategy over JVs formed with non-local partners and perhaps over a wholly-owned subsidiary when a foreign firm invests in unfamiliar markets. However, MNEs with experience in countries of Southeast and East Asia may not need a local partner as parent experience was found to have a significant negative effect on performance in the presence of a local JV partner. An interesting result is the decline in performance that accompanies increasing parent experience in JVs established with a local partner. The redundancy of the local partner's contribution to the JV may impede the performance of the JV rather than benefit the JV as in the case where parent experience is low. Hence, as the foreign partner learns about local market conditions, it may seek a greater role in the JV which can lead to conflict in JV control issues and to lower performance (see Inkpen and Beamish (1997)).[13] JV experience was consistently related to higher performance and this experience could also be an effective replacement for the local knowledge of a local partner.

A JV's own experience is a primary factor influencing its performance. This result is consistent with Chang (1995) who concluded that as Japanese firms operate and learn in foreign environments, they build new capabilities and thereby overcome the disadvantages inherent in being foreign. The learning in Chang (1995) was thought to occur either in a learning by doing process, or in a process of accessing or transferring knowledge from other firms. The results of this study confirm this suspicion and develop the notion of learning from other firms. Where parent and JV experience in a host country are absent, the probability of a JV's success is improved substantively through the utilization of a local partner.[14] However, the utility of a local firm as a means of gaining access to local knowledge decreased as JV and parent experience in the region increased. Thus, a local firm's host country knowledge and a parent firm's host country knowledge (its years of operational experience in that host country) are substitute (complementary) channels for the acquisition of local knowledge when the parent or JV has spent a considerable amount of time (10 years or more) in the host country. An interesting application of this result is to the knowledge-based view on FDI (Kogut and Zander, 1993).

Kogut and Zander (1993) suggest that FDI occurs when knowledge transfer is more efficient within a firm rather than between firms. This line of study is fascinating as it attempts to explain the existence of FDI without assuming opportunism and market failure. However, it cannot fully explain why an alliance would occur from the knowledge transfer perspective. The present study provides reasoning and evidence for the motivation to acquire a local partner. Firms are motivated to form JVs to ameliorate local knowledge deficiencies and complement their existing resource base with a stock of local knowledge. Only in the case in which the foreign firm has significant ownership advantages (Model 2) is it able to sustain high performance in the face of host country inexperience and local knowledge disadvantages. As suggested by Hymer (1976), where the original parent-derived ownership advantage is strong, the JV is able to survive and develop its own capabilities, which may include the acquisition of local knowledge.

In cases in which ownership advantages do not outweigh local knowledge disadvantages, it is possible that foreign firms can be inspired to invest abroad if they can overcome the disadvantage of being foreign. This forgotten half of Hymer's thesis was examined in our analysis. Our results suggest that when FDI takes the form of a JV with a local firm, the relative importance of ownership advantages on JV performance decreases. JV performance is a function of both ownership advantages and those advantages stemming from having local knowledge which is transferred to, or accumulated by, the JV. Thus, explaining the existence of FDI and its performance from one side of Hymer's thesis is not sufficient. To promote a more comprehensive theory of FDI, we examined the other side of Hymer's thesis.

An interesting corollary to the above findings relates expatriate staffing to ownership advantages and location-based disadvantages. In Model 1 and Model 3, the relative intensity of the use of expatriates was significantly negatively related to performance, while in Model 2 the relationship, though still negative, was less pronounced and not significant. Model 2 presents the situation in which a local partner was not used and the intensity of ownership advantages was related positively to performance. Where ownership advantages of the parent firm are greater, there must be a means of transferring intangible know-how to the JV. The deployment of expatriate managers is one means of transferring this firm-specific knowledge to the JV. Indeed, if the knowledge perspective of Kogut and Zander (1992) is adopted, it is necessary for firms to place personnel in the host country to transfer their intangible know-how to that JV.

This study has several limitations. While we discussed knowledge, we did not directly measure knowledge itself in the analysis, nor was its extent of acquisition determined. Knowledge and its acquisition were inferred from years of parent and JV experience and the presence or absence of a local partner. In the local partner channel we assumed that the local partner's knowledge about the host country was being accessed in the JV mode. However, previous literature suggests that JVs are formed with local partners for a variety of reasons (see Contractor and Lorange (1988)). These reasons can be classified into three categories of motives: (1) to gain access to or to acquire a partner's proprietary resources; (2) to achieve economies of scale and scope or to reduce risk; and (3) to respond to local government policies (Makino, 1995). Without an indication of the motive for JV formation, it is difficult to disentangle these motives.[15]

To an extent, the variables for JV size and for the level of host country restrictions control for the second and third motives. However, the first motive elicits the most concern. JVs with local partners can be established for a number of reasons aside from knowledge acquisition (e.g., to access distribution channels, brand names, or even technology). In most circumstances, one reason would be difficult to separate from another in a large sample methodology. However, the composition of our sample allows several generalities about motives to be addressed. The sample comprised Japanese manufacturing JVs in eight developing countries in Asia. The majority of these JVs were formed in the late 1970s and early 1980s (in

1992, the average JV age equaled 12 years) a time at which most Japanese MNEs were making their initial forays into off-shore production. Although the Southeast and East Asian markets have grown rapidly in the last decade, at this time they were at an early stage in their growth. The markets for Japanese manufactures resided in developed countries, not in the developing countries in which Japanese JVs were being located. Thus, location-specific assets like brandnames, distribution channels, and sales forces, while vital reasons for JV formation in many instances, were probably not dominant reasons for partnering with local firms in the JVs established in these Asian countries.

Other limitations are embedded in our methodology. While the study revealed empirical evidence for the acquisition of local knowledge by international JVs, the process by which this knowledge was acquired or transferred remains to be identified (see Tiemessen, Lane, Crossan and Inkpen (1997)). For an extension of our line of inquiry to be made, key attributes and characteristics of local knowledge need to be examined in terms of their association with firm performance. Particularly interesting would be the identification of certain forms of local knowledge that are not readily accumulated either by experience or in a relationship with a local JV partner. Beamish and Inkpen (1995) also provide clarification on another aspect of our study which remains ambiguous. Their study differentiated between two contradicting perspectives on local knowledge transfer: knowledge acquisition and knowledge access. The performance (stability) of JVs depends, in part, on the parent firms' primary purpose in knowledge transfer.

The generalizability of this study must also be discussed. The focus has been on Japanese firms which typically utilize a sequential approach to foreign market entry. It is well recognized that firms from the US have a greater propensity to acquire existing operations (and perhaps a stock of local knowledge). The local knowledge channels and their relationship with firm performance established in this study, may not hold outside of the Japanese company context. It would be interesting to see the nature of these relationships with MNEs based in North America, Europe or Southeast Asia.

NOTES

1. Throughout the chapter, the Japanese partner in the JV is referred to as the parent or foreign parent. Local partner refers to a JV partner based in the host country of the JV.
2. In all JVs one Japanese parent firm held at least 5 percent and no more than 95 percent of the JV's equity. All JVs were established on a greenfield basis. Although there is no consensus on an equity criterion that should be used to distinguish a JV from a wholly-owned subsidiary, the international business literature has used 95 percent as a cut-off point

to differentiate between a JV and a wholly-owned subsidiary (e.g., Franko, 1971; Stopford and Wells, 1972; Anderson and Gatignon, 1986; Gomes-Casseres, 1989, Hennart, 1991a).

3. To test for performance differences across ownership levels, we grouped our sample into three categories: majority, co-owned, and minority ventures (defined by percent equity held by the Japanese parent). In a One-Way ANOVA, there was no significant difference in the performance means of the three groups.

4. See, for example, Hennart (1991a) and Woodcock, Beamish and Makino (1994) for examples of studies which have employed this database for empirical examinations of Japanese FDI.

5. The most recent version (1994) of this survey contains information on 15,200 subsidiaries operating in 92 countries. which represents a little under 10% of the *universe* of the 170,000 foreign affiliates of 37,000 multinational corporations found in the world in 1992. The 1992 version of the Toyo Keizai survey accounts for 42% of Japanese foreign affiliates (Makino, 1995). The survey is published in Japanese under the title *Kaigai Shinshutsu Kigyou Souran.*

6. The dependent variable is a dummy variable in which 0 (low performance) equates to loss and breakeven responses to the performance item in the Toyo Keizai survey. High performance (1) corresponds to a response of gain (i.e., the joint venture was profitable in 1991). This categorization balanced the number of high and low performance observations in the dependent variable inhibiting the logistic regression from over-classifying either to the low or high performance category.

7. In this definition JRA_PAR becomes an employee quality measure (relative number of Japanese employees times parent firm experience).

8. Although several inter-item correlations exceed 0.50, the variance inflation factors for variables in both samples do not exceed 10, and are only greater than 5 when a variable is an interaction term or is part of an interaction term. The interaction terms contribute significantly to the model and multicollinearity does not appear to threaten the regression.

9. While the performance of JVs in this sample may seem high relative to other JVs (see Beamish and Delios (1997a)), it should be noted that these JVs are located in the fast growing economies of Southeast and East Asia and their performance relative to other modes (e.g., acquisitions and wholly-owned subsidiaries) is similar to that of JVs located in North America and Europe.

10. Binomial models have often been used in empirical studies which have involved the examination of entry mode issues (e.g. Gatignon and Anderson, 1988; Gomes-Casseres, 1989; Hennart, 1991a).

11. These outliers had abnormally large observations for the sales measure. Once these abnormal cases were removed from the regression, variance in the sales measure was reduced and the associated coefficient became significant.

12. We thank an anonymous reviewer for assistance with clarification of this point.

13. If lower JV performance is substituted for JV instability, the result depicted in Figure 10.1 is intriguingly similar to the relationship identified in proposition one in Inkpen and Beamish (1997).

14. The degree of local ownership restriction is negatively associated with performance in the absence of a local partner, but this relationship is not significant in the presence of a local partner. This, in part, implies that in a regulatory environment, assistance from a local firm helps the JV attain high performance.

15. We have, based upon our literature review and our sample composition, assumed that JVs in our study were formed to acquire complementary resources. Competing motives do exist (e.g., to attain scale of economies stemming from adding similar or common advantages between partners). The importance of distinguishing between motives has been noted by many scholars (e.g., "X" and "Y" coalitions (Porter and Fuller, 1986); "link" and "scale" JVs (Hennart, 1988); and "complementary" and "scale" alliances (Dussauge and Garrette, 1995)). To isolate the role of a local JV partner as a local knowledge channel, a future study should control for this primary distinction.

ACKNOWLEDGEMENTS

The authors wish to thank Jay Anand, Paul Beamish, Scott Ensign, Peter Killing and two anonymous reviewers for comments on earlier drafts. We also thank the participants of the Global Perspectives on Cooperative Strategies: Asian Conference for their advice and comments. Both authors contributed equally to this chapter and are listed in no particular order.

PART IV

Management Strategy

11. How Japanese MNCs have matched goals and strategies in India and China

Jaideep Anand and Andrew Delios

Japanese MNCs have established strong investment positions in the US, Europe and Asia. China has been a major recipient of Japanese foreign direct investment (FDI), while investment in India has grown much more slowly. We argue that the differences extend much beyond the levels of investment – Japanese involvement in India and China is qualitatively different. Japanese FDI in China was motivated by access to location-specific productive resources, and it involved a high degree of technology, management skills and organizational knowledge transfer. The Japanese subsidiaries in China were integrated with the network of international subsidiaries as a part of the MNC's global strategy. Japanese FDI in India, however, was motivated by the desire to access local markets. It involved less transfer of technology and management skills, and Japanese subsidiaries in India operated independently as part of a multi-domestic strategy. We conclude that foreign entrants to the region should be aware and able to respond to the unique advantages of each host country and to the different strategies and capabilities of the subsidiaries of Japanese multinational companies (MNCs).

INTRODUCTION

The rapidly developing economies of Asia have attracted much interest because of large consumer and industrial markets – and with good reason. This region of the world harbors more than three billion people, five times the population of Western Europe and North America. With economic expansion, the market opportunities are beginning to match this long latent potential, and North American and European companies have been moving into the region with an eye to these markets. However, among countries from the Triad (Europe, Japan and North America), Japan is the dominant investor in Asia. While historically Japanese companies have used a Japanese-based (centralized) manufacturing strategy, with sales offices in foreign countries, this pattern has changed in the last few years and much of Japan's manufacturing has been re-located to Asia. American and other MNCs can draw important lessons from Japanese MNCs in tailoring their subsidiary strategies to their multinational mission.

Japanese MNCs became well known in the 1960s and 1970s for exports of automobiles, motorcycles and electronic equipment. This was not only testimony to their design and manufacturing expertise but also to their ability to penetrate foreign markets. More recently, in the 1980s and 1990s, centralized manufacturing is being replaced by broader based Asian manufacturing. Textiles and other forms of labor intensive manufacture are more frequently taking place in China and Southeast Asia. This is consistent with the observation that footwear, watches and toys commonly bear a "Made in China" label. Curiously, however, China's developing country counterpart, India, is less well known as a site for the manufacture of labor intensive products. The strategies and actions of Japanese MNCs reflect these differences. In investing in China, Japanese MNCs aspired to the goal of developing a globally integrated production system. Consistent with this goal were many of the decisions made by the parent MNC in setting up the subsidiary. In India, however, where the economic policies of the host country did not facilitate economic integration with other countries, but where the market size motivated FDI, Japanese MNCs developed subsidiaries oriented to serving the closed Indian market.

Both host country conditions and the choice of industry are important factors in determining the goals of the FDI and the subsidiary's strategy. Japanese MNCs in Asia provide insight into this relationship. More importantly, the strategies and actions of Japanese MNCs in India and China hold several lessons for managers and public policy makers alike. By exploring the outcomes of Japanese MNCs' international strategies – their subsidiaries – the implementation of the strategies is better understood. By evaluating and understanding the goals of FDI and subsidiary strategies, we can learn how Japanese MNCs compete in China and India and in the Asian continent at large. Of course, whether a MNC's subsidiary is oriented to global or to domestic markets has fundamental implications for the net host country benefits of the foreign investment.

Japanese MNCs in Asia

Japanese MNCs have become dominant figures in the international business landscape. The growth of FDI from Japan has been strong in the last 30 years and Japanese MNCs, now the second largest investor in the US, account for a 20 percent share of all FDI into the US. More strikingly, in the fastest growing economic region of the world – Southeast, South and East Asia – Japanese MNCs dominate foreign investment. A few figures illustrate the pervasiveness of Japanese investment in this region. Developing countries in Asia (excluding West Asia) received $61 billion of FDI in 1994 or 70 percent of FDI inflows to developing countries. In 1993, Japanese MNCs were the largest foreign investor and possessed one and a half times more stock of FDI in Asia than either MNCs from Europe or the US (UNCTAD, 1995). The commanding position of Japanese MNCs in Asia has fostered fears of the growth of an East Asian bloc (Graham and Anzai, 1994) and, in fact, the growth of Japanese FDI in general has generated much concern just as the dominance of Japanese exports did in earlier decades.

Many discussions of Japanese FDI portray Japanese investments abroad as a flight response to the interminable rise of the yen. Japanese foreign ventures are depicted as seeking to ameliorate the competitive disadvantages of rising costs caused by the dogged advance of their home currency. FDI is thus spurred by the yen to the exclusion of other factors and strategies. This portrayal of Japanese MNCs casts them as homogeneous in their strategies, in their responses to resource conditions, and in their treatments of countries around the world as host sites for FDI. Japanese firms lose any uniqueness in this vision of their actions on the world stage, and fears of a Japanese economic juggernaut are compounded. However, Japanese investment in Asia is more complex than is suggested in this simple picture of Japanese MNC activity, and US and European MNCs entering the region need to understand the strategies and activities of their principal rivals (Japanese MNCs).

Despite the need for an understanding of the strategies, activities and host country benefits of Japanese investment in Asia, many myths and fears (such as the above) about Japanese trade and investment still exist. Much of the uncertainty about Japanese activity in the region can be attributed to the infrequency with which Japanese trade and investment with Asia has been studied. The lack of focus on this region is understandable. Prior to the 1990s, FDI was dominated by countries in the Triad markets both as investors and as host sites. International business research tended to reflect the preeminence of the triad markets and focused on business activity between these markets.

Here, we shift examination of MNC activity to the Asian context and argue that the nature and host-country benefits of Japanese FDI are dependent upon the subsidiary strategy employed and the motive of the Japanese MNC's investment; that is, whether FDI is incited by location-specific productive resources or by the desire to access local markets. We use Japanese investments in China and India as cases and investigate the characteristics (strategies) of Japanese foreign subsidiaries in these two countries. China and India present interesting cases for contrast. Both countries are large and similar in size, and both have liberalized their economies albeit at different times. Economic liberalization began in 1978 in China and in 1991 in India. Further, these two countries have received considerable attention in the popular press because of their large and growing markets and their common promotion of export oriented zones (export processing zones in India and special economic zones in China). While the countries are now pursuing similar paths with respect to liberalization and the promotion of foreign investment, the 13-year separation in economic liberalization has contributed to different FDI strategies by Japanese MNCs as we will outline in subsequent sections.

HOST COUNTRY BENEFITS OF MNCs

The rise in Japanese FDI has been followed by a concurrent increase in concern about the impact of Japanese MNCs in developing host countries. However, the outcome of FDI, whether it holds net positive or negative benefits for the host country, is difficult to determine. As Japanese MNCs are becoming dominant institutions in the developing countries of Asia, concern about the effects of Japanese subsidiaries is well founded. The strategies and actions of Japanese MNCs and the characteristics of their subsidiaries established in these countries provide a platform from which the question of net benefits or costs can be examined.

Arguably, the foremost host country benefit of FDI, aside from capital inflows and other potential improvements in the capital account[1], involves the transfer of intangibles like technology, management skills and organizational knowledge. A more recent explanation of FDI suggests that MNCs are able to invest abroad successfully because they possess superior organizing principles (management skills and organizational knowledge) and technological strengths (Kogut, 1991). MNCs bring these skills and organizing knowledge when they invest in a host country. The transfer of superior management skills, for example just-in-time practices or total quality management, involves more than the recording of the details of the practice in a handbook. Many organizational systems are complex and require extensive coordination within the firm and with outside suppliers. Learning of these activities occurs best through the replication of the firm or, in the case of foreign transfers, by the establishment of foreign subsidiaries.

The degree or extent of transfer of these intangibles (technology, management skills, and organizational knowledge) depends upon the mandate under which foreign subsidiaries are established. As we will illustrate in the remainder of the paper, Japanese MNCs have used different strategies in entering India and China, and the MNCs' subsidiaries reflect these differences. Subsidiaries that are established to access local markets and compete with local firms (a multidomestic strategy) tend to involve fewer transfers of intangibles, and where intangibles are transferred, the skills and knowledge embodied in the transfer typically do not represent the best the MNC has to offer. However, when a subsidiary is established to compete in world markets (a global strategy) and exists as part of the network of the MNC's global operations, the best practices and skills of the MNC are transferred to the host country subsidiary. Consequently, the strategic mandate under which subsidiaries are established (the motive for the investment) has important implications for the type and extent of intangible transfers made to the host country, and ultimately, to the net host country benefits of foreign activity.

JAPANESE FDI IN INDIA AND CHINA

The Case of Yamaha

The linkages between the transfer of intangibles and the subsidiary's strategic mandate are highlighted in our investigation of the extensive foreign activities of Yamaha. In its global operations, Yamaha produces motorcycles, marine products and automotive engines, and by 1995, the company had invested more than US$630 million in foreign subsidiaries. In 1995, the sales of Yamaha's foreign affiliates (US$2.8 billion) approached that of domestically based operations (US$4.1 billion)[2]. Two of its foreign subsidiaries were established in India in the 1980s (pre-liberalization) and four in China in 1994 and 1995. One investment in India was a partial acquisition made in 1985. Yamaha possesses 26 percent of the equity in this subsidiary and employs 450 local staff. Yamaha's participation in this facility, which produces and sells engines and related parts, involves little more than a capital investment as the general manager is from India and there are no Japanese expatriate managers.

Yamaha's second investment in India was similar in many respects to the first. The partner in Yamaha's venture in this case is Escorts Ltd. (Escorts),[3] a large Indian conglomerate. Escorts has a fifty year operational history in India. The company began as a distribution outlet for foreign produced consumer goods and gradually integrated backwards in an attempt to indigenize production. To access technology and to develop production capabilities, Escorts engaged in more than 20 technology alliances with foreign firms from Japan, Eastern and Western Europe and North America. The foreign partners were willing to engage in these alliances because they were effectively barred from entry in India during the licensed Raj regime which persisted to 1991. Thus, prior to liberalization, competition in Escorts' sectors was limited to a few domestic competitors whose numbers were further limited because of the licensing regime.

One of Escorts' principal manufactures is motorcycles. The company, which produces its own brand in Faridabad (an industrial zone near New Delhi), India, engaged in a technology partnership with Yamaha in the 1980s and began to produce Yamaha brand motorcycles in Surajpur, India in 1986. The original plant was established and made operational with little assistance from Yamaha. In 1990, with domestic competition in India intensifying (many other Indian firms had partnered with other Japanese manufacturers like Kawasaki, Honda and Suzuki) and liberalization looming on the horizon, a new plant, in which Yamaha increased its equity position to 50 percent, was established in the Surajpur location at an incremental cost of US$8 million. In developing this plant, Yamaha participated much more actively. Yamaha sent teams of ten managers to train Indian employees in Japanese production practices. The plant followed a typical Japanese design, and work was organized on a cellular basis. Numerous Japanese management practices, like just-in-time inventory, were also adopted. In addition, the scope of the plant was expanded to include the full manufacture and assembly of motorcycles.

The results of the Surajpur plant, in comparison to the Faridabad plant, are impressive. The Surajpur plant is much more efficient than its previous incarnation and the plant in Faridabad. It produces nearly the same number of motorcycles as the Faridabad plant with only 15 percent the workforce of the Faridabad plant. Inventories have been reduced from 3-6 months to 15-30 days and the output per worker is more than six times greater.

This case illustrates the benefits that can accrue to local firms and to the host country when FDI occurs under a mandate which promotes the transfer of management and technological skills to the foreign subsidiary. The initial entry into India by Yamaha was completed under the guise of market expansion. Originally, Yamaha committed little to its Indian operation; however, as the specter of increased competition appeared, Yamaha consigned more resources (capital and management time) to the venture and improved its operation.

While intensified domestic competition was the motive for Yamaha's increased involvement in its domestically oriented joint venture with Escorts, a global strategic mandate is the impetus behind Yamaha's active participation in its four subsidiaries in China. From May 1994 to April 1995, Yamaha placed four subsidiaries in three provinces of China. The total investment in these greenfield subsidiaries is approximately US$13.7 million and Yamaha possesses a 50 percent ownership stake in the two largest ventures. The two main manufacturing ventures are located in the large interior province of Sichuan (population 120 million, per capita GDP of US$432) in the industrial cities of Chungking and Chengtu. The stated motives for the establishment of these joint ventures were to access local resources and markets, to maintain ties with existing affiliated companies and to develop production for export to markets other than Japan. A Japanese general manager oversees the Chungking plant and a local Chinese manager supervises the Chengtu operation. Thirty-nine other Japanese expatriates assist the 908 local employees with manufacturing operations. The two smaller affiliates, which have 43 local employees and two Japanese managers, are located in the coastal provinces of Hainan and Shandong. These joint ventures manufacture marine products and engage in the sale of related equipment.

Yamaha's subsidiaries in China represent the extension of its manufacturing capabilities to a lower cost location (access to local resources) while maintaining ties with its global operations. The Chinese subsidiaries are part of Yamaha's global network of operations and were established under a global strategic mandate. The extensive involvement of Yamaha in building new plants and in transferring many expatriate employees suggests that leading edge technology and organizational practices are being transferred to its subsidiaries in China. The potential for host country benefits, in terms of the transfer of intangibles, tends to be greater in subsidiaries established under a global strategic mandate. The dynamics of many of the investments made in India and China are similar to the initial and subsequent investments made by Yamaha in India and China.

The Case of Sumitomo

A surprisingly large number of Japanese MNCs (42 percent) that have made direct investments in India also have invested in China. Interestingly, the nature of these investments differs much in the pattern as Yamaha's investments in India and China. Sumitomo Trading, a part of the Sumitomo group of companies, is involved in more than 300 ventures across the world. Eleven of its subsidiaries are in China and four are in India. The investments are in a number of industries including textiles. In the three textile subsidiaries established in China, Sumitomo and its Japanese partners average a 64 percent equity position; one percent of employees are Japanese expatriates; one of three subsidiary general managers is Japanese; and the average equity involved in each subsidiary is US$1.2 million. Sumitomo's sole textile subsidiary in India stands in contrast to these investments. The Indian subsidiary is three years older than its counterparts in China. The equity involved is much less (US$320,000); the equity position of the Japanese partners is lower (49 percent); and Japanese managerial involvement is limited (0.2 percent of all employees, with the subsidiary general manager from India).

The lesser involvement, in terms of the capital committed, managerial participation, and equity ownership, in the Indian subsidiary by the Japanese partner strongly alludes to the lack of a transfer of technology, managerial skills and organizational knowledge. The capital committed per employee – US$600 per Indian employee versus US$9,000 per Chinese employee – suggests that the technology being transferred to India in the establishment of the subsidiary is different from that transferred to the Chinese subsidiary. Using the case of Sanyo's investments in India and China, we further this argument by illustrating the relation of the motives for subsidiary establishment to levels of managerial involvement, equity ownership and subsidiary capitalization.

The Case of Sanyo

Sanyo Electric and Sanyo Electric Trading have been very active internationally placing 162 subsidiaries in Asia, Europe and North America. Sanyo's sole subsidiary in India manufactures video cassette recorders with a plant established in 1987 and currently run by an Indian general manager. The subsidiary reports market access as its motive for investment in India. The level of ownership of the US$2.2 million facility is low (40 percent) and two Japanese expatriates assist the 174 Indian employees in manufacturing. The facility operates independently and does not have any cross-ownership as do Sanyo's subsidiaries in China.

In the late 1980s, Sanyo placed six subsidiaries in China for the manufacture of tape recorders, radios, CD players, semi-conductors and air conditioners. Each of these subsidiaries reports access to low cost labor as its motive for locating in China. The number of employees per subsidiary is large (833) and the average capitalization is $5.2 million. In these ventures, the Japanese partners possess 50 percent or more of the equity, and ownership is typically shared between the Sanyo parent, a Sanyo subsidiary in other parts of the world, and a local partner. In a more interesting case, a CD manufacturing facility in China has a local partner and three Sanyo affiliated partners (60 percent equity). One of the Japanese partners is Sanyo Electrical Trading Company which established several trade and sales subsidiaries in Hong Kong in the early 1980s. The subsidiary is integrated within the parent's global network, and the high level of involvement by the Japanese partner, both in equity participation and the number of Japanese managers employed (nine per subsidiary), alludes to the transference of technology and management skills. Sanyo's activities in China stand in marked contrast to typical Japanese investments in India.

These cases illustrate the insights that can be gained into the nature and potential effect or benefits of FDI. Intangible transfers to the host country through the foreign subsidiary require extensive participation by the Japanese parent. In the next section, we extend this analysis from the individual case level to a large sample examination of the characteristics of subsidiaries in China and India. From this examination, we identify characteristics unique to subsidiaries in each region and derive several implications about the nature of transfers to the host country and host country benefits.

GENERAL TRENDS IN JAPANESE FDI

Timing and Distribution of Japanese Investment

The first reported case of Japanese FDI in India was in June of 1957. Following this initial investment, Japanese involvement in India has been sporadic; however, since the economic liberalization process was instituted in 1991, there has been a resurgence in Japanese FDI. Even so, in comparison to China FDI in India is still small – the amount of Japanese FDI in China is approximately ten times that in India. The recent surge in Japanese FDI in China has been much more dramatic than that in India. China's share of all Japanese FDI increased from 6 percent in the 1987-91 period to 18 percent in the 1992-93 period. Almost half of the investments in China were formed post-1992, compared with less than 20 percent of all cases of FDI formed in India in the same period. This makes the average age of ventures in China (3 years) much lower than that in India (11 years).

Japanese FDI in India is concentrated in the industrial belts around Bombay and New Delhi and occurs in a few specific industries (Table 11.1). Investments in the manufacture of electronic and transportation equipment account for 58 percent of the incidences of investment. Other prominent sectors are chemicals (12 percent) and industrial machinery and equipment. Clearly, Japanese investment in India is concentrated in capital-intensive manufacturing industries in India. But it is not in China. Japanese FDI in China, which is clustered in the eastern coastal provinces,

Table 11.1 Comparison of Japanese FDI in India, China and the world

Industry	SIC	World % of total	India Count	India %	China Count	China %
Food and kindred products	20	6.7	2	2.6	52	11.5
Textile mill products	22	5.0	1	1.3	26	5.7
Apparel and other textile products	23	3.5	1	1.3	79	17.4
Lumber and wood products	24	1.0	0	0.0	7	1.6
Furniture and fixtures	25	1.2	0	0.0	6	1.4
Paper and allied products	26	1.1	0	0.0	3	0.7
Printing and publishing	27	1.0	0	0.0	0	0.0
Chemicals and allied products	28	12.5	9	11.8	33	7.3
Petroleum and coal products	29	0.1	0	0.0	3	0.7
Rubber and misc. plastics products	30	5.7	0	0.0	8	1.8
Leather and leather products	31	0.4	0	0.0	4	0.9
Stone, clay, and glass products	32	2.5	4	5.3	10	2.3
Primary metal industries	33	4.7	2	2.6	11	2.5
Fabricated metal products	34	7.4	2	2.6	18	3.9
Industrial machinery and equipment	35	9.2	8	10.5	41	9.1
Electronic and electrical equipment	36	17.5	17	22.4	74	16.2
Transportation equipment	37	11.3	26	34.2	26	5.7
Instruments and related products	38	4.7	3	3.9	28	6.2
Miscellaneous manufacturing ind.	39	4.5	1	1.3	23	5.0

Note: In each table percentage column totals may not sum to 100 because of rounding.

has a much more even industrial distribution than that in India. However, FDI in food, textile and clothing industries is most prominent in China while it is least prominent in these sectors in India.

Role of Indian and Chinese Subsidiaries in Japanese MNCs

A global strategy involves multiple linkages among subsidiaries and headquarters, whereas a multidomestic strategy involves more self-sufficient subsidiaries with limited connections to other subsidiaries and headquarters. Subsidiaries that conduct most of their business (sourcing and sales) within the host country have a multidomestic strategic mandate. Subsidiaries that conduct much of their business outside the host country have a global strategic mandate. The role of Indian and Chinese subsidiaries in the worldwide operations of the MNC is examined by looking at two variables: the extent to which the output from these subsidiaries is exported and the extent to which these subsidiaries are dependent on sources of inputs from outside of the host country.[4] We use these variables to judge the level of integration of Indian and Chinese operations in the worldwide system of Japanese MNCs.

A Japanese subsidiary can use any of three possible locations for the sourcing of inputs and the sale of outputs: (1) the local (host) country in which the subsidiary is located, (2) the home country (in this case, Japan), or (3) a third country. Products which are sold in markets outside of the host country suggest that the subsidiary has adopted a global (re-exporting) strategy. Where products are sold within the country, the subsidiary could be characterized as adopting a multidomestic (market penetration) strategy. Similarly, we distinguish between inputs sourced from the host country and those sourced from abroad. Table 11.2 presents the patterns in marketing strategies and the corresponding patterns in input strategies.

In India, products are generally sold domestically, suggesting a market penetration (multidomestic) role for these subsidiaries. This is in contrast to China, where goods are produced for sale in China 48 percent of the time, and for re-export in 52 percent of the cases. Goods are re-exported to both Japan and other countries, unlike the case of India, in which goods, if not sold in India, seem to be exported back to Japan. Subsidiaries in China, on this measure, appear to be more integrated internationally.

The market penetration strategy of Japanese firms in India contrasts sharply with the re-export strategy in other locations with low wages like China. Similarly, the input sourcing pattern of Japanese subsidiaries in India is in contrast to that in China: Japanese subsidiaries in India show a greater reliance on local sourcing than do subsidiaries in China. Only a small percentage of inputs (23 percent) were sourced from outside the host country by Indian subsidiaries. Conversely, inputs for production in China came almost equally from inside and from outside of China reflecting the more global nature of subsidiary strategy in China. The strong relationship between external sourcing and exporting reaffirms the global nature of subsidiaries in China. In India, the sourcing and marketing relationships show that subsidiaries are more oriented to the host market.

Table 11.2 MNE strategies

	Marketing		Sourcing	
	India	**China**	**India**	**China**
Region	**Percentage of respondents**		**Percentage of respondents**	
1. Japan	34.7	38.1	18.2	48.9
2. Host country	65.3	47.6	77.3	48.9
3. Third country	0.0	14.3	4.5	2.2
Strategy				
Multi-domestic (2)	65.3	52.4	77.3	48.9
Global (1+3)	34.7	47.6	22.7	51.1

Note: The strategy items had a lower response rate in the survey (approximately 20%) across both countries. Respondents and non-respondents compared similarly on most of the organizational characteristics identified in this study. Responding firms were generally older and non-respondent firms in China were typically larger by equity and total employment measures.

Investment Motivation

The primary motives for FDI in India were (1) as a response to government invitation (e.g. government investment incentives), and (2) for market expansion (see Table 11.3). Subsidiaries which indicated the market expansion motive were primarily in the transportation equipment industry. Access to local resources was a factor in the chemicals industry, where natural resources and low cost labor are cited as reasons for investment. Whereas market entry is the dominant motivation for FDI in India, low cost labor is the most frequently cited motivation for investment in China (31 percent), with market expansion being of somewhat less importance (27 percent).

To explore the relationship between the motive for subsidiary formation and the subsequent strategy, we examined how these two variables were related to each other. When subsidiaries were established as part of a multidomestic strategy (local market penetration), the primary motives for investment were market expansion and as a response to government invitation. As a rule, inputs were generally sourced in India. However, when the motive for entry was government invitation or market expansion, inputs were sourced from Japan and India.

Table 11.3 Motives for investment

Motive	% responding Yes India	China
Access to raw materials	7.7	7.7
Abundance of natural resources	4.6	5.7
Access to low-cost labor	4.6	30.8
Response to government invitation	33.8	13.5
Expand market	41.5	26.9
Collect information	0.0	0.9
Obtain royalty	4.6	5.7
Establish export base	1.5	3.7
Counter trade friction	1.5	0.9
Raise capital	0.0	0.0
Other motive	0.0	4.8

Note: The response rate for these items was approximately 40% across both countries.

Subsidiaries in China exhibit a somewhat contrasting pattern. These subsidiaries were established to access low cost labor and local markets, and even those subsidiaries motivated by government incentives tended to be oriented to a more global strategy. Japanese firms established ventures in China to reduce labor costs and output from these ventures was both exported and distributed locally. In the manufacture of products in China, inputs also tended to be sourced both locally and from Japan.

These trends in strategies and motives vary somewhat by industry within each country. While input strategies are evenly distributed across industries, marketing strategies exhibit some difference across industries. In India, to the extent that there were transactions with the outside world, they were in industries like chemicals, electronics and instrumentation. In China, on the other hand, there are wider variations between the strategies in different industries. For example, the food, textile and apparel industries sourced exclusively in Japan. However, production from the apparel and textile industries was sold mainly outside of China, while production from the food industry was both exported and sold domestically. These differences in the strategic orientations of Japanese subsidiaries in India and China are reflected in the organizational characteristics (size, entry mode, ownership and employment) of each country's subsidiaries.

Subsidiary Characteristics

Size and productivity
Japanese subsidiaries in India are larger based on the dollar value of sales and the number of employees. However, the average equity invested in subsidiaries in India is less than that invested in China (see Table 11.4). Part of this inconsistency in size measures (equity, employees and sales) arises because subsidiaries in India are older than those in China and the reported equity (which is the book value) is understated in India. A second part of this inconsistency arises because of the distribution of investments across industries in these two countries. Subsidiaries in China tend to be located in low wage, labor intensive industries like textiles, clothing and food manufacture. Typically such plants employ fewer workers than manufacturing operations in heavier, process-intensive industries – transportation and machinery manufacture – in which Japanese firms have invested in India. Also, because the inputs to manufacturing in the heavier industries are component parts, the sales per employee is greater than the output per worker. Consequently, the sales per worker is lower in China ($30,000 per employee) than in India ($63,000 per employee). The high labor component found in the products made in Japanese subsidiaries in China is consistent with MNCs operating with a global strategy. Labor intensive production is located in a low wage country (China) and the labor intensity of this production is reflected in the low sales per employee in subsidiaries in China.

Table 11.4 Subsidiary size and productivity

Measure	India	China
Sales (US$ million)	35	7.20
Equity investment (US$ million)	3.90	8.96
Number of employees	554	240
Sales per employee (US$ '000s)	63	30
Labor intensity (employees / $ million in equity)	142	27

Entry mode
Prior to 1991, local ownership restrictions precluded market entry by a wholly-owned subsidiary in India and, in most situations, restricted foreign equity ownership in a subsidiary to 40 percent. Not surprisingly, there were not any wholly-owned subsidiaries of Japanese firms formed in this pre-July 1991 period. The mode of foreign investment was either that of joint venture or partial acquisition, with the former being preferred in the majority of subsidiaries. Post July-1991 conditions allow foreign investors to freely hold

up to a 51 percent equity share in a joint venture and provisions exist for foreign investors to seek a greater than 51 percent share. In the eight joint ventures formed in the 1991-93 period, the smallest ownership position held by a Japanese partner is 35 percent, and in four of the joint ventures, the Japanese partner(s) hold more than a 50 percent equity share.

Japanese FDI in China displays a greater degree of diversity with respect to the mode of entry, perhaps reflecting the Chinese economic reforms in the 1980s. Joint ventures, partial acquisitions and wholly-owned modes are each used in China with joint ventures implemented most frequently. Wholly-owned subsidiaries are the next most prominent form of market entry in China, representing 10 percent of all subsidiaries established in China. The Japanese partner had at least 50 percent ownership in 40 percent of the foreign subsidiaries established in China, but only 50 percent ownership in 11 percent of subsidiaries established in India.

A subsidiary operating under a global mandate requires its operations to be more highly integrated and requires greater control and coordination by the foreign parent than a subsidiary with a multidomestic orientation (Bartlett and Ghoshal, 1989). The form of entry mode can used as an estimate for the desired level of control. Wholly-owned subsidiaries and acquisitions are high control modes; joint ventures and partial acquisitions are low control modes. Wholly-owned subsidiaries are used more frequently in China, perhaps reflecting the general global orientation of its subsidiaries. However, we cannot conclude that the lack of wholly-owned subsidiaries in India is due to their multidomestic orientation. This conclusion is made uncertain by the presence of local ownership restrictions in India. A more sensitive measure of control is the average equity ownership of the Japanese partner.

Japanese ownership and control
Japanese subsidiaries in China, which are more often globally oriented, have a higher average equity ownership (56 percent) by the Japanese parent(s) than do Japanese subsidiaries in India (30 percent). However, the majority of investments in these two regions is via the joint venture mode. A joint venture operating as part of a global strategy needs to be flexible and responsive in managing activities that are coordinated globally. However, there are inherent managerial difficulties in operating a joint venture, and one method of overcoming these difficulties is to increase the formal level of control by increasing the share of equity ownership (Stopford and Wells, 1972). When joint ventures in China and India are compared, the Japanese partner(s) on average takes a majority ownership position (51 percent) in subsidiaries in China. However, in Japanese joint ventures in India, the position of the Japanese partner remains weak (32 percent) and less than that

prescribed by foreign investment regulations. Further, within China, equity ownership by the Japanese partner increases as the subsidiary's strategic stance moves from a local to a global orientation.

Our observation of ownership positions is consistent with the patterns we observe in the use of Japanese expatriates. The number of Japanese employees in Japanese subsidiaries in Asia tends to be associated with the level of equity ownership. Figure 11.1 demonstrates this relationship in India and China. Higher Japanese employment levels are found in those subsidiaries operating under a global mandate than those operating under a multidomestic strategy.

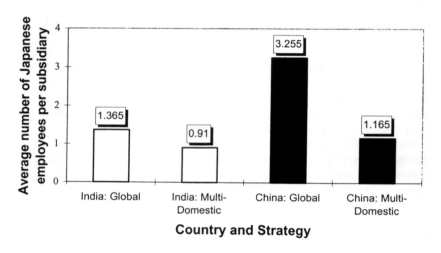

Figure 11.1 Subsidiary strategy and employment of expatriates

The average number of Japanese employees in subsidiaries in China is greater than that in India. Also, in 62 percent of the subsidiaries in India, there were no Japanese employees, while only 33 percent of subsidiaries in China operated without any Japanese employees. When we scale the number of Japanese employees against the total number of employees in the subsidiary, subsidiaries in China employ nearly one expatriate per 100 local employees. On average, Japanese subsidiaries in India employ only one expatriate per 400 local employees. Subsidiaries in China, through the use of home country employees, are better linked with the Japanese parent firm and other subsidiaries and the host country is more likely to receive the benefits of intangible skill transfers.

CONCLUSIONS

We have argued that Japanese firms have adopted different strategic orientations in operating in India and China. Japanese FDI in India and China was motivated by different factors and involved a different strategic stance. The nature of the relationship between investment motive and the host country impact of FDI (the transfer of intangibles), is clarified in this investigation of Japanese investments in China and India. Specifically, we have demonstrated that the transfer of non-monetary benefits – organizational knowledge, management skill and technical knowledge – to the host country is dependent on investment motive and the subsidiary's strategic mandate within the operational labyrinth of the MNC. FDI motivated by country-specific resources, like low cost labor, promotes greater integration of the subsidiary in the MNC's global network and is favorably inclined to the employment of newer technology, and the use of more expatriate managers to assist with the transfer of technology, management skills and organizational knowledge. On the other hand, investment motivated by market expansion (i.e., market access factors) is characterized by independent subsidiaries operating with few expatriate managers in capital intensive, automated industries. The mode of the investment is also affected by the investment motive: Japanese firms exhibit greater equity participation in subsidiaries established to access country-specific resources, while lower equity participation and a more intensive utilization of shared ownership modes are characteristics of investments motivated by market access factors (see Table 11.5).

More succinctly, Japanese ventures in India tended to be market-seeking investments spurred by government incentives and the desire to expand into what was a market protected from exports. Government incentives were effective in attracting inward FDI to India; however, seldom was output from these ventures re-exported and inputs were often sourced outside of India. While FDI resulted in import substitution, such as the replacement of Japanese produced Suzuki automobiles with automobiles produced by the Suzuki-Maruti joint venture in India, imports of component parts countered some of the trade related capital gains.

The Suzuki-Maruti joint venture illustrates how the strategic stance and subsequent organizational characteristics can affect the nature of technology and management skills transferred to the host country through the subsidiary. While some automotive production technology and management skills may have been transferred by the Japanese partner to this joint venture, the original equity stake of the Japanese partner was low (26 percent) as was employment of Japanese managers (7 of 3497 employees or 0.2 percent compared to a worldwide average of 2.4 percent in Japanese automotive subsidiaries). Dispersion of the technology and management skills was restrained by the low level of participation by the Japanese partner. However, in the 1990s, perhaps reflecting reforms in the Indian economy, Suzuki increased its equity involvement to 50 percent, and the number of Japanese managers increased from six to eleven.

Table 11.5 FDI in China and India – organizational characteristics and strategy

Characteristic	India	China
Industries	Industrial machinery Transportation Electronics	Food Textiles Clothing
Subsidiary role	Multi-domestic	Global
FDI motives	Government invitation Market expansion	Access to cheap labor Government invitation
Growth	Fluctuating	Rapid (post 1991)
Subsidiary size	Large	Small
Age	11 years	3 years
Entry mode	Shared mode	Varied modes
Ownership	Lesser equity participation	Greater equity participation
Number of Japanese managers	Lower	Higher
Intangible transfers (technology and organizational skills)	Lesser	Greater

The transfer of intangible organizational skills and technological capabilities, judging by the characteristics of subsidiaries, occurs with greater efficacy in China. FDI in China frequently tended to be part of a global strategy. Subsidiaries were located in China for access to low cost factors of production, and production was frequently in the food, textile, clothing and other such labor intensive industries. Mitsubishi, for example, established a number of subsidiaries in China in the early 1990s. These ventures are in the clothing and textile industries, and ownership is shared by other Mitsubishi subsidiaries, such as Mitsubishi Corporation in Hong Kong. These subsidiaries use newer technology to fully exploit the cost advantages conferred by the locational advantages of China; however, the technology transferred is from technologically less sophisticated industries.

The actions, strategies and benefits of Japanese MNCs, then, differ by host site. For host country public policy makers, key considerations for the evaluation of the potential impact of direct investment by MNCs are the nature of the technology to be transferred *and* the potential for technology, management skills and organizational knowledge transfer. The ideal situation for a host country is well illustrated by the case of Japanese electronic firms like Sanyo, Toshiba and Matsushita, which, in response to demands for globally integrated production, have located numerous manufacturing subsidiaries throughout East and Southeast Asia. When these subsidiaries are placed in China, their degree of integration into the MNC's global production network is high, and the management skills and technology utilized in these subsidiaries, are, by competitive necessity, at the forefront of the company's capability. To date, India houses few subsidiaries of this nature. Rather, India, at least to the early 1990s, remained the domain of heavier industries. Frequently the involvement of manufacturers like Suzuki, Honda and Toyota was to access a closed domestic market which was competitively less intense and, consequently, placed less stringent demands on the quality of technology, management skills and organizational knowledge transfer.

Finally, new foreign entrants to the region need to be aware of the variegated nature of existing Japanese investments. Japanese MNCs have developed a series of local competitors in India and a network of linked global subsidiaries in China. Other Japanese investments in Asia also reflect the different advantages of the different countries. As a result, the integration of industries and economies that has occurred across many of the developed nations of the world is now occurring across these countries of Asia. MNCs from Japan have been the largest contributor to this process, and MNCs from North America and Europe must match the strategies of entrenched Japanese MNCs. Consequently, when entering this region, MNCs must be aware of and respond to the different advantages of each potential host country *and* to the different strategies and capabilities of the network of subsidiaries of well-positioned Japanese MNCs. The motives for investment must be considered in line with the investment strategy, which in turn must account for resident advantages and competitors.

NOTES

1. When MNCs use developing countries as sites for manufacturing to serve world markets, these economies get a new source of foreign exchange. On the other hand, production for

local or domestic markets can reduce net imports when it is a substitute for imports rather than for domestic-based production.

2. Information on Japanese MNCs and foreign subsidiaries is derived from various editions (1986, 1989, 1994, 1995) of *Kaigai Shinshutsu Kigyou Souran* (Japanese Investment Overseas), an annual publication in Japanese by Toyo Keizai, Inc. The most recent edition lists more than 15,000 cases of Japanese overseas investment.

3. Discussion of the Escorts case is based upon research conducted by the authors in India in 1995. A series of teaching cases have been written. The main case is *Escorts Limited, 1993*, and is registered with Western Business School Case and Publication Services, No. 9-95-M009, Teaching Note No. 8-95-M009. Supplementary information is sourced from UNCTAD, *World Investment Report, 1995*.

4. We define Japanese MNCs that reported sourcing their raw materials and marketing their finished products locally as multidomestic. Japanese MNCs are considered to have global strategies if they reported sourcing their raw materials from outside the host country (Japan or third country) or market their products to countries other than the one in which they are situated.

ACKNOWLEDGEMENTS

The authors would like to acknowledge Shige Makino for providing some of the data used in this paper and for comments on the manuscript, and an anonymous reviewer and Daniel London for critiques of earlier drafts.

12. Japanese firms and the decline of the Japanese expatriate

Paul W. Beamish and Andrew C. Inkpen

Conventional wisdom holds that Japanese firms use large numbers of expatriates and are reluctant to allow local nationals a significant role in subsidiary management. Japanese firms have been criticized for their unwillingness to capitalize on the internal diversity in their international managerial ranks. It has been suggested that a rice paper ceiling in Japanese firms restricts local managers from advancement opportunities and involvement in corporate-level decision making. The research reported in this paper directly challenges the notion that Japanese firms are unwilling to reduce their use of expatriates. Using a comprehensive database of Japanese subsidiaries, this paper shows that the number of Japanese expatriates is declining and has been for some time. One explanation for this decline is that Japanese firms have had no choice because of a limited supply of managers for expatriate positions. A second explanation is that Japanese firms are beginning to recognize the importance of empowering local management and are becoming more truly global in how they compete.

INTRODUCTION

To compete in the global arena, multinational enterprises (MNEs) must develop configurations of human resources that take into account diverse cultures, traditions, and educational systems. Various strategic choices will affect the development of international human resources, including the use of expatriate managers, management control systems, and the formation of strategic alliances. In this paper we focus on the use of expatriate managers as a key element of international strategy. Specifically, we examine Japanese firms and their use of expatriates. The use of expatriates by Japanese firms has been a controversial issue because of the widespread view that Japanese firms use large numbers of expatriates and are reluctant to allow local nationals a significant role in subsidiary management. Japanese firms have been charged with deliberately restricting local managers from advancement opportunities and involvement in corporate-level decision making. It has been argued that because of their reluctance to use local managers, Japanese MNEs operate at a competitive disadvantage relative to their American and European competitors (Reich, 1991).

During the 1980s and the 1990s, Japanese foreign direct investment (FDI) levels increased significantly. For the Japanese FDI trend to continue, Japanese firms must either have the depth of human capital necessary to create a pool of expatriates or look to local managers to assume greater responsibility. The primary objective of this paper is to dispel the myth that Japanese MNEs are unwilling to hire local managers. Our research shows a significant decline in the use of Japanese expatriates over the past several years and, therefore, refutes the prevalent contention made by a community of Japanese management scholars. Using a comprehensive database of Japanese subsidiaries, we show that there has been a steady reduction in the use of expatriates by Japanese firms. We propose several reasons to explain why Japanese expatriate influence on MNE operations is declining and should continue to decline.

The decline in the use of expatriates by Japanese firms has an important implication for global competition and for competitors of Japanese MNEs. Contrary to the argument that Japanese firms will ultimately lose out in the race for global talent, our research suggests that Japanese MNEs are increasingly using non-Japanese managers and will continue to do so. As a result, Japanese MNEs are likely to become even stronger global competitors as they move toward truly globalized management structures.

THE ROLE OF JAPANESE EXPATRIATES

Expatriate managers play an important role in representing and implementing the corporate objectives of an MNE. Expatriates often serve as a control mechanism to ensure that the affiliate adheres to corporate goals and objectives (Sohn and Paik, 1996). Expatriates are used for a variety of other reasons: to transfer technology skills, to test high-potential managers in a general management position, to provide staff with management development experience, and to provide international experience for future senior managers (Peterson, Sargent, Napier, and Shim, 1996).

Japan is one of the leading source nations of FDI outflows on a worldwide level. In many regions of the world, Japanese MNEs are among the most active foreign investors. In the United States, for example, Japan is the second largest investing nation following the United Kingdom. According to a survey in 1996 by JETRO, the Japanese External Trade Organization, there were 1,709 Japanese-affiliated manufacturing plants in the United States. Japanese firms hold the largest stock of FDI in Asia and Japan has a leading FDI position in many European countries. To manage and control their foreign investments, Japanese firms have traditionally relied extensively on the use of expatriates, particularly in senior management positions. For example, Japanese firms in the automobile industry have invested heavily in North America, both at the supplier and OEM levels. Several hundred Japanese joint venture (JV) automotive suppliers have been formed in North America. In a typical Japanese automotive JV with 150 to 200 employees, an expatriate structure would include: the JV president or general manager, one or two engineering managers, a quality manager, a sales manager, and possibly a manufacturing manager. According to Rozenzweig (1994), Japanese firms explained their preference for Japanese managers as necessary given the subtle and unique nature of communication between headquarters and subsidiary. It has been argued that the set of relationships between Japanese managers is the result of years of training and education in a homogenous culture. Because these relationships are alien to managers from more heterogeneous and diverse cultures, Japanese firms must rely extensively on expatriates.

The business press and various research studies suggest that Japanese firms use more expatriates than American and European firms (e.g., Pucik, Hanada, and Fifield, 1989; Putti and Chong, 1985). In a survey of MNEs from Europe, Japan, and the United States, Kopp (1984) found that 74% of top managers in Japanese firms were Japanese nationals. Comparative figures for the European and United States firms were 45% and 31%. According to Kawakami (1996) and based on a study by the Japan Overseas Enterprises Association, the percentage of expatriates at Japanese companies is substantially higher than the equivalent for European or American companies. The proportional differences were the highest in Asia. Reasons cited for the lack of local nationals in management positions in Japanese subsidiaries include the inability of locals to communicate effectively with headquarters; the tendency of local managers to switch jobs; and language and cultural differences. A further argument is that the international expansion preference of Japanese firms is through greenfield investments that "transplant" Japanese systems and processes to subsidiaries. The transplants require Japanese expatriate managers because they are so closely linked with Japanese parent firms.

Beechler and Iaquinto (1994) concluded that the internationalization of Japanese firms is not proceeding along the lines of the "Western" model of development. They suggested that changing global competitive conditions and a need for greater integration in MNEs could lead to an increased use of

Japanese expatriates. Pucik (1994), highly pessimistic as to the willingness of Japanese MNEs to hire more local managers, suggested that Japanese firms may reduce the number of expatriates when the business is successful. When difficulties arise, a "re-Japanization" with increased expatriates will occur. Pucik dismissed the argument that the dominance of Japanese managers in subsidiary decision making was because Japanese MNEs were "young" compared to Western MNEs. In fact, Pucik suggested that for many Japanese firms, the slogan "think globally, act locally" referred to the division of labor: the Japanese do the thinking, while the acting is left to the locals. Based on data from 32 Japanese affiliates in the United States, Pucik concluded that in many cases, Japanese managers were increasing their involvement in affiliate decision making.

In the current paper, our primary objective is to show that the number of Japanese expatriates is declining and has been for some time. We discuss the reason for the decline and then consider the implications for Japanese firms' international strategies. Based on the preceding discussion, our arguments challenge the generally accepted view found in the research on Japanese MNEs and expatriate management. To support our position, we track Japanese expatriate employment using a comprehensive Japanese database that previously has not been used to study Japanese expatriate trends.

THE RESEARCH STUDY

The primary source of data for this study was *Kaigai Shinshutsu Kigyou Souran*, a publication of Toyo Keizai Shinposha (Toyo Keizai, 1994).[1] The company Toyo Keizai (Oriental Economist) was formed in 1895, first publishing a weekly journal of political economy entitled *Toyo Keizai*. In 1934 the company introduced its first English language publication, known today as *Tokyo Business Today*. Toyo Keizai publishes more than 100 volumes annually as well as a variety of corporate and economic data covering economic conditions, stock markets, and Japanese corporations. The Corporate Quarterly Handbook (published in Japanese as Kaisha Shikiho) contains data on more than 2,500 firms and has a circulation of more than four million.

Kaigai Shinshutsu Kigyou Souran (Japanese Investments Overseas), the publication used in this study, provides information on the foreign affiliates of Japanese companies listed on the major stock exchanges in Japan as well as on the overseas subsidiaries of other Japanese companies. We used data from the database published in 1994. The database was developed with questionnaires sent through Japanese parent firms to the general managers of these firms' overseas subsidiaries. The survey information was

pronounced in Japanese subsidiaries than in US and European subsidiaries, would reduce the number of expatriates in the older subsidiaries.

Table 12.1 shows expatriates per subsidiary. The table shows that the two largest categories, 6-10 and more than 10 expatriates, declined with the most recently formed subsidiaries. The smallest categories, 0 and 1-2 expatriates, represented an increasingly large number of subsidiaries. The two smallest categories accounted for 54% of subsidiaries formed in the most recent period, 1991-93.

To ensure that the size of the subsidiaries was not influencing the data, we also looked at the number of Japanese expatriates expressed as a percentage of total subsidiary employees. Four categories were used: 0%, 1-5%, 6-10%, and 11-100%. Table 12.2 shows a trend similar to that in Table 12.1. The number of firms in the two smallest percentage categories increased over time and the number of firms in the largest percentage category declined. Looking at the column for no expatriates shows some surprising results. Of the 419 (surviving) subsidiaries formed in the 1976-80 period, 12.6% had no Japanese expatriates. This is slightly more than the percentage for subsidiaries formed in 1986-90 during the huge wave of Japanese FDI. For subsidiaries formed in 1991-93, there were *more* organizations on a percentage basis with no expatriates than in five of the seven earlier periods.

Table 12.2 is also interesting in that it shows that older subsidiaries continued to use a high number of expatriates. For example, of the 580 subsidiaries formed in 1971-75, expatriates constituted 11% or more of total employees in 98 subsidiaries (16.9%). In that respect, the analysis supports the argument that historically, Japanese firms have used a high number of expatriates. One has to question why, after existing for 20 or more years, Japanese subsidiaries continue to use such a large number of expatriates. A possible explanation is that many of the older, more established subsidiaries with high numbers of expatriates are trading companies and service industry firms. In particular, the large Japanese trading companies, the *sogo shosha,* are unique to Japan and, therefore, may require a larger number of expatriates. The trading companies have centuries of traditions and practices to draw on that are difficult to copy and transfer internationally. It is likely that the trading companies have been, and continue to be, resistant to changing from an expatriate to a local management system (McMillan, 1989). A further explanation for the high number of expatriates is the structure of trading company JVs. These JVs are typically three-way JVs between the trading company, another Japanese firm (usually a manufacturer), and a local firm. When there are two Japanese partners the number of Japanese expatriates is often higher than in two-partner JVs.

Our analysis of the trading companies supports the previous argument. In the sample of 3,263 subsidiaries, 622 were classified as wholesale trade

Table 12.1 Number of expatriates per subsidiary by subsidiary entry date

Entry date	Number of expatriate employees					Number of subsidiaries
	0	1-2	3-5	6-10	over 10	
pre-1960	5	9	8	8	17	47
	10.6%	19.1%	17.0%	17.0%	36.2%	
1961-65	11	18	18	19	16	82
	13.4%	22.0%	22.0%	23.2%	19.5%	
1966-70	42	59	49	39	31	220
	19.1%	26.8%	22.3%	17.7%	14.1%	
1971-75	83	164	142	111	80	580
	14.3%	28.3%	24.5%	19.1%	13.8%	
1976-80	53	143	122	60	41	419
	12.6%	34.1%	29.1%	14.3%	9.8%	
1981-85	87	156	109	90	52	494
	17.6%	31.6%	22.1%	18.2%	10.5%	
1986-90	148	406	346	184	113	1,197
	12.4%	33.9%	28.9%	15.4%	9.4%	
1991-93	35	85	66	25	13	224
	15.6%	37.9%	29.5%	11.2%	5.8%	
All subsidiaries	464	1,040	860	536	363	3,263
	14.2%	31.9%	26.4%	16.4%	11.1%	

Note: The first number in a cell is a count of the number of subsidiaries, the second is a row percentage.

Table 12.2 Number of expatriates employed per 100 subsidiary employees by subsidiary entry date

Entry date	Percentage of expatriate employees				Number of subsidiaries
	0%	1–5%	6–10%	11–100%	
pre-1960	5	19	5	18	47
	10.6%	40.4%	10.6%	38.3%	
1961–65	11	41	17	13	82
	13.4%	50.0%	20.7%	15.9%	
1966–70	42	119	24	35	220
	19.1%	54.1%	10.9%	15.9%	
1971–75	83	328	71	98	580
	14.3%	56.6%	12.2%	16.9%	
1976–80	53	233	65	68	419
	12.6%	55.6%	15.5%	16.2%	
1981–85	87	245	75	87	494
	17.6%	49.6%	15.2%	17.6%	
1986–90	148	756	161	132	1197
	12.4%	63.2%	13.5%	11.0%	
1991–93	35	128	34	27	224
	15.6%	57.1%	15.2%	12.1%	
All subsidiaries	**464**	**1,869**	**452**	**478**	**3,263**
	14.2%	57.3%	13.9%	14.6%	

Note: The first number in a cell is a count of the number of subsidiaries, the second is a row percentage.

firms. On a percentage basis, these subsidiaries had much higher levels of expatriates than the manufacturing subsidiaries. For example, expatriates made up more than 11% of total employees in 24% of the trading subsidiaries formed in 1986-90 and 28% of the subsidiaries formed in 1991-93. The percentages for manufacturing subsidiaries were 5% and 8% respectively (Table 12.4) and for the complete sample, 11% and 12% (Table 12.2). For the 0 expatriate category, the percentages were very small for the older trading subsidiaries: 6% of 71 subsidiaries formed in 1966-70, 8% of 118 subsidiaries formed in 1971-75, and 6% of 108 subsidiaries formed in 1976-80. Table 12.3 shows that for manufacturing firms, comparable figures were 27%, 18% and 17%.

Despite the higher numbers of expatriates in the trading firms, this group of firms has also experienced a decline in expatriates in recent periods. The percentage of firms in the 0 expatriate category was 15% for 1986-90 and 12% for 1990-93, versus figures of 10% or less for all but one of the earlier periods. For the category of 11% or more expatriates, the percentage of firms was 42% for 1966-70 subsidiaries and 45% for 1971-75. Beginning with the 1976-80 period, there has been a steady decline in the percentages of firms with 11% or more expatriates. It should also be reiterated that these are surviving subsidiaries and that the 45% for 1971-75 means that after about 20 years of existence, expatriates still make up 11% or more of total employees in these subsidiaries.

We also speculate that the firms using fewer expatriates are newer Japanese multinationals that do not have as entrenched an expatriate culture and are not as bound to traditional Japanese management practices. Undoubtedly, many of these firms are manufacturing firms, forced to move offshore because of high manufacturing costs in Japan. Tables 12.3 and 12.4 show results for manufacturing firms only. Table 12.3 shows that 15.6% of the manufacturing subsidiaries formed in 1991-93 had no expatriates and 35.5% had only 1-2 expatriates. Table 12.4, based on the percentage of expatriates in each subsidiary, shows similar trends. The 6-10% category had a lower percentage of firms for the most recent period than for the three immediately preceding periods, including 1976-80. The figure for the 0% category in 1991-93 was higher than the corresponding figure for two of the previous periods and very close to two others. Like the previous tables, Table 12.4 shows no clear upward trend for recently formed subsidiaries, which is what we would expect if Japanese firms were using a consistent percentage of expatriates for new subsidiaries. What all of the data consistently show is that the number of expatriates in recently formed subsidiaries is on a downward trend.

Table 12.3 Number of expatriates per subsidiary by subsidiary entry date, manufacturing subsidiaries only

| Entry date | Number of expatriate employees | | | | | Number of subsidiaries |
	0	1-2	3-5	6-10	over 10	
pre-1960	4	2	3	6	1	16
	25.0%	12.5%	18.8%	37.5%	6.3%	
1961-65	7	13	11	11	4	46
	15.2%	28.3%	23.9%	23.9%	8.7%	
1966-70	35	36	29	20	8	128
	27.3%	28.1%	22.7%	15.6%	6.3%	
1971-75	61	103	90	56	29	339
	18.0%	30.4%	26.5%	16.5%	8.6%	
1976-80	39	72	69	33	14	227
	17.2%	31.7%	30.4%	14.5%	6.2%	
1981-85	39	79	60	36	24	238
	16.4%	33.2%	25.2%	15.1%	10.1%	
1986-90	95	274	258	132	76	835
	11.4%	32.8%	30.9%	15.8%	9.1%	
1991-93	22	50	48	15	6	141
	15.6%	35.5%	34.0%	10.6%	4.3%	
All subsidiaries	**302**	**629**	**568**	**309**	**162**	**1,970**
	15.3%	31.9%	28.8%	15.7%	8.2%	

Note: The first number in a cell is a count of the number of subsidiaries, the second is a row percentage.

Table 12.4   Number of expatriates employed per 100 subsidiary employees by subsidiary entry date, manufacturing subsidiaries only

Entry date	Percentage of expatriate employees				Number of subsidiaries
	0%	1-5%	6-10%	11-100%	
pre-1960	4 / 25.0%	11 / 68.8%	1 / 6.3%	0 / 0%	16
1961-65	7 / 15.2%	32 / 69.6%	6 / 13.0%	1 / 2.2%	46
1966-70	35 / 27.3%	87 / 68.0%	3 / 2.3%	3 / 2.3%	128
1971-75	61 / 18.0%	248 / 73.2%	21 / 6.2%	9 / 2.7%	339
1976-80	39 / 17.2%	150 / 66.1%	28 / 12.3%	10 / 4.4%	227
1981-85	39 / 16.4%	161 / 67.6%	24 / 10.1%	14 / 4.4%	238
1986-90	95 / 11.4%	591 / 70.8%	107 / 12.8%	42 / 5.9%	835
1991-93	22 / 15.6%	93 / 66.0%	14 / 9.9%	12 / 5.0%	141
All subsidiaries	**302** / 15.3%	**1,373** / 69.7%	**204** / 10.4%	**91** / 8.5%	**1,970**
	10.4%				

Note: The first number in a cell is a count of the number of subsidiaries, the second is a row percentage.

Regional Analysis

To provide additional support for our main argument, we conducted some analysis at the regional level. In 439 manufacturing JVs in East and South East Asia that were in existence in both 1989 and 1994, the mean number of Japanese expatriates declined from 4.10 to 3.46. As a percentage of total joint venture employment, the number of expatriates declined from 4.35% to 3.07%. Our examination of Japanese expatriates in Canada was also consistent with the overall trend toward fewer expatriates. In 242 Japanese subsidiaries in 1986, the mean number of Japanese expatriates was 4.13. In 339 subsidiaries in 1994, the mean number of expatriates decreased to 3.02. At the same time, the size of subsidiaries increased from a mean of 100 employees in 1986 to 126 employees in 1994. Interestingly, although the number of expatriates declined, the percentage of subsidiaries with Japanese general managers remained at about 80%. As well, of the subsidiaries that exited Canada during this period, only 60% had Japanese general managers.

WHY IS THE NUMBER OF JAPANESE EXPATRIATES DECLINING?

Conventional wisdom and reports from the business press notwithstanding, the number of Japanese expatriates per subsidiary is declining. The first, and most obvious, explanation for this trend is that the increase in the number of Japanese subsidiaries has made it impossible for Japanese firms to use expatriates at the same level as in the past. Japanese firms may simply not have the managerial resources to send expatriates to new subsidiaries. In part, this may be the result of Japanese demographics and an aging population with little or no population growth. As Japanese FDI has grown, Japanese firms have had little choice but to cut back on the number of expatriates and rely more on local managers. A second explanation, and one consistent with our analysis, is that using local managers makes good business sense. In the Toyo Keizai data there is a performance variable with three categories: loss, break-even, and gain. Our analysis of performance for the large sample of 5,843 subsidiaries showed that better performance was associated with fewer expatriates. This is consistent with other research (Pucik, 1994) showing a positive relationship between increased input from local managers and subsidiary profitability and market share. In particular, the involvement of local managers in corporate strategy planning and new product development were strong indicators of subsidiary performance.

A third possible explanation is that Japanese firms are no longer willing to pay the high costs of maintaining an expatriate workforce when local managers can be hired at a fraction of the cost. We have observed in other research in China that many firms – Japanese and other – are being pressured by their JV partners to reduce the number and duration of expatriate stays in order to maintain financial competitiveness (Beamish, 1993).

The fourth, and most intriguing explanation, is that the Japanese "rice paper ceiling" is being dismantled. To explain Japanese human resource management policies with respect to non-Japanese employees, the term rice paper ceiling has been coined (Kopp, 1994). This ceiling is an artificial barrier to advancement for non-Japanese employees of Japanese firms. The ceiling has been criticized as a means for Japanese firms to keep authority and power in the hands of Japanese firms and out of the reach of local employees. This ceiling has also been suggested as one of the explanatory factors for the poor performance of Japanese subsidiaries, particularly in the United States. For a discussion of some of the problems associated with Japanese expatriate managers in US factories, see Kamiyama (1994). According to some observers, this preference for Japanese managers has been the "Achilles heel" of Japanese MNEs (Bartlett and Yoshihara, 1988). In a study of Japanese JVs in the United States, financial performance problems plagued many of the JVs, as did a situation of two "camps" of managers within the JV organization (Inkpen, 1995). In many of these JVs, the Japanese partner was clearly unwilling to reduce the number of Japanese managers in senior positions, despite the cost of expatriates and availability of qualified American managers.

DeNero (1990) identified various areas where Japanese subsidiaries in the United States had weaknesses: lack of product fine-tuning for US customers; failure to tailor marketing approaches to different customer segments; and lack of speed, flexibility, and responsiveness. DeNero argued that each of these weaknesses could probably have been alleviated through the effective use of local managers. In our JV research, a number of managers described organizational practices as costly and wasteful because of their failure to follow common American practices (Inkpen, 1995).

The observed decline in Japanese expatriates means that non-Japanese must be taking on more managerial responsibilities in Japanese subsidiaries. What we don't yet know is why. Is it because the rice ceiling is coming down for rational business reasons or is it because demographics and a shortage of Japanese managers has created a situation of no choice – local managers must be used if Japanese FDI is to continue.

We ruled *out* two explanations for the decline in expatriates. The first is the argument that Japanese firms were using more JVs and hence, more local managers. The general trend observed in our analysis was that the greater the equity holding of the Japanese partner, the greater the use of Japanese expatriates. If there were more JVs and fewer WOS being formed, there would also be fewer expatriate managers. Our analysis of Japanese firms' international entry modes did not indicate a growing preference for JVs rather than WOS. Over time, the Japanese preference for JVs appears to be cyclical (Beamish, Delios, and Lecraw, 1997). Except for subsidiaries formed prior to 1960, which were 77% WOS, from 1961 to 1993 the percentage of WOS showed no clear trend. There was a weak trend towards acquisitions in the most recent periods, which if anything, suggests more expatriates would be used rather than less.

A second explanation that is not supportable is the argument that Japanese firms are moving resources and operations back to Japan and, therefore, have less need for expatriates. During the 1980s and the 1990s, Japanese FDI levels increased remarkably. In this period, the rapid expansion of Japanese firms' investment positions in international markets positioned Japan as the second leading source of FDI flows, behind only the United States, but beyond the United Kingdom and Germany (UNCTAD, 1996). Both the equity capital of many Japanese foreign subsidiaries and their functional scope has increased in recent years. In many Hong Kong and Singapore subsidiaries, for example, there has been a shift in the mandate of subsidiaries from a manufacturing operation to a regional headquarters. From 1993 to 1996, the stock of Japanese FDI grew at an average annual rate of 7-8% per year, and while this growth was concentrated in Asia and China, no region, other than perhaps Africa, saw a net decline in Japanese investment.

WHAT ARE THE IMPLICATIONS FOR FUTURE JAPANESE FDI?

Japanese firms have been criticized for their failure to use local nationals in their subsidiaries. Kopp (1994) suggested that the Japanese ethnocentric style of MNE management can lead to a combination of short-term cultural misunderstandings and the long-term effects of limited advancement opportunities for local nationals. According to Reich (1991), former US labor secretary:

> In the competition for global talent, corporations that are reluctant to consider foreign talent for top managerial positions will lose out: the most talented people simply will not join an organization that holds out no promise of promotion. Japanese-owned corporations that have been notoriously slow to open their top executive ranks to non-Japanese will operate at a competitive disadvantage.

Although it is too early to tell if Japanese firms are willing to open the most senior executive positions to non-Japanese, our research shows that at the subsidiary level, Japanese firms are using fewer expatriates. We have identified two possible future scenarios associated with Japanese MNEs, their use of expatriates, and their role in global business. The Toyo Keizai data indicates a link between subsidiary performance and the use of local nationals. On this basis, a possible scenario for Japanese FDI could unfold as follows. As Japanese firms continue to expand internationally, the shortage of qualified Japanese expatriates will force Japanese firms to hire more local nationals for senior managerial positions. As well, enlightened firms will realize that the rice paper ceiling is an obsolete concept. Over time, Japanese MNEs will shed their ethnocentric bias and hire the best managers they can find, Japanese or non-Japanese. Non-Japanese managers will find their way to the most senior executive ranks. As a result, Japanese MNEs become even stronger competitors around the world.

An alternative scenario is far less positive from a Japanese firm perspective. The inability to find high quality expatriates and the reluctance to abandon an ethnocentric view will limit Japanese MNEs' ability to grow. The increasing use of local managers will impact only middle and lower manager levels. Top management positions in both headquarters and subsidiaries will be reserved for Japanese nationals. As a result, Japanese FDI will stagnate and probably decline. Japanese firms will gradually play a less important role in the global environment.

If we were to bet, our money would be on the first scenario. Although some Japanese firms may prefer to muddle along with an outdated management approach, leading firms such as Toyota, Sony, Fujitsu, and Nomura will surely see the folly in not changing. Toyota, for example, is embarking on a massive global expansion through the year 2000. Although Toyota's Chairman has conceded that making Toyota more multinational will take years, hiring more non-Japanese is one of Toyota's objectives (Bremmer, 1997). Sony is another example of a firm that appears committed to greater use of local managers. Consider the comments of Sony's executive vice president concerning Sony's expansion in Malaysia:

> It is a Sony policy to think global and act local. . . . It is not economically viable for Sony to send people out to every country it sets up a production base in. Since we have already developed the local expertise in Malaysia a fair deal, we will boost this further to enable them to train others in the region. Sony intends to gradually decrease the number of Japanese expatriates working in Malaysia. (Kaur, 1995)

When Fujitsu Korea started operations in 1974, more than half of the 50 employees were Japanese expatriates. By 1994, Fujitsu had transferred responsibility for marketing and R&D to local staff and in 1993 a Korean became president. Of the 500 Fujitsu Korea employees, only three were Japanese expatriates (McGrath, 1994). At the investment firm Nomura

International, a major restructuring in Europe created new opportunities for non-Japanese managers. Prior to the restructuring, Nomura operated with 16 European offices reporting to Tokyo. These offices had one primary objective – to distribute products from Japan to European investors. Each office was headed by a Japanese expatriate operating as a country manager and there was limited coordination between European offices. With the new structure, the European offices would report to a London office and greater cross-border integration was anticipated, increasing promotion opportunities for non-Japanese managers. Eventually, Nomura expected its European business to be headed by a non-Japanese executive and to establish its own capital base and distinctive operating culture (Gapper, 1994).

CONCLUSION

In considering Japanese firms and their commitment to global egalitarianism in their management ranks, March (1992) noted that for this to happen, significant changes in the culture of Japanese firms and in the core values of senior Japanese managers would have to occur. Our data show that Japanese MNEs have begun the process of reducing expatriate managers. Accordingly, we would argue that a cultural change in Japanese firms is already underway. Interestingly, this cultural change has gone largely unnoticed by researchers and observers of Japanese business practice.

If Japanese firms truly recognize that using local managers leads to better subsidiary performance, changes in Japanese MNE operating policies could have a significant impact on global competition in many industries. Several intriguing questions remain unanswered. For example, why do subsidiaries established in the 1960s, 1970s, and early 1980s continue to use so many expatriates? If Japanese firms that internationalized later can succeed with fewer expatriates, why don't older Japanese MNEs emulate the newer firms and localize their management. Our analysis suggests superior performance for locally managed subsidiaries and there is no question that local managers will always be less expensive than Japanese expatriates.

Another question is to what extent a shift to fewer expatriates is simply a reaction to a lack of supply or a determined effort to adopt a new human resource management strategy. A further question is to what extent subsidiary top management positions are and will become accessible to local managers. Our Canadian data show that although the number of Japanese expatriates per firm is declining, the number of Japanese general managers has remained constant. If Japanese firms refuse to allow non-Japanese managers into top executive positions in their subsidiaries, the problems of ethnocentrism discussed earlier will continue to prevail. Finally, if there is greater use of local managers, will Japanese firms be more willing to engage in international mergers and acquisitions?

If the trend does reflect a shift in Japanese firm management practices, there are two important implications. The first is that there will be more management opportunities in Japanese subsidiaries for non-Japanese and by implication, even more competition for the existing supply of effective global managers. The second implication is that this trend represents a move toward genuine globalization for Japanese firms. On the assumption that localization improves subsidiary performance, many Japanese firms will become even stronger international competitors. For their North American, European, and Asian competitors, let this serve as a wake-up call.

NOTE

1. The Toyo Keizai data have been used in a number of studies, including Anderson and Noguchi (1995), Hennart (1991a), Sachwald (1995), and Yamawaki (1991). In the volume edited by Sachwald (1995), the appendix lists various sources of data on Japanese FDI activity and concludes that the Toyo Keizai data is the most extensive data source of Japanese firms' investments abroad.

ACKNOWLEDGEMENTS

We are grateful for the research assistance of Andrew Delios, helpful comments from Shige Makino, and the financial support provided by the Social Sciences and Humanities Research Council of Canada, and Business Research Center at Thunderbird, The American Graduate School of International Management.

13. Matching strategy with ownership structure in Japanese joint ventures

Shige Makino and Paul W. Beamish

Although many international joint ventures (JVs) are formed in the traditional way between foreign and local firms, nontraditional forms are increasingly being utilized. We identify four distinct types of JV ownership structure, based on partner nationality and affiliation. Senior executives of two large Japanese firms with joint ventures in Asia suggested three distinct strategies corresponding to the choice of JV ownership structure. These involve exploiting the competitive advantage specific to a parent firm, or to a pre-existing relationship, and complementing local partners' competitive advantage. We consider several key issues regarding JV partner selection and the development of a sustainable relationship between JV partners that are relevant to both American executives and those from other countries.

INTRODUCTION

The joint venture has become an increasingly popular form of foreign direct investment. Indeed, many successful firms are JVs between companies from different countries. An international JV has traditionally been considered one between a foreign and a local firm. However, some international JVs have partners from three or more countries. Others involve partnerships between firms from the same country, such as a JV formed in China by Japanese parent firms.

A FRAMEWORK FOR JV OWNERSHIP STRUCTURE

This study examines international JVs established by Japanese multinational enterprises (MNEs) in Asia. We define JV ownership structure in terms of partner nationality and partner affiliation. Partner nationality is determined by whether JV equity is owned by home-, host-, or third-country-based firms. Partner affiliation is determined by equity relatedness between partners. A partner is considered affiliated if it owns the equity of other partners. Otherwise, the partner is considered unaffiliated. JVs formed between affiliated partners are those JVs formed between a parent and its subsidiary and those between firms that are separate but have a cross-ownership relationship.

The classification scheme we have developed for JV ownership structures is outlined in Table 13.1. Intrafirm JVs are JVs formed between affiliated Japanese firms. An example is Newlong Singapore Private Ltd., a venture formed by the firms Newlong and its subsidiary, Newlong Kogyo. Cross-national domestic JVs are formed between unaffiliated Japanese firms. This type is represented by CMK Singapore Pte. Ltd., which was formed by two unaffiliated Japanese companies, Sumitomo Bakelite and CMK. Traditional international JVs are formed between Japanese and local firms. The US-based NUMMI, a JV between Toyota and General Motors, is an example. Trinational international JVs are formed between Japanese and third-country-based firms. An example is Thailand's FDK Tatung Co. Ltd., formed in Thailand by the Japanese firm FDK, and the Taiwanese firm Tatung. Both parents are unaffiliated, and both the home and third countries are represented in the partnership structure.

These forms of JV are characterized according to two dimensions – local access through partners and cultural distance between partners at national and corporate levels. The existing literature suggests that foreign firms are at a disadvantage with a local competitors. The formation of a JV with a local partner has often been considered an effective means to acquire local knowledge and overcome such disadvantages, particularly when such knowledge is difficult to acquire. The traditional international JV provides the greatest opportunity for a firm to acquire local knowledge from its partners.

Cultural distance exists in JVs formed by firms with different national and corporate cultures. National cultural distance occurs when JV partners are from different countries. Corporate cultural distance occurs when JV partners are unafiliated organizations with different historical backgrounds. Cultural distance often makes communication and learning between partners difficult.[1] National and corporate cultural distance contribute to management complexity. The overall level of complexity is highest in the traditional international JV and trinational international JV, which have great cultural distance at both levels. Moderate complexity is found in the cross-national domestic JV, which has high cultural distance at the corporate level but low distance at the national level. It is lowest in the intrafirm JV, which has low cultural distance at both levels.

Table 13.1 Joint venture ownership structure options for Japanese MNEs

Equity affiliation	Partner nationality	JV ownership structures	Descriptions of JV types
Affiliated	Japan	Intrafirm JVs	JVs formed outside Japan between a Japanese parent and its own subsidiary JVs formed outside Japan between Japanese firms that have a cross ownership holding
Affiliated	Japan	Cross-national domestic JVs	JVs formed outside Japan between Japanese firms that do not have an equity relationship
Unaffiliated	Local	Traditional international JVs	JVs formed outside Japan between a Japanese and a local firm
Unaffiliated	Thirds	Trinational international JVs	JVs formed outside Japan between a Japanese and a third-country firm that originates neither in Japan nor the host country

Table 13.2 Local access and cultural distance in joint venture ownership structures

	Intrafirm JV	Cross-national domestic JV	Traditional international JV	Trinational international JV
Local access through partners	No	No	Yes	No
National cultural distance	Low	Low	High	High
Corporate cultural distance	Low	High	High	High

Table 13.2 shows that a traditional international JV provides the best opportunity for a firm to gain local access through its local partner, despite high cultural distance at both levels between partners. An intrafirm JV, although it has the least interpartner cultural distance, provides no local access through local partners. A cross-national domestic JV also provides no

local access, and involves low national- and high corporate-cultural distance. A trinational international JV provides no local access and is subject to high cultural distance at both levels.

Why do some Japanese firms choose culturally distant JV partners – the traditional international JV and the trinational international JV – when they can choose culturally similar partners? And, why do Japanese firms choose nonlocal firms as their JV partners – intrafirm JV, cross-national domestic JV, and trinational international JV – when those JVs create disadvantages in the host country? To answer these questions, we interviewed five senior JV managers of two major Japanese MNEs, two from S-Electric Industries and three from M-Automotive Industries.[2] The two MNEs had a total of 25 JVs. Their profiles are provided in Table 13.3. The research methodology is described in the Appendix.

Table 13.3 Profiles of Japanese MNEs surveyed

	M-Auto		**S-Electric**	
Year founded	1970		1911	
Employees	26,470		14,833	
Total net sales	2,798		1,114	
(Japanese yen in billions)				
Export sales (%)	48		10	
Businesses (%)	Compact cars	47	Electric wires & cables	53
	Sub-compact cars	7	Special steel wires	5
	Tracks & buses	25	Sintered alloy products	10
	Auto parts	7	Brake products	6
	Others	14	Hybrid products	4
			Others	21
Overseas	Asia	18	Asia	26
subsidiaries and	Europe	7	Europe	10
affiliates including	North America	8	North America	15
JVs (all industries)	Others	3	Others	10
	Total	36	Total	61

Note: This table is based on data from 1991.

JV PRACTICES IN TWO JAPANESE FIRMS

Ownership Structure and Strategies

Of the 25 JVs, 16 (64 percent) were traditional international JVs. Four were intrafirm JVs, three were cross-national domestic JVs, and two were trinational international JVs. Three strategies influenced the choice of JV ownership structure:

- exploiting the competitive advantage specific to a parent firm;
- exploiting the competitive advantage specific to a pre-existing business relationship between the firms;
- complementing each partner's comparative advantage relative to the other.

The first strategy was associated with an intrafirm JV; the second with cross-national domestic and trinational international JVs; and the third with a traditional international JV (see Table 13.4).

Matching Strategies to Ownership Structure

Intrafirm JV

At the JV formed between S-Electric and its foreign subsidiary in Malaysia to produce cable wires, the Japanese managers suggested that an intrafirm JV was usually preferred when the benefits of coordinating internationally dispersed activities were high. According to the S-Electric manager, an intrafirm JV has virtually the same function as a wholly-owned subsidiary in that it is used to save production costs, hedge exchange rate risk, export products and components to its home-country-based parent, or substitute the parent firm's exports to a third country. An intrafirm JV is a miniature replica of the Japanese parent. It is expected to replicate its parent's strategy and to contribute to the benefits of internalization of global activities. The manager of S-Electric stated:

> This type of JV is used to implement our global strategy: to produce products where the manufacturing costs are cheaper, to sell products where the margins are higher, and to report profits where the taxes are lower.

The senior manager of M-Auto suggested another benefit of forming an Intrafirm JV: sharing the same corporate values. This facilitates the normative integration between a parent and its subsidiaries. He stated:

If we can manufacture standard cars in ASEAN countries and sell them without restriction, the establishment of a wholly-owned subsidiary or a JV formed with our affiliates may be the best way to proceed. Although there may be many merits of forming this latter type of venture, I personally feel that the most important thing is that it is easier to share our manufacturer's mind-set [with our partners] when we have such ventures.

The advantages of an intrafirm JV are its ability to exploit a Japanese parent firm's competitive superiority and to internalize its global production and marketing systems on a consolidated basis. An intrafirm JV produces the least management complexity because the JV partners are the same company. Since the JV partners share the same corporate values, partner conflicts or misperceptions are less likely to result in termination of the partnership.

Cross-national domestic JV

JVs like that in the Philippines between M-Auto and a Japanese trading company are often formed to transfer an established domestic buyer-supplier relationship into the host country, or to gain access to the local market information of a firm with the same nationality. The first type is usually formed when the firm cannot find desirable suppliers or buyers in the host country. The M-Auto manager said:

Our suppliers often follow us into foreign markets. In most cases, we set up a JV with a supplier, partly to disperse the capital risk to the supplier. Also, by carrying on the manufacturer-supplier relationship from Japan to the foreign country, we can make sure that technical cooperation between the two companies is strengthened. In many cases, it's quite difficult to find a comparative parts supplier in Asian countries. And probably most important, it is easier to manage a JV with a familiar Japanese business partner.

The second type of cross-national domestic JV is usually formed with *sogo shosha* general trading companies that possess huge market networks across the world and are a source of local market information for the firm. Most of the cross-national domestic JVs formed by M-Auto and S-Electric were with sogo shosha. Joint ventures between Japanese manufacturing firms and sogo shosha are quite popular, but unique to Japanese multinationals.[3] The M-Auto manager explained the merits of such JVs:

The reason why a sogo shosha is sometimes chosen as a JV partner is to let them take care of export operations. Especially when entering an unfamiliar market, the information on the world market which they have is very useful.

Table 13.4 Strategies and major reasons for JV ownership structure

Ownership structure	Number of JVs		Strategy	Major reasons for ownership structure
Intrafirm JV (JV of affiliated Japanese partners)	M-Auto S-Electric	3 1	Exploit a Japanese parent's competitive advantage.	To internalize a firm's global value activities. To share the same corporate value and culture.
Cross-national domestic JV (JV of unaffiliated Japanese firms)	M-Auto S-Electric	2 1	Exploit competitive advantages of the established business relationship between Japanese firms.	To disperse investment risks. To avoid possible partner conflict. To avoid possible partner conflict with a partner of different national background. To use partner's previous international experience. To transfer an existing domestic business relationship (a buyer-supplier between two or more Japanese firms) when a desirable local firm cannot be found.
Traditional international JV (JV of a Japanese and a local firm)	M-Auto S-Electric	8 8	Complement comparative advantages between a Japanese firm and a local firm.	To disperse investment risks. To circumvent local ownership restrictions in a host country. To get access to local partner's capability of marketing, negotiating with the government and managing local labour forces.
Trinational international JV (JV of a Japanese and a third-country firm)	M-Auto S-Electric	1 1	Exploit competitive advantages of the established business relationship between a Japanese firm and a third-country firm.	To disperse investment risks. To circumvent local ownership restrictions through the investment agreement between the host-country and the third-country governments. To transfer the existing international business relationship between a Japanese firm and a third-country firm when a desirable local firm cannot be found.

He was echoed by the S-Electric manager:

> By having a sogo shosha as a JV partner we can hedge the sales risk by asking them
> to engage in the sales, and we can hedge the risk of foreign currency restrictions,
> where they apply, through their participation in the partnership.

The managers suggested that the merits of the cross-national domestic JV are in dispersing investment risks and gaining access to partners' proprietary resources without incurring conflicts with a partner with a different national background. While an intrafirm JV tends to be used to exploit the parent firm's own competitive advantages, the cross-national domestic JV is often used to exploit the advantages of an established relationship between Japanese firms.

Managers often chose a cross-national domestic JV when the firm needed to establish a JV in the host country, and a suitable local firm was not available. In this way, a cross-national domestic JV can be a secondary option to a traditional international JV. However, the cross-national domestic JV may produce less management complexity than a traditional international JV. Since the JV partners have the same country of origin, the cross-national domestic JV can incur less management complexity than JVs formed between firms of different nationalities.

Traditional international JV

A Taiwan JV that produced electric cables was formed by S-Electric and a local cable manufacturer when local ownership was required by the host government and when S-Electric needed the local firm's assistance. The S-Electric manager explained:

> Establishment of a JV usually results from either of the two following
> circumstances: First, when it is impossible to establish a 100 percent subsidiary
> because of local regulations; and second, when there is no existing local market for
> the product we are going to manufacture. In the latter case, we need to form a JV in
> order to develop the market.

The managers of both companies suggested that a local partner plays a critical role in accessing local distribution networks, negotiating with local government, and hiring, educating and managing local labor forces. The M-Auto manager suggested that this type of capability cannot be obtained merely by spending years in the local country:

> Although we have long international experience in Asia, we still feel we have
> limited ability in negotiating with the local government and developing the local
> distribution network. In that sense, a JV with a local company has a big advantage
> in terms of complementarity.

If the local access is necessary, then why does a firm choose a local firm, not sogo shosha? While both a local firm and a general trading company provide the Japanese firm with general and specific local knowledge, sogo shosha may result in less management complexity than a local firm. The M-Auto manager commented:

> In terms of usefulness as an information source, local companies are superior to any *Shosha*. For example, using the information network of a local company is more effective for marketing than using the network of a *Shosha*. In addition, we have to pay dividends and commissions to the *Shosha*, so we try to avoid *Shosha* partners as much as possible.

While a traditional international JV can provide both partners with access to each other's resources, it is more likely to produce management complexity than an intrafirm JV or a cross-national domestic JV. The M-Auto manager, however, insisted that ease of management and business results did not always coincide:

> Our company set up a JV with a Chinese company which had majority ownership. Although our business plans have almost never been easily accepted by our Chinese partner, the business is very successful in terms of results. We cannot deny the considerable advantage of having a local partner, though other Japanese companies may want to have Japanese partners and be eager to obtain majority ownership.

The source of advantage of most traditional international JVs seems to be their ability to complement the comparative advantages of Japanese and local firms. Most traditional international JVs of both M-Auto and S-Electric are in fact formed to complement Japanese parent's technical advantages and a local firm's specific knowledge and skills. In choosing a JV partner, both M-Auto and S-Electric managers were concerned primarily with economic compatibility, such as complementary resources, and secondarily with organizational compatibility, such as management complexity. Economic compatibility needs to be developed in a relatively early stage of the JV's formation, while organizational compatibility can be developed as the JV endures. Thus, while the short-term success of the traditional international JV may depend on resource complementarity, the long-term success may depend on how quickly JV partners can develop, and how long they can maintain, a viable trust relationship with one another. Both managers agreed that traditional international JVs had the highest potential to attain financial performance, yet the highest likelihood of termination.

Trinational international JV

A Thailand JV that produced electric cables was formed by S-Electric and a US-based electronic company to transfer the established international business relationship between the Japanese firm and the US-based firm to another market. This type of JV is often preferred when a desirable local partner cannot be found and when the host country government has a special investment agreement with the third country government. The M-Auto manager explained:

> Our policy in choosing a JV partner is to find the best in the country. However, this is not always easy. For example, even if it is best in the long term to set up a JV with a certain local company, in the short term we sometimes have to choose second best, owing to regulations imposed by the foreign government and the existing relationship of our company with the other company in the area. In fact, we are currently trying to go into Vietnam. As we could not find an attractive local company, we gave up our plan to establish a JV with a Vietnamese company. Instead we decided to set up a JV with a Malaysian company with which we had already established a business relationship. Malaysia has a national investment agreement with Vietnam. Therefore, the JV with the Malaysian company enabled us to receive preferential treatment for our investment in Vietnam.

A trinational international JV is able to exploit the competitive advantages of the established business relationship between the Japanese firm and the third-country-based firm. A trinational international JV is usually considered a secondary option to traditional international and cross-national domestic JVs, and is often chosen when the parent firm can find neither an ideal local firm nor a potential Japanese partner. The M-Auto manager noted:

> This JV is a special case in our past foreign investments. Frankly, we were not so excited about the project.... We might have never considered forming this type of JV unless the Vietnam government provided subsidies for the investment.

A trinational international JV is the most complex form of the four types of JV ownership structure because both location of the operation and partner nationality are different. JV partners have different countries of origin, and none is familiar with local conditions. Managers generally agree that a trinational international JV is the least frequent form of JV ownership structure.

MANAGING INTERNATIONAL JV PARTNERS

A JV is formed by two or more firms that often disagree on just about anything.[4] Partner conflicts are more likely to occur when partners have different corporate or national cultures, as is usually the case in international JVs. This may lead to a concern with a shared management JV in an international context. As one observer notes, "A shared management venture should not be established unless it is abundantly clear that the extra benefit of having two parents managerially involved will more than offset the extra difficulty which will result."[5]

However, Japanese firms tend to form more traditional international JVs than JVs with culturally similar partners. Then why do so many traditional international JVs still exist? Did the Japanese managers make a wrong decision?

The interviews with the Japanese managers suggested that Japanese firms tended to weigh the potential benefits of having a local partner against the potential costs. JV success involves not only whether to have a local partner, but also how to build a relationship based on trust.

Trust and Contracts

Theoretically, trust plays an important role in preventing JV partners from behaving opportunistically,[6] which creates potential management complexity, and increases the necessity of monitoring. Opportunism can be avoided either by specific contract penalties or by building trust between partners. Managers of both companies suggested that contracts were less effective than a relationship built on trust. The S-Electric manager noted:

Since the contract is after all only paper, we can hardly say that preparing a complete contract is a sufficient precondition for success. I think it is important to establish a relationship of trust between the two parties so the partner may not violate the provisions. This is more effective than specifying penalties in the contract if the terms of the original agreement are violated.

And the M-Auto manager said:

Some people argue that it is important to include rules of behavior in the contract in order to prevent the partner from taking opportunistic action. According to our experience, this has not proved to be very effective. For example, we had a JV that exported products even though contract provisions prohibited it. We did not try to resolve this by referring to the contract, because that could have hurt the relationship, although we might have been able to resolve the problem temporarily. We believe that it is basically more important to try to avoid break-up than prepare detailed contracts to abide by.

Most economic studies of MNEs are based on the implicit assumption that a JV partner is essentially opportunistic, and therefore, that monitoring or controlling the partner's activity is critical for maintaining a good partnership.[7] The managers we interviewed seemed to make the opposite assumption: A JV partner is inherently cooperative at least initially, and trust is therefore critical for maintaining a good partnership. As the M-Auto manager commented: "After all, a JV is a kind of token to enforce our trust-based relationship."

Trust and Resource-Access Incentives

Trust, a partner's long-term commitment to maintaining a good partnership, is likely to occur when the firm's incentive is to gain access to resources rather than to acquire them.[8] In the first instance, each partner attempts to gain access to missing resources to attain a joint outcome. Toppan Moore, a Japanese-Canadian JV that lasted over 25 years, was formed to share North American technology and Japanese market knowledge. In the second instance, each partner attempts to acquire missing resources from the other to achieve its own strategic goal. When either of the JV partners has such a motivation, the JV is likely to be terminated or acquired by that partner. US-based Borden, for example, ended its partnership with Japan's Meiji Milk in 1991 after 20 years. Borden formed the alliance to gain access to the Japanese market for its ice cream. Borden eventually developed its own marketing know-how and decided to set up its own sales subsidiary in Japan. The managers of S-Electric and M-Auto had the same view of such actions. The S-Electric manager commented:

> Our policy for the relationship between our company and the local partner is not to acquire something from the partner, but to create something new to both of us together by each bringing something necessary.

The M-Auto manager concurred:

> The responsibility of a parent company should essentially be to support its local JV to become the best in the area. However, some managers of the Japanese company do not support the JV for the sake of the JV, but try to use the JV for the sake of the profit of the parent company. Such an attitude could hurt the relationship based on trust between the two partners. In order to establish a good partnership, it is sometimes necessary to be unselfish in order to build trust in the long term.

The managers suggest that trust is a special form of psychological commitment between JV partners that facilitates their mutual resource-access incentive. Without trust, each of them would focus merely on maximizing self-interest, or acquiring partner resources, resulting in conflict.

Trust, Ownership, and Control

Although the level of ownership has long been considered one of the most important mechanisms for control, the responses from the managers did not confirm this. Both Japanese managers repeatedly emphasized the importance of informal control mechanisms, such as shared values and shared commitment. The M-Auto manager suggested that these informal control systems reduce the importance of the size of ownership, yet facilitate the autonomous decision-making process with the JV. The M-Auto manager said:

> We think a JV evolves. Since we are an automobile manufacturer, we think the key to success is to share our manufacturer's mind-set with our partners. If a JV develops the capacity to think with the same mind-set as the parent company, it is time for that JV to act independently. By that time, the JV may have grown to be independent enough to even be able to support the parent company.... If we achieve this sharing of the mind-set, the next objective of the JV is to be the best in the country. Therefore, the equity of ownership percentage of the parent company itself becomes less important in terms of management control.

The S-Electric manager explained that decisions should be made not by majority rule, but by unanimous agreement based on trust. He noted:

> There are many ways to maintain a good relationship. I think the most important thing is, no matter how high our equity is in the JV, one should not make management decisions by majority rule. If we force the partner to accept our majority decision, the minority holder will inevitably resist us by saying, for example, 'We will sell our stock to a third party if you force us to comply'. Thus the relationship based on trust will collapse. A JV is like an arranged marriage. Often we do not know the partner until after we are married. That is why we have to free ourselves from the amount of ownership and make sure we have commitment and the right attitude on which to build trust. We are not making management decisions by majority but by unanimous agreement.

Both managers suggest that a homogenous decision-making context would be created through sharing values, while an autonomous decision-making context would be created by the parents' keeping hands off the JV. Interestingly, while research has focused on the importance of equity ownership and control, neither was used by these managers to achieve JV success. Rather, the managers believed that ownership and control become less critical as the partners build trust for each other.

HOW UNIQUE IS THE JAPANESE JV OWNERSHIP STRATEGY?

Is the Japanese ownership strategy of joint ventures unique? Previous studies have generally suggested yes, that North American firms tended to secure either full- or minority-ownership positions in their subsidiaries, while Japanese firms preferred a shared yet dominant ownership position.[9] The primary interest of North American firms may be either to secure full control by establishing a wholly-owned subsidiary or to minimize investment risks by holding a minority position in a JV.[10] On the contrary, as the Japanese managers suggested, the primary interest of Japanese firms was to gain favourable local access through their JV partners, not to secure control or dissipate investment risks. Partly for this reason, the Japanese firms have been more likely to share ownership with local firms than North American firms,[11] implying that Japanese managers have different attitudes and perceptions on foreign activities from North American managers.

Asian Versus American Partners

Japanese managers do not always see their JV partners as trustworthy friends. One manager noted that Japanese firms tended to have different attitudes towards Asian and American partners. The M-Auto manager noted:

> There are some unique customs in Asia where the ideal and the reality are different and there is no strict distinction in management control based on the equity ownership. The reason we do not want to set up a JV with American companies is because they think very strictly that equity ownership equals control. If we were to set up a JV in, say, Thailand with an American company where our equity was 49 percent and theirs 51 percent, I do not think such a JV would be successful.

This attitude towards American JV partners is consistent with previous studies,[12] which suggested that many Japanese firms form JVs with American MNEs to acquire their proprietary skills and knowledge and build their own competitive advantages over rivals including their American partners. Our study suggests that Japanese firms form JVs with local partners because they need their assistance with regard to market access and local knowledge in the host country, and are satisfied with having access to, rather than acquiring these contributions.

These differing attitudes arise for several reasons. First, it is more likely for established Japanese multinational enterprises such as M-Auto and S-Electric to find comparable JV partners in North America, rather than in Asia, that potentially become competitors to the Japanese firms. Second, given a lucrative market opportunity in Asia, forming a cooperative relationship with local partners is more critical in Asia than in North America as a means to gain quick access to the local market and build legitimacy and recognition in a host country. Finally, Japanese managers, as Asians, may share similar cultural values and norms with Asian partners. Thus, Japanese firms tend to form a more friendly, cooperative relationship with Asian partners than with those in North America.

CHOOSING AND KEEPING GOOD PARTNERS

This study considered two questions: Why do firms choose different JV ownership structures and how do they maintain or enforce good partnerships? The detailed interviews with the senior executives of two Japanese MNEs suggest that each of the four JV ownership structures has a distinct strategic orientation. An intrafirm JV differs from the other three forms in that partners provide similar elements of resources to the venture. In the other forms of JVs, partners make independent or complementary contributions to the venture. Competitive advantages in the intrafirm JV are specific to a single parent firm, while those of the other forms are specific to the relationship between partners.

A traditional international JV also has distinctive characteristics in the way it attains competitive advantage. The competitive advantages of JVs having other ownership structures seem to originate in the transfer, or exploitation, of ownership advantage of either a single firm or an established relationship between firms in a host country. In contrast, those of the traditional international JV seem to involve the creation of a new advantage by complementing comparative advantages between partners in the host country. A cross-national domestic JV and a trinational international JV both seem to have similar strategic orientation. The competitive advantage of both JV ownership structures is in the exploitation of relationship-based advantages. They differ in that cross-national domestic JV partners share the same nationality, while partners in trinational international JVs have different nationalities.

These findings provide several implications for the choice of JV ownership structure. First, if a firm is confident that its skills, brand reputation, and other attributes are strong enough to outweigh its lack of local knowledge about indigenous competitors, one promising option is to form an intrafirm JV. This option may enable the firm to reduce the likelihood of conflicts between JV partners. Second, if a firm is confident that it can outperform indigenous competitors by transferring an established relationship into the host country, rather than investing in the host country by itself, it may be able to use either a cross-national domestic JV, when a JV partner is of the same nationality, or a trinational international JV, when a JV partner is of a different nationality. Finally, if a firm's primary purpose is to gain access to a local firm's proprietary knowledge of local conditions, a traditional international JV will be the best choice.

With regard to maintaining good partnerships, our study suggested that partnerships in traditional international JVs were developed, maintained, and enforced in a way that was different from that suggested previously in the economics literature.   Japanese practitioners had a different view of corporate behavior and a very positive attitude towards development of cooperative relationships with local partners.   To sustain the JV's success, each partner should have a strong commitment to overcoming the managerial complexity that results when interests and activities are dissimilar.

APPENDIX

Research Methodology

We interviewed five executives of two Japanese parent firms who are or were senior managers in JVs.   The sample firms, selected from the Toyo Keizai database (*Kaigai Shinshutsu Kigyou Souran*), were S-Electric Industries and M-Automotive Industries.   Both firms provide complete coverage of all four of the JV ownership structures.

Generally, Japanese senior executives are reluctant to be interviewed, particularly when an interviewer is non-Japanese or has no link to the company.   Even though one of the authors is Japanese, this does not provide access to senior executives.   The successful approach was to contact people with strong personal connections to senior managers in each firm.   A senior professor at the business school of a major Japanese university with graduates at most large Japanese companies helped us approach executives.

Most senior managers we contacted were managers involved in the international planning department at headquarters.   We asked them why the firm chose a particular JV ownership structure and what was the intended goal of the JV.   We also interviewed other managers involved in front-line JV management.   We asked this group about the difficulties of managing the partner relationship, and what their firms had gained from and given to the JV.   The questions were asked in an unstructured setting.   All interviews were conducted in Japanese and taped and documented with the permission of the respondents.

NOTES

1. See for example, Barkema, Bell, and Pennings (1996), Brown, Rugman, and Verbeke (1989), and Lane and Beamish (1990).
2. The names of the companies are disguised.
3. Sogo shosha also gain benefits by forming a JV with a Japanese manufacturer. Anazawa noted that sogo shosha "enhanced their businesses by exporting machinery and production equipment before starting [JV] operation and supplying materials for production thereafter. They also made use of their business networks in the host country." See Anazawa, (1994), p. 99.
4. Many studies have suggested that the termination rate of an international JV was quite high. See for example, Franko (1971), Harrigan (1985), Kogut (1988b), and Geringer and Hebert (1989).
5. Killing, (1983).
6. Opportunism has been one of the central behavioral assumptions in transaction cost economics. The concept of opportunism generally refers to "a condition of a self-interest seeking with guile." See Williamson, (1985). Some studies discussed the relationship between trust and opportunism in a JV context. See for example, Beamish and Banks (1987), and Buckley and Casson (1988).
7. Transaction cost economists share this view. For example, Williamson, op. cit., p. 7, noted that "any issue that can be formulated as a contracting problem can be investigated to advantage in transaction cost economizing terms." Hennart also adopts this contracting orientation in the study of international JVs: "Whenever partners have conflicting goals which cannot be reconciled by contract, their actions will lower the profits available for sharing, and the joint venture mode of organization will prove to be very costly for one or both parties." Hennart, (1991b), p. 99-100.
8. A detailed practitioner-oriented discussion of the resource-acquisition and resource-access view is provided in Beamish and Inkpen, (1995). A conceptual framework is provided in Inkpen and Beamish, (1997).
9. For the latest evidence, see Beamish and Delios (1997b) and Pan (1997).
10. Anderson and Gatignon, (1986) provided a theoretical model that supports this evidence. They suggested that the choice of desired level of equity ownership would be based on the trade-off between risks of resource commitment and control.
11. See Beamish, Delios and Lecraw, (1997).
12. See, for example, Hamel, Doz, and Prahalad (1989), and Inkpen (1992).

References

Abegglen, J. C. and G. Stalk (1985), *Kaisha, the Japanese Corporation,* New York: Basic Books.

Adler, Nancy J. and J. L. Graham (1989), 'Cross-cultural integration: The international comparison fallacy?', *Journal of International Business Studies,* **20** (3), 515-537.

Agarwal, Sanjeev (1994), 'Socio-cultural distance and the choice of joint ventures: A contingency perspective', *Journal of International Marketing,* **2** (2), 63-80.

Agarwal, Sanjeev and Sridhar N. Ramaswami (1992), 'Choice of foreign market entry mode: Impact of ownership, location and internalization factors', *Journal of International Business Studies,* **23** (1), 1-28.

Alstom, L. J. and W. Gillespie (1989), 'Resource coordination and transaction costs: A framework for analyzing the firm/market boundary', *Journal of Economic Behavior and Organization,* **11** (2), 191-212.

Amit, Raphael, J. Livnat and P. Zarowin (1989), 'The mode of corporate diversification: Internal ventures versus acquisitions', *Managerial and Decision Economics,* **10,** 89-100.

Anand, B. and T. Khanna (2000), 'Do firms learn to create value? The case of alliances', *Strategic Management Journal,* **21** (3), 295-315.

Anand, Jaideep and Andrew Delios (1997), 'Location specificity and the transferability of downstream assets to foreign subsidiaries', *Journal of International Business Studies,* **28** (3), 579-604.

Anand, Jaideep and Bruce Kogut (1997), 'Technological capabilities of countries, firm rivalry and foreign direct investment', *Journal of International Business Studies,* **28** (3), 445-465.

Anand, Jaideep and H. Singh (1997), 'Asset redeployment, acquisitions and corporate strategy in declining industries', *Strategic Management Journal,* **18** (Special Issue), 99-118.

Anazawa, M. (1994), 'Japanese manufacturing investment in Malaysia', in K.S. Jomo (ed.), *Japan and Malaysian development: In the shadow of the rising sun,* New York: Routledge.

Anderson, A. D. and K. Noguchi (1995), 'An analysis of the intra-firm sales activities of Japanese multinational enterprises in the United States: 1977-1989', *Asia Pacific Journal of Management,* **12,** 69-90.

Anderson, E. (1985), 'The salesperson as outside agent or employee: A transaction cost analysis', *Marketing Science,* **4**, 234-254.

Anderson, E. and A. T. Coughlan (1987), 'International market entry and expansion via independent or integrated channels of distribution', *Journal of Marketing,* **51** (1), 71-82.

Anderson, E. and H. Gatignon (1986), 'Modes of foreign entry: A transaction cost analysis and propositions', *Journal of International Business Studies,* **17** (3), 1-26.

Anderson, E. and D. C. Schmittlein (1984), 'Integration of the sales force: An empirical examination', *Rand Journal of Economics,* **15**, 385-395.

Andrews, K. R. (1971), *The Concept of Corporate Strategy,* Homewood, IL: Irwin.

Ansoff, H. I. (1965), *Corporate Strategy,* New York: McGraw Hill.

Arrow, K. J. (1971), *Essays in the Theory of Risk-Bearing,* Chicago: Markham.

Asheghian, Parviz (1982), 'Comparative efficiencies of foreign firms and local firms in Iran', *Journal of International Business Studies,* **13** (3), 113-19.

Balakrishnan, Srinivasan (1988), 'The prognostics of diversifying acquisitions', *Strategic Management Journal,* **9** (2), 185-196.

Barclay, D., R. Thompson and C. Higgins (1995), 'The partial least squares (PLS) approach to causal modeling: Personal computer adoption and use as an illustration', *Technology Studies,* **2** (Special Issue), 285-324.

Barkema, H. G., J. H. J. Bell and J. M. Pennings (1996), 'Foreign entry, cultural barriers, and learning', *Strategic Management Journal,* **17** (2), 151-166.

Barkema, H. G., O. Shenkar, F. Vermeulen and J. H. J. Bell (1996), 'Working abroad, working with others: How firms learn to operate international joint ventures', *Academy of Management Journal,* **40**, 426-442.

Barkema, H. G. and F. Vermeulen (1998), 'International expansion through start-up or acquisition: A learning perspective', *Academy of Management Journal,* **41**, 7-27.

Barkema, H. G. and Freek Vermeulen (1997), 'What differences in the cultural backgrounds of partners are detrimental for international joint ventures?', *Journal of International Business Studies,* **28** (4), 845-64.

Barney, Jay B. (1991), 'Firm resources and sustained competitive advantage', *Journal of Management,* **17** (1), 99-120.

Barney, Jay B. (1988a), 'Returns to bidding firms in mergers and acquisitions: Reconsidering the relatedness hypothesis', *Strategic Management Journal,* **9** (Summer), 71-78.

Barney, Jay B. (1988b), 'Types of competition and the theory of strategy: Toward an integrative framework', *Academy of Management Review*, **11** (4), 791-800.

Bartlett, Christopher A. and Sumantra Ghoshal (1989), *Managing Across Borders: The Transnational Solution*, Boston: Harvard Business School Press.

Bartlett, Christopher A. and H. Yoshihara (1988), 'New challenges for Japanese multinationals: Is organizational adaptation their Achilles heel?', *Human Resource Management*, **27** (1), 19-43.

Baum, Joel A. C. and Helaine J. Korn (1996), 'Competitive dynamics of interfirm rivalry', *Academy of Management Journal*, **39** (2), 255-291.

Beamish, Paul W. (1993), 'The characteristics of joint ventures in the People's Republic of China', *Journal of International Marketing*, **1**, 29-48.

Beamish, Paul W. (1988), *Multinational joint ventures in developing countries*, New York: Routledge.

Beamish, Paul W. (1985), 'The characteristics of joint ventures in developed and developing countries', *Columbia Journal of World Business*, **20** (3), 13-19.

Beamish, Paul W. (1984), *Joint venture performance in developing countries*, unpublished Ph.D. dissertation, Ontario, Canada: The University of Western Ontario.

Beamish, Paul W. and John C. Banks (1987), 'Equity joint ventures and the theory of the multinational enterprise', *Journal of International Business Studies*, **18** (2), 1-16.

Beamish, Paul W. and R. C. daCosta (1984), 'Factors affecting the comparative performance of multinational enterprises', *European International Business Association Conference Proceedings*, Rotterdam, Holland.

Beamish, Paul W. and Andrew Delios (1997a), 'Improving joint venture performance through congruent measures of success', in P. W. Beamish and J. Peter Killing (eds), *Cooperative strategies: European perspectives*, San Francisco: The New Lexington Press.

Beamish, Paul W. and Andrew Delios (1997b), 'Incidence and propensity of alliance formation by US, Japanese and European MNEs', in P. W. Beamish and J. P. Killing (eds), *Cooperative strategies: Asian perspectives*, San Francisco: The New Lexington Press.

Beamish, Paul W., Andrew Delios and Donald J. Lecraw (1997), *Japanese Multinationals in the Global Economy*, Cheltenham, UK and Lyme, US: Edward Elgar Publishing.

Beamish, Paul W. and Andrew Inkpen (1995), 'Keeping joint ventures stable and profitable', *Long Range Planning*, **28** (3), 26-36.

Beechler, S. and A. L. Iaquinto (1994), 'A longitudinal study of staffing patterns in US affiliates of Japanese transnational companies', paper presented at Academy of Management Meetings, Dallas.

Belderbos, R. and L. Sleuwaegen (1996), 'Japanese firms and the decision to invest abroad: Business groups and regional core networks', *Review of Economics and Statistics,* **78** (2), 214-220.

Bell, John H. J. (1996), *Joint or single venturing? An eclectic approach to foreign entry mode,* Aldershot, UK: Avebury.

Bernheim, B. Douglas and Michael D. Whinston (1990), 'Multimarket contact and collusive behavior', *RAND Journal of Economics,* **21** (1), 1-26.

Bettis, R. A. (1981), 'Performance differences in related and unrelated diversified firms', *Strategic Management Journal,* **2** (3), 379-393.

Bettis, R A. and W. K. Hall (1982), 'Diversification strategy, accounting determined risk, and accounting determined return', *Academy of Management Journal,* **25** (2), 254-264.

Bettis, R. A. and V. Mahajan (1985), 'Risk/return performance of diversified firms', *Management Science,* **31**, 785-799.

Birkinshaw, J., A. Morrison and J. Hulland (1995), 'Structural and competitive determinants of a global integration strategy', *Strategic Management Journal,* **16**, 637-655.

Bleeke, Joel and David Ernst (1993), *Collaborating to compete: Using strategic alliances and acquisitions in the global marketplace,* New York, NY: Wiley.

Blodgett, Linda L. (1992), 'Factors in the instability of international joint ventures: An event history analysis', *Strategic Management Journal,* **13** (6), 475-81.

Blodgett, Linda L. (1991), 'Partner contributions as predictors of equity share in international joint ventures', *Journal of International Business Studies,* **22** (1), 63-78.

Boddewyn, Jean J., Marsha Baldwin Halbrich and A. C. Perry (1986), 'Service multinationals: Conceptualization, measurement and theory', *Journal of International Business Studies,* **17** (3), 41-57.

Bowman, E. H. (1982), 'Risk seeking by troubled firms', *Sloan Management Review,* **23**, 33-42.

Bradley, D. (1977), 'Managing against expropriation', *Harvard Business Review* (July-Aug.), 75-83.

Bremmer, B. (1997), 'Toyota's crusade: Hiroshi Okuda is retooling the company in an all-out bid to turn Toyota into the world's premier carmaker', *Business Week,* **April 7**, 104-114.

Brouthers, Keith D. (1995), 'The influence of international risk on entry mode strategy in the computer software industry', *Management International Review,* **35** (1), 7-28.

Brouthers, Keith D. and Gary J. Bamossy (1997), 'The role of key stakeholders in international joint venture negotiations: Case studies from eastern Europe', *Journal of International Business Studies,* **28** (2), 285-308.

Brown, L., Alan Rugman and Alain Verbeke (1989), 'Japanese joint ventures with Western multinationals: Synthesizing the economic and cultural explanations of failure', *Asia Pacific Jounral of Management,* **6**, 225-242.

Brown, Paul R., Virginia E. Soybel and Clyde P. Stickney (1994), 'Comparing US and Japanese corporate-level operating performance using financial statement data', *Strategic Management Journal,* **15** (1), 75-83.

Buckley, Peter J. and Mark C. Casson (1998), 'Analyzing foreign market entry strategies: Extending the internationalization approach', *Journal of International Business Studies,* **29** (3), 539-561.

Buckley, Peter J. and Mark C. Casson (1996), 'An economic model of international joint venture strategy', *Journal of International Business Studies,* **27** (5), 849-76.

Buckley, Peter J. and Mark C. Casson (1988), 'A theory of cooperation in international business', in Farok J. Contractor and Peter Lorange (eds), *Cooperative strategies in international business,* Lexington, MA: Lexington, pp. 31-51.

Buckley, Peter J. and Mark C. Casson (1976), *The future of the multinational enterprise,* London: Macmillan.

Burgleman, Robert A. (1985), 'Managing the internal development division: Research findings and implications for strategic management', *Strategic Management Journal,* **6**, 36-54.

Burgleman, Robert A. (1983), 'A process model of internal corporate venturing in the diversified major firm', *Administrative Science Quarterly,* **28**, 223-244.

Burton, F. N. and H. Inoue (1987), 'A country risk appraisal model of foreign asset expropriation in developing countries, *Applied Economics,* **19**, 1009-1048.

Burton, F. N. and F. H. Saelens (1982), 'Partner choice and linkage characteristics of international joint ventures in Japan', *Management International Review,* **22** (2), 20-9.

Busija, E. C. and H. M. O'Neill (1997), 'Diversification strategy, entry mode, and performance: Evidence of choice and constraints', *Strategic Management Journal,* **18** (4), 321-327.

Calvet, A. Louis (1984), 'A synthesis of foreign direct investment theories and theories of the multinational enterprise', *Journal of International Business Studies,* **12**, 43-59.

Cardozo, Richard, P. Reynolds, B. Miller and D. Phillips (1989), 'Empirical evidence on developmental trajectories of new businesses', in R. Brockhaus, N. Churchill, J. Katz, B. Kirchhoff, K. Vesper and W. Wetzel (eds), *Frontiers of Entrepreneurship Research,* St. Louis University: Babson College, pp. 360-369.

Carman, James M. and Eric Langeard (1980), 'Growth strategies for service firms', *Strategic Management Journal,* **1** (1), 7-22.

Carpenter, G. S. and K. Nakamoto (1989), 'Consumer preference formation and pioneering advantage', *Journal of Marketing Research,* **26** (3), 285-298.

Carr, D. L., J. R. Markusen and K. E. Maskus (1998), 'Estimating the knowledge-capital model of the multinational enterprise', *NBER Working Paper,* 6773.

Casson, Mark (1992), 'Internalization theory and beyond', in P. J. Buckley (ed), *New directions in international business: Research priorities for the 1990s,* Aldershot, UK and Brookfield, US: Edward Elgar.

Caves, Richard E. (1998), 'Research in international business: Problems and prospects', *Journal of International Business Studies,* **29** (1), 5-19.

Caves, Richard E. (1996), *Multinational enterprise and economic analysis,* second edition, Cambridge, MA: Cambridge University Press.

Caves, Richard E. (1989), 'Mergers, takeovers, and economic efficiency: Foresight vs. hindsight', *International Journal of Industrial Organization,* **7**, 151-174.

Caves, Richard E. (1982), *'Multinational enterprise and economic analysis',* New York, NY: Cambridge University Press.

Caves, Richard E. (1974), 'Causes of direct investment: Foreign firms' shares in Canadian and United Kingdom manufacturing industries', *Review of Economics and Statistics,* **56**, 279-293.

Caves, Richard E. (1971), 'International corporations: The industrial economics of foreign investment', *Economica,* **38**, 1-27.

Caves, Richard E. and S. K. Mehra (1986), 'Entry of foreign multinationals into US manufacturing industries', in M. E. Porter (ed.), *Competition In Global Industries,* Boston: Harvard Press.

Chang, S. J. (1995), 'International expansion strategy of Japanese firms: Capability building through sequential entry', *Academy of Management Journal,* **38** (2), 383-407.

Chang, S. J. (1992), *A Knowledge-Based Perspective on Corporate Growth: Entry, Exit, and Economic Performance During 1981-1989,* Unpublished PhD dissertation, Philadelphia, PA: University of Pennsylvania.

Chatterjee, Sanjit (1996), 'Types of synergy and economic value: The impact of acquisitions on merging and rival firms', *Strategic Management Journal,* **7**, 119-139.

Chatterjee, Sanjit (1992), 'Sources of value in takeovers: Synergy or restructuring - implications for target and bidder firms', *Strategic Management Journal,* **13** (4), 267-286.

Chatterjee, Sanjit (1990), 'Excess resources, utilization costs, and mode of entry', *Academy of Management Journal*, **33** (4), 780-800.

Chatterjee, Sanjit, M. H. Lubatkin, D. M. Schweiger and Y. Weber (1992), 'Cultural differences and shareholder value in related mergers: Linking equity and human capital', *Strategic Management Journal*, **13** (5), 319-334.

Chatterjee, Sanjit and B. Wernerfelt (1991), 'The link between resources and type of diversification: Theory and evidence', *Strategic Management Journal*, **12** (1), 33-48.

Chen, Ming-jer and Donald C. Hambrick (1995), 'Speed, stealth, and selective attack: How small firms differ from large firms in competitive behavior', *Academy of Management Journal*, **38** (2), 453-482.

Chen, Ming-jer, Ken G. Smith and Curtis M. Grimm (1992), 'Action characteristics as predictors of competitive responses', *Management Science*, **38** (3), 439-455.

Chi, Tailan (1994), 'Trading in strategic resources: Necessary conditions, transaction cost problems, and choice of exchange structure', *Strategic Management Journal*, **15** (4), 271-290.

Chowdhury, Jafor (1992), 'Performance of international joint ventures and wholly owned foreign subsidiaries: A comparative perspective', *Management International Review*, **32** (2), 115-133.

Christensen, H. K. and C. A. Montgomery (1981), 'Corporate economic performance: Diversification strategy versus market structure', *Strategic Management Journal*, **2** (3), 327-343.

Chu, Wujin and Erin M. Anderson (1992), 'Capturing ordinal properties of categorical dependent variables: A review with application to modes of foreign entry', *International Journal of Research in Marketing*, **9**, 149-160.

Cohen, Wesley M. and Daniel A. Levinthal (1990), 'Absorptive capacity: A new perspective on learning and innovation', *Administrative Science Quarterly*, **35** (1), 128-152.

Collis, D. J. (1991), 'A resource-based analysis of global competition: The case of the bearings industry', *Strategic Management Journal*, **12** (Special Issue Summer), 49-68.

Conn, R. L. and F. Connell (1990), 'International mergers: Returns to US and British firms', *Journal of Business Finance & Accounting*, **17** (5), 689-712.

Contractor, Farok J. (1990), 'Ownership patterns of US joint ventures abroad and the liberalization of foreign government regulation in the 1980s: Evidence from the benchmark surveys', *Journal of International Business Studies*, **21** (1), 55-73.

Contractor, Farok J. and Peter Lorange (1988), 'Why should firms cooperate? The strategy and economics basis for cooperative ventures', in

F. J. Contractor and P. Lorange (eds), *Cooperative strategies in international business,* New York: Lexington Books.

Cool, K., Dierickx, I. and Jemison D. (1989), 'Business strategy, market structure and risk-return relationships: A structural approach', *Strategic Management Journal,* **10**, 507-522.

Cosset, J. C. and J. Roy (1991), 'The determinants of country risk ratings', *Journal of International Business Studies,* **22** (1), 135-142.

Cullen, John B., Jean L. Johnson and Tomoyuki Sakano (1995), 'Japanese and local partner commitment to IJVs: Psychological consequences of outcomes and investments in the IJV relationship', *Journal of International Business Studies,* **26** (1), 91-115.

Curhan, J. P., W.H. Davidson and R. Suri (1977), *Tracing the multinationals: A sourcebook on US-based enterprises,* Cambridge, MA: Ballinger Publishing Co.

Cyert, Richard M. and James G. March (1963), *A behavioral theory of the firm,* Englewood Cliffs, NJ: Prentice-Hall.

Daiwa Institute of Research Limited (1996), *Analyst's guide,* Tokyo, Japan: Daiwa Securities Co., Ltd.

Daniels, John D. (1970), 'Recent foreign direct manufacturing investment in the United States', *Journal of International Business Studies,* **1** (1), 125-132.

Daniels, John D. and S. H. Magill (1991), 'The utilization of international joint ventures by United States firms in high technology industries', *The Journal of High Technology Management Research,* **2** (1), 113-131.

Daniels, John D., Ernest W. Ogram and Lee H. Radebaugh (1976), *International business: Environments and operations,* Reading, Massachusetts: Addison-Wesley.

Datta, Deepak K. (1991), 'Organizational fit and acquisition performance: Effects of post-acquisition integration', *Strategic Management Journal,* **12** (4), 281-297.

Datta, Deepak K., N. Rajagopalan and A. M. A. Rasheed (1991), 'Diversification and performance: Critical review and future directions', *Journal of Management Studies,* **28** (5), 529-558.

Davidson, William H. (1982), *Global Strategic Management,* New York, NY: John Wiley and Sons.

Davidson, William H. (1980a), *Experience effects in international transfer and technology transfer,* Ann Arbor, Michigan: UMI Research Press.

Davidson, William H. (1980b), 'The location of foreign direct investment activity: Country characteristics and experience effects', *Journal of International Business Studies,* **11** (1), 9-22.

Davidson, William H. and D. G. McFetridge (1985), 'Key characteristics in the choice of international technology transfer', *Journal of International Business Studies,* **16** (2), 5-21.

Davidson, William H. and Donald G. McFetridge (1984), 'Recent directions in international strategies: Production rationalization or portfolio adjustment?', *Columbia Journal of World Business*, Summer, **19** (2), 95-101.

Davies, Keri and Fergus Fergusson (1995), 'The international activities of Japanese retailers', *Service Industries Journal,* **15** (4), 97-117.

de Figueiredo, J. M. and D. J. Teece (1996), 'Mitigating procurement hazards in the context of innovation', *Industrial and Corporate Change*, **5**, 1-23.

Delios, Andrew and Paul W. Beamish (1999), 'Ownership strategy of Japanese firms: Transactional, institutional and experience influences', *Strategic Management Journal*, **20** (10), 915-933.

DeNero, H. (1990), 'Creating the 'hyphenated' corporation', *McKinsey Quarterly,* **4**, 153-174.

Dess, G. G., A. Gupta, J. F. Hennart and C. W. L. Hill (1995), 'Conducting and integrating strategy research at the international, corporate, and business levels: Issues and directions', *Journal of Management*, **21** (3), 357-393.

Dess, G. G., R. D. Ireland and M. A. Hitt (1990), 'Industry effects and strategic management research', *Journal of Management*, **16** (1), 7-27.

Dierickx, Ingemar and Karel Cool (1989), 'Asset stock accumulation and sustainability of competitive advantage', *Management Science*, **35** (12), 1504-10.

DiMaggio, Paul J. and Walter W. Powell (1983), 'The iron cage revisited: Institutional isomorphism and collective rationality in organizational fields', *American Sociological Review*, **48**, 147-160.

Dodwell (1996/1997), *Industrial groupings in Japan: The anatomy of the keiretsu* (12th ed.), Tokyo, Japan: Dodwell Marketing Consultants.

Drucker, Peter (1974), *Management: Tasks, responsibilities, promise*, New York: Harper & Row.

Dubin, Michael (1975), *Foreign acquisitions and the spread of the multinational firm*, Unpublished Doctoral Dissertation, Harvard.

Dun and Bradstreet (1995), *Principal international businesses: The world marketing directory 1996,* Bethlehem, PA: Dun & Bradstreet, Inc.

Dunning, John H. (1998), 'Location and the multinational enterprise: A neglected factor?', *Journal of International Business Studies*, **29** (1), 45-66.

Dunning, John H. (1993), *Multinational enterprises and the global economy,* Wokingham, England: Addison-Wesley Publishing Company.

Dunning, John H. (1989), 'Multinational enterprises and the growth of services: Some conceptual and theoretical issues', *Service Industries Journal,* **9** (1), 5-39.

Dunning, John H. (1988a), 'The Eclectic Paradigm of international production: A restatement and some possible extensions'; *The Journal of International Business Studies,* **19** (1), 1-31.

Dunning, John H. (1988b), *Explaining international production*, London: Unwin Hyman.

Dunning, John H. (1980), 'Toward an eclectic theory of international production: Some empirical tests', *Journal of International Business Studies*, **11** (2), 9-31.

Dunning, John H. (1977), 'Explaining changing patterns of international production: In defence of the eclectic theory', *Oxford Bulletin of Economics and Statistics*, **41** (4), 269-295.

Dussauge, Pierre and Bernard Garrette (1995), 'Determinants of success in international strategic alliances: Evidence from the global aerospace industry', *Journal of International Business Studies,* **26** (3), 505-30.

Economist (1996), 'The lesson the locals learnt a little too quickly', *The Economist,* **340** (7985), 71-72.

Edwards, Corwin D. (1955), 'Conglomerate bigness as a source of power', in the National Bureau of Economics Research conference report', *Business Concentration and Price Policy*, Princeton, NJ: Princeton University Press.

Eisenhardt, Kathleen M. (1989), 'Making fast strategic decisions in high-velocity environments', *Academy of Management Journal*, **32**, 533-576.

Enderwick, Peter (1990), 'The international competitiveness of Japanese service industries', *California Management Review,* **32** (4), 22-37.

Enderwick, Peter (1988), 'Between markets and hierarchies: The multinational operations of Japanese general trading companies', *Managerial and Decision Economics,* **9**, 35-40.

Erramilli, M. Krishna (1996), 'Nationality and subsidiary ownership patterns in multinational corporations', *Journal of International Business Studies*, **27** (2), 225-48.

Erramilli, M. Krishna (1991), 'The experience factor in the foreign market entry behaviour of service firms', *Journal of International Business Studies*, **22** (3), 479-501.

Erramilli, M. Krishna and Chatrathi P. Rao (1993), 'Service firms' entry-mode choice: A modified transaction-cost analysis approach', *Journal of Marketing*, **57** (3), 19-38.

Erramilli, M. Krishna and C. P. Rao (1990), 'Choice of foreign market entry modes by service firms: Role of market knowledge', *Management International Review*, **30** (2), 135-150.

European Round Table of Industrialists (1994), *Survey on Improvements of Conditions for Investment in the Developing World*, Vevey, Switzerland: Nestec Ltd.

Evans, Wendy, Henry W. Lane and Shawna O'Grady (1992), *Border crossings: Doing business in the US,* Scarborough, ON: Prentice-Hall.

Fagre, Nathan and Louis T. Wells, Jr. (1982), 'Bargaining power of multinationals and host governments', *Journal of International Business Studies,* **13** (2), 9-23.

Fisman, R. and T. Khanna (1998), 'Facilitating development: The role of business groups', *Harvard Business School Working Paper,* 98.

Fligstein, Neil (1991), 'The structural transformation of American industry: The causes of diversification in the largest firms, 1919-1979', in Walter W. Powell and Paul J. DiMaggio (eds), *The new institutionalism in organizational analysis,* Chicago: University of Chicago Press, pp. 311-336.

Fligstein, Neil (1985), 'The spread of the multidivisional form among large firms, 1919-1979', *American Sociological Review,* **59**, 377-391.

Flowers, E. B. (1976), 'Oligopolistic reactions in European and Canadian direct investment in the United States', *Journal of International Business Studies,* **7** (Fall/Winter), 43-55.

Fornell, C. and D. Larcker (1981), 'Evaluating structural equation models with unobservable variables and measurement error', *Journal of Marketing Research,* **18**, 39-50.

Forsgren, Mats (1989), *Managing the internationalization process: The Swedish case,* London, U.K.: Routledge.

Franko, Lawrence G. (1989), 'Use of minority and 50-50 joint ventures by United States multinationals during the 1970s: The interaction of host country policies and corporate strategies', *Journal of International Business Studies,* **20** (1), 19-40.

Franko, Lawrence G. (1987), 'New forms of investment in developing countries by US companies: A five industry comparison', *Columbia Journal of World Business,* **22** (2), 39-56.

Franko, Lawrence G. (1971), *Joint venture survival in multinational corporations,* New York: Praeger Publishers.

Freund, John E., and R. E. Walpole (1980), *Mathematical Statistics* 3rd ed., Englewood Cliffs, New Jersey: Prentice-Hall Inc.

Friedman, Wolfgang G. and John-Pierre Beguin (1971), *Joint international business ventures in developing countries,* New York, NY: Columbia University Press.

Gapper, J. (1994), 'Taking Japan out of Nomura International - The broker is quietly restructuring its European arm to serve clients better and shift the power away from Tokyo', *Financial Times,* **April 14**, 30.

Gatignon, Hubert and E. Anderson (1988), 'The multinational corporation's degree of control over foreign subsidiaries: An empirical test of a transaction cost explanation', *Journal of Law, Economics, and Organization*, **4** (2), 305-336.

Gatignon, Hubert and E. Anderson (1987), 'The multinational corporation's degree of control over foreign subsidiaries: An empirical test of a transaction cost explanation', in *Report Number 87-103, Marketing Science Institute*, Cambridge, MA.

Geringer, J. Michael (1991), 'Strategic determinants of partner selection criteria in international joint ventures', *Journal of International Business Studies*, **22** (1), 41-62.

Geringer, J. Michael, Paul W. Beamish and R. C. daCosta (1989), 'Diversification strategy and internationalization: Implications for MNE performance', *Strategic Management Journal*, **10**, 109-119.

Geringer, J. Michael and Louis Hebert (1991), 'Measuring performance of international joint ventures', *Journal of International Business Studies*, **22** (2), 249-263.

Geringer, J. Michael and Louis Hebert (1989), 'Control and performance of international joint ventures', *Journal of International Business Studies*, **20** (2), 235-254.

Gerlach, M. L. (1992), *Alliance capitalism: The social organization of Japanese business*, Berkeley, CA: University of California Press.

Gerlach, M. L. (1987), 'Business alliances and the strategy of the Japanese firm', *California Management Review*, **30** (1), 126-142.

Ghoshal, S. and P. Moran (1996), 'Bad for practice: A critique of transaction cost theory', *Academy of Management Review*, **21** (1), 13-47.

Gimeno, Javier and Carolyn Y. Woo (1996), 'Hypercompetition in a multimarket environment: The role of strategic similarity and multimarket contact in competitive de-escalation', *Organization Science*, **7** (3), 322-341.

Gomes-Casseres, Benjamin (1990), 'Firm ownership preferences and host government restrictions: An integrated approach', *Journal of International Business Studies*, **21** (1), 1-22.

Gomes-Casseres, Benjamin (1989), 'Ownership structures of foreign subsidiaries: Theory and evidence', *Journal of Economic Behavior and Organization*, **11** (1), 1-26.

Gomes-Casseres, Benjamin (1988), 'Joint venture cycles: The evolution of ownership strategies of US MNEs, 1945-75', in Farok J. Contractor and Peter Lorange (eds), *Cooperative Strategies in International Business*, Lexington Books, New York.

Gomes-Casseres, Benjamin (1987), 'Joint venture instability: Is it a problem?', *Columbia Journal of World Business*, **22** (2), 97-101.

Gort, M. (1962), *Diversification and Integration in American Industry,* Princeton University Press, Princeton, NJ.

Graham, Edward M. and Naoko T. Anzai (1994), 'The myth of a *de facto* East Asian Bloc', *Columbia Journal of World Business* (Fall 1994), 7-20.

Grant, R. M. (1987), 'Multinationality and performance among British manufacturing companies', *Journal of International Business Studies,* **18** (1), 79-89.

Grant, R. M., A. P. Jammine and H. Thomas (1988), 'Diversity, diversification, and profitability among British manufacturing companies, 1972-84', *Academy of Management Journal,* **31**, 771-801.

Green, R. T. and W. Cunningham (1975), 'The determinants of US foreign investment: An empirical examination', *Management International Review,* **15** (2-3), 113-120.

Greene, William H. (1997), *Econometric analysis,* third edition, Upper Saddle River, NJ: Prentice Hall.

Grossman, Sanford J. and Oliver D. Hart (1986), 'The costs and benefits of ownership: A theory of vertical and lateral integration', *Journal of Political Economy,* **94** (4), 691-719.

Grubaugh, Stephen G. (1987), 'Determinants of foreign direct investment', *Review of Economics and Statistics,* **69**, 149-152.

Guillen, M. (2000), 'Business groups in emerging economies: A resource-based view', *Academy of Management Journal,* **43**, 362-380.

Guillen, M. (1999), *Business Groups in Emerging Economies: A resource-based view,* Mimeo.

Guisinger, Stephen E. and Associates (1985), *Investment Incentives and Performance Requirements: Pattern of International Trade, Production, and Investment,* New York, Praeger Publishers.

Haar, Jerry (1989), 'A comparative analysis of the profitability performance of the largest US, European and Japanese multinational enterprises', *Management International Review,* **29** (3), 5-18.

Habib, Ghazi (1987), 'Measures of manifest conflict in international joint ventures', *Academy of Management Journal,* **30** (4), 808-16.

Hamel, Gary (1991), 'Competition for competencies and inter-partner learning within international strategic alliances', *Strategic Management Journal,* **12** (Special Issue, Summer), 83-103.

Hamel, G., Y.L. Doz and C.K. Prahalad (1989), 'Collaborate with your competitors – and win', *Harvard Business Review,* **67**, 133-39.

Hamel, Gary and K. C. Prahalad (1990), 'The core competence of the corporation', *Harvard Business Review* (May/June), 79-93.

Hannan, Michael T. and Glenn R. Carrol (1992), *The dynamics of organizational populations,* New York: Oxford University Press.

Hannan, Michael T. and John Freeman (1989), *Organizational ecology,*

Cambridge, MA: Harvard University Press.

Harrigan, Kathryn R. (1988), 'Joint ventures and competitive strategies', *Strategic Management Journal*, **9**, 141-158.

Harrigan, Kathryn R. (1986), *Managing for joint venture success,* Lexington, MA: Lexington.

Harrigan, Kathryn R. (1985), *Strategies for joint ventures*, Lexington, MA: Lexington Books.

Harrison, J. S., M. A. Hitt, R. E. Hoskisson and R. D. Ireland (1991), 'Synergies and post-acquisition performance: Differences versus similarities in resource allocations', *Journal of Management*, **17** (1), 173-190.

Haveman, Heather A. (1993), 'Follow the leader: Mimetic isomorphism and entry into new markets', *Administrative Science Quarterly*, **38**, 593-627.

Hebert, Louis (1994), 'Division of control: Relationship dynamics and joint venture performance', unpublished Ph.D. dissertation, London, Ontario, Canada: University of Western Ontario.

Helou, A. (1991), 'The nature and competitiveness of Japan's keiretsu', *Journal of World Trade*, **25** (3), 99-129.

Henisz, W. J. (2000a), *The institutional environment for multinational investment*, Reginald H. Jones Center for Management Policy, Strategy and Organization working paper, 2000(1).

Henisz, W. J. (2000b), 'The institutional environment for economic growth', *Economics and Politics*, **12** (1), 1-31.

Hennart, J. F. (1991a), 'The transaction cost theory of joint ventures: An empirical study of Japanese subsidiaries in the United States', *Management Science,* **37** (4), 483-497.

Hennart, J. F. (1991b), 'The transaction costs theory of the multinational enterprise', in C.N. Pitelis and S. Rogert (eds), *The nature of the transnational firm*, New York: Routledge.

Hennart, J. F. (1988), 'A transaction costs theory of equity joint ventures', *Strategic Management Journal,* **9** (4), 361-374.

Hennart, J. F. (1982), *A Theory of Multinational Enterprise,* Ann Arbor, MI: The University of Michigan Press.

Hennart, J. F. and Y.R. Park (1994), 'Location, governance and strategic determinants of Japanese manufacturing investment in the United States', *Strategic Management Journal*, **15**, 418-437.

Hennart, J. F. and Y. R. Park (1993), 'Greenfield vs. acquisition: The strategy of Japanese investors in the United States', *Management Science*, **39**, 1054-70.

Hill, C. W. L., P. Hwang and W. C. Kim (1990), 'An eclectic theory of the choice of international entry mode', *Strategic Management Journal*, **11** (2), 117-128.

Hill, C. W. L. and G. R. Jones (1989), *Strategic management: An integrated approach,* Boston: Houghton Mifflin Co.

Hirsch, Seev (1993), 'The globalization of services and service-intensive goods industries', in Y. Aharoni (ed.), *Coalitions and competitions: The globalization of professional business services,* London: Routledge.

Hirsch, Seev (1988), 'International transactions in services and in service-intensive goods', in H. Giersch (ed.), *Services in world economic growth,* Tel Aviv, Israel: Tel Aviv University.

Hisey, K. B. and R. E. Caves (1985), 'Diversification strategy and the choice of country: Diversifying acquisitions abroad by US multinationals, 1978-1980', *Journal of International Business Studies,* **16** (Summer), 51-64.

Hitt, M. A., R. E. Hoskisson and H. Kim (1997), 'International diversification: Effects on innovation and firm performance in product-diversified firms', *Academy of Management Journal,* **40** (4), 767-798.

Hopkins, H. Donald (1987), 'Acquisition strategy and the market position of acquiring firms', *Strategic Management Journal,* **8**, 535-547.

Horaguchi, Haruo (1992), *Nihon kigyo no kaigai chokusetsu toushi: Asia eno shinshutsu to tettai* [Foreign direct investment of Japanese firms: Investment and divestment in Asia], University of Tokyo Press, Tokyo, Japan.

Horst, T. (1972), 'Firm and industry determinants of the decision to invest abroad: An empirical study', *Review of Economics and Statistics,* **54**, 258-266.

Hoskisson, R. E. and M. A. Hitt (1990), 'Antecedents and performance outcomes of diversification: A review and critique of theoretical perspectives', *Journal of Management,* **16**, 461-509.

Hoskisson, R. E. and M. A. Hitt (1988), 'Strategic control systems and relative R&D investment in large multiproduct firms', *Strategic Management Journal,* **9**, 605-621.

Hosmer, David W., Jr. and Stanley Lemeshow (1987), *Applied logistic regression,* New York: John Wiley and Sons.

Hulland, J. H. (1999), 'The use of partial least squares (PLS) in strategic management research: A review of four recent studies', *Strategic Management Journal,* **20** (2), 195-204.

Hymer, Stephen H. (1976), *The international operations of national firms: A study of direct foreign investment,* Cambridge, Massachusetts: MIT Press. Original thesis produced in 1960.

Imai, K. (1987), 'The corporate network in Japan', *Japanese Economic Studies,* **16**, 1-37.

IMD International and World Economic Forum (1995), *The World Competitiveness Report 1995,* The Foundation, Geneva, Switzerland.

IMD and World Economic Forum (1994), *World Competitiveness Report,* Geneva, Switzerland: EMF Foundation.

Inkpen, Andrew C. (1995), *The management of international joint ventures: An organizational learning perspective*, London: Routledge Press.

Inkpen, Andrew C. (1992), *Learning and collaboration: An examination of North American-Japanese joint ventures*, unpublished Ph.D. dissertation, Ontario, Canada: The University of Western Ontario.

Inkpen, Andrew C. and Paul W. Beamish (1997), 'Knowledge, bargaining power, and the instability of international joint ventures', *Academy of Management Review*, **22** (1), 177-202.

Isobe, Takehiko, Shige Makino and David B. Montgomery (2000), 'Resource commitment, entry timing, and market performance of foreign direct investments in emerging economies: The case of Japanese international joint ventures in China', *Academy of Management Journal*, **43** (3), 468-484.

Janger, Allen R. (1980), *Organization of international joint ventures*, New York: Conference Board.

Jemison, David B. and Sim B. Sitkin (1986), 'Corporate acquisitions: A process perspective', *Academy of Management Review*, **11** (1), 145-163.

Jensen, Michael C. and R. S. Ruback (1983), 'The market for corporate control: The scientific evidence', *Journal of Financial Economics*, **11**, 5-50.

Johanson, Jan and Lars-Gunnar Mattson (1987), 'Interorganizational relations in industrial systems: A network approach compared with the transaction-cost approach', *International Studies of Management and Organization*, **XVII** (1), 34-48.

Johanson, J. and J. E. Vahlne (1977), 'The internationalization process of the firm: A model of knowledge development and increasing foreign market commitments', *Journal of International Business Studies*, **8** (1), 23-32.

Johanson, J. and F. Wiedersheim-Paul (1975), 'The internationalization of the firm: Four Swedish cases', *Journal of Management Studies*, **12** (3), 305-322.

Johansson, Johny K. (1990), 'Japanese service industries and their overseas potential', *Service Industries Journal*, **10** (1), 85-109.

Juul, Monika and P. G. P. Walters (1987), 'The internationalization of Norwegian firms - A study of the U.K. experience', *Management International Review*, **27** (1), 58-66.

Kamiyama, K. (1994), 'The typical Japanese overseas factory', in T. Abo (ed.), *Hybrid Factory: The Japanese Production System in the United States*, Oxford: Oxford University Press, pp. 58-81.

Kaur, L. (1995), 'Malaysia stands to gain from Sony shift', *Business Times*, Malaysia, February 3, 18.

Kawakami, S. (1996), 'Local problems', *Far Eastern Economic Review*, July 4, 44-46.

Khanna, Tarun and Krishna Palepu (1999), 'Policy shocks, market intermediaries, and corporate strategy: The Evolution of Business Groups in Chile and India', *Journal of Economics and Management Strategy*, **8** (2), 271-310.

Killing, J. Peter (1983), *Strategies for joint venture success*, New York, NY: Praeger.

Kim, W. Chan and P. Hwang (1992), 'Global strategy and multinationals' entry mode choice', *Journal of International Business Studies*, **23** (1), 29-54.

Kim, W. C., P. Hwang and W. P. Burgers (1993), 'Multinationals' diversification and the risk-return trade-off', *Strategic Management Journal*, **14**, 257-286.

Kim, W. C., P. Hwang and W. P. Burgers (1989), 'Global diversification strategy and corporate profit performance', *Strategic Management Journal*, **10**, 45-57.

Klein, B. and K. B. Leffler (1981), 'The role of market forces in assuring contractual performance', *Journal of Political Economy*, **89**, 615-641.

Knickerbocker, F. T. (1973), *Oligopolistic reaction and the multinational enterprise*, Boston, MA: Graduate School of Business Administration, Harvard University.

Kobrin, Stephen J. (1988), 'Trends in ownership of US manufacturing subsidiaries in developing countries: An interindustry analysis', in Farok J. Contractor and Peter Lorange (eds), *Cooperative Strategies in International Business*, Lexington Books, New York.

Kobrin, S. (1978), 'When does political instability result in increased investment risk?', *Columbia Journal of World Business* (Fall), 113-122.

Kobrin, S. (1976), 'The environmental determinants of foreign manufacturing investment: An ex post empirical analysis', *Journal of International Business Studies*, **7** (1), 29-42.

Kogut, Bruce (1991), 'Country capabilities and the permeability of borders', *Strategic Management Journal*, **12**, 33-47.

Kogut, Bruce (1989), 'The stability of joint ventures: Reciprocity and competitive rivalry', *Journal of Industrial Economics*, **38** (2), 183-198.

Kogut, Bruce (1988a), 'Joint ventures: Theoretical and empirical perspectives', *Strategic Management Journal*, **9** (4), 319-332.

Kogut, Bruce (1988b), 'A study of the life cycle of joint ventures', in Farok J. Contractor and Peter Lorange (eds), *Cooperative strategies in international business*, Lexington, MA: Lexington.

Kogut, Bruce (1983), 'Foreign direct investment as a sequential process', in C. P. Kindleberger (ed.), *The multinational corporations in the 1980s*, Cambridge, MA: MIT Press, pp. 35-56.

Kogut, Bruce and S. J. Chang (1991), 'Technological capabilities and Japanese foreign direct investment in the United States', *Review of Economics and Statistics*, **73** (3), 401-413.

Kogut, Bruce and Harbir Singh (1988), 'The effect of national culture on the choice of entry mode', *Journal of International Business Studies*, **19** (3), 411-32.

Kogut, Bruce and U. Zander (1996), 'What firms do? Coordination, identity and learning', *Organization Science*, **7**, 502-518.

Kogut, Bruce and Udo Zander (1995), 'Knowledge, market failure and the multinational enterprise: A reply', *Journal of International Business Studies*, **26** (2), 417-426.

Kogut, Bruce and Udo Zander (1993), 'Knowledge of the firm and the evolutionary theory of the multinational corporation', *Journal of International Business Studies*, **24** (4), 625-645.

Kogut, Bruce and Udo Zander (1992), 'Knowledge of the firm, combinative capabilities, and the replication of technology', *Organizational Science*, **3** (August), 383-397.

Koh, Jeongsuk and N. Venkatraman (1991), 'Joint venture formation and stock market reactions: An assessment in the information technology sector', *Academy of Management Journal*, **34** (4), 869-892.

Kohn, T. O. (1988), *International Entrepreneurship: Foreign Direct Investment by Small US-based Manufacturing Firms*, Unpublished DBA thesis, Harvard University, Cambridge, MA.

Kojima, Kiyoshi (1978), *Direct foreign investment: A Japanese model of multinational business operations*, London: Croom Helm.

Kojima, K. and T. Ozawa (1984), *Japan's general trading companies: Merchants of economic development*, Paris: OECD Press.

Kopp, R. (1994), *The Rice-Paper Ceiling: Breaking Through Japanese Corporate Culture*, Berkeley, CA: Stone Bridge Press.

Kopp, R. (1984), 'International human resource policies and practices in Japanese, European, and United States multinationals', *Human Resource Management*, **4**, 581-599.

Kumar, N. (1990), *Multinational Enterprises in India: Industrial Distribution, Characteristics and Performance*, London: Routledge.

Lall, S. (1980), 'Monopolistic advantages and foreign involvement by US manufacturing industry', *Oxford Economics Papers*, **32**, 102-22.

Lane, H.W. and P.W. Beamish (1990), 'Cross-cultural cooperative behaviour in joint ventures in LDCs', *Management International Review*, **30**, 87-102.

Lane, Henry W. and Terry Hildebrand (1990), 'How to survive in US retail markets', *Business Quarterly*, **54** (3), 62-66.

Lecraw, Donald J. (1984), 'Bargaining power, ownership, and profitability of transnational corporations in developing countries', *Journal of International*

Business Studies, **15** (1), 27-44.

Lee, Chol and Paul W. Beamish (1995), 'The characteristics and performance of Korean joint ventures in LDCs', *Journal of International Business Studies,* **26** (3), 637-54.

Levitt, B. and J. March (1988), 'Organizational learning', *Annual Review of Psychology,* **14**, 319-340.

Li, Jiatao (1995), 'Foreign entry and survival: Effects of strategic choices on performance in international markets', *Strategic Management Journal,* **16** (5), 333-351.

Li, Jiatao (1994), 'Experience effects and international expansion: Strategies of service MNCs in the Asia-Pacific region', *Management International Review,* **34** (3), 217-234.

Li, Jiatao and Stephen Guisinger (1991), 'Comparative business failures of foreign-controlled firms in the United States', *Journal of International Business Studies,* **22** (2), 209-224.

Li, Jiatao and Stephen Guisinger (1992), 'The globalization of service multinationals in the 'triad' regions: Japan, Western Europe and North America', *Journal of International Business Studies,* **23** (4), 675-696.

Lieberman, Marvin B. and David B. Montgomery (1998), 'First-mover (dis)advantages: Retrospective and link with the resource-based view', *Strategic Management Journal,* **19**, 1111-1125.

Lieberman, Marvin B. and David B. Montgomery (1988), 'First-mover advantages', *Strategic Management Journal,* **9** (Summer Special Issue), 41-58.

Lippman, S. A. and R. P. Rumelt (1982), 'Uncertain imitability: An analysis of interfirm differences in efficiency under competition', *Bell Journal of Economics,* **13** (2), 418-438.

Lorange, Peter and Gilbert J. B. Probst (1987), 'Joint ventures as self-organizing systems: A key to successful joint venture design and implementation', *Columbia Journal of World Business,* **22** (2), 71-7.

Love, James H. (1995), 'Knowledge, market failure and the multinational enterprise: A theoretical note', *Journal of International Business Studies,* **26** (2), 399-408.

Luo, Yadong (1997), 'Partner selection and venturing success: The case of joint ventures with firms in the People's Republic of China', *Organization Science,* **8** (6), 648-62.

Lyles, Marjorie A. and Inga S. Baird (1994), 'Performance of international joint ventures in two Eastern European countries: The case of Hungary and Poland', *Management International Review,* **34** (4), 313-29.

Lyles, Marjorie A. and Jane E. Salk (1996), 'Knowledge acquisition from foreign parents in international joint ventures: An empirical examination in the Hungarian context', *Journal of International Business Studies,* **27** (5),

877-903.

MacMillan, Ian C., Mary L. McCaffery and Gilles Van Wijk (1985), 'Competitor's responses to easily imitated new products: Exploring commercial banking product introductions', *Strategic Management Journal,* **6** (1), 75-86.

Maddala, G. S. (1983), *Limited dependent and qualitative variables in econometrics*, New York, NY: Cambridge University Press.

Madhok, A. (1997), 'Cost, value and foreign market entry mode: The transaction and the firm', *Strategic Management Journal,* **18** (1), 39-61.

Madhok, Anoop (1995), 'Revisiting multinational firms' tolerance for joint ventures: A trust-based approach', *Journal of International Business Studies*, **26** (1), 117-137.

Magee, Stephen P. (1977), 'Information and the multinational corporation: An appropriability theory of direct foreign investment', in J. N. Bhagwati (ed.), *The new international economic order,* Cambridge, Mass.: MIT Press.

Makhija, Mona V. and Usha Ganesh (1997), 'The relationship between control and partner learning in learning-related joint ventures', *Organization Science*, **8** (5), 508-27.

Makino, Shige (1995), *Joint venture ownership structure and performance: Japanese joint ventures in Asia,* unpublished Ph.D. dissertation, Ontario, Canada: The University of Western Ontario.

Makino, Shige and Paul W. Beamish (1999), 'Matching strategy with the choice of joint venture ownership structure', *Academy of Management Executive,* **12** (4), 17-27.

Makino, Shige and Paul Beamish (1998), 'Performance and survival of joint ventures with non-conventional ownership structures', *Journal of International Business Studies*, **29** (4), 797-818.

Makino, Shige and Andrew Delios (1996), 'Local knowledge transfer and performance: Implications for alliance formation in Asia', *Journal of International Business Studies,* **27** (5), 905-928.

Malnight, Thomas W. (1995), 'Globalization of an ethnocentric firm: An evolutionary perspective', *Strategic Management Journal,* **16** (2), 119-132.

March, James G. (1981), 'Decisions in organizations and theories of choice', in Andrew H. Van de Ven and William F. Joyce (eds) *Perspectives on organization design and behavior,* New York: Wiley: pp. 205-244.

March, R. M. (1992), *Working For A Japanese Company*, Tokyo: Kodansha.

Markides, Constantinos C. and Christopher D. Ittner (1994), 'Shareholder benefits from corporate international diversification: Evidence from US international acquisitions', *Journal of International Business Studies,* **25** (2), 343-366.

Markides, Constantinos C. and P. J. Williamson (1994), 'Related diversification, core competencies and corporate performance', *Strategic Management Journal*, **15** (2), 149-165.

Martin, Xavier, Anand Swaminathan and Will Mitchell (1998), 'Organizational evolution in the interorganizational environment: Incentives and constraints on international expansion strategy', *Administrative Science Quarterly*, **43** (3), 566-601.

Mascarenhas, Briance (1997), 'The order and size of entry into international markets', *Journal of Business Venturing*, **12** (4), 287-299.

Mascarenhas, Briance (1992a), 'First-mover effects in multiple dynamic markets', *Strategic Management Journal*, **13** (3), 237-243.

Mascarenhas, Briance (1992b), 'Order of entry and performance in international markets', *Strategic Management Journal*, **13** (7), 499-510.

Masten, S. E. (1994), 'Empirical research in transaction cost economics: Challenges, progress, directions', Working Paper, Ann Arbor, MI: School of Business Administration, The University of Michigan.

Mayer, K. (1999), 'Buyer-supplier relationships in high technology industries', unpublished doctoral dissertation, Berkeley: Haas School of Business, University of California.

McCardle, K. F. and S. Viswanathan (1994), 'The direct entry versus takeover decision and stock price performance around takeovers', *Journal of Business*, **67** (1), 1-43.

McFetridge, Donald G. (1995), 'Knowledge, market failure and the multinational enterprise: A comment', *Journal of International Business Studies*, **26** (2), 409-416.

McGrath, N. (1994), 'Why HQ should relax its grip', *Asian Business*, June, 46-48.

McMillan, C. J. (1989), *The Japanese Industrial System*, second edition, Berlin: Walter de Gruyter.

Meyer, John W., W. Richard Scott and Terence E. Deal (1983), 'Institutional and technical sources of organizational structure', in John W. Meyer and W. Richard Scott (eds), *Organizational environments: Ritual and rationality*, Beverly Hills, CA: Sage, pp. 45-67

Milgrom, Paul and John Roberts (1992), *Economics, Organization and Management*, Englewood Cliffs, NJ: Prentice-Hall.

Miller, D. and J. Shamsie (1996), 'The resource-based view of the firm in two environments: The Hollywood film studios from 1936 to 1965', *Academy of Management Journal*, **39**, 519-539.

Miller, R. A. (1973), 'Concentration and marginal concentration, advertising and diversity: Three issues in structure performance tests', *Industrial Organization Review*, **1**, 15-24.

Minor, Michael S. (1994), 'The demise of expropriation as an instrument of LDC policy, 1980-1992,' *Journal of International Business Studies,* **25** (1), 177-188.

Mitchell, Will (1994), 'The dynamics of evolving markets: The effects of business sales and age on dissolutions and divestitures', *Administrative Science Quarterly,* **39** (4), 575-602.

Mitchell, Will (1991), 'Dual clocks: Entry order influences on incumbent and newcomer market share and survival when specialized assets retain their value', *Strategic Management Journal,* **12** (2), 85-100.

Mitchell, Will, J. Myles Shaver and Bernard Yeung (1994), 'Foreign entrant survival and foreign market share: Canadian companies' experience in United States medical sector markets', *Strategic Management Journal,* **15** (7), 555-567.

Mjoen, Hans and Stephen Tallman (1997), 'Control and performance in international joint ventures', *Organization Science,* **8** (3), 257-74.

Mody, A. (1993), 'Learning through alliances', *Journal of Economic Behavior and Organization,* **20**, 151-170.

Montgomery, C. A. (1985), 'Product-market diversification and market power', *Academy of Management Journal,* **28** (4), 789-798.

Montgomery, C. A. and B. Wernerfelt (1988), 'Diversification, Ricardian rents and Tobin's *q'*, *Rand Journal of Economics,* **19** (4), 623-632.

Morck, R. and B. Yeung (1991), 'Why investors value multinationality', *Journal of Business,* **64**, 165-87.

Mowery, David C., Joanne E. Oxley and Brian S. Silverman (1996), 'Strategic alliances and interfirm knowledge transfer', *Strategic Management Journal,* **17** (Winter special issue), 77-91.

Mowery, David C. and N. Rosenberg (1989), *Technology and the pursuit of economic growth,* Cambridge: Cambridge University Press.

Murtha T. (1991), 'Surviving industrial targeting - state credibility and public policy contingencies in multinational subcontracting', *Journal of Law Economics & Organization,* **7**, 117-143.

Nahavandi, Afsaneh and A. Maleksadeh (1988), 'Acculturation in mergers and acquisitions', *Academy of Management Review,* **13** (1), 79-90.

Nayyar, Praveen R. (1993), 'Stock market reactions to related diversification moves by service firms seeking benefits from information asymmetry and economies of scope', *Strategic Management Journal,* **14** (8), 569-591.

Nelson, Richard R. and Sydney Winter (1982), *An evolutionary theory of economic change,* Cambridge, MA: Belknap Press.

Newbould, Gerald D., Peter J. Buckley and J. C. Thurwell (1978), *Going international - The experiences of smaller companies overseas,* New York, NY: John Wiley & Sons.

Nitsch, Detlev, Paul W. Beamish and Shige Makino (1996), 'Entry mode and performance of Japanese FDI in Western Europe', *Management International Review*, **36** (1), 27-43.

North, D. C. (1990), *Institutions, institutional change, and economic performance*, Cambridge: Cambridge University Press.

North, D. C. (1981), *Structure and change in economic history*, New York: W. W. Norton and Company.

North, D. and B. Weingast (1989), 'Constitutions and commitment: The evolution of institutions governing public choice in 17th century England', *Journal of Economic History*, **49**, 803-832.

Olk, Paul and Candace Young (1997), 'Why members stay in or leave an R&D consortium: Performance and conditions of membership as determinants of continuity', *Strategic Management Journal*, **18** (11), 855-877.

Oman, Charles P. (1988), 'Cooperative strategies in developing countries: The new forms of investment', in Farok J. Contractor and Peter Lorange (eds), *Cooperative Strategies in International Business*, New York: Lexington Books.

Osborn, R. N. and C. C. Baughn (1990), 'Forms of interorganizational governance for multinational alliances', *Academy of Management Journal*, **33** (3), 503-519.

Oxley, J. E. (1999), 'Institutional environment and the mechanisms of governance: The impact of intellectual property protection on the structure of inter-firm alliances', *Journal of Economic Behavior and Organization*, **38**, 283-310.

Oxley, J. E. (1997), 'Appropriability hazards and governance in strategic alliances: A transaction cost approach', *Journal of Law, Economics and Organization*, **13**, 387-409.

Oxley, J. E. (1995), *International Hybrids: A Transaction Cost Treatment and Empirical Study*, unpublished PhD Dissertation, Berkeley: University of California.

Ozawa, T. (1979), *Multinationalism, Japanese style: The political economy of outward dependence*, Princeton, New Jersey: Princeton University Press.

Padmanabhan, Prasad and Kang Rae Cho (1996), 'Ownership strategy for a foreign affiliate: An empirical investigation of Japanese firms', *Management International Review*, **36** (1), 45-65.

Palepu, K. (1985), 'Diversification strategy, profit performance, and the entropy measure of diversification', *Strategic Management Journal*, **6**, 239-255.

Pan, Yigang (1997), 'The formation of Japanese and US equity joint ventures in China', *Strategic Management Journal*, **18** (3), 247-54.

Pan, Yigang (1996), 'Influences on foreign equity ownership level in joint ventures in China', *Journal of International Business Studies,* **27** (1), 1-26.

Pan, Yigang and David K. Tse (1996), 'Cooperative strategies between foreign firms in an overseas country', *Journal of International Business Studies*, **27** (5), 929-46.

Park, Seung H. and Gerardo R. Ungson (1997), 'The effect of national culture, organizational complementarity, and economic motivation on joint venture dissolution', *Academy of Management Journal*, **40** (2), 279-307.

Parkhe, Arvind (1993), 'Partner nationality and the structure-performance relationship in strategic alliances', *Organization Science*, **4** (2), 301-24.

Parkhe, Arvind (1991), 'Interfirm diversity, organizational learning, and longevity in global strategic alliances', *Journal of International Business Studies*, **22** (4), 579-601.

Pearce, R. D. (1989), *The Internationalisation of Research and Development by Multinational Enterprises,* New York: St. Martin's Press.

Pearce, Robert J. (1997), 'Toward understanding joint venture performance and survival: A bargaining and influence approach to transaction cost theory', *Academy of Management Review*, **22** (1), 203-225.

Pennings, J. M., H. G. Barkema and S. Douma (1994), 'Organizational learning and diversification', *Academy of Management Journal*, **37**, 608-627.

Penrose, E. T. (1959), *The Theory of the Growth of the Firm,* Oxford, UK: Basil Blackwell Publishers Ltd.

Penrose, E. T. (1956), 'Foreign investment and the growth of the firm', *Economic Journal,* **66**, 220-235. Reprinted in J. H. Dunning, ed. (1972), *International Investment: Selected Readings,* Penguin Books, Middlesex, England, pp. 243-264.

Peterson, R. B., J. Sargent, N. K. Napier and W. S. Shim (1996), 'Corporate expatriate HRM policies, internationalization, and performance in the world's largest MNCs', *Management International Review*, **36**, 215-230.

Pisano, G. P. (1991), 'The governance of innovation: Vertical integration and collaborative arrangements in the biotechnology industry', *Research Policy*, **20**, 237-249.

Pisano, G. P. (1990), 'The R&D boundaries of the firm: An empirical analysis', *Administrative Science Quarterly,* **35**, 153-176.

Pisano, G. P. (1989), 'Using equity participation to support exchange: Evidence from the biotechnology industry', *Journal of Law, Economics and Organization*, **5**, 109-126.

Porter, Michael E. (1990), *The competitive advantage of nations,* London: Macmillan.

Porter, Michael E. (1987), 'From competitive advantage to corporate strategy', *Harvard Business Review*, **65** (3), 43-59.

Porter, Michael E. (1976), *Interbrand Choice, Strategy, and Bilateral Market Power,* Cambridge, MA: Harvard University Press.

Porter, Michael E. and Mark B. Fuller (1986), 'Coalitions and global strategy', in M. E. Porter (ed.), *Competition in global industries,* Boston, Mass: Harvard Business School Press, pp. 315-44.

Poynter, Thomas A. (1985), *Multinational Enterprises & Government Intervention,* London, U.K.: Croom Helm.

Poynter, Thomas A. (1982), 'Government intervention in less developed countries: The experience of multinational companies, *Journal of International Business Studies,* **13** (1), 9-25.

Prahalad, C. K. and R. A. Bettis (1986), 'The dominant logic: A new linkage between diversity and performance', *Strategic Management Journal,* **7** (6), 485-501.

Pucik, V. (1994), 'The challenges of globalization: The strategic role of local managers in Japanese-owned US subsidiaries', in N. Campbell and F. Burton (eds), *Japanese Multinationals: Strategies and Management in the Global Kaisha,* London: Routledge, pp. 218-239.

Pucik, V., M. Hanada, and G. Fifield (1989), *Management Cultures and the Effectiveness of Local Executives in Japanese-Owned US Corporations,* Tokyo: Egon Zehnder International.

Pugel, T. A. (1978), *International Market Linkages and US Manufacturing: Prices, Profits and Patterns,* Cambridge, MA: Ballinger.

Putti, J. and T. Chong (1985), 'American and Japanese management practices in their Singapore Subsidiaries', *Asia Pacific Journal of Management,* **2,** 106-114.

Ramanujam, V. and P. Varadarajan (1989), 'Research on corporate diversification: A synthesis', *Strategic Management Journal,* **10,** 523-552.

Ravenscraft, D. J. and F. Scherer (1989), 'The profitability of mergers', *International Journal of Industrial Organization,* **7,** 101-116.

Reddy, S. B., R. N. Osborn and A. Pratap (1998), 'Japanese keiretsu and the formation and survival of US/Japanese strategic alliances', paper presented at the annual meeting of the Academy of International Business, Vienna.

Reich, R. B. (1991), 'Who is them?', *Harvard Business Review,* **69** (2), 77-88.

Reynolds, John I. (1984), 'The "pinched shoe" effect of international joint ventures', *Columbia Journal of World Business,* **19** (2), 23-9.

Rivoli, Pietra and Eugene Salorio (1996), 'Foreign direct investment and investment under uncertainty', *Journal of International Business Studies,* **27** (2), 335-354.

Robinson, W. T., Claus Fornell and M. Sullivan (1992), 'Are market pioneers intrinsically stronger than later entrants?', *Strategic Management Journal,* **13** (8), 609-624.

Root, F. R. (1987), *Entry Strategies for International Markets,* Lexington, MA: Lexington Books.

Rozenzweig, P. M. (1994), 'The new "American challenge": Foreign multinationals in the United States', *California Management Review,* **36** (3), 107-123.

Rugman, Alan M. (1982), *New theories of the multinational enterprise,* New York: St. Martin's Press.

Rugman, Alan M. (1981), *Inside the multinationals: The economics of internal markets,* New York: Columbia University Press.

Rugman, Alan M. (1979), *International Diversification and the Multinational Enterprise,* Lexington, MA: Lexington Books.

Rugman, Alan M. and Alain Verbeke (1992), 'A note on the transnational solution and the transaction cost theory of multinational management', *Journal of International Business Studies,* **23** (4), 761-71.

Rumelt, R. P. (1982), 'Diversification strategy and profitability', *Strategic Management Journal,* **3** (3), 359-369.

Rumelt, R. P. (1974), *Strategy, Structure, and Economic Performance,* Harvard University Press, Cambridge, MA.

Sachwald, F. (1995), *Japanese firms in Europe,* Luxembourg: Harwood Academic Publishers.

Schaan, Jean-Louis (1988), 'How to control a joint venture even as a minority partner', *Journal of General Management,* **14** (1), 4-16.

Schaan, Jean-Louis (1983), 'Parent control and joint venture success: The case of Mexico', unpublished Ph.D. dissertation, London, Ontario, Canada: University of Western Ontario.

Schaan, Jean-Loius and P.W. Beamish (1988), 'Joint venture general managers in developing countries', in F. Contractor and P. Lorange (eds), *Cooperative Strategies in International Business,* Lexington, MA: Lexington Books, D.C. Heath & Co.

Scherer, F. M. and David Ross (1990), *Industrial market structure and economic performance,* third edition, Boston, MA: Houghton Mifflin Co.

Schmalensee, T. (1985), 'Do markets differ much?', *American Economic Review,* **75**, 341-351.

Scholhammer, H. and D. Nigh (1984), 'The effects of political events on foreign direct investments by German multinational corporations', *Management International Review,* **24** (1), 18-40.

Scott, John T. (1982), Multimarket contact and economic performance. *Review of Economics and Statistics,* **64**, 368-375.

Shan, Weijian (1991), 'Environmental risks and joint venture sharing arrangements', *Journal of International Business Studies,* **22** (4), 555-578.

Shan, Weijian and William Hamilton (1991), 'Country-specific advantage and international cooperation', *Strategic Management Journal,* **12** (6), 419-

32.

Shane, Scott. A. (1994), 'The effect of national culture on the choice between licensing and direct foreign investment', *Strategic Management Journal*, **15** (8), 627-642.

Shane, Scott A. (1993), 'The effect of cultural distances in perceptions of transactions costs on national differences in the preference for international joint ventures', *Asia Pacific Journal of Management*, **10** (1), 57-69.

Shane, Scott A. (1992), 'The effect of cultural differences in perceptions of transaction costs on national differences in the preference for licensing', *Management International Review*, **32**, 295-311.

Sharma, Dharma Deo and Jan Johanson (1987), 'Technical consultancy in internationalization', *International Marketing Review*, **4** (4), 20-29.

Shaver, J. M. (1998), 'Accounting for endogeneity when assessing strategy performance: Does entry mode choice affect FDI survival?', *Management Science*, **44** (4), 571-585.

Shaver, J. M., W. Mitchell and B. Yeung (1997), 'The effect of own-firm and other-firm experience on foreign direct investment survival in the United States, 1987-92', *Strategic Management Journal*, **18**, 811-824.

Shenkar, Oded and Stephen B. Tallman (1993), 'Formation of international cooperative ventures: An organizational perspective', *Advances in International Comparative Management*, **8**, 101-117.

Shenkar, Oded and Yoram Zeira (1992), 'Role of conflict and role ambiguity of chief executive officers in international joint ventures', *Journal of International Business Studies*, **23** (1), 55-75.

Shenkar, Oded and Yoram Zeira (1987), 'Human resources management in international joint ventures: Directions for research', *Academy of Management Review*, **12** (3), 546-57.

Silverman, B. (1998), 'Technological resources and the direction of corporate diversification: Toward an integration of the resource-based view and transaction cost economics', working paper no. 99-019, Cambridge, MA: Harvard Business School.

Simmonds, Paul G. (1990), 'The combined diversification breadth and mode dimensions and the performance of large diversified firms', *Strategic Management Journal*, **11**, 399-410.

Simon, H. A. (1997/1947), *Administrative behavior: A study of decision making processes in administrative organizations* (4th ed.), New York: The Free Press.

Singh, Harbir and Bruce Kogut (1989), 'Industry and competitive effects on the choice of entry mode', in *Academy of Management Best Paper Proceedings*, 116-120.

Sohn, J. H. D. and Y. Paik (1996), 'More is better? Expatriate managers and MNCs' ability to control international subsidiaries', working paper.

Stalk, George, P. Evans and L. E. Shulman (1992), 'Competing on capabilities: The new rules of corporate strategy', *Harvard Business Review*, **70** (2), 57-69.

Stalk, George and Thomas M. Hout (1990), *Competing against time: How time-based competition is reshaping global markets,* New York: Free Press.

Stimpert, J. L. and I. M. Duhaime (1997), 'Seeing the big picture: The influence of industry, diversification and business strategy on performance', *Academy of Management Journal*, **40**, 560-583.

Stinchcombe, Arthur L. (1965), 'Social structure and organizations', in James G. March (ed.), *Handbook of organizations*, Chicago, IL: Rand McNally, pp. 142-92.

Stopford, John M. and Louis T. Wells, Jr. (1972), *Managing the multinational enterprise: Organization of the firm and ownership of the subsidiaries,* New York, NY: Basic Books.

Sullivan, M. (1991), 'Brand extension and order of entry', *Marketing Science Institute*, 91-105.

Swedenborg, B. (1979), *The Multinational Operations of Swedish Firms: An Analysis of Determinants and Effects,* Stockholm: Industrial Institute for Economic and Social Research.

Swenson, Deborah (1993), 'Foreign mergers and acquisitions in the United States', in K. A. Froot (ed.), *Foreign direct investment,* Chicago, IL: University of Chicago Press.

Tallman, S. and J. T. Li (1996), 'Effects of international diversity and product diversity on the performance of multinational firms', *Academy of Management Journal,* **39**, 179-196.

Tallman, S. B. and O. Shenkar (1994), 'A managerial decision model of international cooperative venture formation', *Journal of International Business Studies*, **25**, 91-115.

Teagarden, L. F., D. E. Hatfield and A. E. Echols (1999), 'Doomed from the start: What is the value of selecting a future dominant design?', *Strategic Management Journal*, **20** (6), 495-518.

Teece, David J. (1992), 'Competition, cooperation, and innovation: Organizational arrangements for regimes of rapid technological progress', *Journal of Economic Behavior and Organization*, **18**, 1-25.

Teece, David J. (1986a), 'Transactions cost economics and the multinational enterprise: An assessment', *Journal of Economic Behavior and Organization,* **7** (1), 21-45.

Teece, David J. (1986b), 'Profiting from technological innovation', *Research Policy,* **15**, 285-305.

Teece, David J. (1982), 'Towards an economic theory of the multiproduct firm', *Journal of Economic Behavior and Organization*, **3**, 39-63.

Telser, Lester G. (1969), 'Another look at advertising and concentration',

Journal of Industrial Economics, **XVIII** (1), 90-104.

Telser, Lester G. (1960), 'Why should manufacturers want fair trade?', *Journal of Law & Economics*, **3**, 34-55.

Terpstra, V. and C. Yu (1988), 'Determinants of foreign investment of US advertising agencies', *Journal of International Business Studies*, **19** (1), 33-46.

Tiemessen, Iris, Henry W. Lane, Mary M. Crossan and Andrew Inkpen (1997), 'Knowledge management in international joint ventures', in P. W. Beamish and J. P. Killing (eds), *Cooperative strategies: North American perspectives*, San Francisco: The New Lexington Press.

Tomlinson, James W. C. (1970), *The Joint Venture process in international business: India and Pakistan*, Cambridge, MA: MIT Press.

Toyo Keizai (1999), *Kaigai Shinshutsu Kigyou Souran – kuni betsu, 1999* (Japanese Overseas Investments – by country), Tokyo, Japan: Toyo Keizai, Inc.

Toyo Keizai (1998), *Kaisha Zaimu Karute* (Corporate Financial Listing), Tokyo, Japan: Toyo Keizai, Inc.

Toyo Keizai (1997), *Kaigai Shinshutsu Kigyou Souran – kuni betsu, 1997* (Japanese Overseas Investments – by country), Tokyo, Japan: Toyo Keizai, Inc.

Toyo Keizai (1996), *Japan Company Handbook*, Tokyo, Japan: Toyo Keizai, Inc.

Toyo Keizai (1995), *Kaigai Shinshutsu Kigyou Souran – kuni betsu, 1995* (Japanese Overseas Investments – by country), Tokyo, Japan: Toyo Keizai, Inc.

Toyo Keizai (1994), *Kaigai Shinshutsu Kigyou Souran – kuni betsu, 1994* (Japanese Overseas Investments – by country), Tokyo, Japan: Toyo Keizai, Inc.

Toyo Keizai (1992a), *Kaigai Shinshutsu Kigyou Souran – kuni betsu, 1992* (Japanese Overseas Investments – by country), Tokyo, Japan: Toyo Keizai, Inc.

Toyo Kezai (1992b), *Kigyou Keiretsu Souran*, Tokyo, Japan: Toyo Keizai, Inc.

Toyo Keizai (1991), *Kaisha Shikiho* (in Japanese), Tokyo, Japan: Toyo Keizai, Inc.

Toyo Keizai (1990), *Kaigai Shinshutsu Kigyou Souran – kuni betsu, 1990* (Japanese Overseas Investments – by country), Tokyo, Japan: Toyo Keizai, Inc.

Toyo Keizai (1989), *Kaigai Shinshutsu Kigyou Souran – kuni betsu, 1989* (Japanese Overseas Investments – by country), Tokyo, Japan: Toyo Keizai, Inc.

Toyo Keizai (1988), *Kaigai Shinshutsu Kigyou Souran – kuni betsu, 1988* (Japanese Overseas Investments – by country), Tokyo, Japan: Toyo Keizai, Inc.

Toyo Keizai (1987), *Kaigai Shinshutsu Kigyou Souran – kuni betsu, 1987* (Japanese Overseas Investments – by country), Tokyo, Japan: Toyo Keizai, Inc.

Toyo Keizai (1986), *Kaigai Shinshutsu Kigyou Souran – kuni betsu, 1986* (Japanese Overseas Investments – by country), Tokyo, Japan: Toyo Keizai, Inc.

Tsurumi, Yoshihiro (1976), *The Japanese are coming: A multinational interaction of firms and politics,* Cambridge, MA: Ballinger Publishing Company.

UNCTAD (1997), *World Investment Report, 1997,* New York and Geneva: United Nations.

UNCTAD (1996), *World Investment Report, 1996: Investment, trade and international policy arrangements,* New York and Geneva: United Nations.

UNCTAD (1995), *World Investment Report, 1995,* New York and Geneva: United Nations.

US Department of Labor (1992), *Occupational employment statistics,* Washington, DC 20212: Bureau of Labor Statistics.

Van de Ven, W. P. M. M. and B. M. S. Van Praag (1981), 'The demand for deductibles in private health insurance', *Journal of Econometrics,* **17,** 229-252.

van Witteloostuijn, Arjen and Marc van Wegberg (1992), 'Multimarket competition: Theory and evidence', *Journal of Economic Behavior and Organizations,* **18,** 273-282.

Venkatraman, N. and V. Ramanujam (1986), 'Measurement of business performance in strategy research: A comparison of approaches,' *Academy of Management Review,* **11,** 801-814.

Vernon, Raymond (1995), 'Contributing to an international business curriculum: An approach from the flank', *Journal of International Business Studies,* **25** (2), 215-27.

Vernon, Raymond (1983), 'Organizational and institutional responses to international risk', in R. Herring (ed.), *Managing international risk,* Cambridge: Cambridge University Press.

Vernon, Raymond (1979), 'The product cycle hypothesis in the new international environment', *Oxford Bulletin of Economics and Statistics,* **41,** 255-267.

Vernon, Raymond and L. T. Wells, Jr. (1976), *Manager in the International Economy,* Englewood Cliffs, NJ: Prentice Hall.

Vesey, Joseph T. (1991), 'The new competitors: They think in terms of speed to market', *Academy of Management Executive,* **5** (2), 23-33.

Walter, Gordon A. and J. B. Barney (1990), 'Management objectives in mergers and acquisitions', *Strategic Management Journal*, **11** (1), 79-86.

Wernerfelt, Birger (1984), 'A resource-based view of the firm', *Strategic Management Journal*, **5**, 171-180.

Wernerfelt, Birger and C. A. Montgomery (1988), 'Tobin's Q and the importance of focus in firm performance', *American Economic Review*, **78** (1), 246-250.

Westney, E. D. (1988), 'Domestic and foreign learning curves in managing international cooperative strategies', in F. J. Contractor and P. Lorange (eds), *Cooperative Strategies in International Business*, Lexington: Lexington Books, pp. 339-346.

Williamson, O. E. (1996), *The Mechanisms of Governance*, New York, NY: Oxford University Press.

Williamson, O. E. (1985), *The Economic Institutions of Capitalism*, New York, NY: The Free Press.

Williamson, O. E. (1975), *Markets and Hierarchies: Analysis and Antitrust Implications*, New York, NY: The Free Press.

Wilson, Brent (1980), 'The propensity of multinational companies to expand through acquisitions', *Journal of International Business Studies*, **12** (Spring/Summer), 59-65.

Wind, Y. and H. Perlmutter (1977), 'On the identification of frontier issues in international marketing', *Columbia Journal of World Business*, **12** (4), 131-139.

Wolf, B. M (1975), 'Size and profitability among US manufacturing firms. Multinational versus purely domestic firms', *Journal of Economics and Business*, **28** (1), 15-22.

Woodcock, Patrick (1994), *An Eclectic Theory Model of Wholly-owned Entry Mode Selection and Performance*, unpublished Doctoral Dissertation, London, Ontario: University of Western Ontario.

Woodcock, C. Patrick, Paul W. Beamish and Shige Makino (1994), 'Ownership-based entry mode strategies and international performance', *Journal of International Business Studies*, **25** (2), 253-273.

Yamawaki, Hideki (1991), 'Exports and foreign distributional activities: Evidence on Japanese firms in the United States', *The Review of Economics and Statistics*, **73** (2), 294-300.

Yan, Aimin and Barbara Gray (1994), 'Bargaining power, management control, and performance in United States-China joint ventures: A comparative case study', *Academy of Management Journal*, **37** (6), 1478-1517.

Yip, George S. (1982), 'Diversification entry: Internal development versus acquisition', *Strategic Management Journal*, **3**, 331-345.

Yoshida, M. (1986), *Japanese direct manufacturing investment in the United States*, New York: Praeger.

Yoshino, M. Y. (1976), *Japan's multinational enterprises*, Cambridge, MA: Harvard University Press.

Yu, Chwo-Ming J. and Kiyohiko Ito (1988), 'Oligopolistic reaction and foreign direct investment: The case of the US tire and textile industries', *Journal of International Business Studies*, **19** (3), 449-460.

Zejan, Mario C. (1990), 'Internal developments or acquisitions: The choice of Swedish multinational enterprises', *The Journal of Industrial Economics*, **38** (3), 349-355.

Index